morningglories
volumeten

expulsion

D0917224

WORDS
NICK SPENCER

ART
JOE EISMA

COVERS
RODIN ESQUEJO

PAUL LITTLE
COLORS

JOHNNY LOWE
LETTERS

TIM DANIEL
DESIGN

IMAGE COMICS, INC.
Robert Kirkman – Chief Operating Officer
Erik Larsen – Chief Financial Officer
Todd McFarlane – President
Marc Silvestri – Chief Executive Officer
Jim Valentino – Vice-President

Eric Stephenson – Publisher
Corey Murphy – Director of Sales
Jeff Boison – Director of Publishing Planning & Book Trade Sales
Jeremy Sullivan – Director of Digital Sales
Kat Salazar – Director of PR & Marketing
Branwyn Bigglestone – Controller
Drew Gill – Art Director
Jonathan Chan – Production Manager
Meredith Wallace – Print Manager
Briah Skelly – Publicist
Sasha Head – Sales & Marketing Production Designer
Randy Okamura – Digital Production Designer
David Brothers – Branding Manager
Olivia Ngai – Content Manager
Addison Duke – Production Artist
Vincent Kukua – Production Artist
Tricia Ramos – Production Artist
Jeff Stang – Direct Market Sales Representative
Emilio Bautista – Digital Sales Associate
Leanna Caunter – Accounting Assistant
Chloe Ramos-Peterson – Library Market Sales Representative
IMAGECOMICS.COM

fortyseven

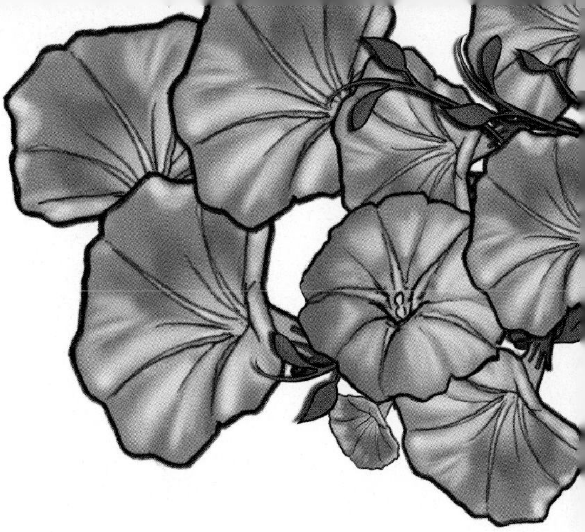

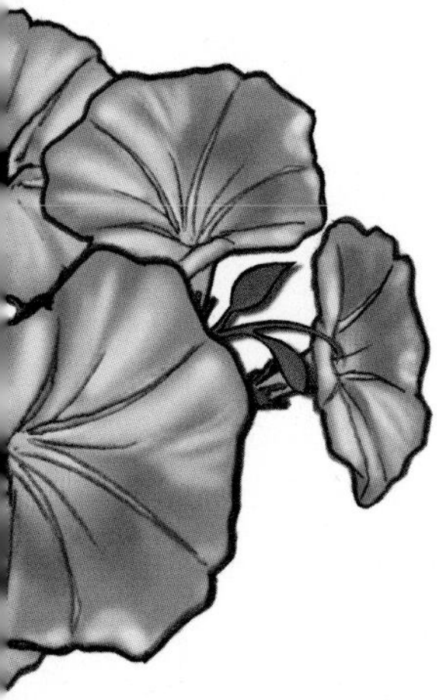

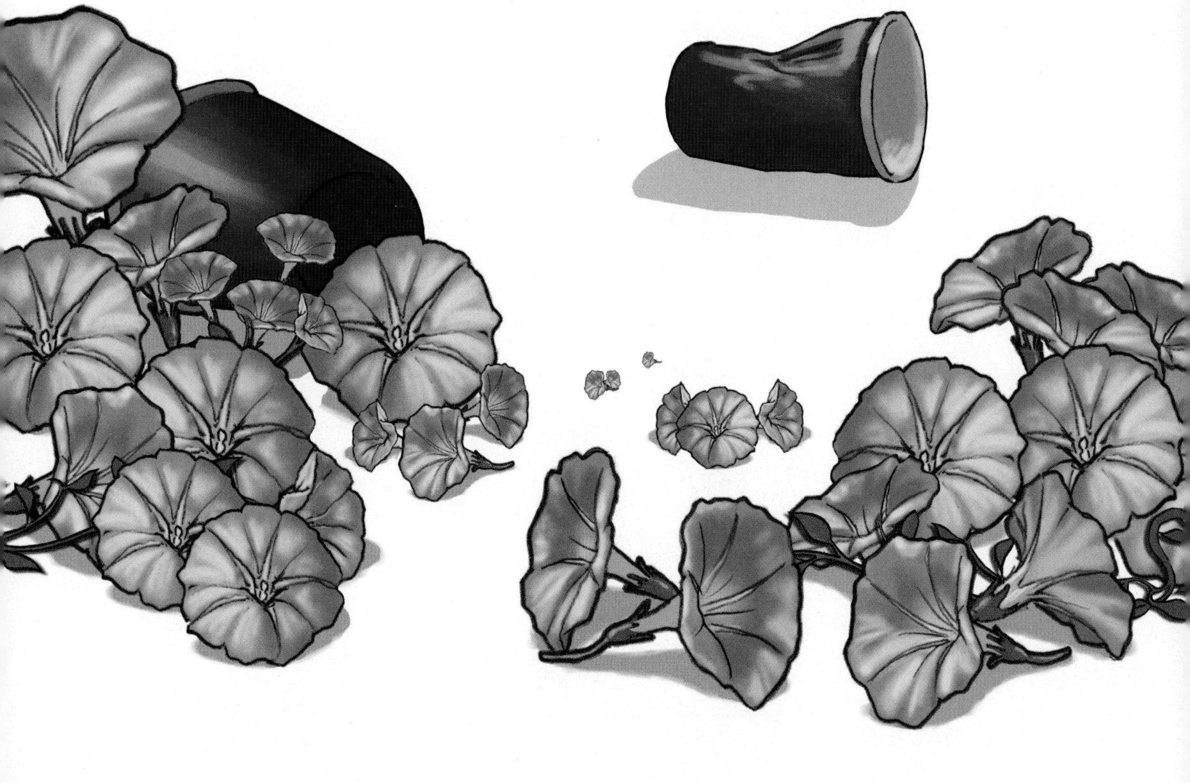

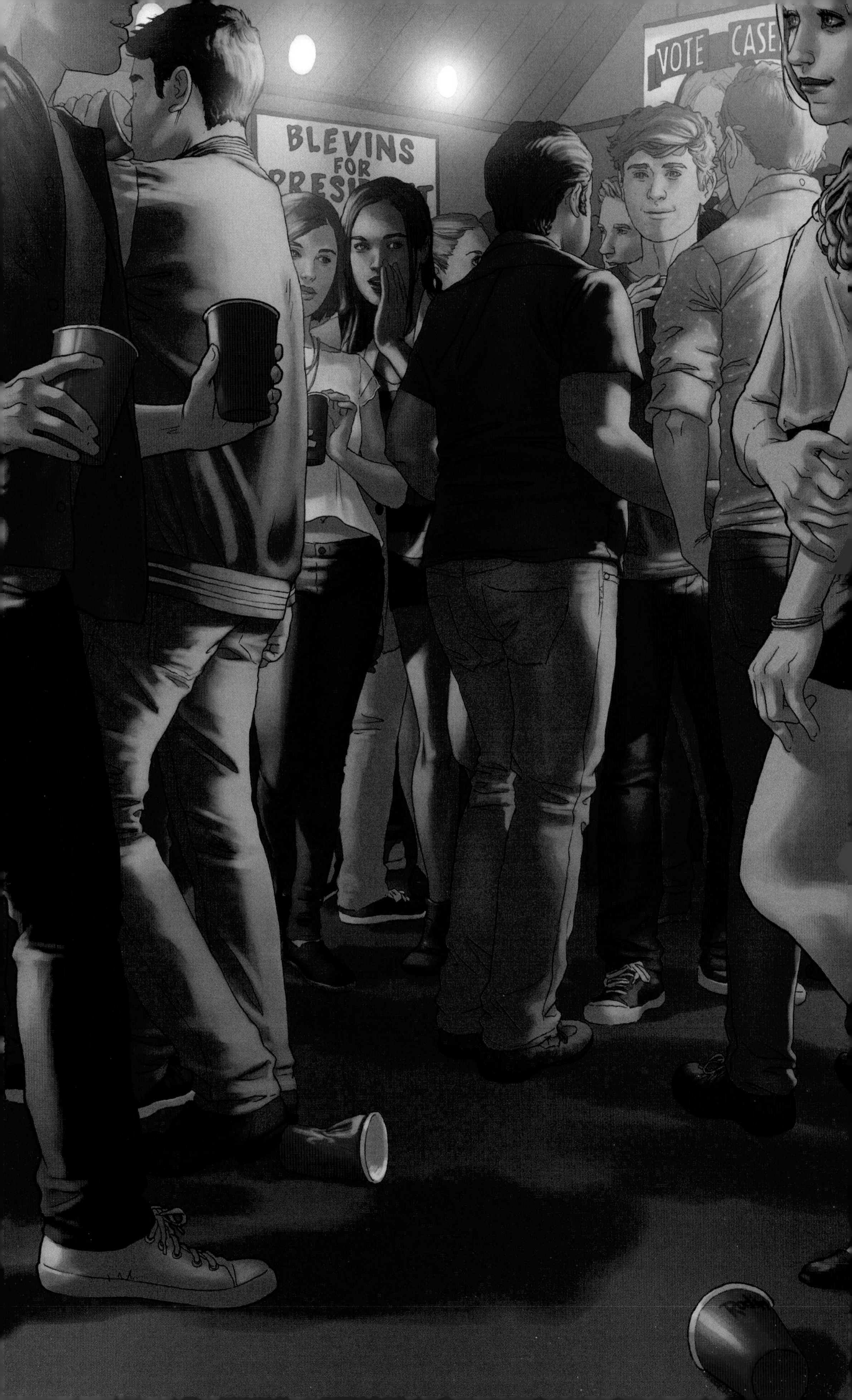
BLEVINS
FOR
VOTE
CASE

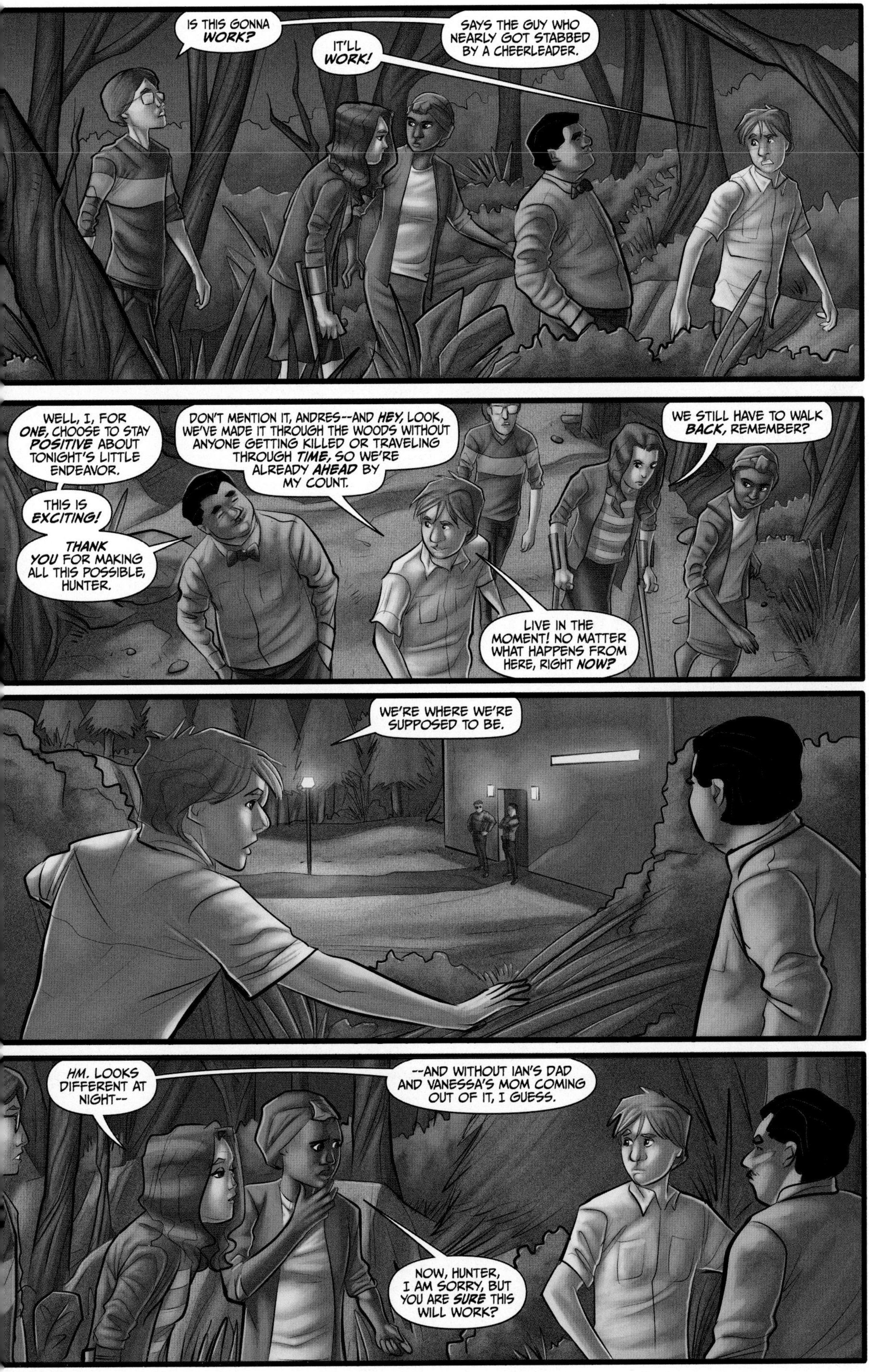
IS THIS GONNA WORK?
IT'LL WORK!
SAYS THE GUY WHO NEARLY GOT STABBED BY A CHEERLEADER.
WELL, I, FOR ONE, CHOOSE TO STAY POSITIVE ABOUT TONIGHT'S LITTLE ENDEAVOR.
THIS IS EXCITING!
THANK YOU FOR MAKING ALL THIS POSSIBLE, HUNTER.
DON'T MENTION IT, ANDRES--AND HEY, LOOK, WE'VE MADE IT THROUGH THE WOODS WITHOUT ANYONE GETTING KILLED OR TRAVELING THROUGH TIME, SO WE'RE ALREADY AHEAD BY MY COUNT.
WE STILL HAVE TO WALK BACK, REMEMBER?
LIVE IN THE MOMENT! NO MATTER WHAT HAPPENS FROM HERE, RIGHT NOW?
WE'RE WHERE WE'RE SUPPOSED TO BE.
HM. LOOKS DIFFERENT AT NIGHT--
--AND WITHOUT IAN'S DAD AND VANESSA'S MOM COMING OUT OF IT, I GUESS.
NOW, HUNTER, I AM SORRY, BUT YOU ARE SURE THIS WILL WORK?

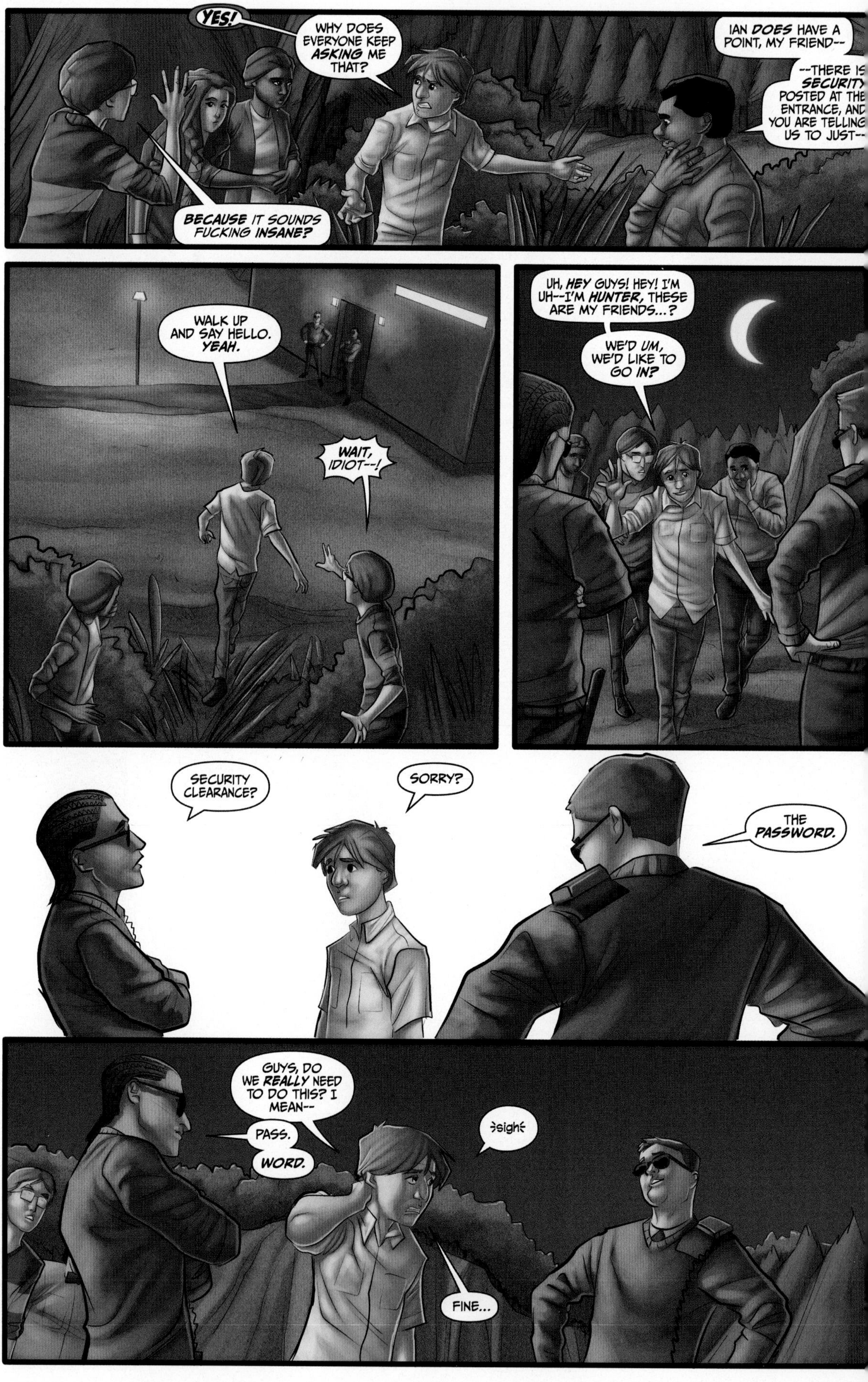
YES!
WHY DOES EVERYONE KEEP ASKING ME THAT?
BECAUSE IT SOUNDS FUCKING INSANE?
IAN DOES HAVE A POINT, MY FRIEND--
--THERE IS SECURITY POSTED AT THE ENTRANCE, AND YOU ARE TELLING US TO JUST--
WALK UP AND SAY HELLO. YEAH.
WAIT, IDIOT--!
UH, HEY GUYS! HEY! I'M UH--I'M HUNTER, THESE ARE MY FRIENDS...?
WE'D UM, WE'D LIKE TO GO IN?
SECURITY CLEARANCE?
SORRY?
THE PASSWORD.
GUYS, DO WE REALLY NEED TO DO THIS? I MEAN--
PASS.
WORD.
sigh
FINE...

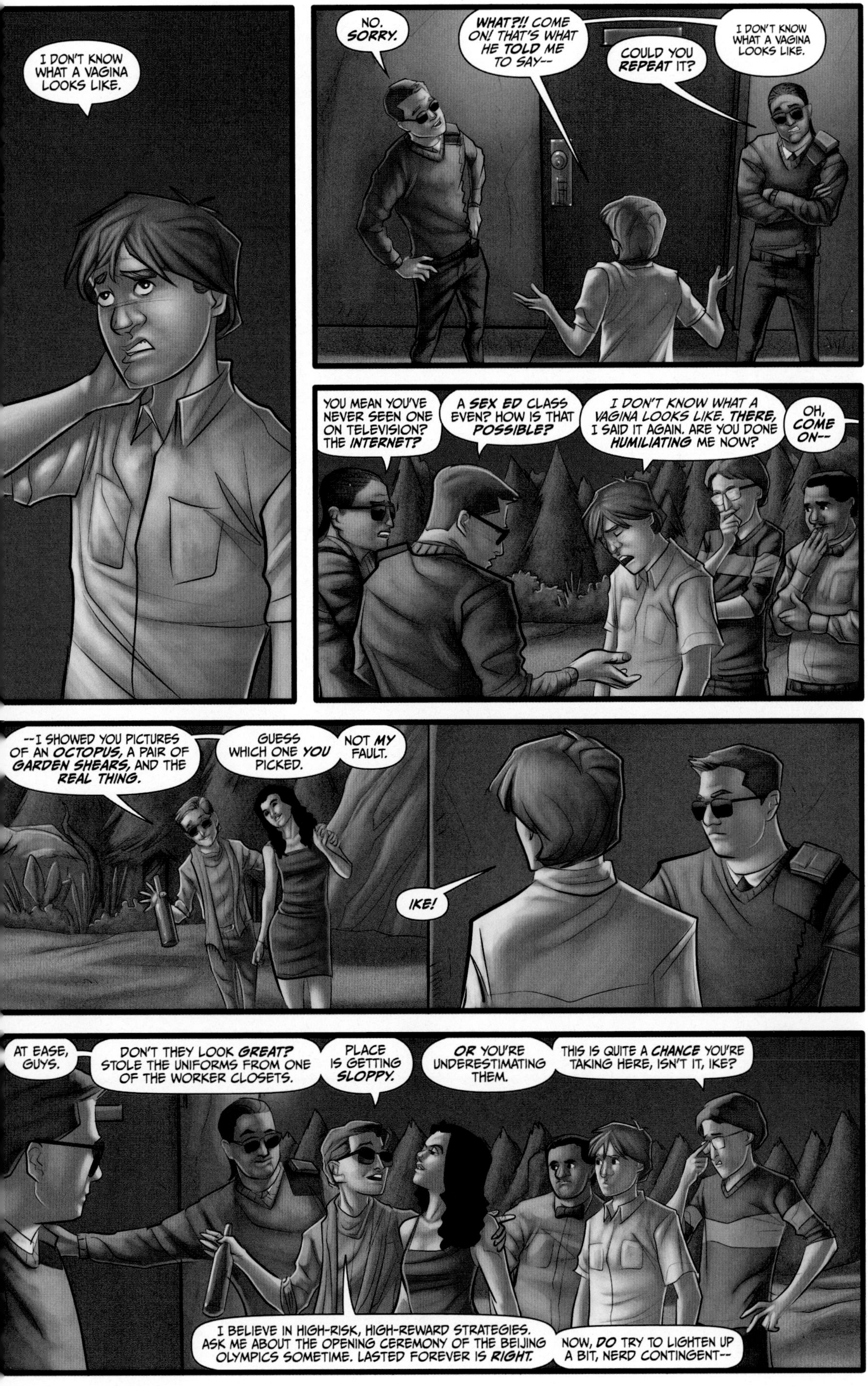
I DON'T KNOW WHAT A VAGINA LOOKS LIKE.
NO. SORRY.
WHAT?!! COME ON! THAT'S WHAT HE TOLD ME TO SAY--
COULD YOU REPEAT IT?
I DON'T KNOW WHAT A VAGINA LOOKS LIKE.
YOU MEAN YOU'VE NEVER SEEN ONE ON TELEVISION? THE INTERNET?
A SEX ED CLASS EVEN? HOW IS THAT POSSIBLE?
I DON'T KNOW WHAT A VAGINA LOOKS LIKE. THERE, I SAID IT AGAIN. ARE YOU DONE HUMILIATING ME NOW?
OH, COME ON--
--I SHOWED YOU PICTURES OF AN OCTOPUS, A PAIR OF GARDEN SHEARS, AND THE REAL THING.
GUESS WHICH ONE YOU PICKED.
NOT MY FAULT.
IKE!
AT EASE, GUYS.
DON'T THEY LOOK GREAT? STOLE THE UNIFORMS FROM ONE OF THE WORKER CLOSETS.
PLACE IS GETTING SLOPPY.
OR YOU'RE UNDERESTIMATING THEM.
THIS IS QUITE A CHANCE YOU'RE TAKING HERE, ISN'T IT, IKE?
I BELIEVE IN HIGH-RISK, HIGH-REWARD STRATEGIES. ASK ME ABOUT THE OPENING CEREMONY OF THE BEIJING OLYMPICS SOMETIME. LASTED FOREVER IS RIGHT.
NOW, DO TRY TO LIGHTEN UP A BIT, NERD CONTINGENT--

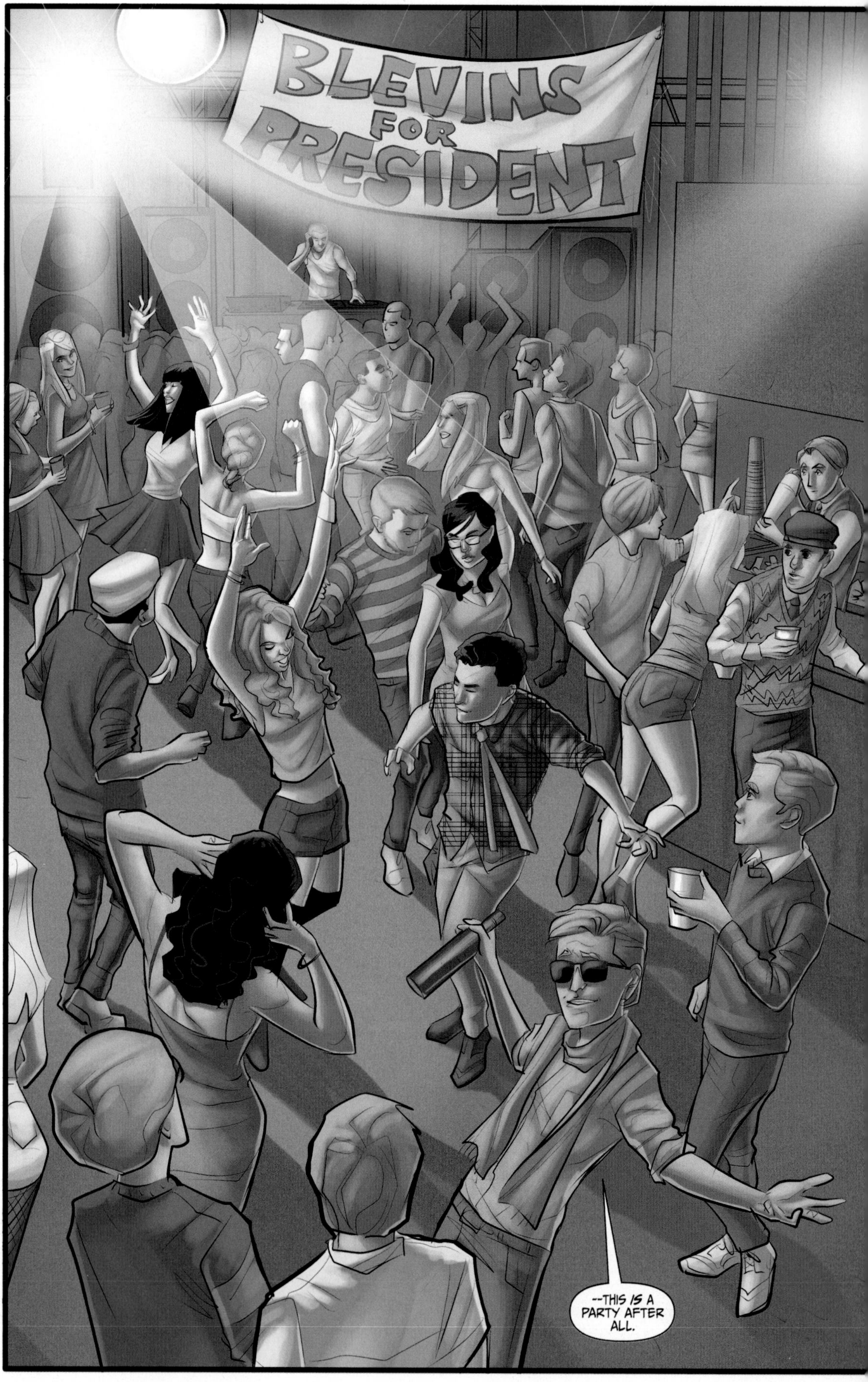
BLEVINS FOR PRESIDENT
--THIS *IS* A PARTY AFTER ALL.

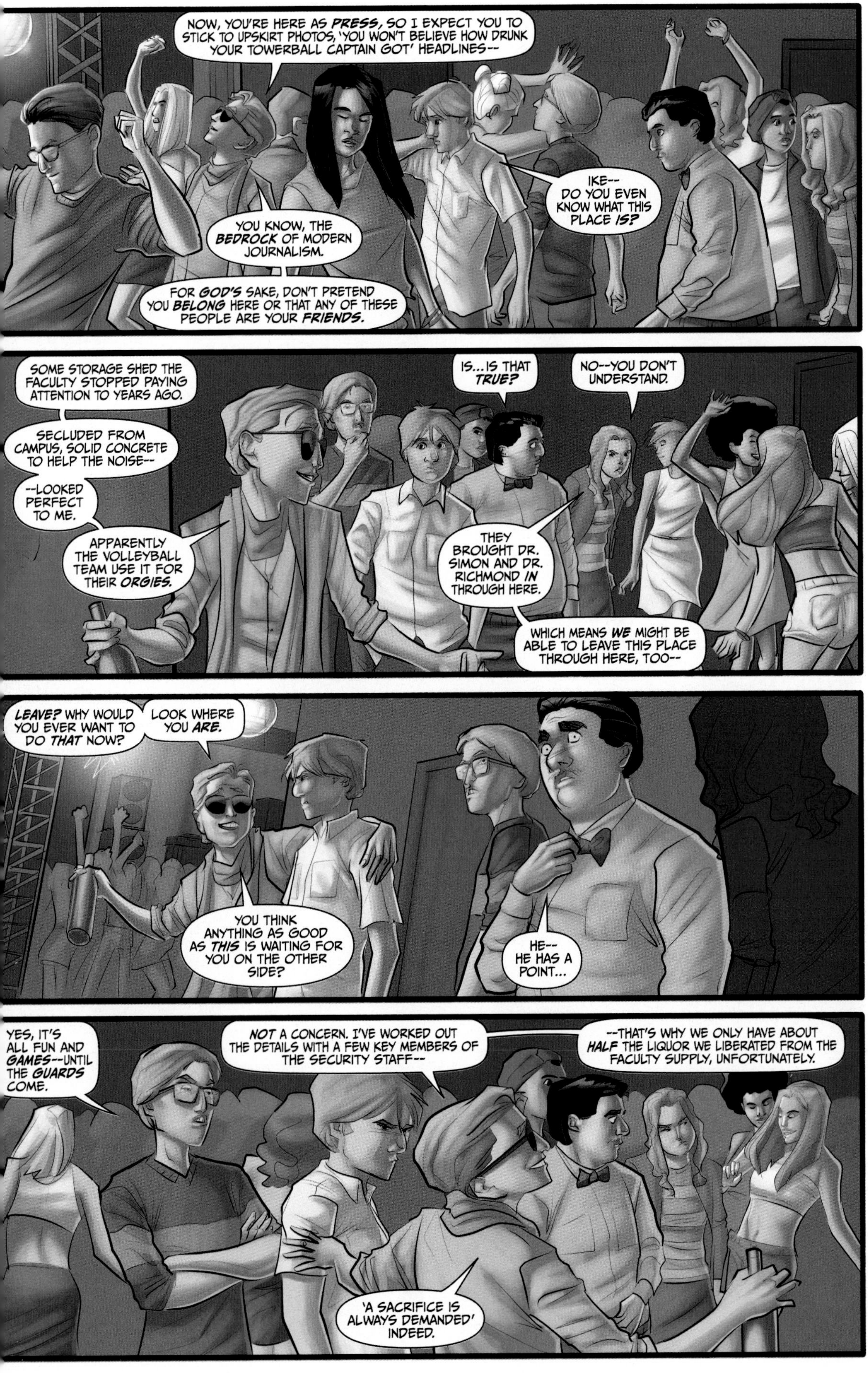
NOW, YOU'RE HERE AS PRESS, SO I EXPECT YOU TO STICK TO UPSKIRT PHOTOS, 'YOU WON'T BELIEVE HOW DRUNK YOUR TOWERBALL CAPTAIN GOT' HEADLINES--
YOU KNOW, THE BEDROCK OF MODERN JOURNALISM.
FOR GOD'S SAKE, DON'T PRETEND YOU BELONG HERE OR THAT ANY OF THESE PEOPLE ARE YOUR FRIENDS.
IKE-- DO YOU EVEN KNOW WHAT THIS PLACE IS?
SOME STORAGE SHED THE FACULTY STOPPED PAYING ATTENTION TO YEARS AGO.
SECLUDED FROM CAMPUS, SOLID CONCRETE TO HELP THE NOISE--
--LOOKED PERFECT TO ME.
APPARENTLY THE VOLLEYBALL TEAM USE IT FOR THEIR ORGIES.
IS...IS THAT TRUE?
NO--YOU DON'T UNDERSTAND.
THEY BROUGHT DR. SIMON AND DR. RICHMOND IN THROUGH HERE.
WHICH MEANS WE MIGHT BE ABLE TO LEAVE THIS PLACE THROUGH HERE, TOO--
LEAVE? WHY WOULD YOU EVER WANT TO DO THAT NOW?
LOOK WHERE YOU ARE.
YOU THINK ANYTHING AS GOOD AS THIS IS WAITING FOR YOU ON THE OTHER SIDE?
HE-- HE HAS A POINT...
YES, IT'S ALL FUN AND GAMES--UNTIL THE GUARDS COME.
NOT A CONCERN. I'VE WORKED OUT THE DETAILS WITH A FEW KEY MEMBERS OF THE SECURITY STAFF--
--THAT'S WHY WE ONLY HAVE ABOUT HALF THE LIQUOR WE LIBERATED FROM THE FACULTY SUPPLY, UNFORTUNATELY.
'A SACRIFICE IS ALWAYS DEMANDED' INDEED.

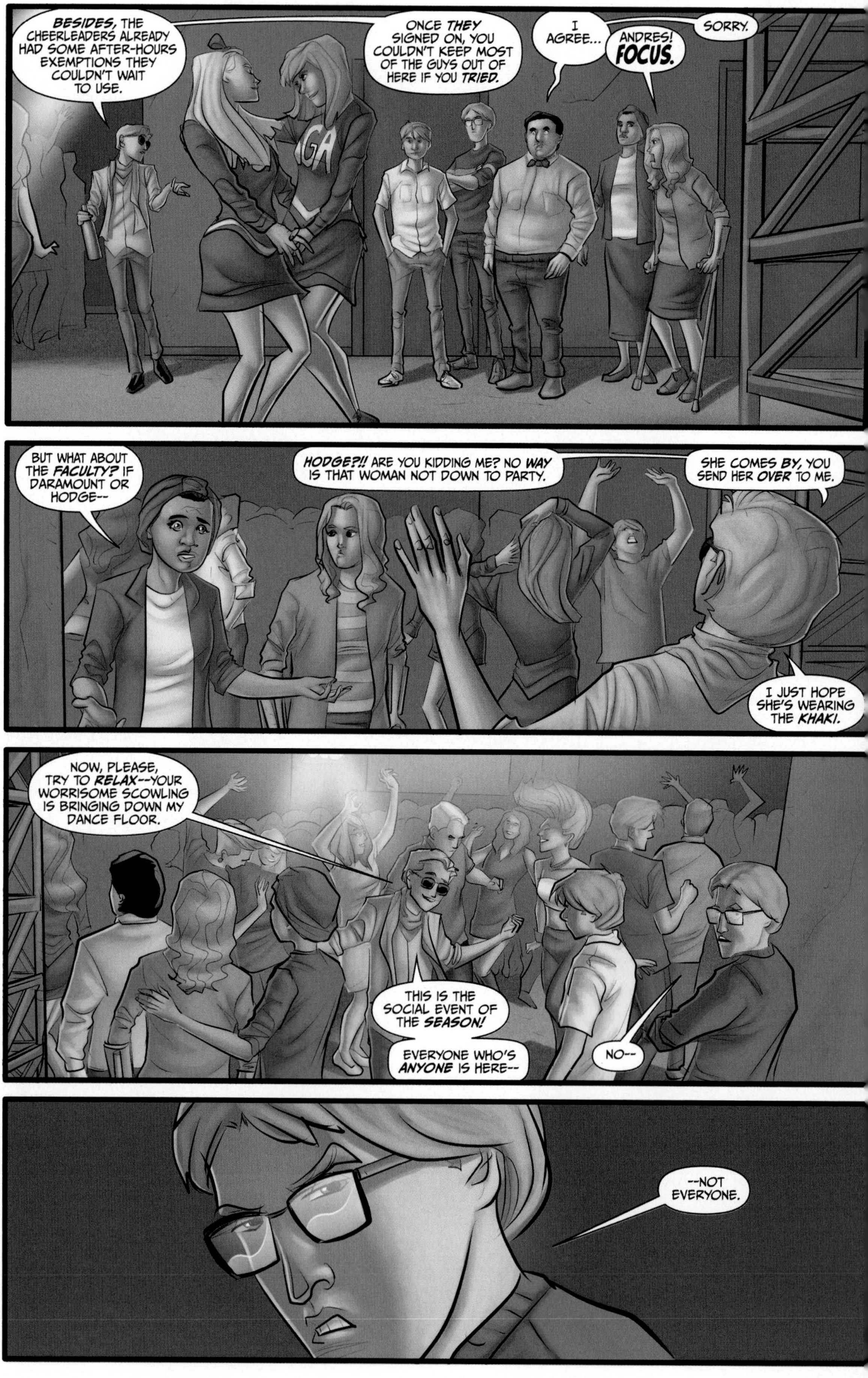

BESIDES, THE CHEERLEADERS ALREADY HAD SOME AFTER-HOURS EXEMPTIONS THEY COULDN'T WAIT TO USE.
ONCE THEY SIGNED ON, YOU COULDN'T KEEP MOST OF THE GUYS OUT OF HERE IF YOU TRIED.
I AGREE...
ANDRES! FOCUS.
SORRY.
BUT WHAT ABOUT THE FACULTY? IF DARAMOUNT OR HODGE--
HODGE?!! ARE YOU KIDDING ME? NO WAY IS THAT WOMAN NOT DOWN TO PARTY.
SHE COMES BY, YOU SEND HER OVER TO ME.
I JUST HOPE SHE'S WEARING THE KHAKI.
NOW, PLEASE, TRY TO RELAX--YOUR WORRISOME SCOWLING IS BRINGING DOWN MY DANCE FLOOR.
THIS IS THE SOCIAL EVENT OF THE SEASON!
EVERYONE WHO'S ANYONE IS HERE--
NO--
--NOT EVERYONE.

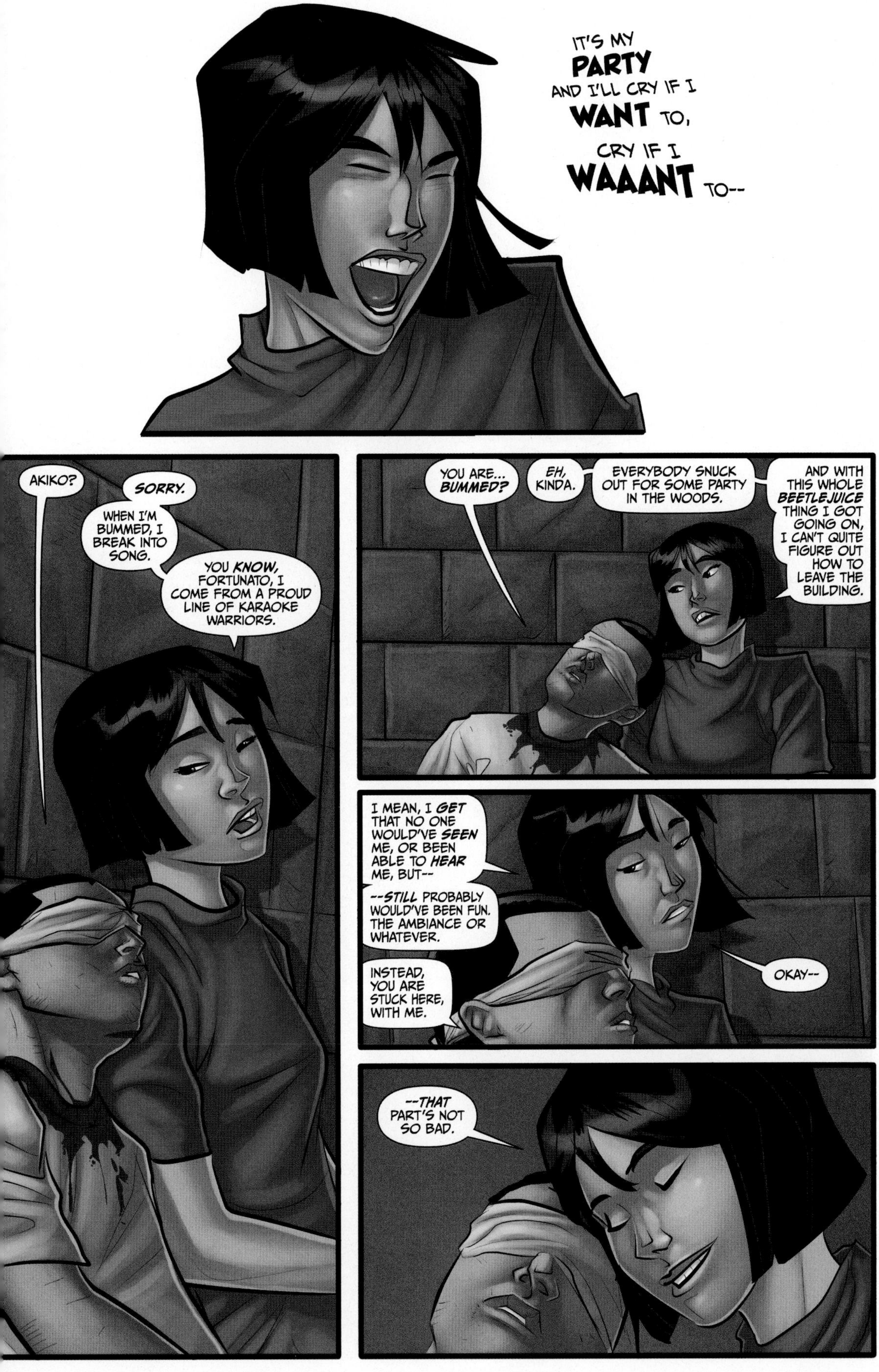
IT'S MY PARTY AND I'LL CRY IF I WANT TO, CRY IF I WAAANT TO--
AKIKO?
SORRY.
WHEN I'M BUMMED, I BREAK INTO SONG.
YOU KNOW, FORTUNATO, I COME FROM A PROUD LINE OF KARAOKE WARRIORS.
YOU ARE... BUMMED?
EH, KINDA.
EVERYBODY SNUCK OUT FOR SOME PARTY IN THE WOODS.
AND WITH THIS WHOLE BEETLEJUICE THING I GOT GOING ON, I CAN'T QUITE FIGURE OUT HOW TO LEAVE THE BUILDING.
I MEAN, I GET THAT NO ONE WOULD'VE SEEN ME, OR BEEN ABLE TO HEAR ME, BUT--
--STILL PROBABLY WOULD'VE BEEN FUN. THE AMBIANCE OR WHATEVER.
INSTEAD, YOU ARE STUCK HERE, WITH ME.
OKAY--
--THAT PART'S NOT SO BAD.

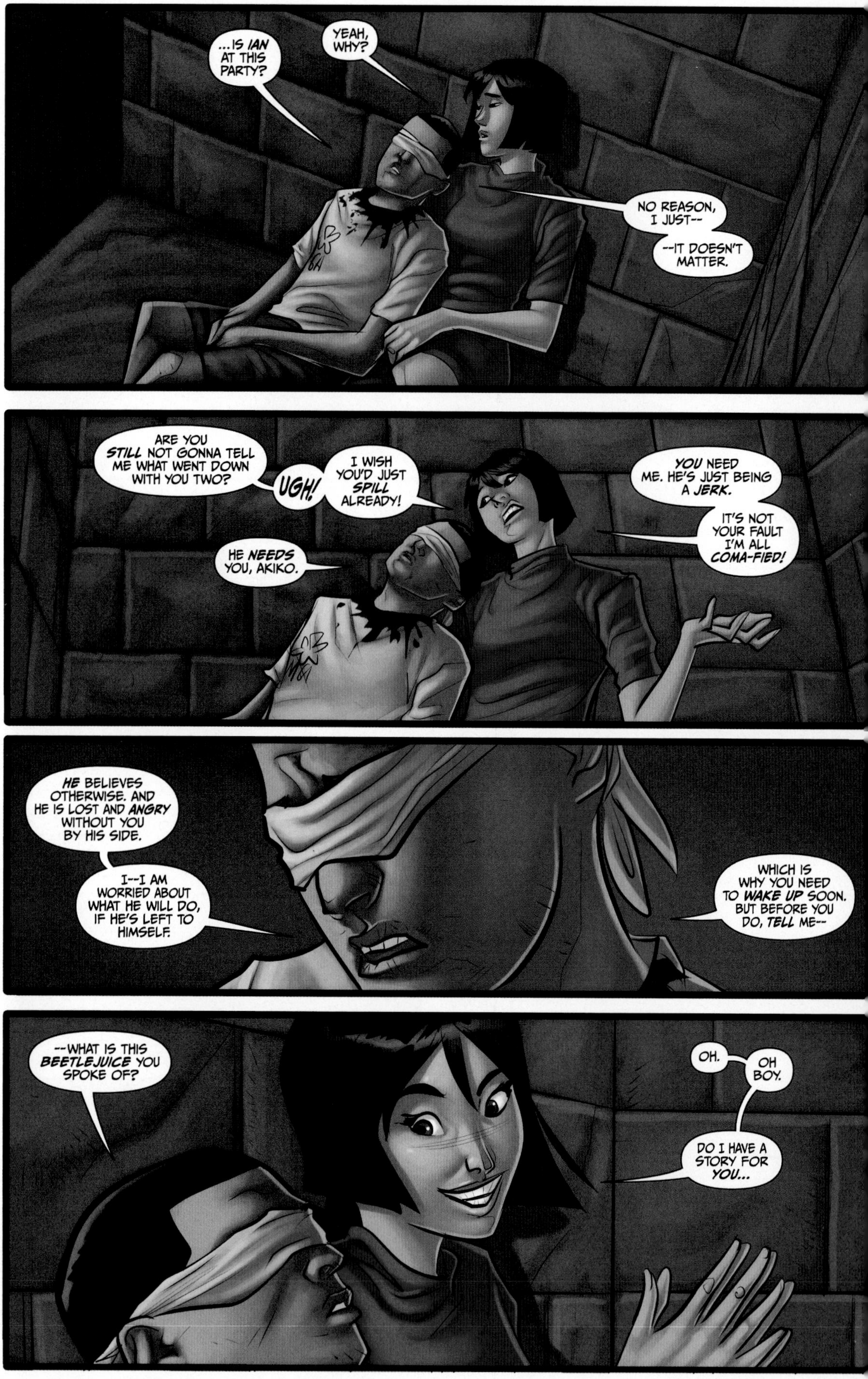

...IS IAN AT THIS PARTY?
YEAH, WHY?
NO REASON, I JUST--
--IT DOESN'T MATTER.
ARE YOU STILL NOT GONNA TELL ME WHAT WENT DOWN WITH YOU TWO?
UGH!
I WISH YOU'D JUST SPILL ALREADY!
YOU NEED ME. HE'S JUST BEING A JERK.
IT'S NOT YOUR FAULT I'M ALL COMA-FIED!
HE NEEDS YOU, AKIKO.
HE BELIEVES OTHERWISE. AND HE IS LOST AND ANGRY WITHOUT YOU BY HIS SIDE.
I--I AM WORRIED ABOUT WHAT HE WILL DO, IF HE'S LEFT TO HIMSELF.
WHICH IS WHY YOU NEED TO WAKE UP SOON. BUT BEFORE YOU DO, TELL ME--
--WHAT IS THIS BEETLEJUICE YOU SPOKE OF?
OH.
OH BOY.
DO I HAVE A STORY FOR YOU...

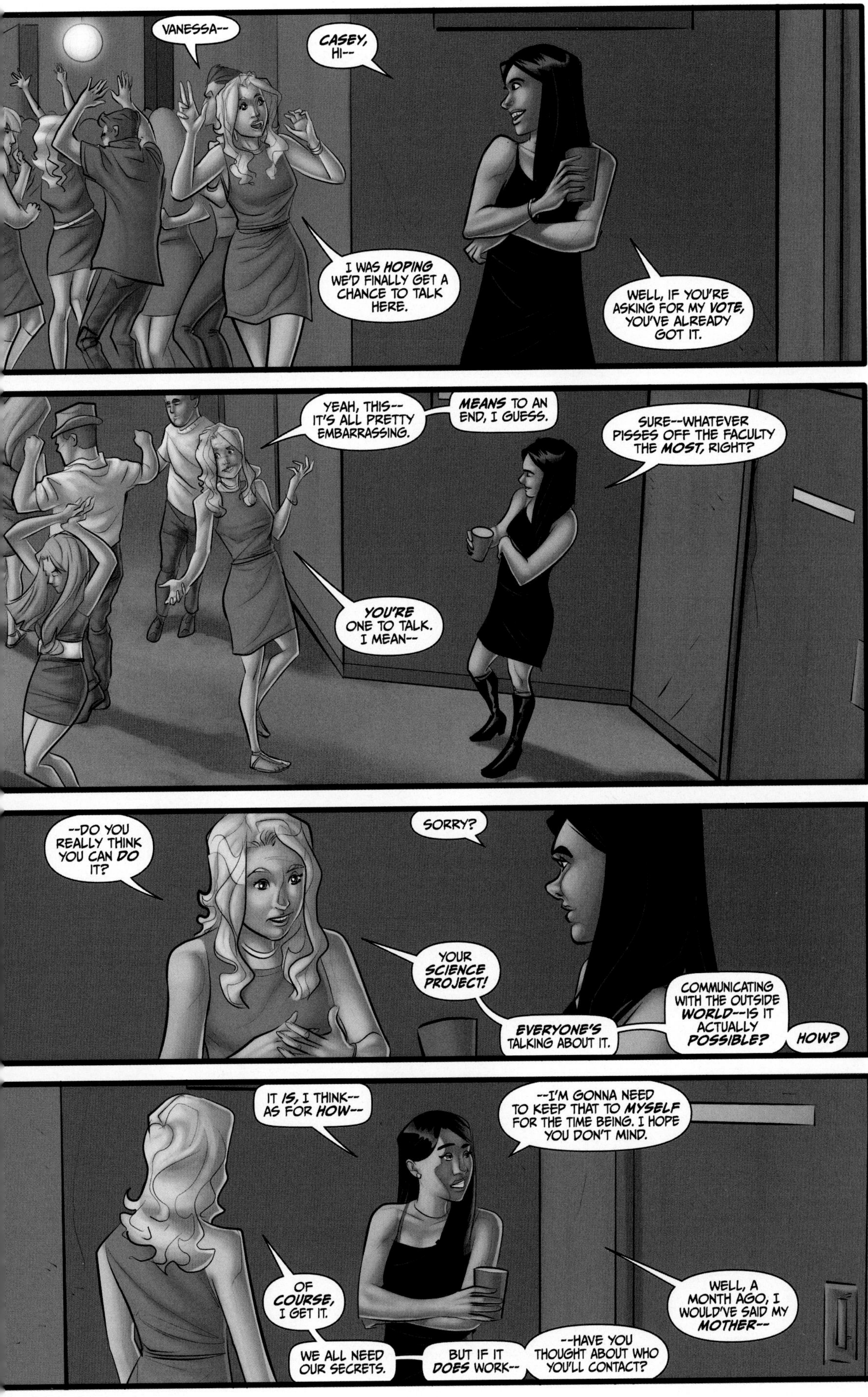
VANESSA--
CASEY, HI--
I WAS HOPING WE'D FINALLY GET A CHANCE TO TALK HERE.
WELL, IF YOU'RE ASKING FOR MY VOTE, YOU'VE ALREADY GOT IT.
YEAH, THIS-- IT'S ALL PRETTY EMBARRASSING.
MEANS TO AN END, I GUESS.
SURE--WHATEVER PISSES OFF THE FACULTY THE MOST, RIGHT?
YOU'RE ONE TO TALK. I MEAN--
--DO YOU REALLY THINK YOU CAN DO IT?
SORRY?
YOUR SCIENCE PROJECT!
EVERYONE'S TALKING ABOUT IT.
COMMUNICATING WITH THE OUTSIDE WORLD--IS IT ACTUALLY POSSIBLE?
HOW?
IT IS, I THINK-- AS FOR HOW--
--I'M GONNA NEED TO KEEP THAT TO MYSELF FOR THE TIME BEING. I HOPE YOU DON'T MIND.
OF COURSE, I GET IT.
WE ALL NEED OUR SECRETS.
BUT IF IT DOES WORK--
--HAVE YOU THOUGHT ABOUT WHO YOU'LL CONTACT?
WELL, A MONTH AGO, I WOULD'VE SAID MY MOTHER--

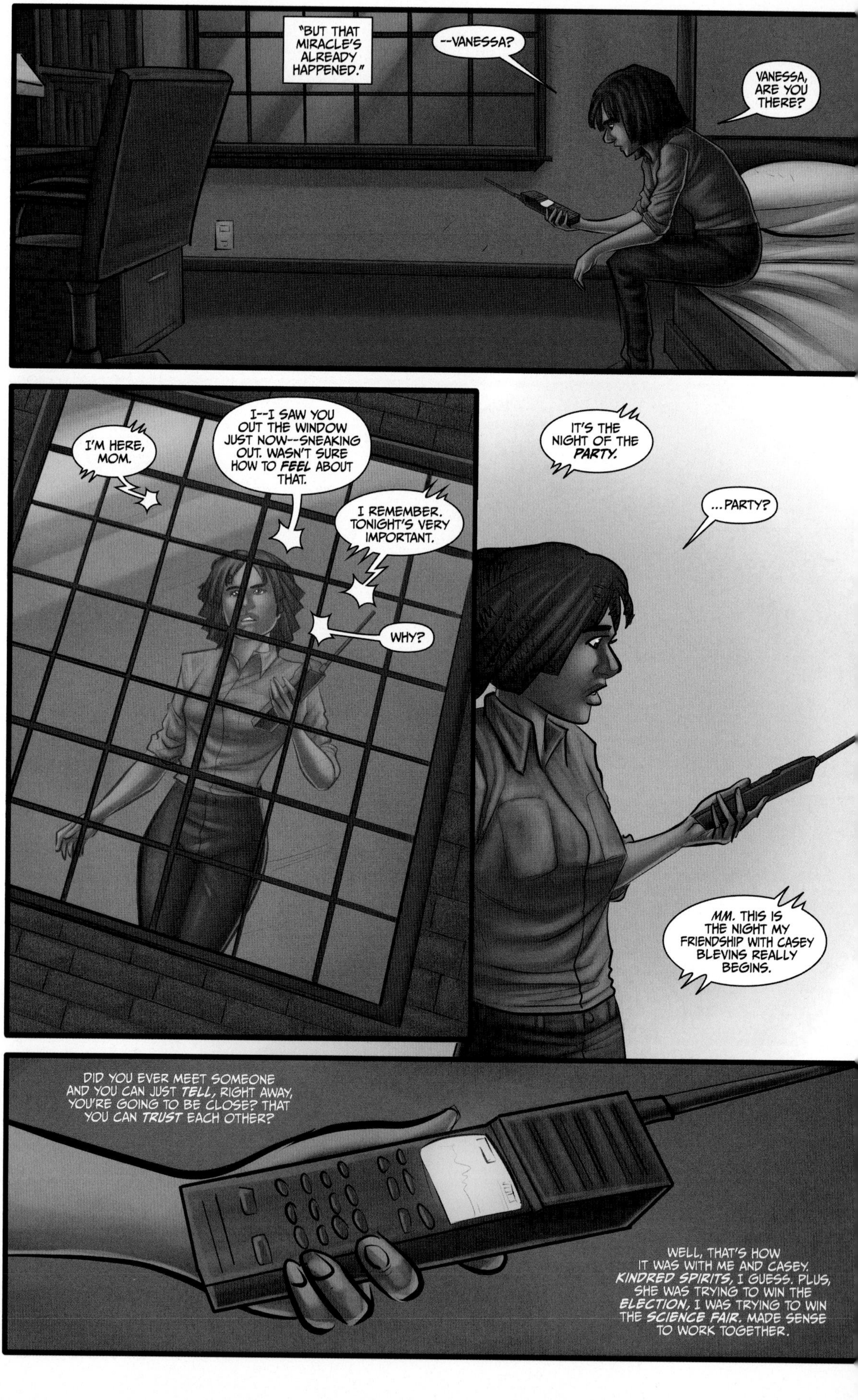
"BUT THAT MIRACLE'S ALREADY HAPPENED."
--VANESSA?
VANESSA, ARE YOU THERE?
I'M HERE, MOM.
I--I SAW YOU OUT THE WINDOW JUST NOW--SNEAKING OUT. WASN'T SURE HOW TO *FEEL* ABOUT THAT.
I REMEMBER. TONIGHT'S VERY IMPORTANT.
WHY?
IT'S THE NIGHT OF THE *PARTY.*
...PARTY?
MM. THIS IS THE NIGHT MY FRIENDSHIP WITH CASEY BLEVINS REALLY BEGINS.
DID YOU EVER MEET SOMEONE AND YOU CAN JUST *TELL*, RIGHT AWAY, YOU'RE GOING TO BE CLOSE? THAT YOU CAN *TRUST* EACH OTHER?
WELL, THAT'S HOW IT WAS WITH ME AND CASEY. *KINDRED SPIRITS,* I GUESS. PLUS, SHE WAS TRYING TO WIN THE *ELECTION,* I WAS TRYING TO WIN THE *SCIENCE FAIR.* MADE SENSE TO WORK TOGETHER.

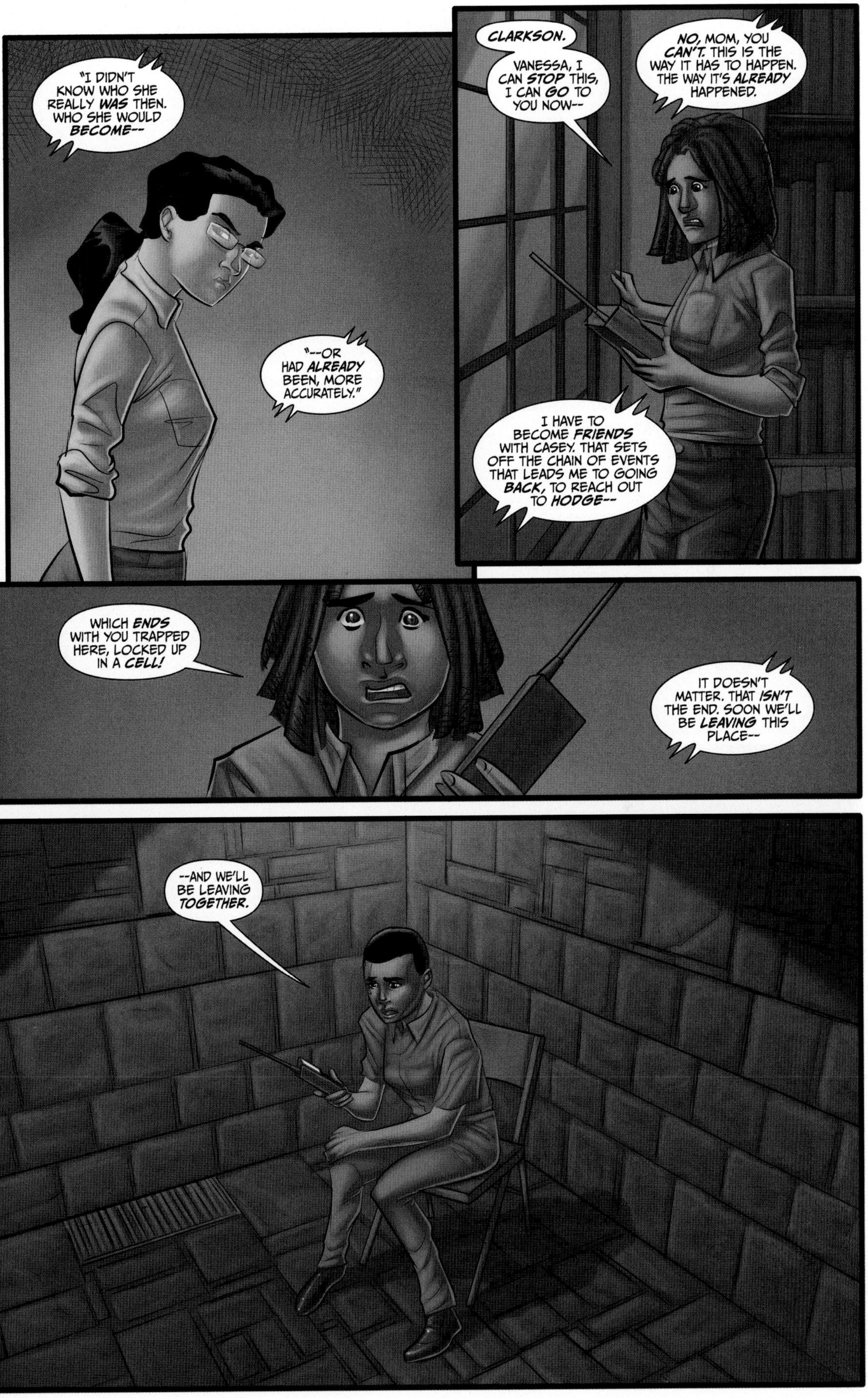
"I DIDN'T KNOW WHO SHE REALLY WAS THEN. WHO SHE WOULD BECOME--
"--OR HAD ALREADY BEEN, MORE ACCURATELY."
CLARKSON.
VANESSA, I CAN STOP THIS, I CAN GO TO YOU NOW--
NO, MOM, YOU CAN'T. THIS IS THE WAY IT HAS TO HAPPEN. THE WAY IT'S ALREADY HAPPENED.
I HAVE TO BECOME FRIENDS WITH CASEY. THAT SETS OFF THE CHAIN OF EVENTS THAT LEADS ME TO GOING BACK, TO REACH OUT TO HODGE--
WHICH ENDS WITH YOU TRAPPED HERE, LOCKED UP IN A CELL!
IT DOESN'T MATTER. THAT ISN'T THE END. SOON WE'LL BE LEAVING THIS PLACE--
--AND WE'LL BE LEAVING TOGETHER.

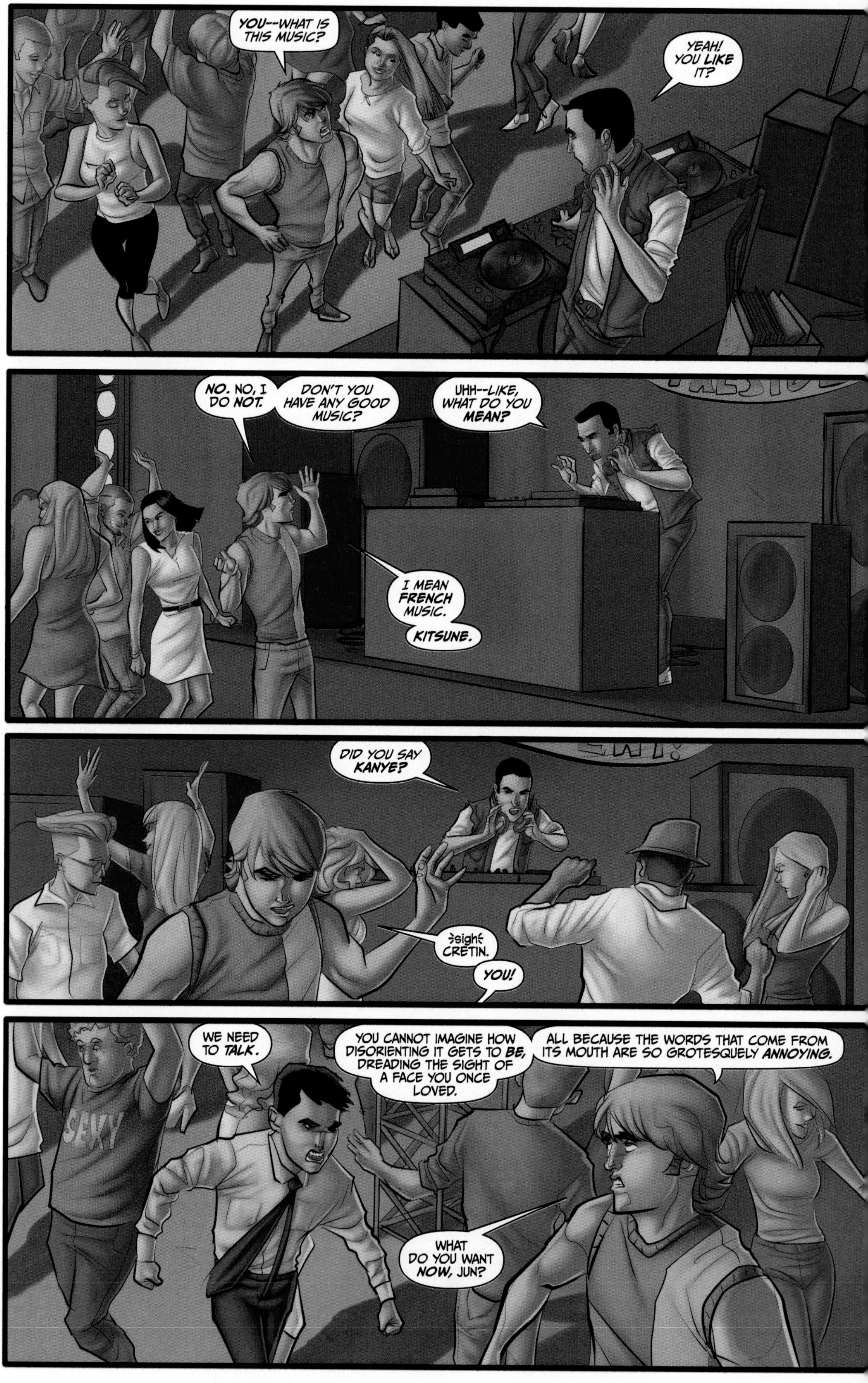
YOU--WHAT IS THIS MUSIC?
YEAH! YOU LIKE IT?
NO. NO, I DO NOT.
DON'T YOU HAVE ANY GOOD MUSIC?
UHH--LIKE, WHAT DO YOU MEAN?
I MEAN FRENCH MUSIC.
KITSUNE.
DID YOU SAY KANYE?
sigh CRETIN.
YOU!
WE NEED TO TALK.
YOU CANNOT IMAGINE HOW DISORIENTING IT GETS TO BE, DREADING THE SIGHT OF A FACE YOU ONCE LOVED.
ALL BECAUSE THE WORDS THAT COME FROM ITS MOUTH ARE SO GROTESQUELY ANNOYING.
WHAT DO YOU WANT NOW, JUN?
SEXY

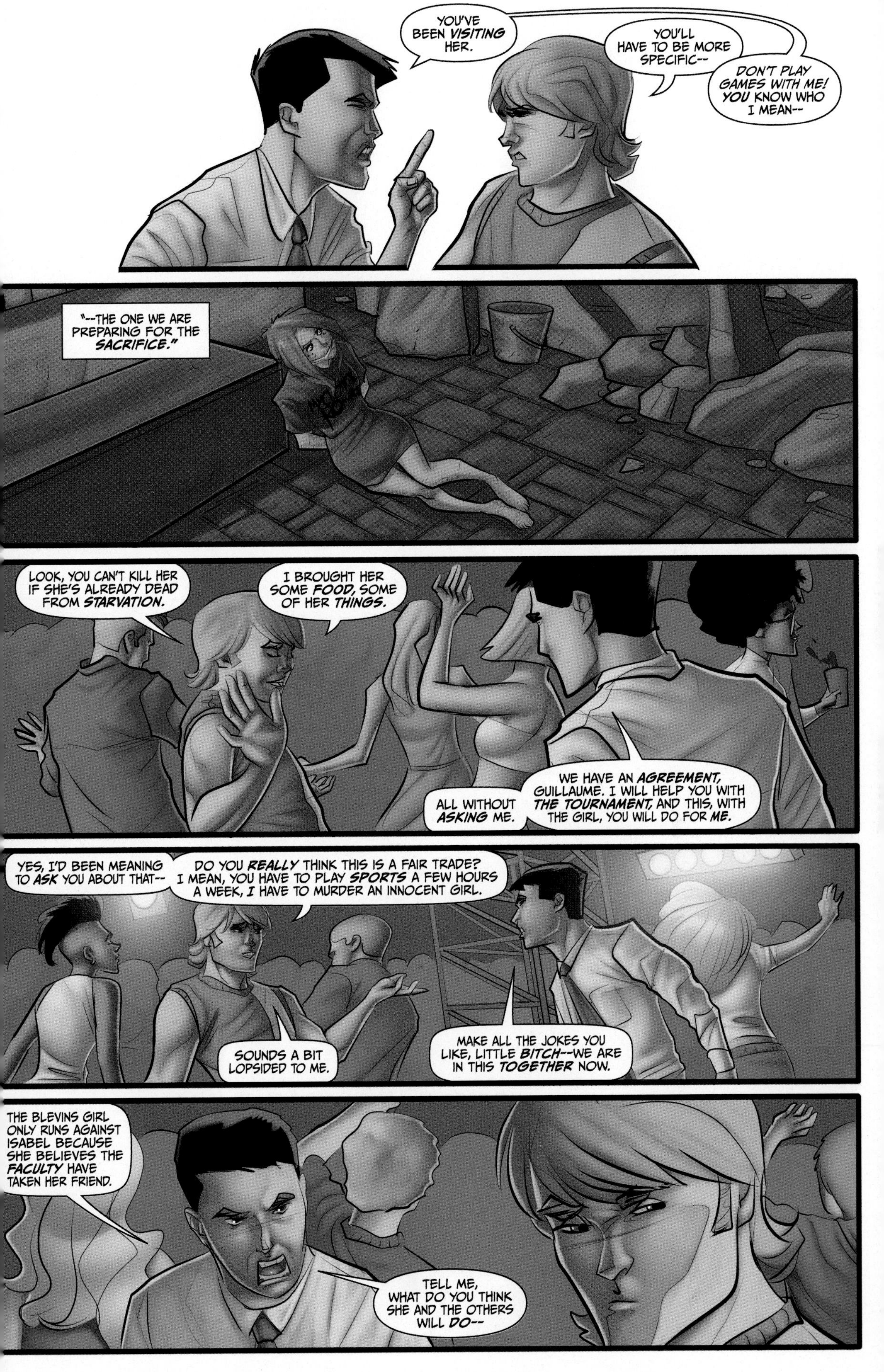

YOU'VE BEEN VISITING HER.
YOU'LL HAVE TO BE MORE SPECIFIC--
DON'T PLAY GAMES WITH ME! YOU KNOW WHO I MEAN--
"--THE ONE WE ARE PREPARING FOR THE SACRIFICE."
LOOK, YOU CAN'T KILL HER IF SHE'S ALREADY DEAD FROM STARVATION.
I BROUGHT HER SOME FOOD, SOME OF HER THINGS.
ALL WITHOUT ASKING ME.
WE HAVE AN AGREEMENT, GUILLAUME. I WILL HELP YOU WITH THE TOURNAMENT, AND THIS, WITH THE GIRL, YOU WILL DO FOR ME.
YES, I'D BEEN MEANING TO ASK YOU ABOUT THAT--
DO YOU REALLY THINK THIS IS A FAIR TRADE? I MEAN, YOU HAVE TO PLAY SPORTS A FEW HOURS A WEEK, I HAVE TO MURDER AN INNOCENT GIRL.
SOUNDS A BIT LOPSIDED TO ME.
MAKE ALL THE JOKES YOU LIKE, LITTLE BITCH--WE ARE IN THIS TOGETHER NOW.
THE BLEVINS GIRL ONLY RUNS AGAINST ISABEL BECAUSE SHE BELIEVES THE FACULTY HAVE TAKEN HER FRIEND.
TELL ME, WHAT DO YOU THINK SHE AND THE OTHERS WILL DO--

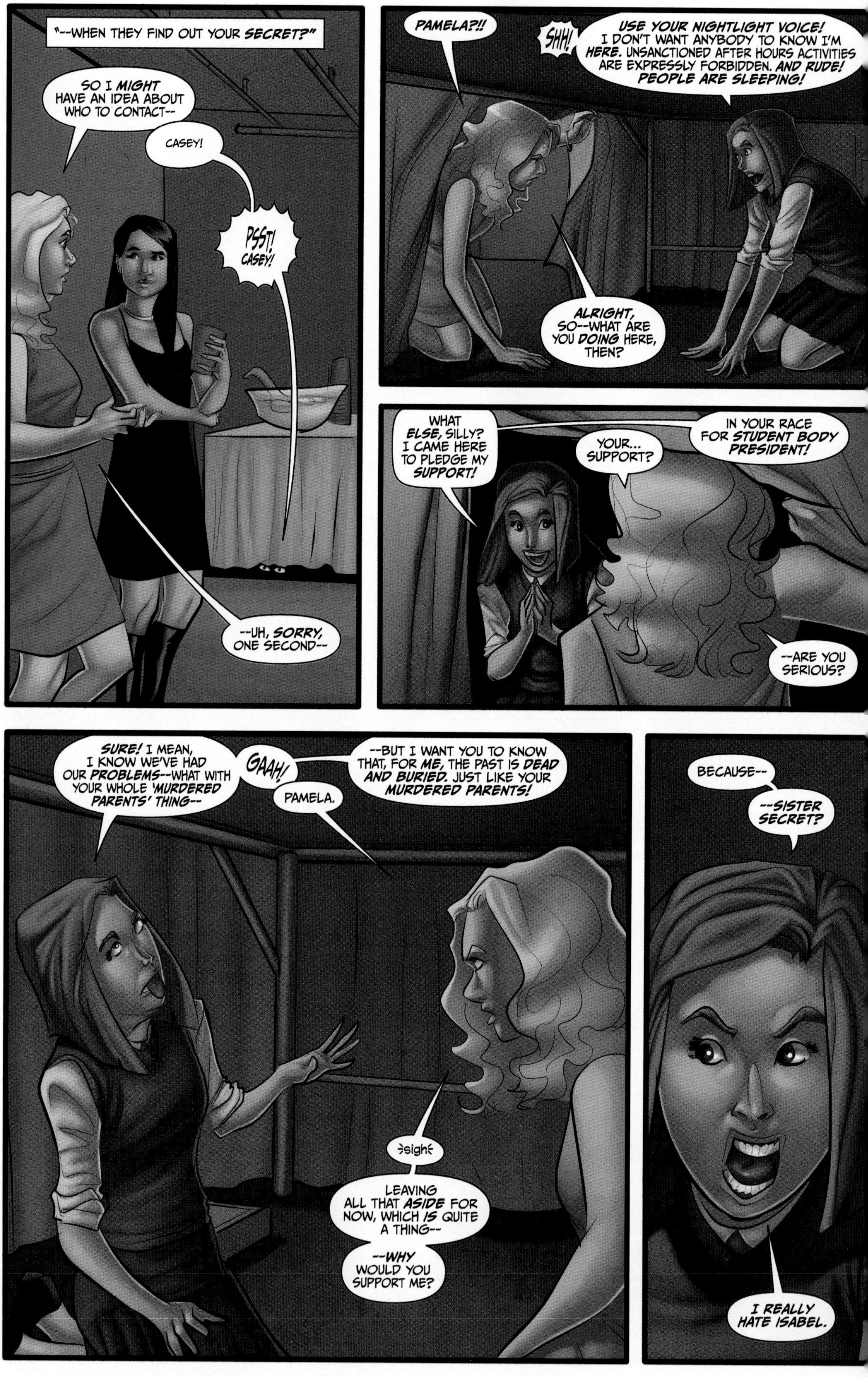
"--WHEN THEY FIND OUT YOUR SECRET?"
SO I MIGHT HAVE AN IDEA ABOUT WHO TO CONTACT--
CASEY!
PSST! CASEY!
--UH, SORRY, ONE SECOND--
PAMELA?!!
SHH!
USE YOUR NIGHTLIGHT VOICE! I DON'T WANT ANYBODY TO KNOW I'M HERE. UNSANCTIONED AFTER HOURS ACTIVITIES ARE EXPRESSLY FORBIDDEN. AND RUDE! PEOPLE ARE SLEEPING!
ALRIGHT, SO--WHAT ARE YOU DOING HERE, THEN?
WHAT ELSE, SILLY? I CAME HERE TO PLEDGE MY SUPPORT!
YOUR... SUPPORT?
IN YOUR RACE FOR STUDENT BODY PRESIDENT!
--ARE YOU SERIOUS?
SURE! I MEAN, I KNOW WE'VE HAD OUR PROBLEMS--WHAT WITH YOUR WHOLE 'MURDERED PARENTS' THING--
GAAH!
PAMELA.
--BUT I WANT YOU TO KNOW THAT, FOR ME, THE PAST IS DEAD AND BURIED. JUST LIKE YOUR MURDERED PARENTS!
sigh
LEAVING ALL THAT ASIDE FOR NOW, WHICH IS QUITE A THING--
--WHY WOULD YOU SUPPORT ME?
BECAUSE--
--SISTER SECRET?
I REALLY HATE ISABEL.

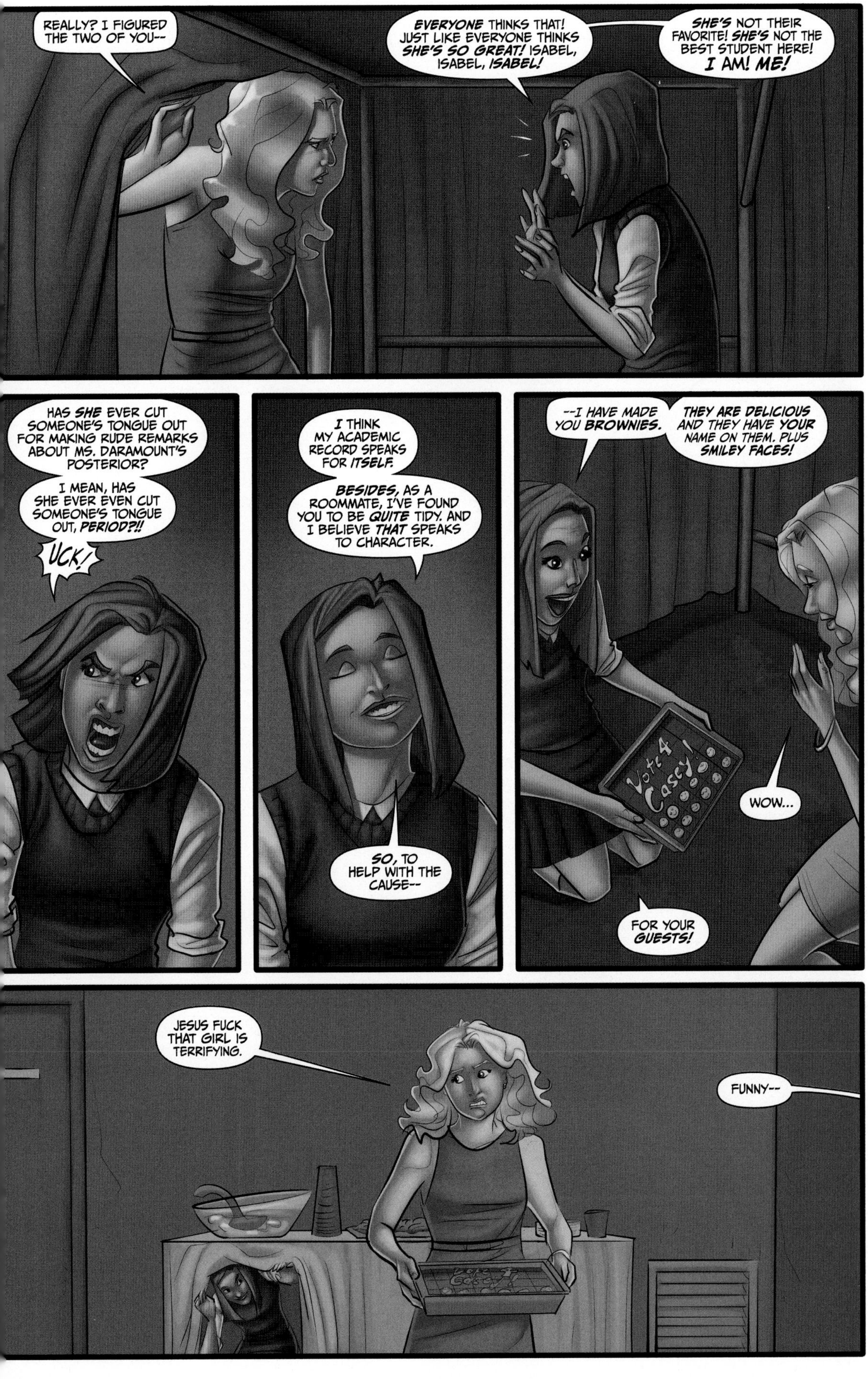
REALLY? I FIGURED THE TWO OF YOU--
EVERYONE THINKS THAT! JUST LIKE EVERYONE THINKS SHE'S SO GREAT! ISABEL, ISABEL, ISABEL!
SHE'S NOT THEIR FAVORITE! SHE'S NOT THE BEST STUDENT HERE! I AM! ME!
HAS SHE EVER CUT SOMEONE'S TONGUE OUT FOR MAKING RUDE REMARKS ABOUT MS. DARAMOUNT'S POSTERIOR?
I MEAN, HAS SHE EVER EVEN CUT SOMEONE'S TONGUE OUT, PERIOD?!!
UCK!
I THINK MY ACADEMIC RECORD SPEAKS FOR ITSELF.
BESIDES, AS A ROOMMATE, I'VE FOUND YOU TO BE QUITE TIDY. AND I BELIEVE THAT SPEAKS TO CHARACTER.
SO, TO HELP WITH THE CAUSE--
--I HAVE MADE YOU BROWNIES.
THEY ARE DELICIOUS AND THEY HAVE YOUR NAME ON THEM. PLUS SMILEY FACES!
Vote 4 Casey!
WOW...
FOR YOUR GUESTS!
JESUS FUCK THAT GIRL IS TERRIFYING.
FUNNY--

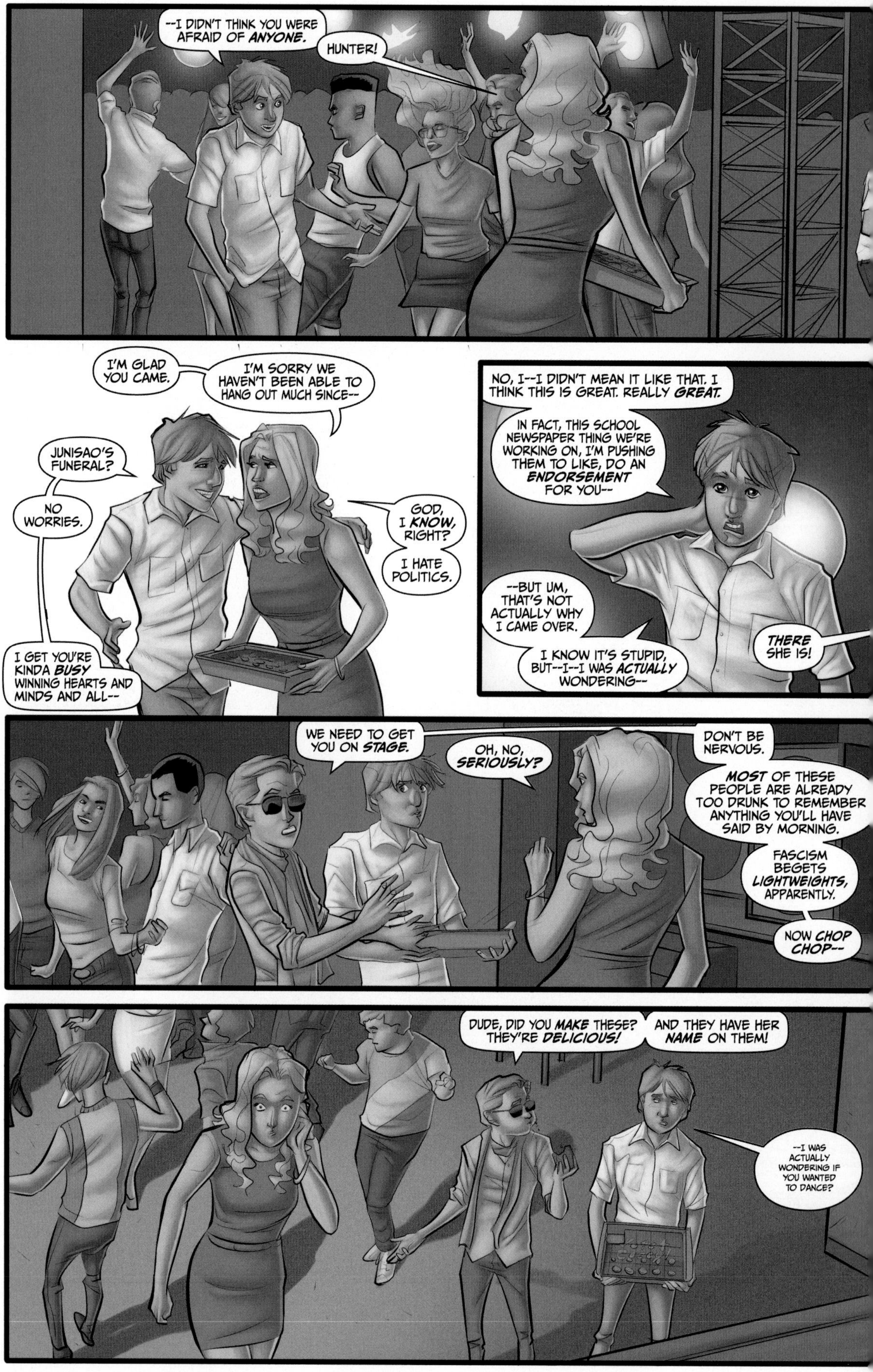
--I DIDN'T THINK YOU WERE AFRAID OF ANYONE.
HUNTER!
I'M GLAD YOU CAME.
I'M SORRY WE HAVEN'T BEEN ABLE TO HANG OUT MUCH SINCE--
JUNISAO'S FUNERAL?
NO WORRIES.
I GET YOU'RE KINDA BUSY WINNING HEARTS AND MINDS AND ALL--
GOD, I KNOW, RIGHT?
I HATE POLITICS.
NO, I--I DIDN'T MEAN IT LIKE THAT. I THINK THIS IS GREAT. REALLY GREAT.
IN FACT, THIS SCHOOL NEWSPAPER THING WE'RE WORKING ON, I'M PUSHING THEM TO LIKE, DO AN ENDORSEMENT FOR YOU--
--BUT UM, THAT'S NOT ACTUALLY WHY I CAME OVER.
I KNOW IT'S STUPID, BUT--I--I WAS ACTUALLY WONDERING--
THERE SHE IS!
WE NEED TO GET YOU ON STAGE.
OH, NO, SERIOUSLY?
DON'T BE NERVOUS.
MOST OF THESE PEOPLE ARE ALREADY TOO DRUNK TO REMEMBER ANYTHING YOU'LL HAVE SAID BY MORNING.
FASCISM BEGETS LIGHTWEIGHTS, APPARENTLY.
NOW CHOP CHOP--
DUDE, DID YOU MAKE THESE? THEY'RE DELICIOUS!
AND THEY HAVE HER NAME ON THEM!
--I WAS ACTUALLY WONDERING IF YOU WANTED TO DANCE?

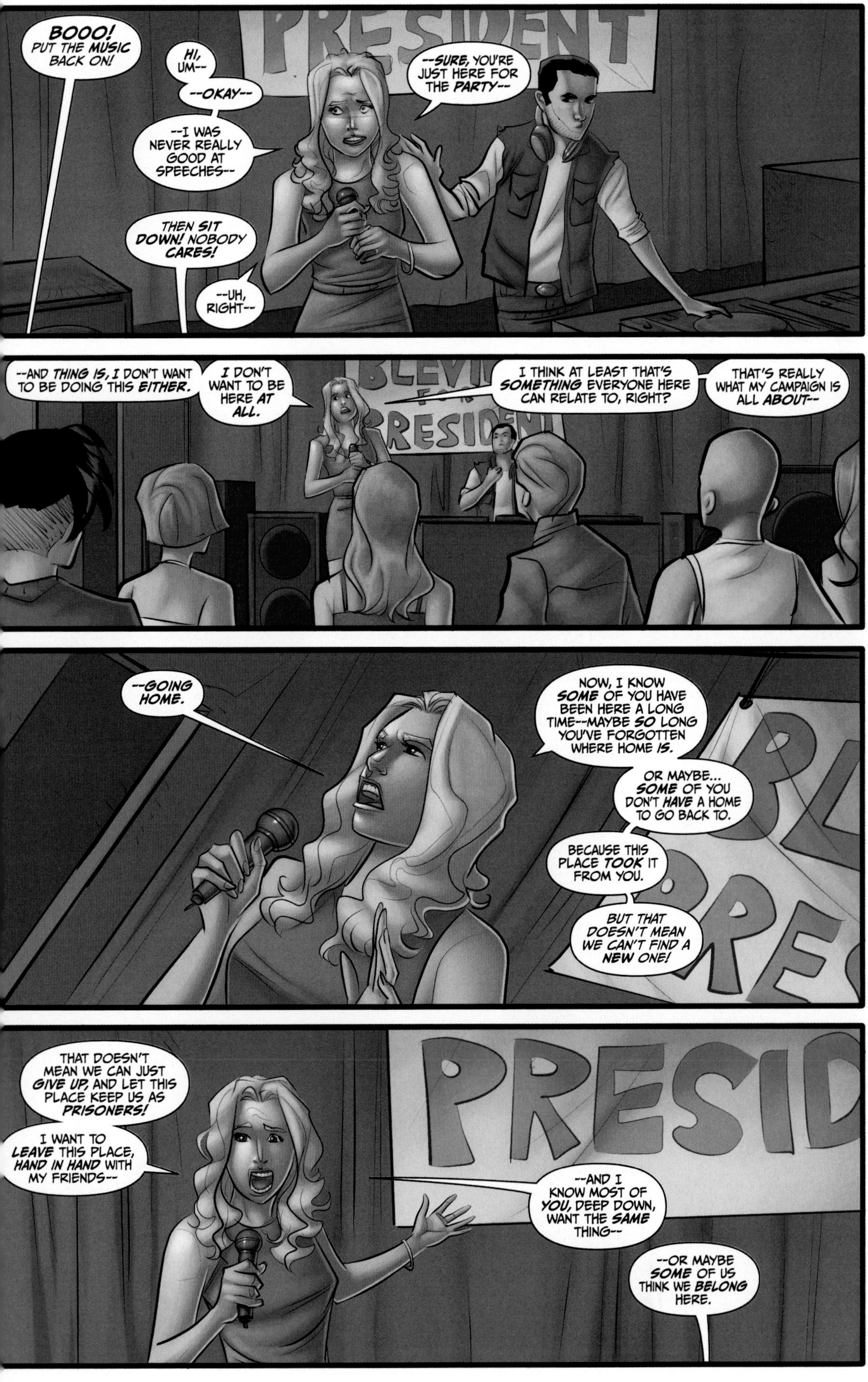
PRESIDENT
BOOO! PUT THE MUSIC BACK ON!
HI, UM--
--OKAY--
--I WAS NEVER REALLY GOOD AT SPEECHES--
--SURE, YOU'RE JUST HERE FOR THE PARTY--
THEN SIT DOWN! NOBODY CARES!
--UH, RIGHT--
--AND THING IS, I DON'T WANT TO BE DOING THIS EITHER.
I DON'T WANT TO BE HERE AT ALL.
I THINK AT LEAST THAT'S SOMETHING EVERYONE HERE CAN RELATE TO, RIGHT?
THAT'S REALLY WHAT MY CAMPAIGN IS ALL ABOUT--
--GOING HOME.
NOW, I KNOW SOME OF YOU HAVE BEEN HERE A LONG TIME--MAYBE SO LONG YOU'VE FORGOTTEN WHERE HOME IS.
OR MAYBE... SOME OF YOU DON'T HAVE A HOME TO GO BACK TO.
BECAUSE THIS PLACE TOOK IT FROM YOU.
BUT THAT DOESN'T MEAN WE CAN'T FIND A NEW ONE!
PRESID
THAT DOESN'T MEAN WE CAN JUST GIVE UP, AND LET THIS PLACE KEEP US AS PRISONERS!
I WANT TO LEAVE THIS PLACE, HAND IN HAND WITH MY FRIENDS--
--AND I KNOW MOST OF YOU, DEEP DOWN, WANT THE SAME THING--
--OR MAYBE SOME OF US THINK WE BELONG HERE.

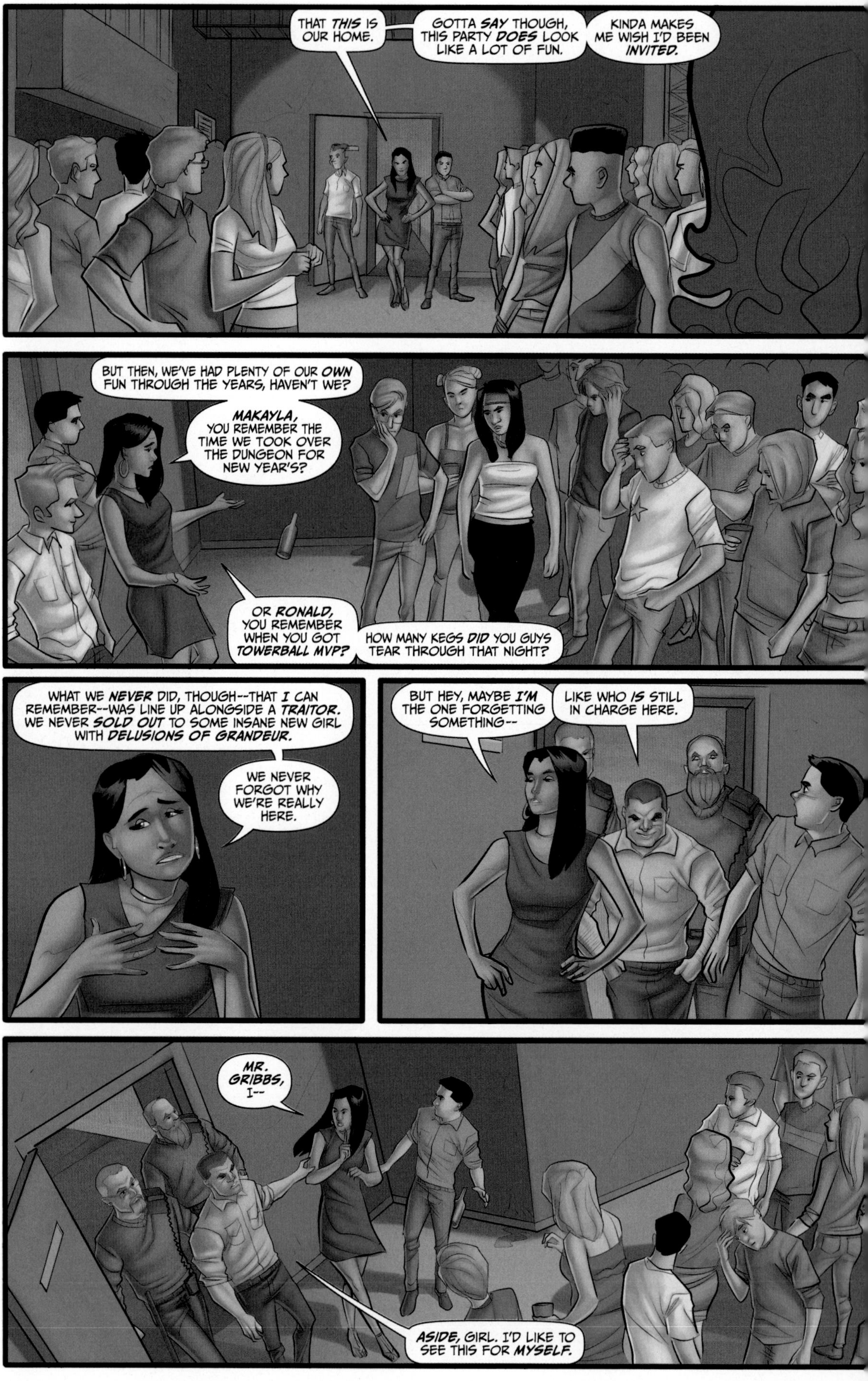
THAT *THIS* IS OUR HOME.
GOTTA *SAY* THOUGH, THIS PARTY *DOES* LOOK LIKE A LOT OF FUN.
KINDA MAKES ME WISH I'D BEEN *INVITED.*
BUT THEN, WE'VE HAD PLENTY OF OUR *OWN* FUN THROUGH THE YEARS, HAVEN'T WE?
MAKAYLA, YOU REMEMBER THE TIME WE TOOK OVER THE DUNGEON FOR NEW YEAR'S?
OR *RONALD,* YOU REMEMBER WHEN YOU GOT *TOWERBALL MVP?*
HOW MANY KEGS *DID* YOU GUYS TEAR THROUGH THAT NIGHT?
WHAT WE *NEVER* DID, THOUGH--THAT *I* CAN REMEMBER--WAS LINE UP ALONGSIDE A *TRAITOR.* WE NEVER *SOLD OUT* TO SOME INSANE NEW GIRL WITH *DELUSIONS OF GRANDEUR.*
WE NEVER FORGOT WHY WE'RE REALLY HERE.
BUT HEY, MAYBE *I'M* THE ONE FORGETTING SOMETHING--
LIKE WHO *IS* STILL IN CHARGE HERE.
MR. GRIBBS, I--
ASIDE, GIRL. I'D LIKE TO SEE THIS FOR *MYSELF.*

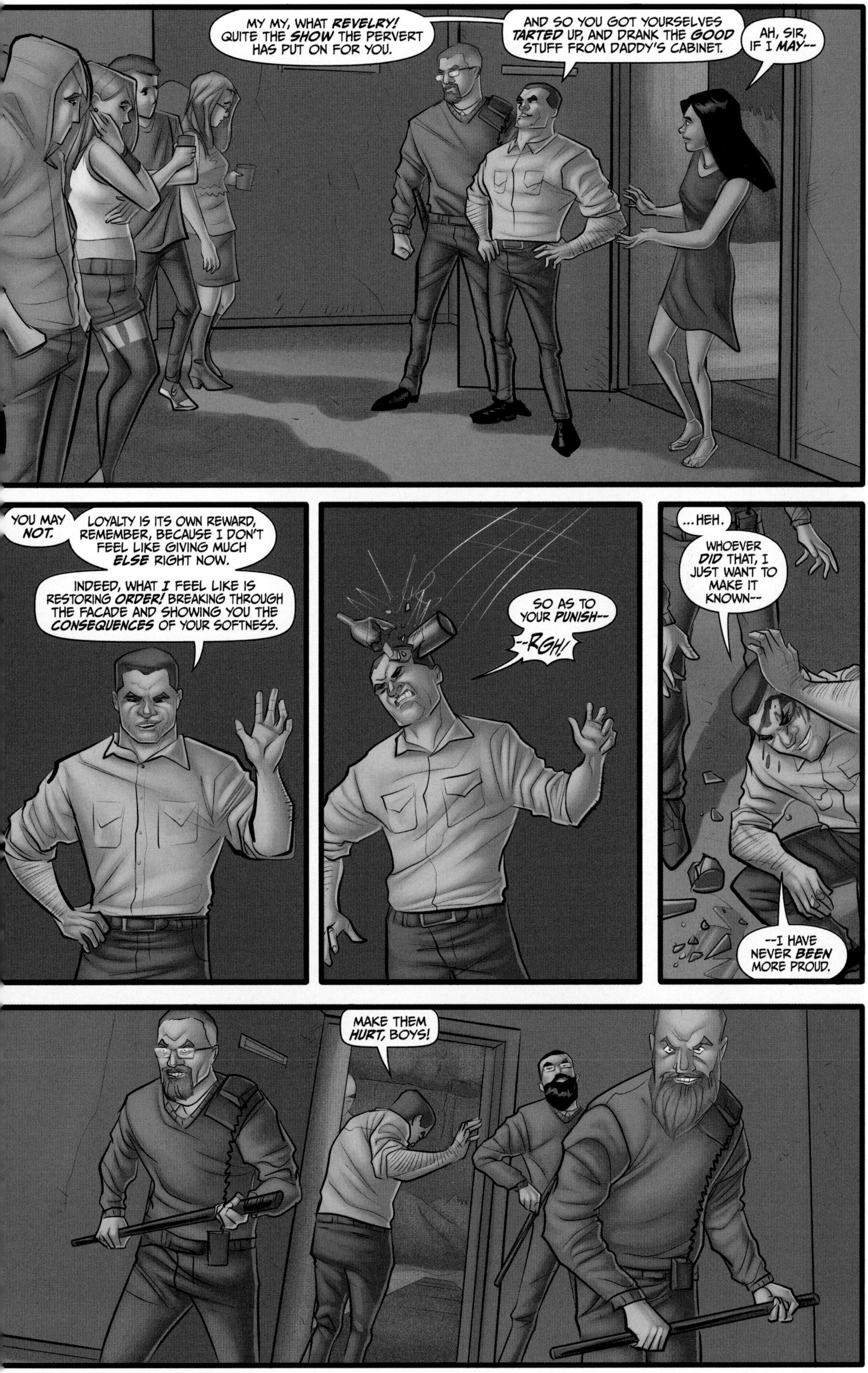
MY MY, WHAT REVELRY! QUITE THE SHOW THE PERVERT HAS PUT ON FOR YOU.
AND SO YOU GOT YOURSELVES TARTED UP, AND DRANK THE GOOD STUFF FROM DADDY'S CABINET.
AH, SIR, IF I MAY--
YOU MAY NOT.
LOYALTY IS ITS OWN REWARD, REMEMBER, BECAUSE I DON'T FEEL LIKE GIVING MUCH ELSE RIGHT NOW.
INDEED, WHAT I FEEL LIKE IS RESTORING ORDER! BREAKING THROUGH THE FACADE AND SHOWING YOU THE CONSEQUENCES OF YOUR SOFTNESS.
SO AS TO YOUR PUNISH--
--RGH!
...HEH.
WHOEVER DID THAT, I JUST WANT TO MAKE IT KNOWN--
--I HAVE NEVER BEEN MORE PROUD.
MAKE THEM HURT, BOYS!

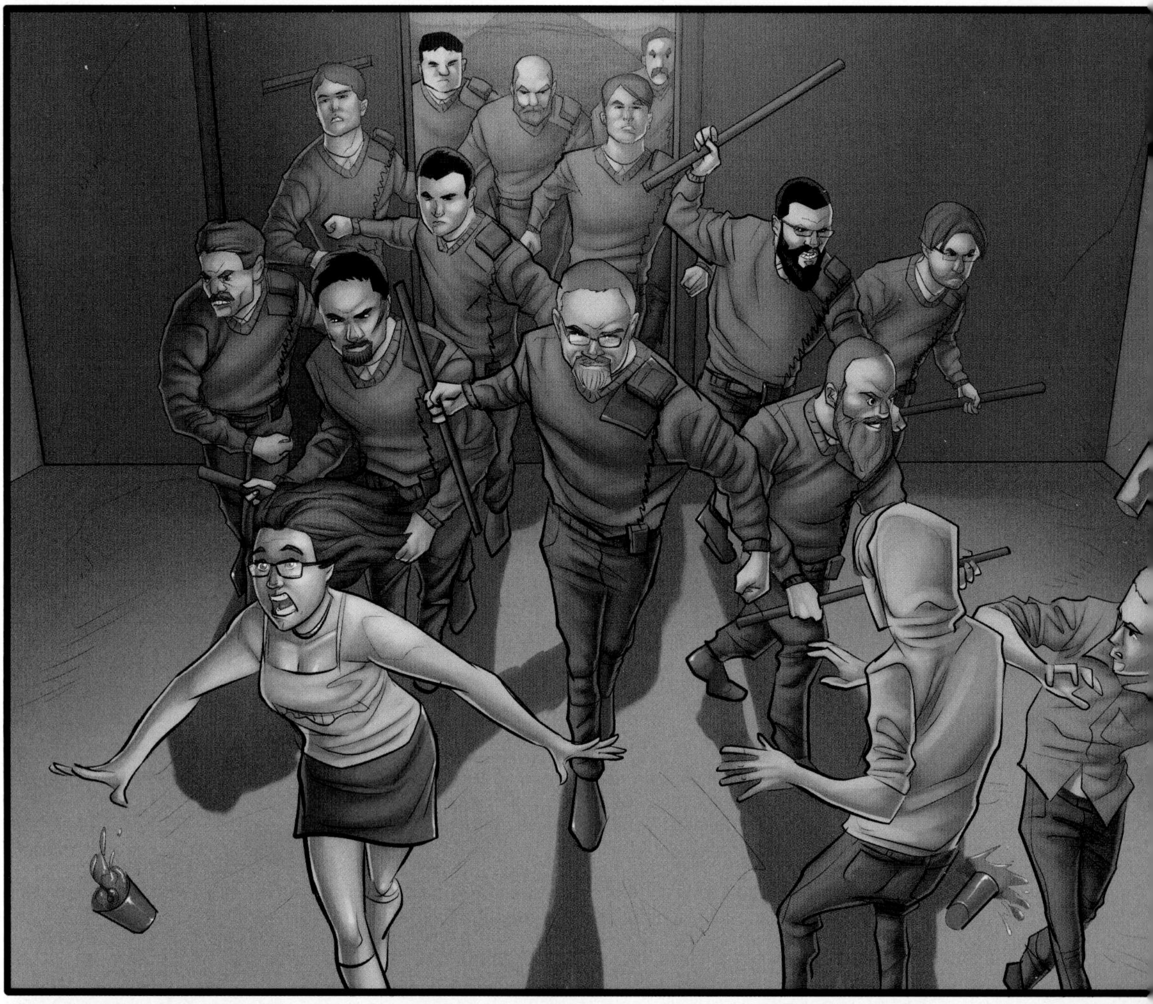
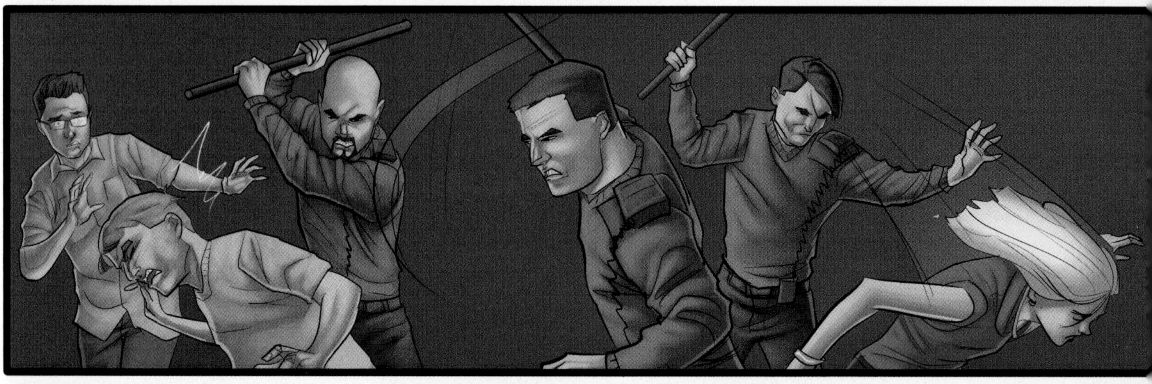
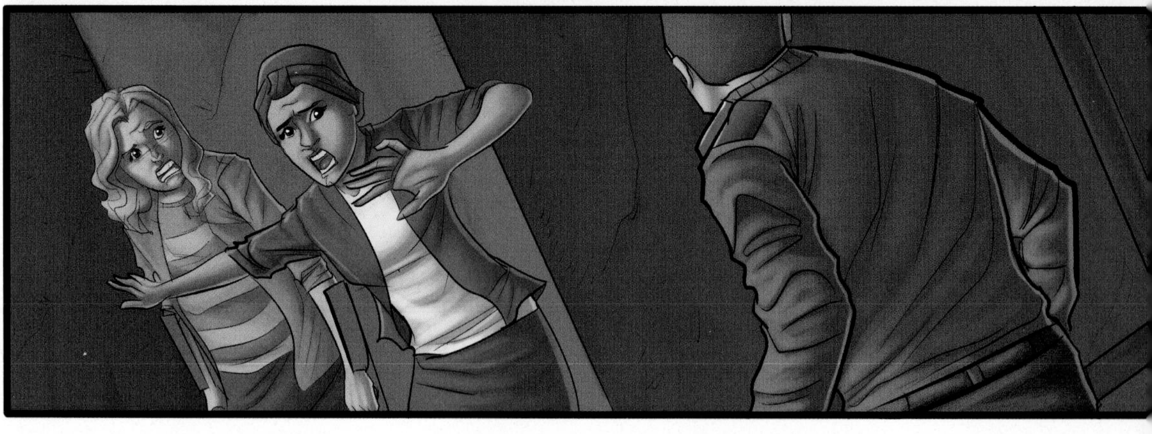

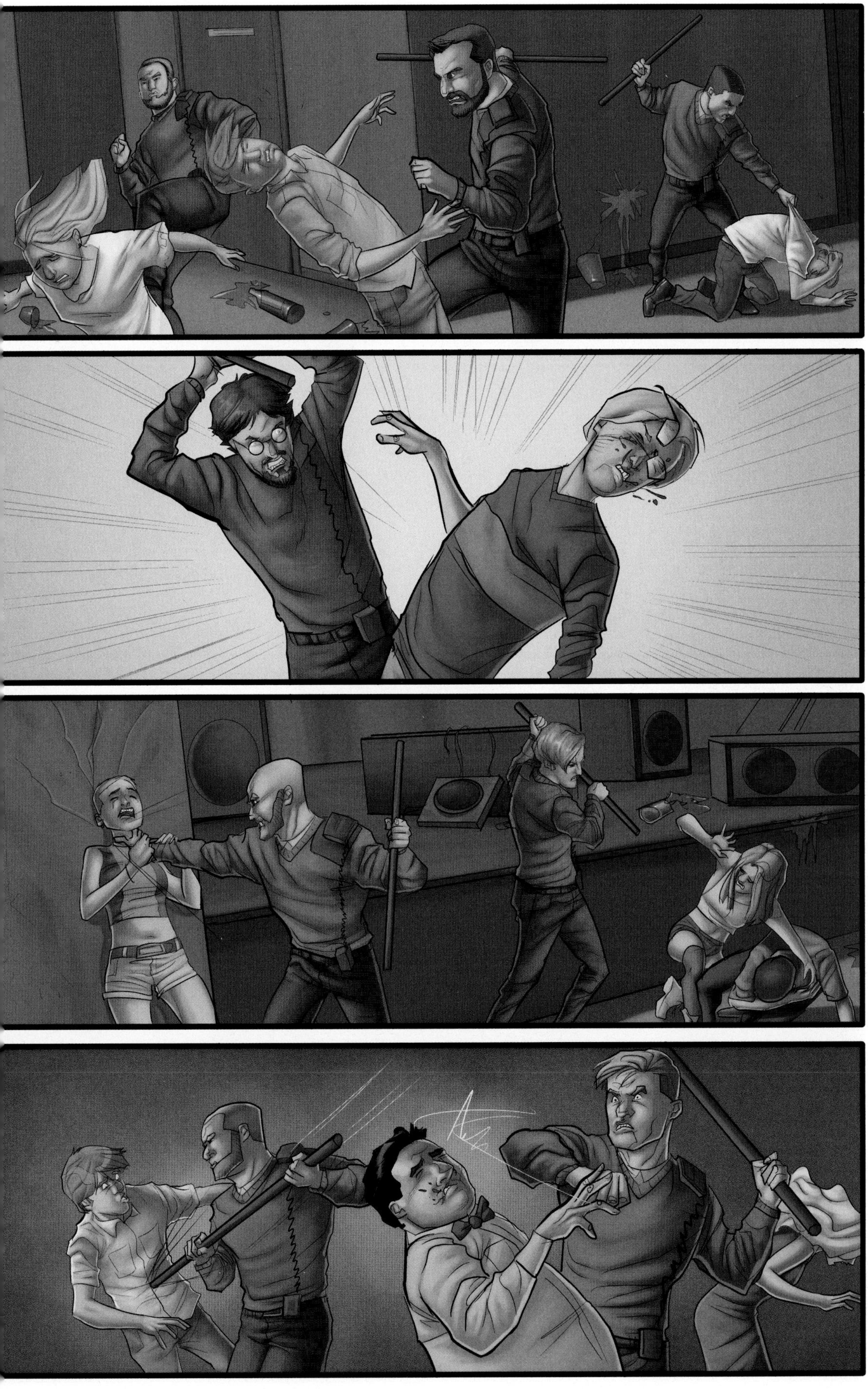

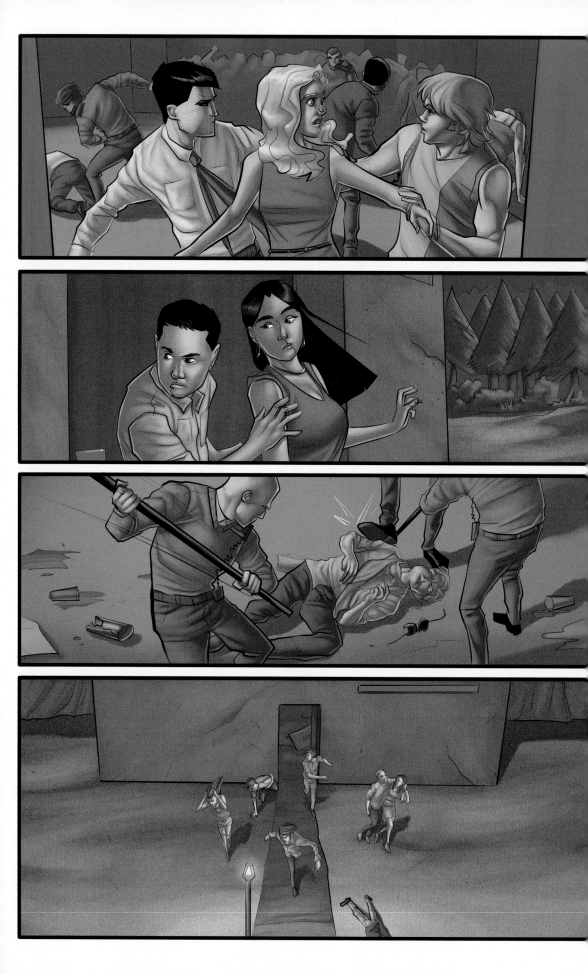

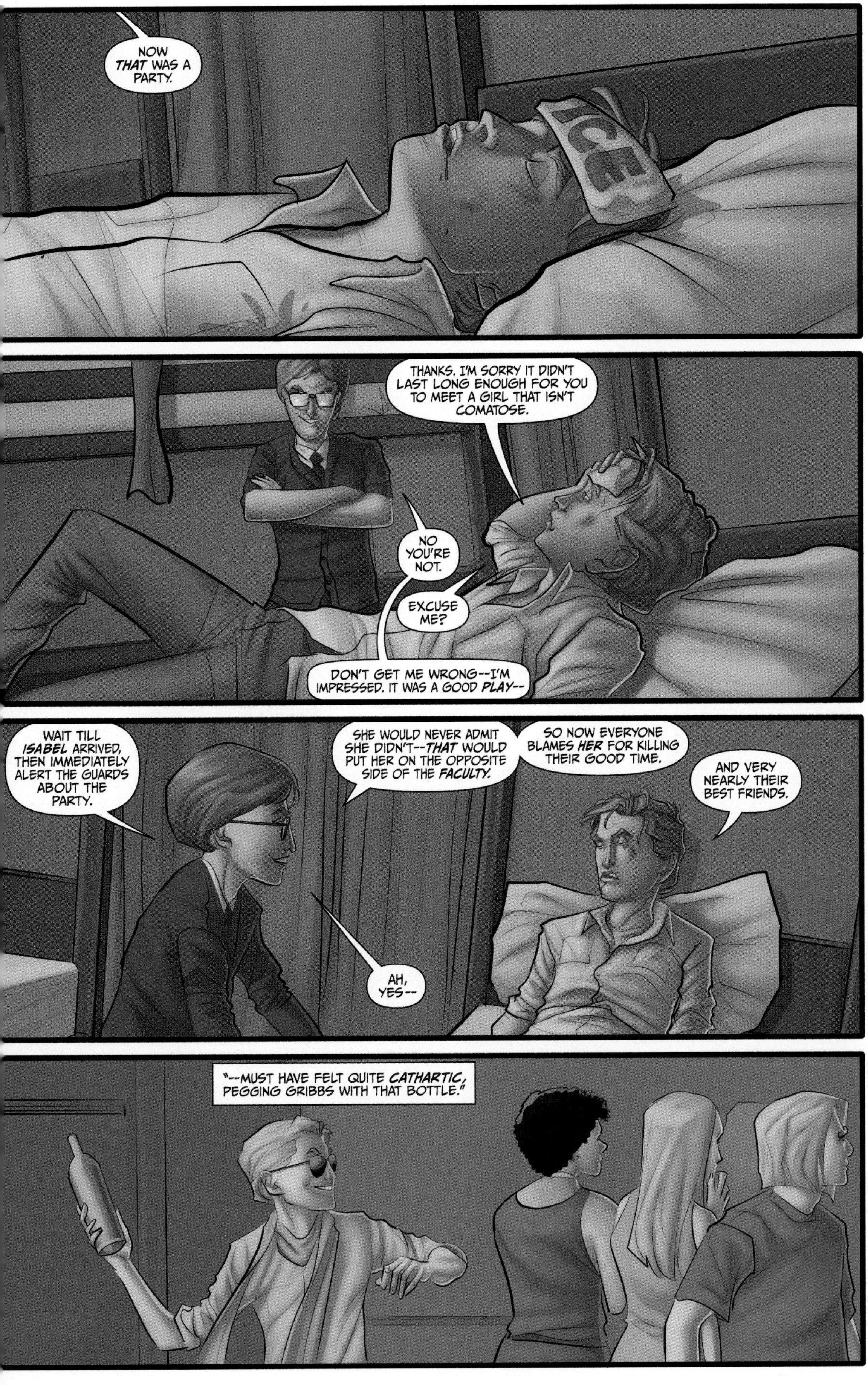
NOW THAT WAS A PARTY.
THANKS. I'M SORRY IT DIDN'T LAST LONG ENOUGH FOR YOU TO MEET A GIRL THAT ISN'T COMATOSE.
NO YOU'RE NOT.
EXCUSE ME?
DON'T GET ME WRONG--I'M IMPRESSED. IT WAS A GOOD PLAY--
WAIT TILL ISABEL ARRIVED, THEN IMMEDIATELY ALERT THE GUARDS ABOUT THE PARTY.
AH, YES--
SHE WOULD NEVER ADMIT SHE DIDN'T--THAT WOULD PUT HER ON THE OPPOSITE SIDE OF THE FACULTY.
SO NOW EVERYONE BLAMES HER FOR KILLING THEIR GOOD TIME.
AND VERY NEARLY THEIR BEST FRIENDS.
"--MUST HAVE FELT QUITE CATHARTIC, PEGGING GRIBBS WITH THAT BOTTLE."

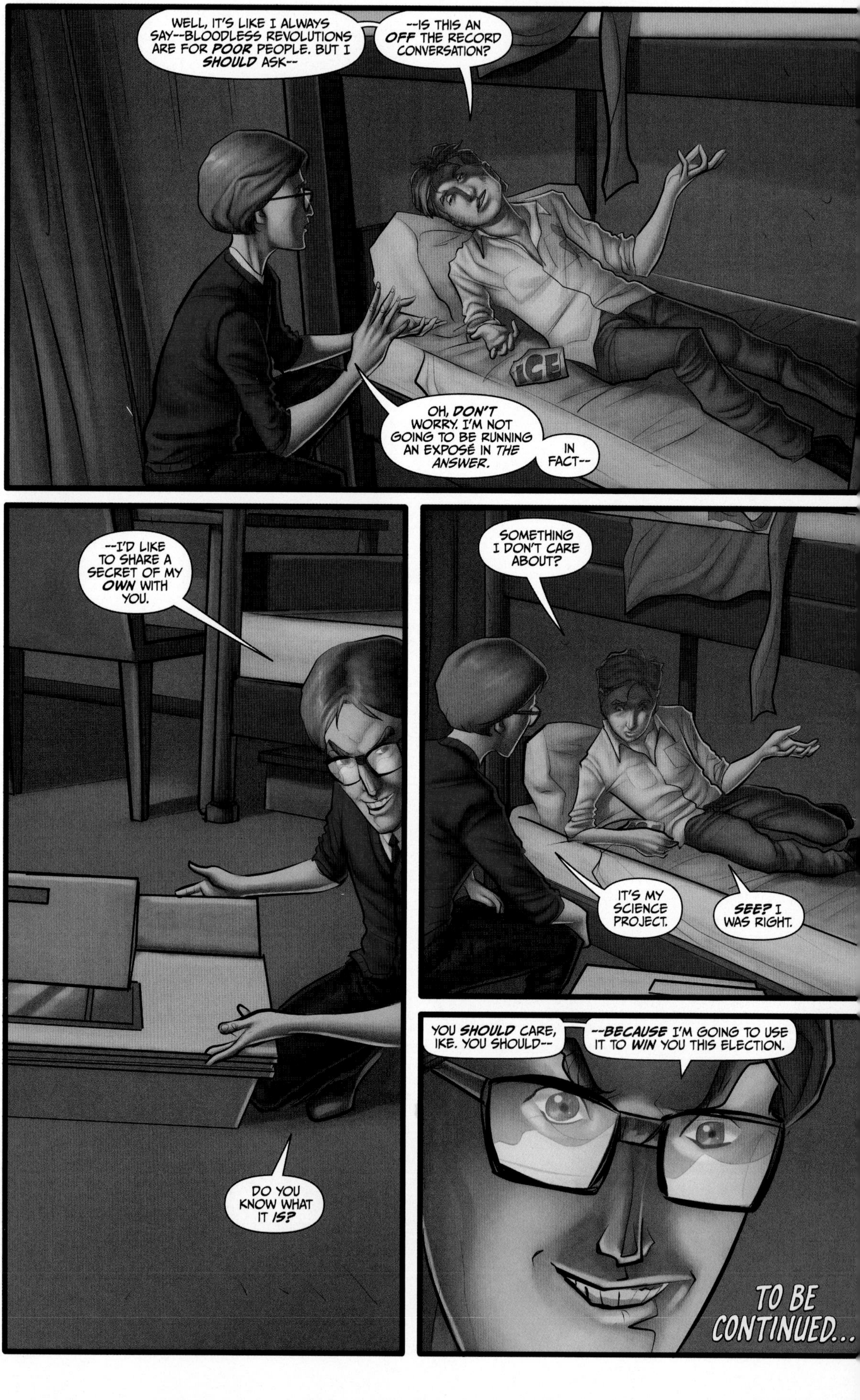
WELL, IT'S LIKE I ALWAYS SAY--BLOODLESS REVOLUTIONS ARE FOR POOR PEOPLE. BUT I SHOULD ASK--
--IS THIS AN OFF THE RECORD CONVERSATION?
OH, DON'T WORRY. I'M NOT GOING TO BE RUNNING AN EXPOSÉ IN THE ANSWER.
IN FACT--
--I'D LIKE TO SHARE A SECRET OF MY OWN WITH YOU.
DO YOU KNOW WHAT IT IS?
SOMETHING I DON'T CARE ABOUT?
IT'S MY SCIENCE PROJECT.
SEE? I WAS RIGHT.
YOU SHOULD CARE, IKE. YOU SHOULD--
--BECAUSE I'M GOING TO USE IT TO WIN YOU THIS ELECTION.
TO BE CONTINUED...

fortyeight

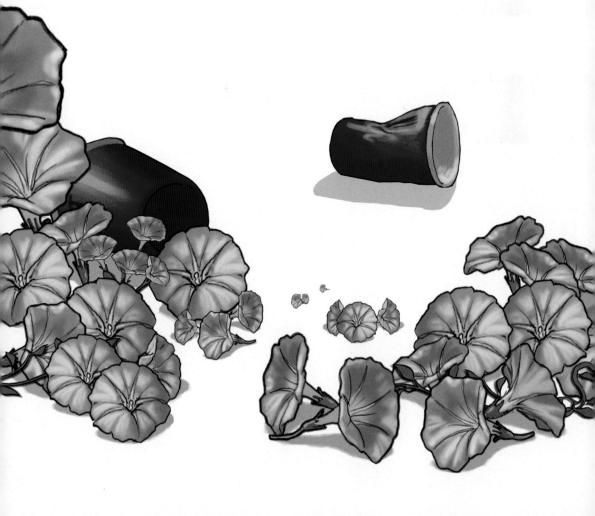

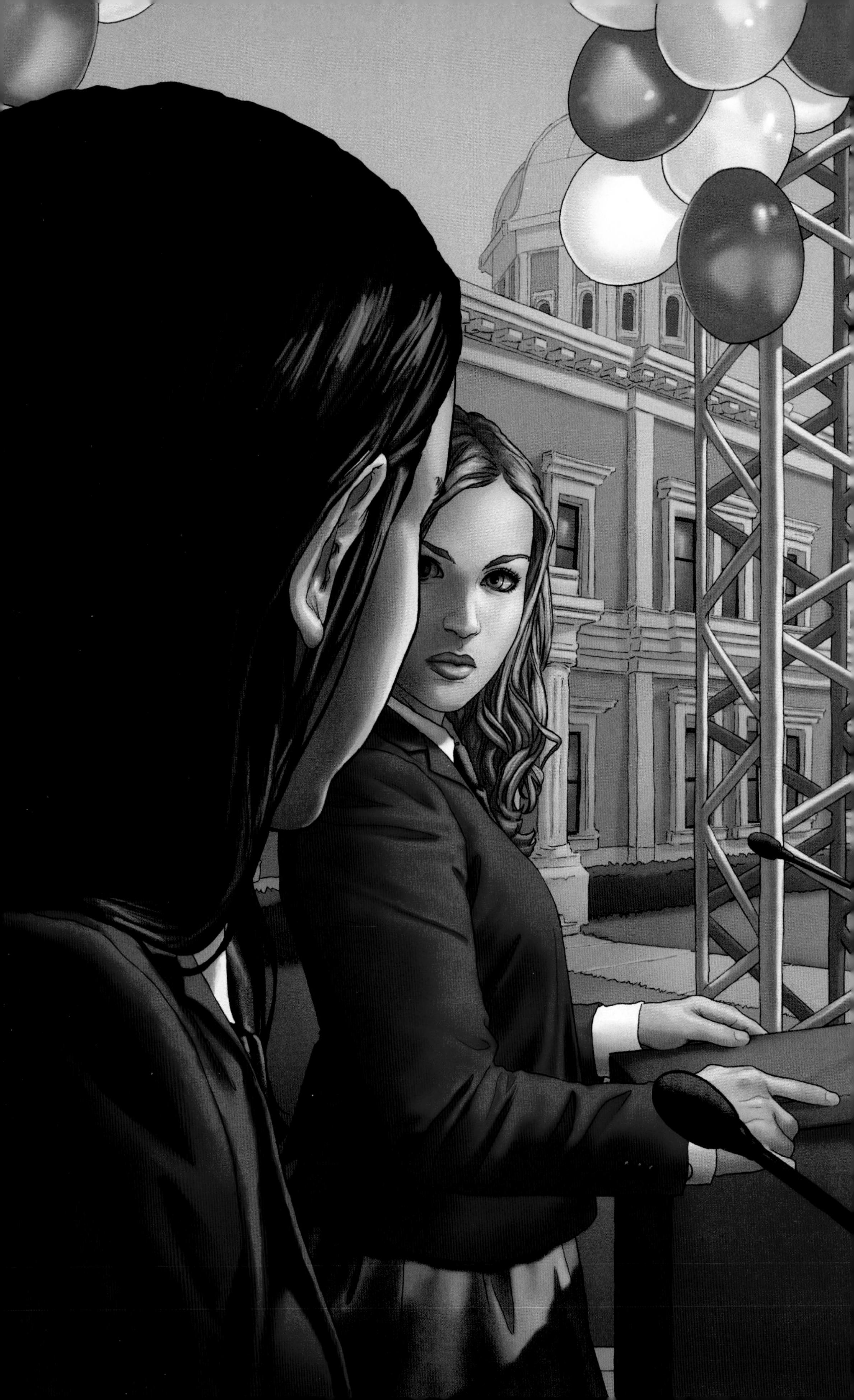

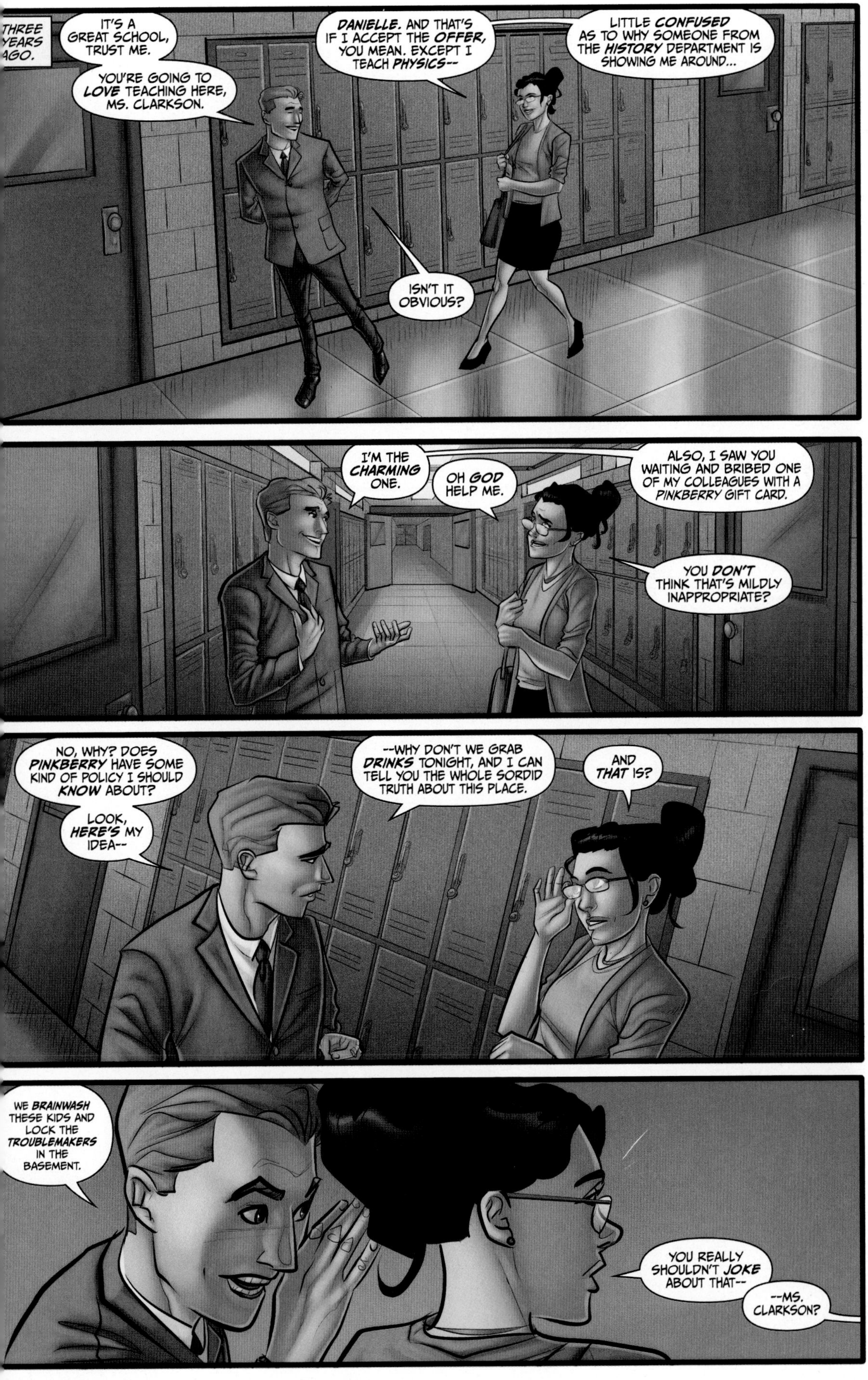
THREE YEARS AGO.
IT'S A GREAT SCHOOL, TRUST ME.
YOU'RE GOING TO LOVE TEACHING HERE, MS. CLARKSON.
DANIELLE. AND THAT'S IF I ACCEPT THE OFFER, YOU MEAN. EXCEPT I TEACH PHYSICS--
LITTLE CONFUSED AS TO WHY SOMEONE FROM THE HISTORY DEPARTMENT IS SHOWING ME AROUND...
ISN'T IT OBVIOUS?
I'M THE CHARMING ONE.
OH GOD HELP ME.
ALSO, I SAW YOU WAITING AND BRIBED ONE OF MY COLLEAGUES WITH A PINKBERRY GIFT CARD.
YOU DON'T THINK THAT'S MILDLY INAPPROPRIATE?
NO, WHY? DOES PINKBERRY HAVE SOME KIND OF POLICY I SHOULD KNOW ABOUT?
LOOK, HERE'S MY IDEA--
--WHY DON'T WE GRAB DRINKS TONIGHT, AND I CAN TELL YOU THE WHOLE SORDID TRUTH ABOUT THIS PLACE.
AND THAT IS?
WE BRAINWASH THESE KIDS AND LOCK THE TROUBLEMAKERS IN THE BASEMENT.
YOU REALLY SHOULDN'T JOKE ABOUT THAT--
--MS. CLARKSON?

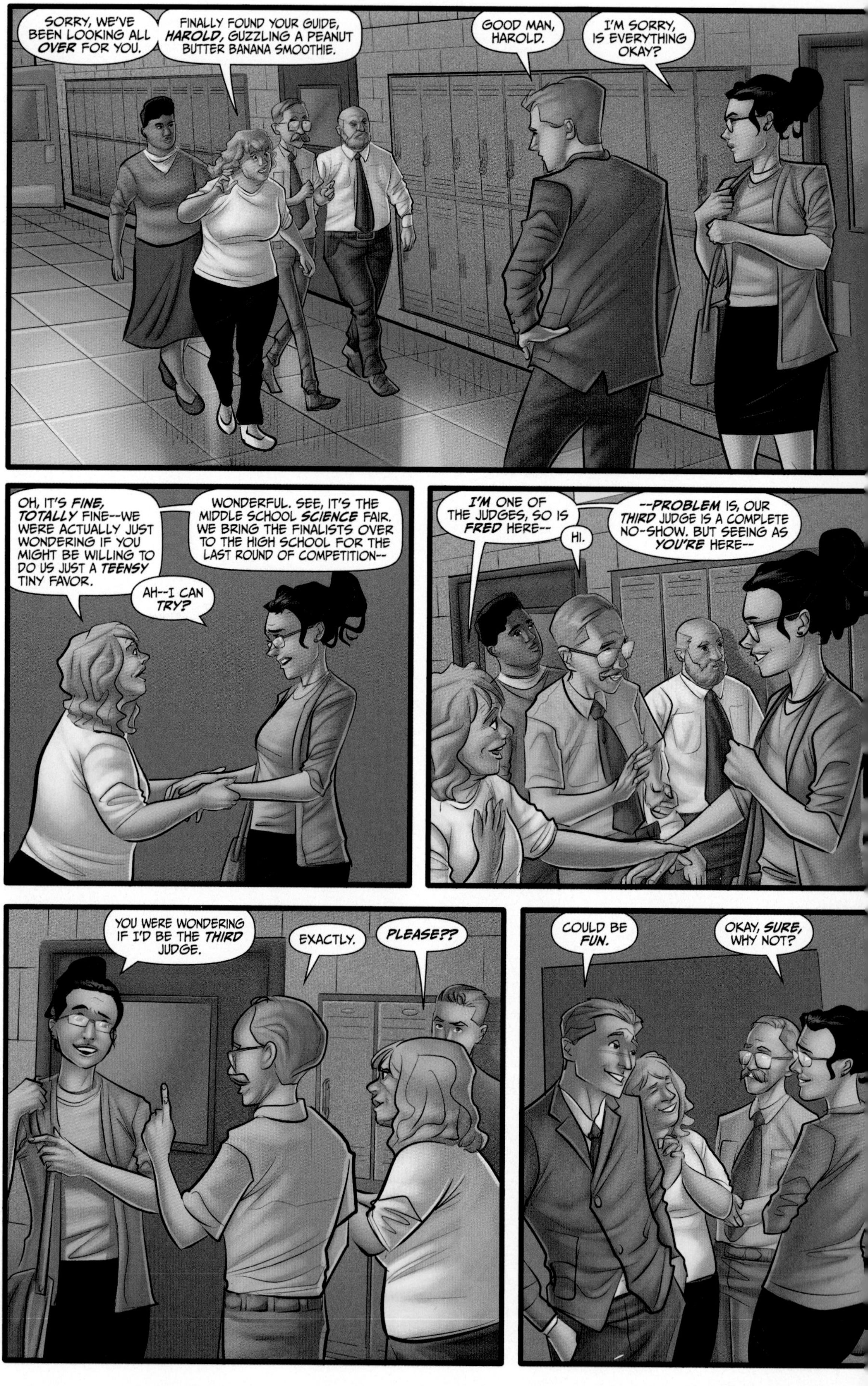
SORRY, WE'VE BEEN LOOKING ALL OVER FOR YOU.
FINALLY FOUND YOUR GUIDE, HAROLD, GUZZLING A PEANUT BUTTER BANANA SMOOTHIE.
GOOD MAN, HAROLD.
I'M SORRY, IS EVERYTHING OKAY?
OH, IT'S FINE, TOTALLY FINE--WE WERE ACTUALLY JUST WONDERING IF YOU MIGHT BE WILLING TO DO US JUST A TEENSY TINY FAVOR.
WONDERFUL. SEE, IT'S THE MIDDLE SCHOOL SCIENCE FAIR. WE BRING THE FINALISTS OVER TO THE HIGH SCHOOL FOR THE LAST ROUND OF COMPETITION--
AH--I CAN TRY?
I'M ONE OF THE JUDGES, SO IS FRED HERE--
HI.
--PROBLEM IS, OUR THIRD JUDGE IS A COMPLETE NO-SHOW. BUT SEEING AS YOU'RE HERE--
YOU WERE WONDERING IF I'D BE THE THIRD JUDGE.
EXACTLY.
PLEASE??
COULD BE FUN.
OKAY, SURE, WHY NOT?

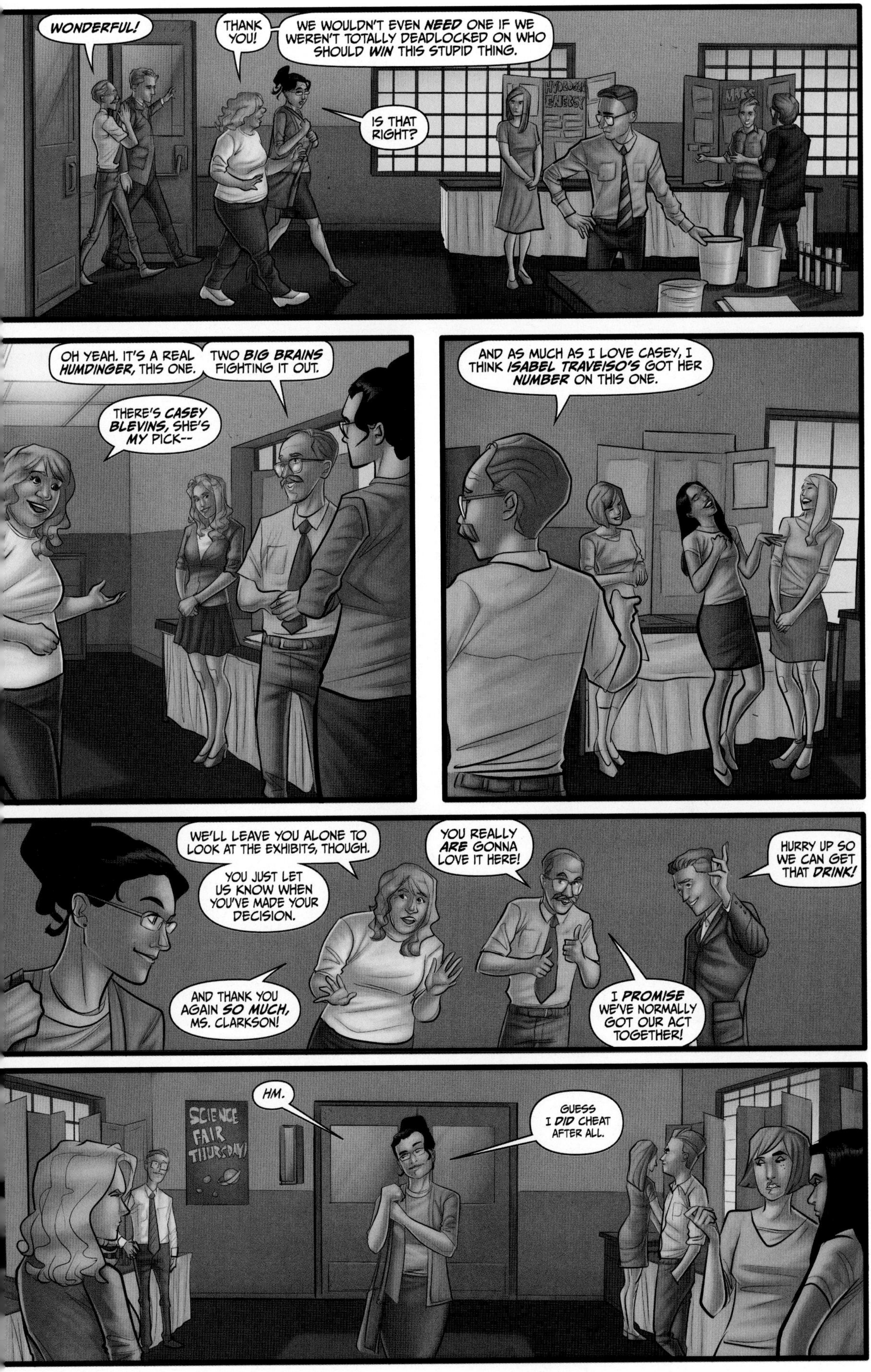
WONDERFUL!
THANK YOU!
WE WOULDN'T EVEN NEED ONE IF WE WEREN'T TOTALLY DEADLOCKED ON WHO SHOULD WIN THIS STUPID THING.
IS THAT RIGHT?
HYDROGEN ENERGY
OH YEAH. IT'S A REAL HUMDINGER, THIS ONE.
TWO BIG BRAINS FIGHTING IT OUT.
THERE'S CASEY BLEVINS, SHE'S MY PICK--
AND AS MUCH AS I LOVE CASEY, I THINK ISABEL TRAVEISO'S GOT HER NUMBER ON THIS ONE.
WE'LL LEAVE YOU ALONE TO LOOK AT THE EXHIBITS, THOUGH.
YOU JUST LET US KNOW WHEN YOU'VE MADE YOUR DECISION.
AND THANK YOU AGAIN SO MUCH, MS. CLARKSON!
YOU REALLY ARE GONNA LOVE IT HERE!
I PROMISE WE'VE NORMALLY GOT OUR ACT TOGETHER!
HURRY UP SO WE CAN GET THAT DRINK!
HM.
SCIENCE FAIR THURSDAY!
GUESS I DID CHEAT AFTER ALL.

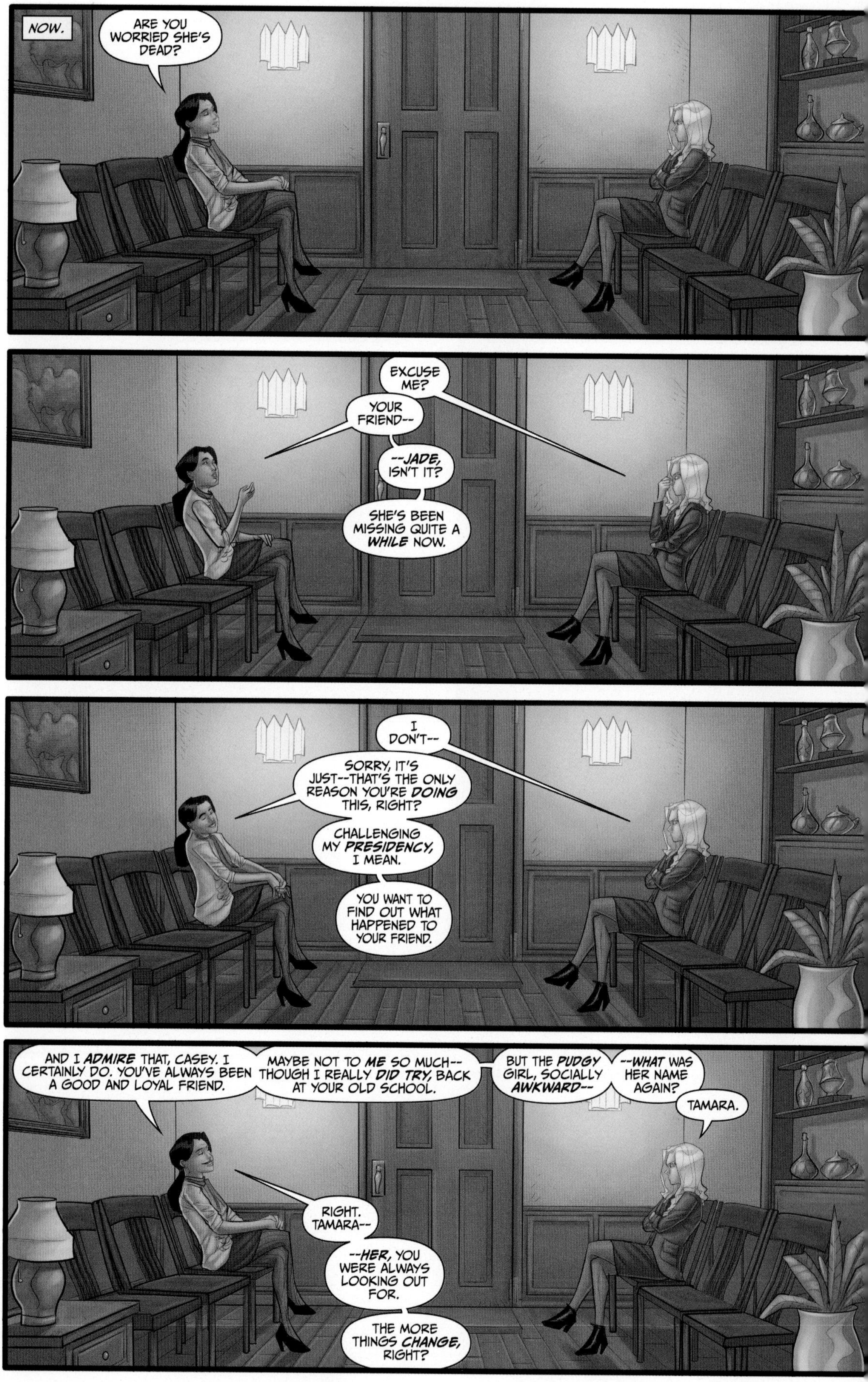
NOW.
ARE YOU WORRIED SHE'S DEAD?
EXCUSE ME?
YOUR FRIEND--
--JADE, ISN'T IT?
SHE'S BEEN MISSING QUITE A WHILE NOW.
I DON'T--
SORRY, IT'S JUST--THAT'S THE ONLY REASON YOU'RE DOING THIS, RIGHT?
CHALLENGING MY PRESIDENCY, I MEAN.
YOU WANT TO FIND OUT WHAT HAPPENED TO YOUR FRIEND.
AND I ADMIRE THAT, CASEY. I CERTAINLY DO. YOU'VE ALWAYS BEEN A GOOD AND LOYAL FRIEND.
MAYBE NOT TO ME SO MUCH-- THOUGH I REALLY DID TRY, BACK AT YOUR OLD SCHOOL.
BUT THE PUDGY GIRL, SOCIALLY AWKWARD--
--WHAT WAS HER NAME AGAIN?
TAMARA.
RIGHT. TAMARA--
--HER, YOU WERE ALWAYS LOOKING OUT FOR.
THE MORE THINGS CHANGE, RIGHT?

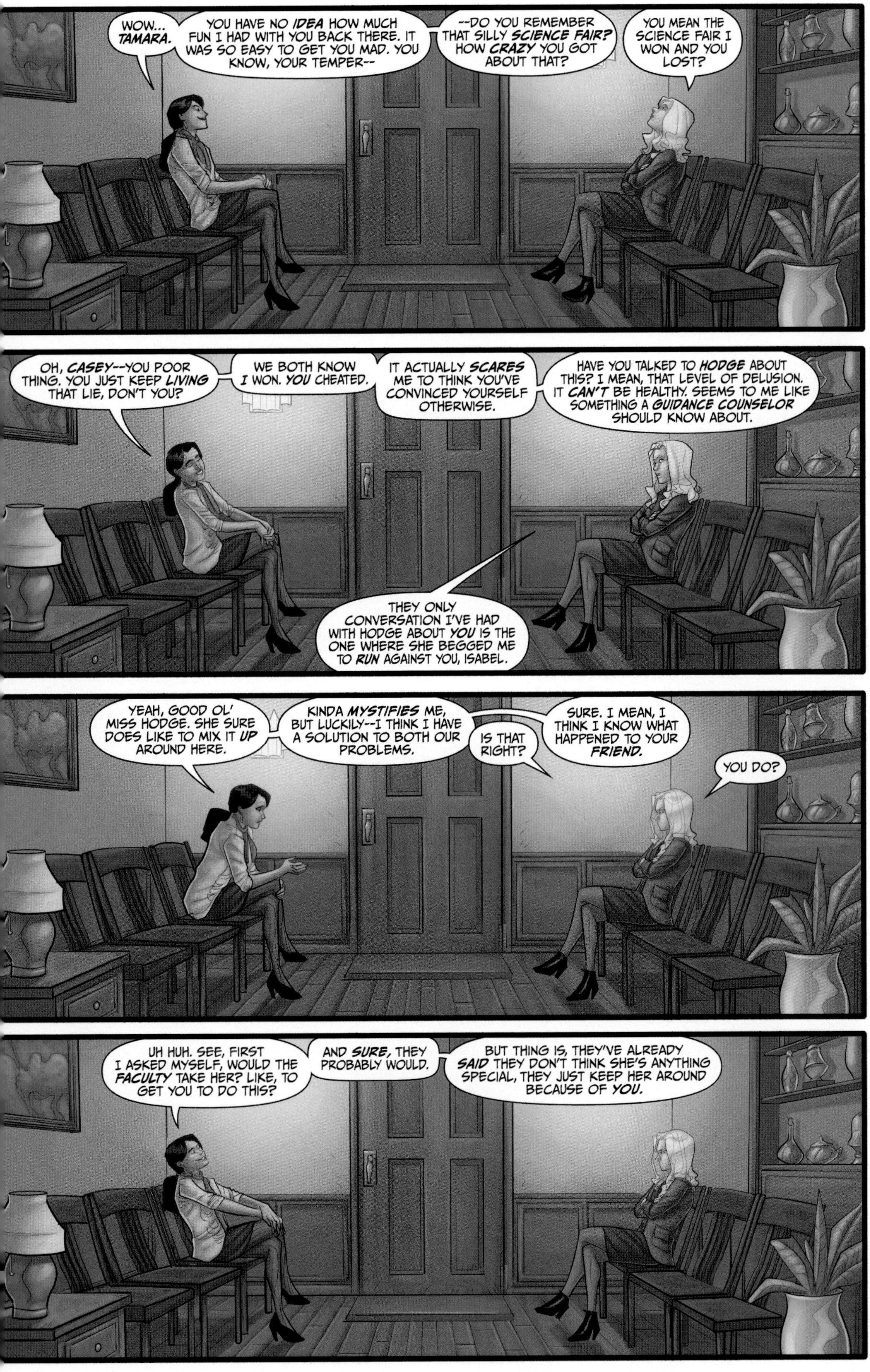
WOW... TAMARA.
YOU HAVE NO IDEA HOW MUCH FUN I HAD WITH YOU BACK THERE. IT WAS SO EASY TO GET YOU MAD. YOU KNOW, YOUR TEMPER--
--DO YOU REMEMBER THAT SILLY SCIENCE FAIR? HOW CRAZY YOU GOT ABOUT THAT?
YOU MEAN THE SCIENCE FAIR I WON AND YOU LOST?
OH, CASEY--YOU POOR THING. YOU JUST KEEP LIVING THAT LIE, DON'T YOU?
WE BOTH KNOW I WON. YOU CHEATED.
IT ACTUALLY SCARES ME TO THINK YOU'VE CONVINCED YOURSELF OTHERWISE.
HAVE YOU TALKED TO HODGE ABOUT THIS? I MEAN, THAT LEVEL OF DELUSION. IT CAN'T BE HEALTHY. SEEMS TO ME LIKE SOMETHING A GUIDANCE COUNSELOR SHOULD KNOW ABOUT.
THEY ONLY CONVERSATION I'VE HAD WITH HODGE ABOUT YOU IS THE ONE WHERE SHE BEGGED ME TO RUN AGAINST YOU, ISABEL.
YEAH, GOOD OL' MISS HODGE. SHE SURE DOES LIKE TO MIX IT UP AROUND HERE.
KINDA MYSTIFIES ME, BUT LUCKILY--I THINK I HAVE A SOLUTION TO BOTH OUR PROBLEMS.
IS THAT RIGHT?
SURE. I MEAN, I THINK I KNOW WHAT HAPPENED TO YOUR FRIEND.
YOU DO?
UH HUH. SEE, FIRST I ASKED MYSELF, WOULD THE FACULTY TAKE HER? LIKE, TO GET YOU TO DO THIS?
AND SURE, THEY PROBABLY WOULD.
BUT THING IS, THEY'VE ALREADY SAID THEY DON'T THINK SHE'S ANYTHING SPECIAL, THEY JUST KEEP HER AROUND BECAUSE OF YOU.

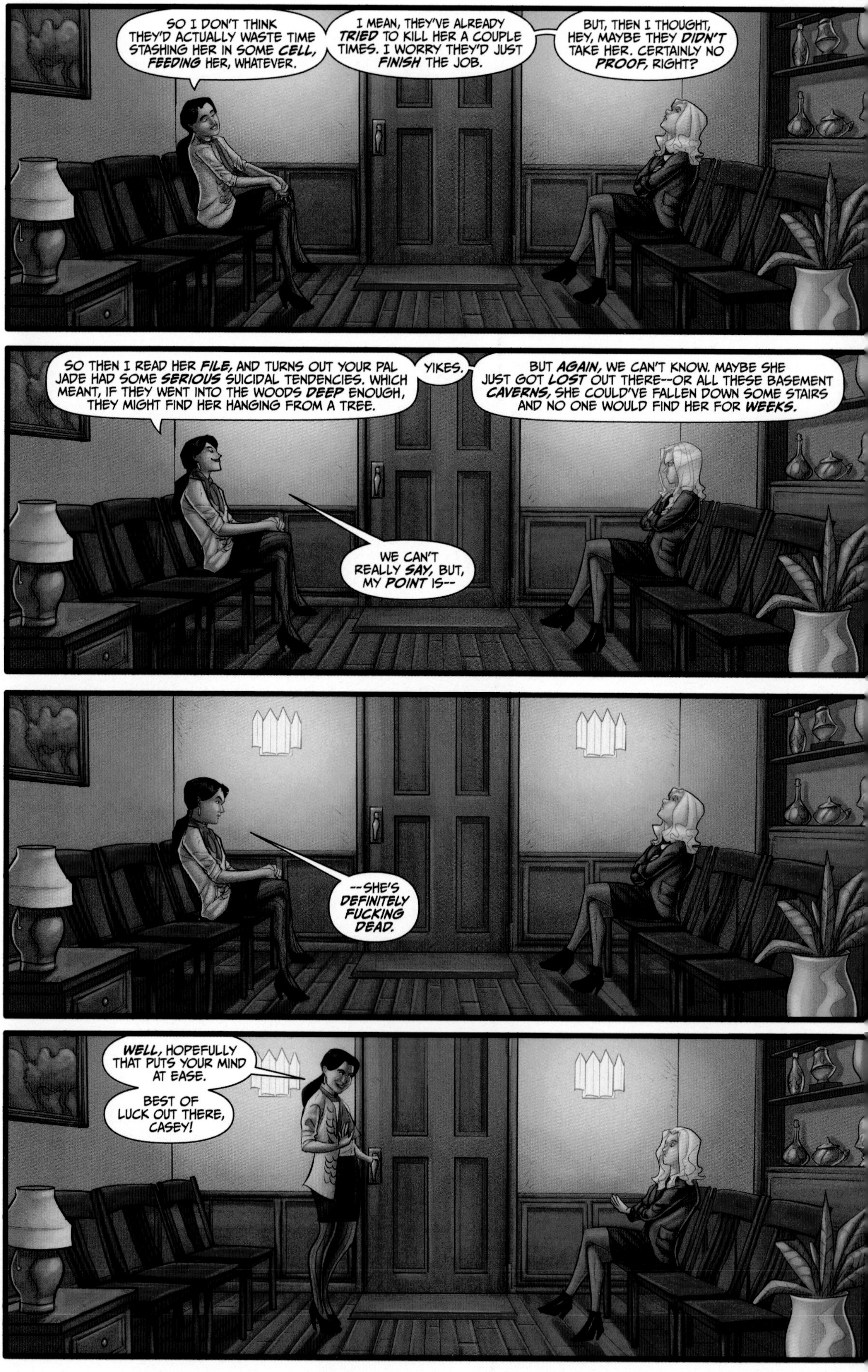
SO I DON'T THINK THEY'D ACTUALLY WASTE TIME STASHING HER IN SOME CELL, FEEDING HER, WHATEVER.
I MEAN, THEY'VE ALREADY TRIED TO KILL HER A COUPLE TIMES. I WORRY THEY'D JUST FINISH THE JOB.
BUT, THEN I THOUGHT, HEY, MAYBE THEY DIDN'T TAKE HER. CERTAINLY NO PROOF, RIGHT?
SO THEN I READ HER FILE, AND TURNS OUT YOUR PAL JADE HAD SOME SERIOUS SUICIDAL TENDENCIES. WHICH MEANT, IF THEY WENT INTO THE WOODS DEEP ENOUGH, THEY MIGHT FIND HER HANGING FROM A TREE.
YIKES.
BUT AGAIN, WE CAN'T KNOW. MAYBE SHE JUST GOT LOST OUT THERE--OR ALL THESE BASEMENT CAVERNS, SHE COULD'VE FALLEN DOWN SOME STAIRS AND NO ONE WOULD FIND HER FOR WEEKS.
WE CAN'T REALLY SAY, BUT, MY POINT IS--
--SHE'S DEFINITELY FUCKING DEAD.
WELL, HOPEFULLY THAT PUTS YOUR MIND AT EASE.
BEST OF LUCK OUT THERE, CASEY!

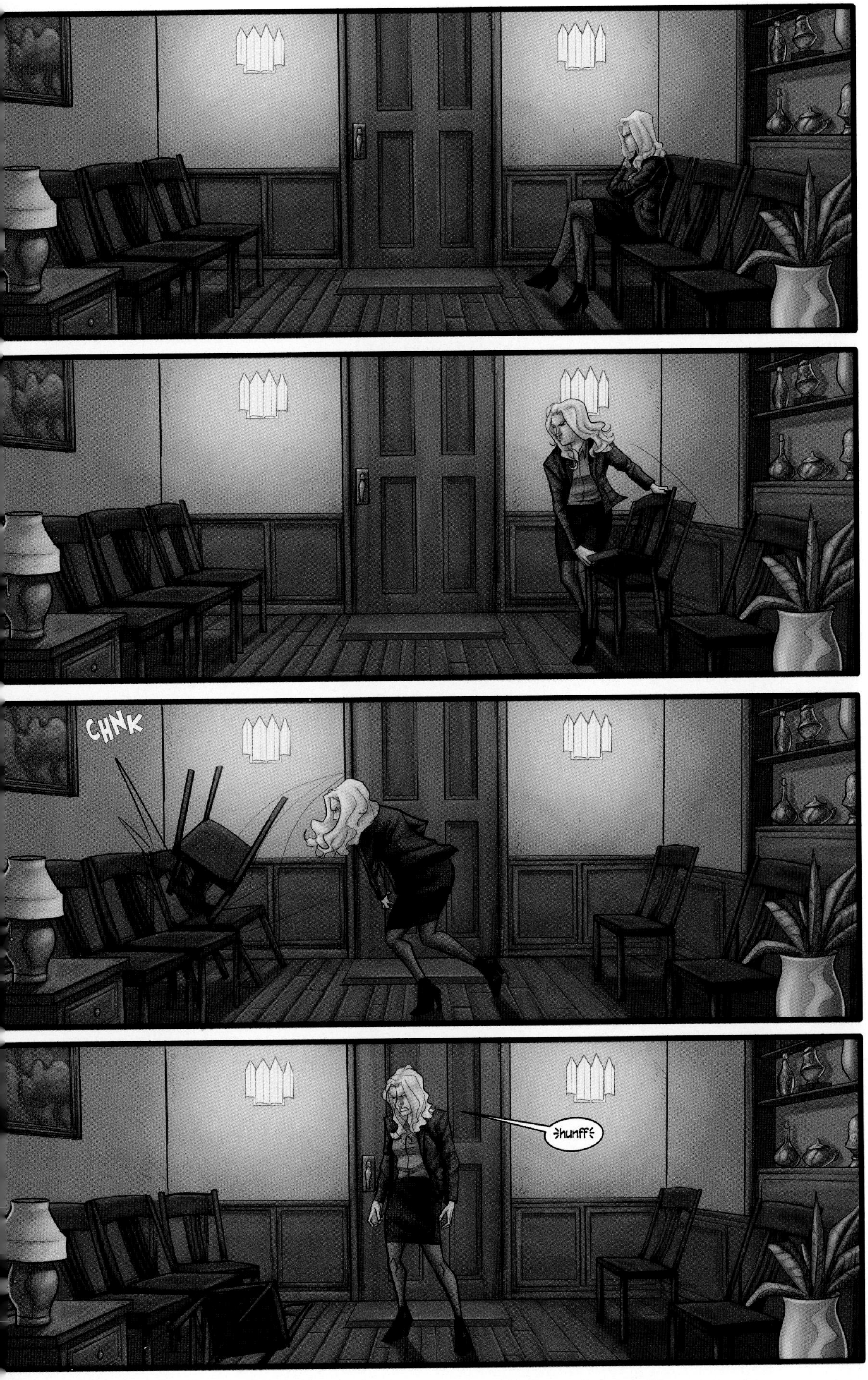
CHNK
hunff

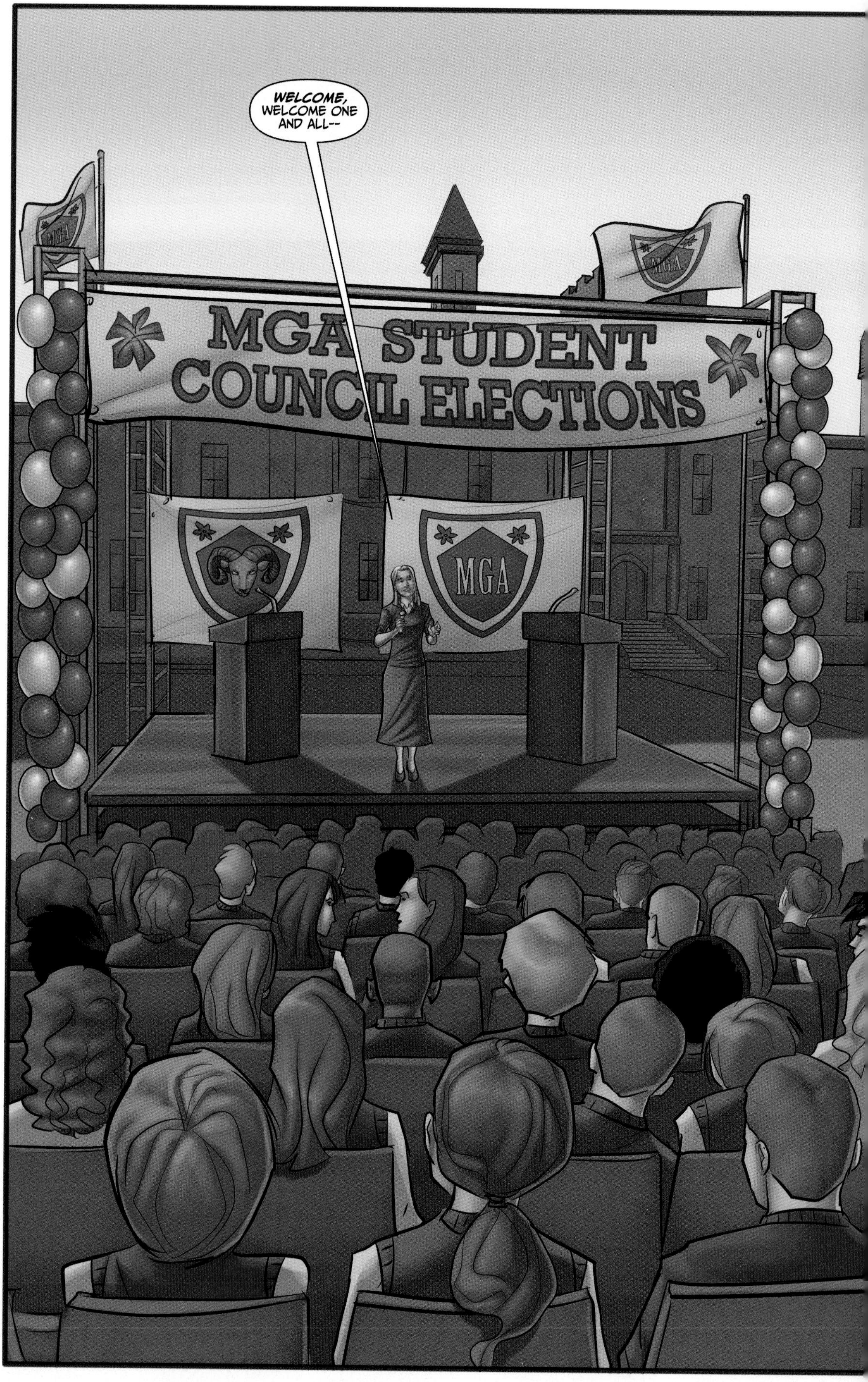
WELCOME, WELCOME ONE AND ALL--
MGA STUDENT COUNCIL ELECTIONS
MGA
MGA
MGA
MGA

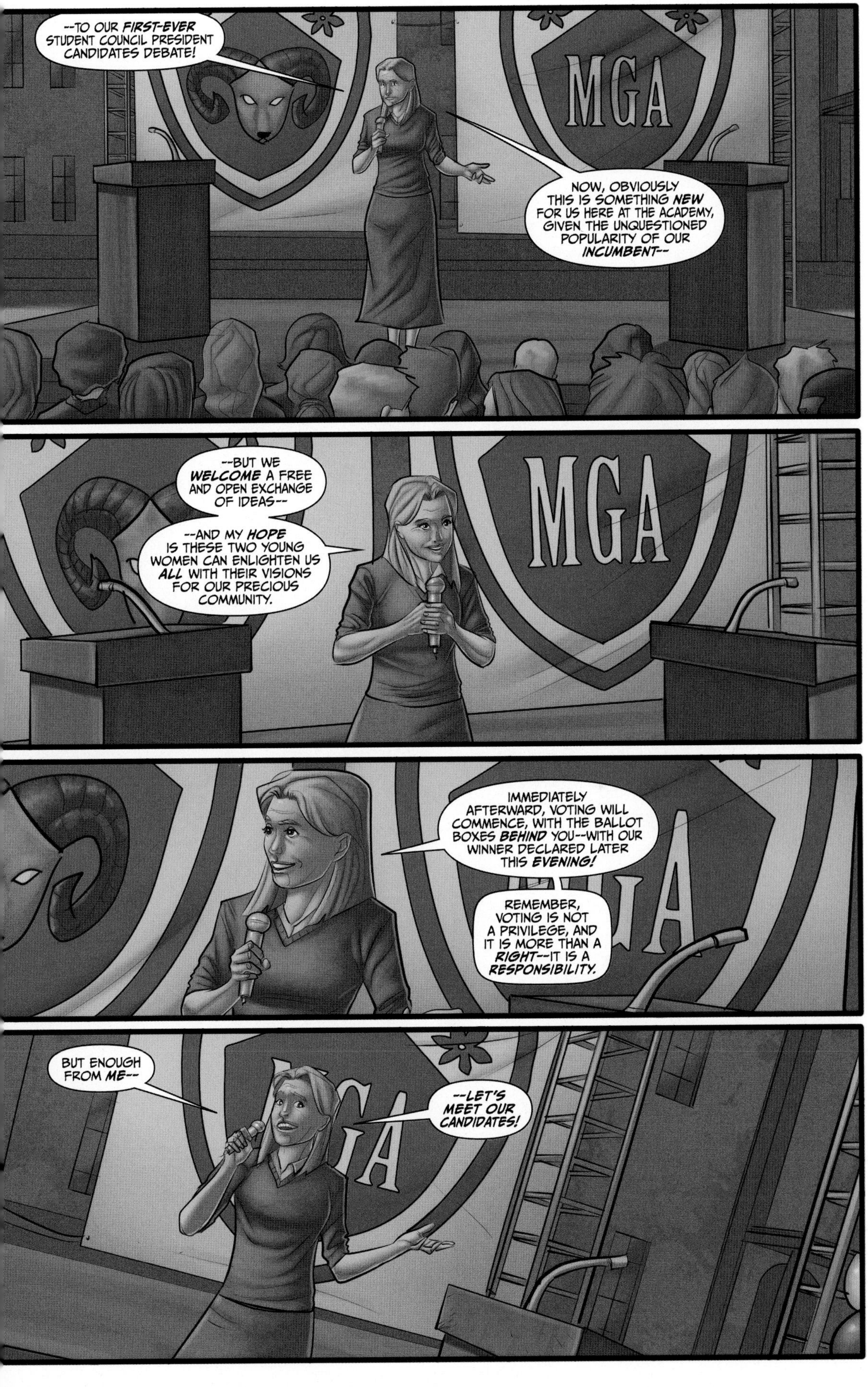
--TO OUR FIRST-EVER STUDENT COUNCIL PRESIDENT CANDIDATES DEBATE!
NOW, OBVIOUSLY THIS IS SOMETHING NEW FOR US HERE AT THE ACADEMY, GIVEN THE UNQUESTIONED POPULARITY OF OUR INCUMBENT--
MGA
--BUT WE WELCOME A FREE AND OPEN EXCHANGE OF IDEAS--
--AND MY HOPE IS THESE TWO YOUNG WOMEN CAN ENLIGHTEN US ALL WITH THEIR VISIONS FOR OUR PRECIOUS COMMUNITY.
IMMEDIATELY AFTERWARD, VOTING WILL COMMENCE, WITH THE BALLOT BOXES BEHIND YOU--WITH OUR WINNER DECLARED LATER THIS EVENING!
REMEMBER, VOTING IS NOT A PRIVILEGE, AND IT IS MORE THAN A RIGHT--IT IS A RESPONSIBILITY.
BUT ENOUGH FROM ME--
--LET'S MEET OUR CANDIDATES!

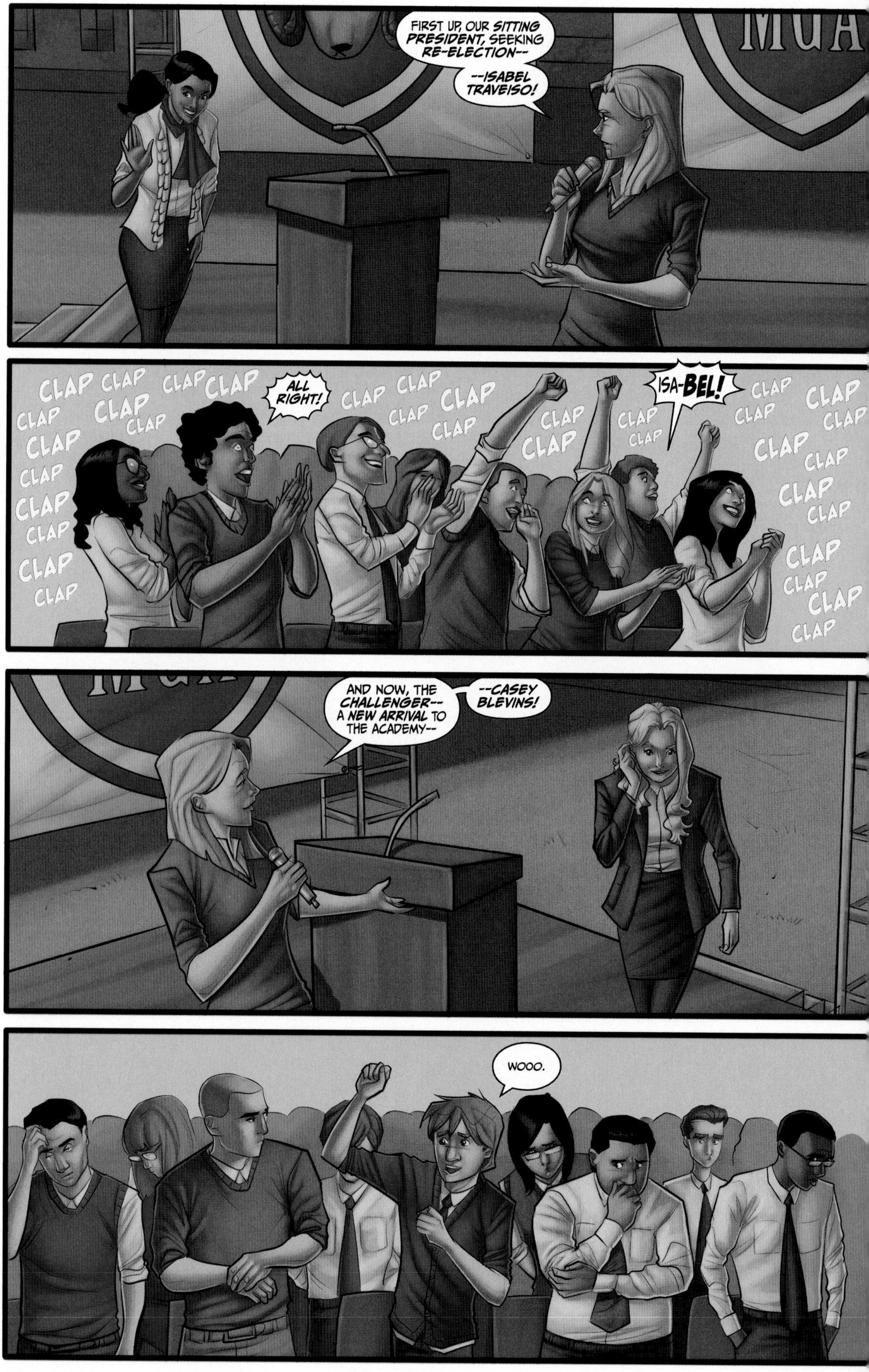
FIRST UP, OUR SITTING PRESIDENT, SEEKING RE-ELECTION--
--ISABEL TRAVEISO!
CLAP CLAP CLAP CLAP CLAP CLAP CLAP CLAP CLAP CLAP CLAP CLAP CLAP
ALL RIGHT!
CLAP CLAP CLAP CLAP CLAP CLAP CLAP CLAP CLAP
ISA-BEL!
CLAP CLAP CLAP CLAP CLAP CLAP CLAP CLAP CLAP CLAP CLAP CLAP CLAP CLAP
AND NOW, THE CHALLENGER-- A NEW ARRIVAL TO THE ACADEMY--
--CASEY BLEVINS!
WOOO.

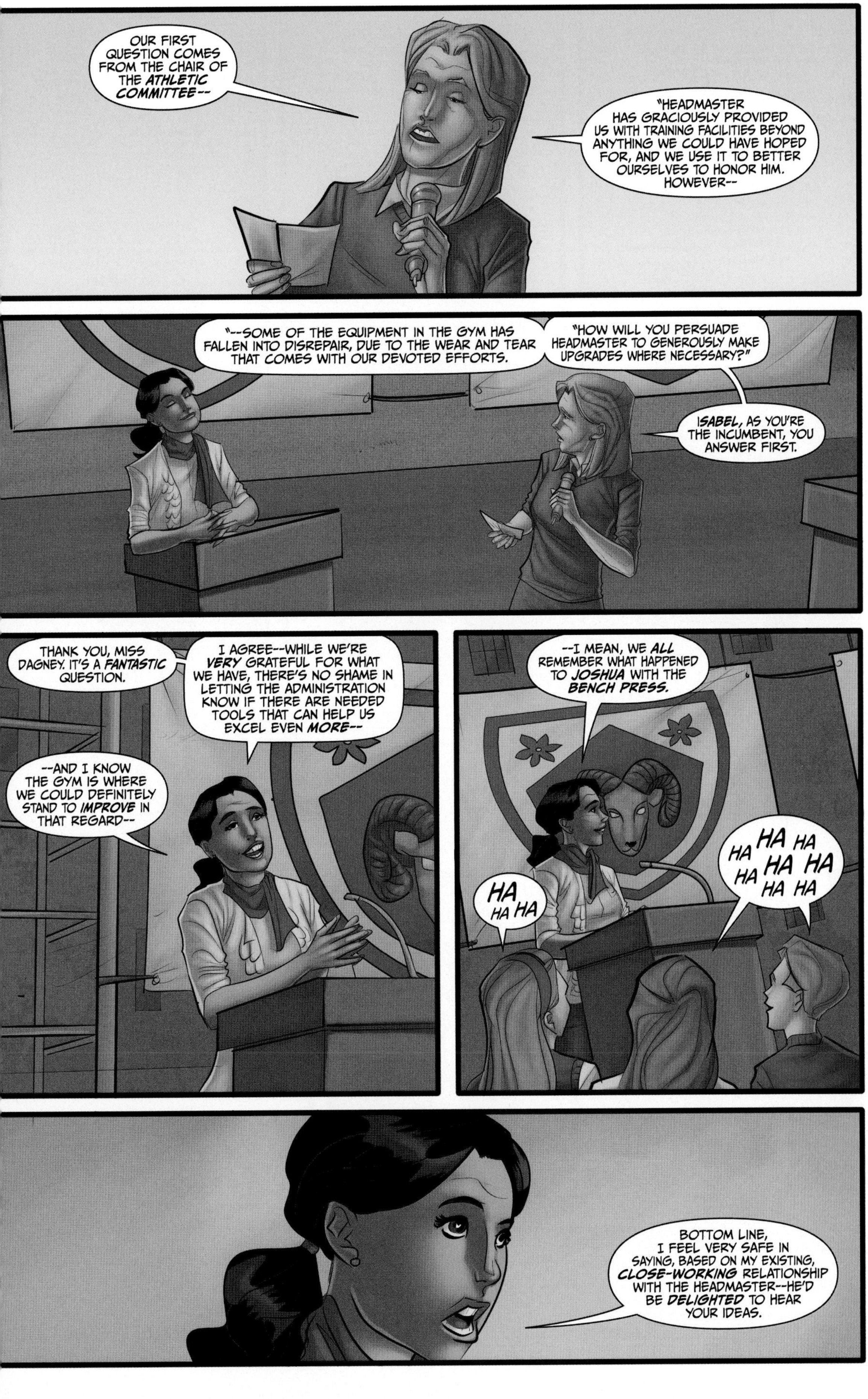
OUR FIRST QUESTION COMES FROM THE CHAIR OF THE ATHLETIC COMMITTEE--
"HEADMASTER HAS GRACIOUSLY PROVIDED US WITH TRAINING FACILITIES BEYOND ANYTHING WE COULD HAVE HOPED FOR, AND WE USE IT TO BETTER OURSELVES TO HONOR HIM. HOWEVER--
"--SOME OF THE EQUIPMENT IN THE GYM HAS FALLEN INTO DISREPAIR, DUE TO THE WEAR AND TEAR THAT COMES WITH OUR DEVOTED EFFORTS.
"HOW WILL YOU PERSUADE HEADMASTER TO GENEROUSLY MAKE UPGRADES WHERE NECESSARY?"
ISABEL, AS YOU'RE THE INCUMBENT, YOU ANSWER FIRST.
THANK YOU, MISS DAGNEY. IT'S A FANTASTIC QUESTION.
I AGREE--WHILE WE'RE VERY GRATEFUL FOR WHAT WE HAVE, THERE'S NO SHAME IN LETTING THE ADMINISTRATION KNOW IF THERE ARE NEEDED TOOLS THAT CAN HELP US EXCEL EVEN MORE--
--AND I KNOW THE GYM IS WHERE WE COULD DEFINITELY STAND TO IMPROVE IN THAT REGARD--
--I MEAN, WE ALL REMEMBER WHAT HAPPENED TO JOSHUA WITH THE BENCH PRESS.
HA HA HA
HA HA HA HA HA HA HA HA
BOTTOM LINE, I FEEL VERY SAFE IN SAYING, BASED ON MY EXISTING, CLOSE-WORKING RELATIONSHIP WITH THE HEADMASTER--HE'D BE DELIGHTED TO HEAR YOUR IDEAS.

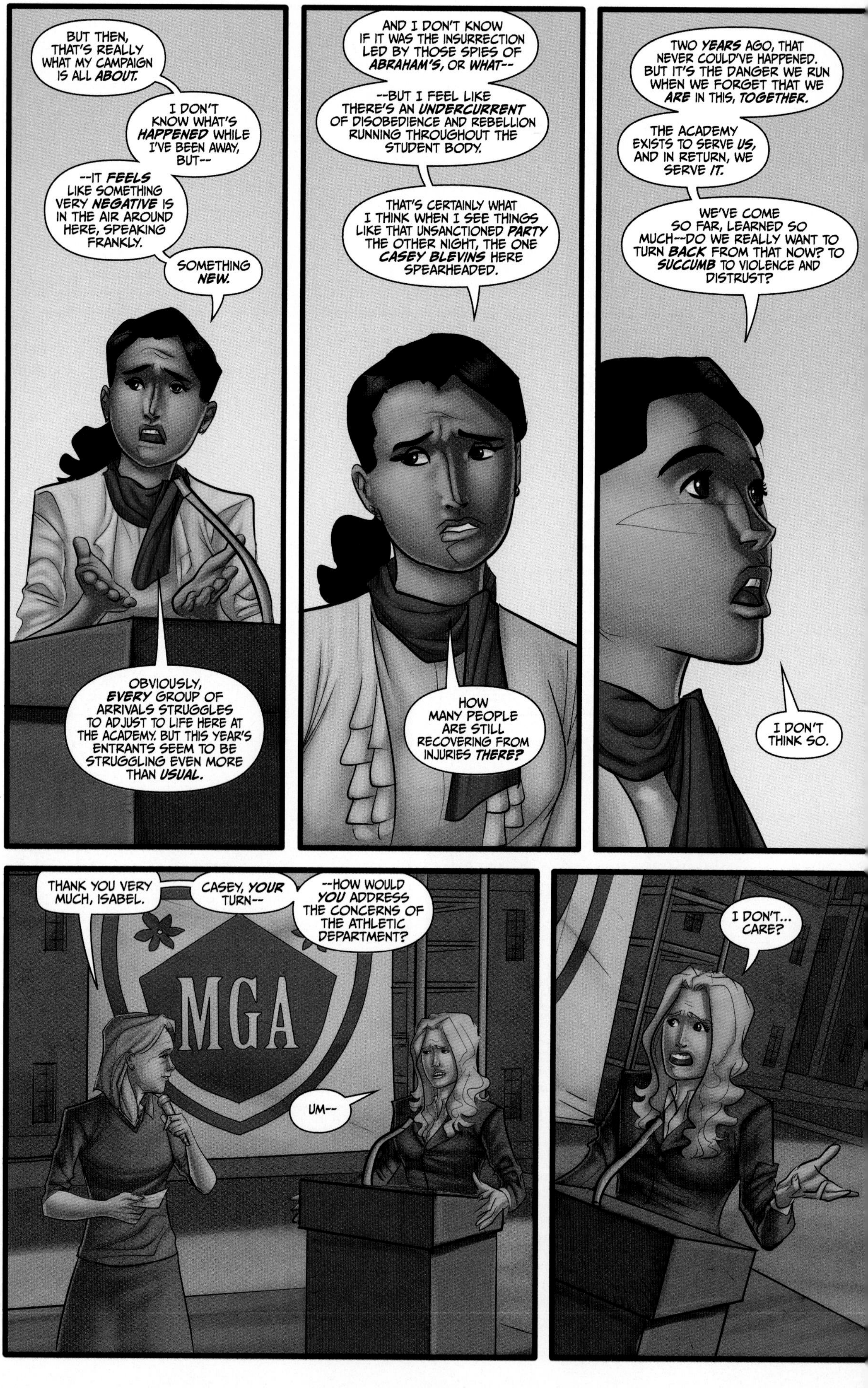
BUT THEN, THAT'S REALLY WHAT MY CAMPAIGN IS ALL ABOUT.
I DON'T KNOW WHAT'S HAPPENED WHILE I'VE BEEN AWAY, BUT--
--IT FEELS LIKE SOMETHING VERY NEGATIVE IS IN THE AIR AROUND HERE, SPEAKING FRANKLY.
SOMETHING NEW.
OBVIOUSLY, EVERY GROUP OF ARRIVALS STRUGGLES TO ADJUST TO LIFE HERE AT THE ACADEMY. BUT THIS YEAR'S ENTRANTS SEEM TO BE STRUGGLING EVEN MORE THAN USUAL.
AND I DON'T KNOW IF IT WAS THE INSURRECTION LED BY THOSE SPIES OF ABRAHAM'S, OR WHAT--
--BUT I FEEL LIKE THERE'S AN UNDERCURRENT OF DISOBEDIENCE AND REBELLION RUNNING THROUGHOUT THE STUDENT BODY.
THAT'S CERTAINLY WHAT I THINK WHEN I SEE THINGS LIKE THAT UNSANCTIONED PARTY THE OTHER NIGHT, THE ONE CASEY BLEVINS HERE SPEARHEADED.
HOW MANY PEOPLE ARE STILL RECOVERING FROM INJURIES THERE?
TWO YEARS AGO, THAT NEVER COULD'VE HAPPENED. BUT IT'S THE DANGER WE RUN WHEN WE FORGET THAT WE ARE IN THIS, TOGETHER.
THE ACADEMY EXISTS TO SERVE US, AND IN RETURN, WE SERVE IT.
WE'VE COME SO FAR, LEARNED SO MUCH--DO WE REALLY WANT TO TURN BACK FROM THAT NOW? TO SUCCUMB TO VIOLENCE AND DISTRUST?
I DON'T THINK SO.
THANK YOU VERY MUCH, ISABEL.
CASEY, YOUR TURN--
--HOW WOULD YOU ADDRESS THE CONCERNS OF THE ATHLETIC DEPARTMENT?
MGA
UM--
I DON'T... CARE?

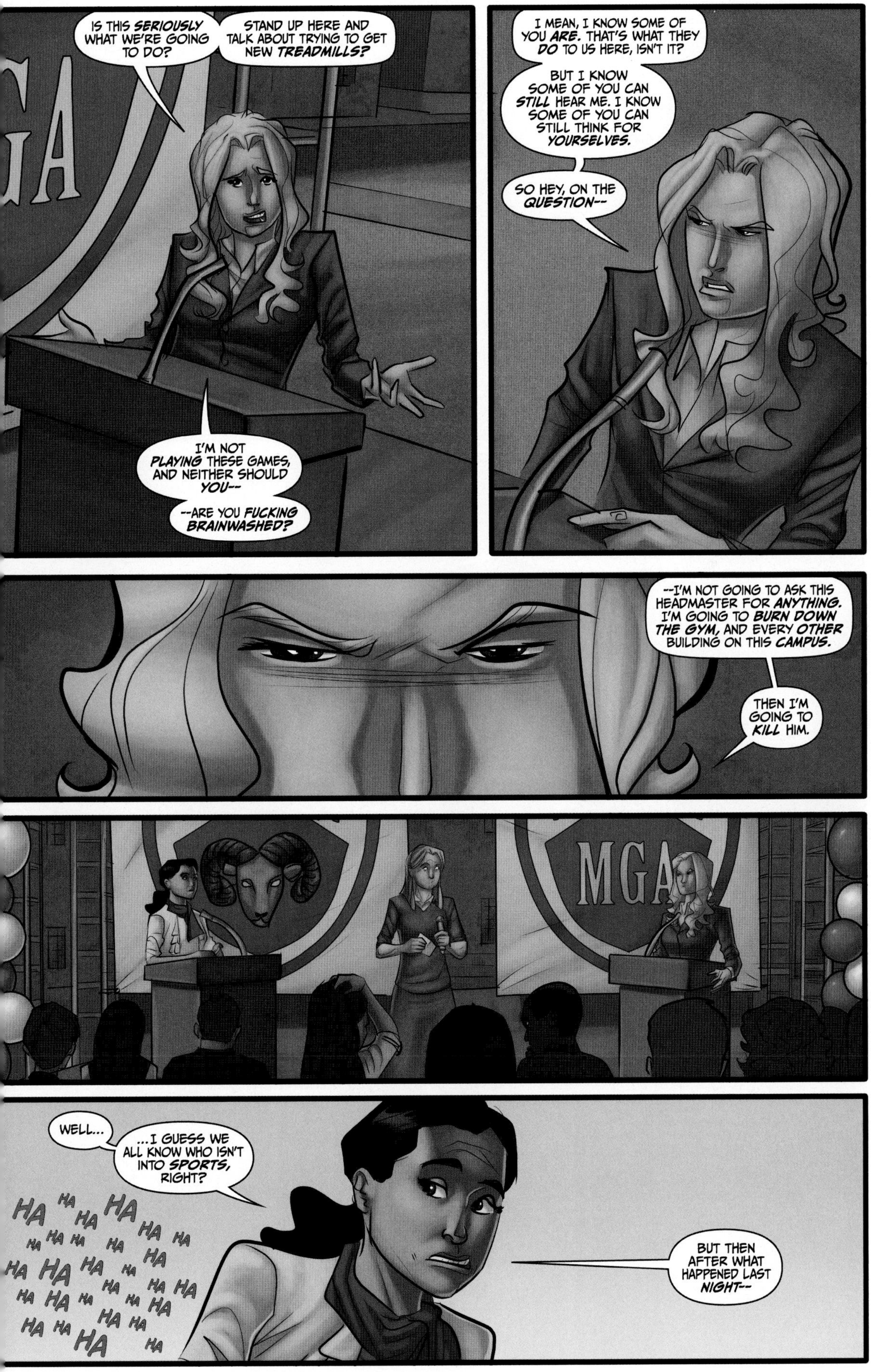

IS THIS SERIOUSLY WHAT WE'RE GOING TO DO?
STAND UP HERE AND TALK ABOUT TRYING TO GET NEW TREADMILLS?
I'M NOT PLAYING THESE GAMES, AND NEITHER SHOULD YOU--
--ARE YOU FUCKING BRAINWASHED?
I MEAN, I KNOW SOME OF YOU ARE. THAT'S WHAT THEY DO TO US HERE, ISN'T IT?
BUT I KNOW SOME OF YOU CAN STILL HEAR ME. I KNOW SOME OF YOU CAN STILL THINK FOR YOURSELVES.
SO HEY, ON THE QUESTION--
--I'M NOT GOING TO ASK THIS HEADMASTER FOR ANYTHING. I'M GOING TO BURN DOWN THE GYM, AND EVERY OTHER BUILDING ON THIS CAMPUS.
THEN I'M GOING TO KILL HIM.
MGA
WELL...
...I GUESS WE ALL KNOW WHO ISN'T INTO SPORTS, RIGHT?
HA HA HA HA HA HA HA HA HA HA HA HA HA HA HA HA HA HA HA HA HA HA HA HA HA HA HA HA HA HA HA HA HA HA
BUT THEN AFTER WHAT HAPPENED LAST NIGHT--

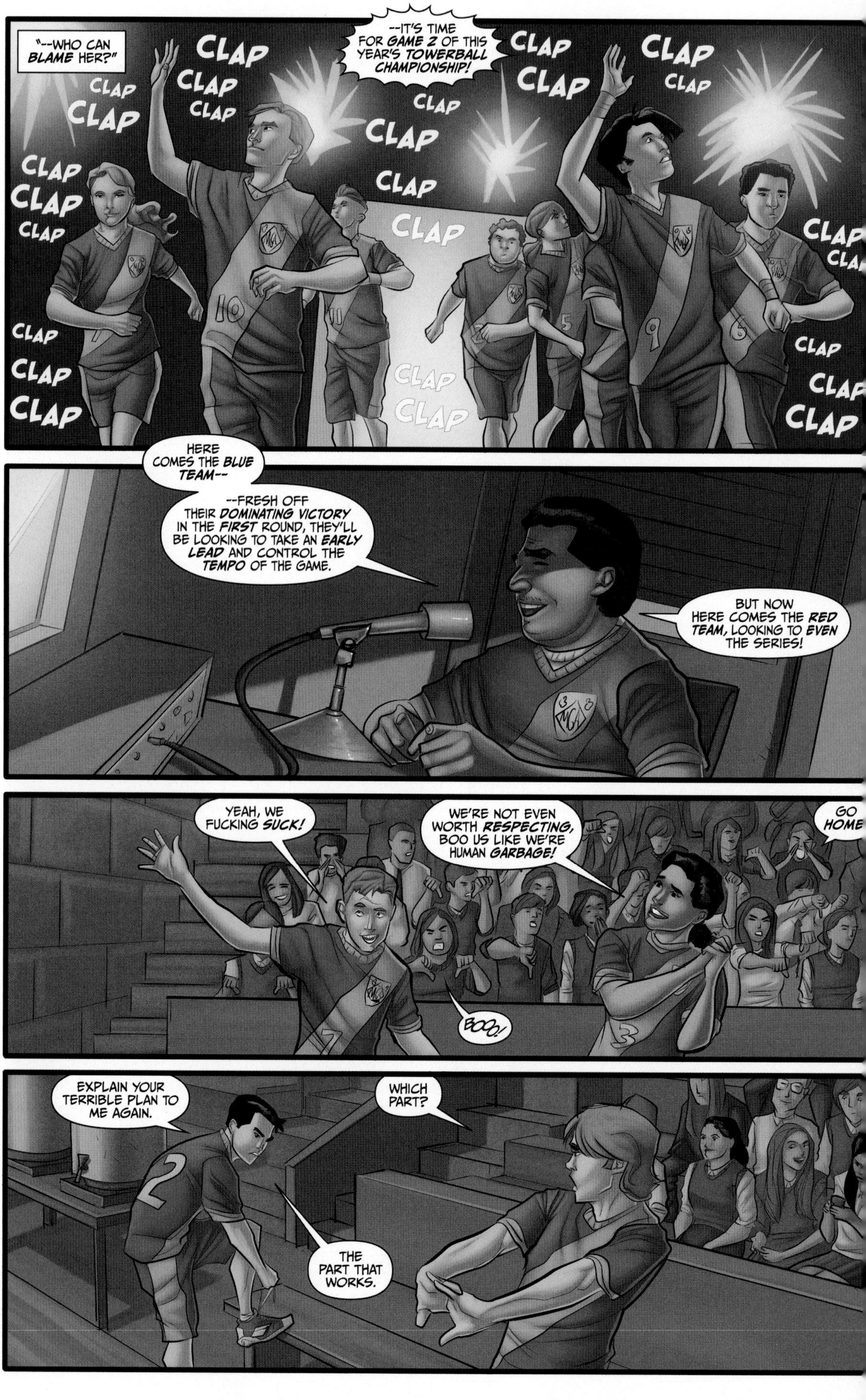
"--WHO CAN BLAME HER?"
--IT'S TIME FOR GAME 2 OF THIS YEAR'S TOWERBALL CHAMPIONSHIP!
CLAP CLAP CLAP CLAP CLAP CLAP CLAP CLAP
HERE COMES THE BLUE TEAM--
--FRESH OFF THEIR DOMINATING VICTORY IN THE FIRST ROUND, THEY'LL BE LOOKING TO TAKE AN EARLY LEAD AND CONTROL THE TEMPO OF THE GAME.
BUT NOW HERE COMES THE RED TEAM, LOOKING TO EVEN THE SERIES!
YEAH, WE FUCKING SUCK!
WE'RE NOT EVEN WORTH RESPECTING, BOO US LIKE WE'RE HUMAN GARBAGE!
GO HOME
BOOO!
EXPLAIN YOUR TERRIBLE PLAN TO ME AGAIN.
WHICH PART?
THE PART THAT WORKS.

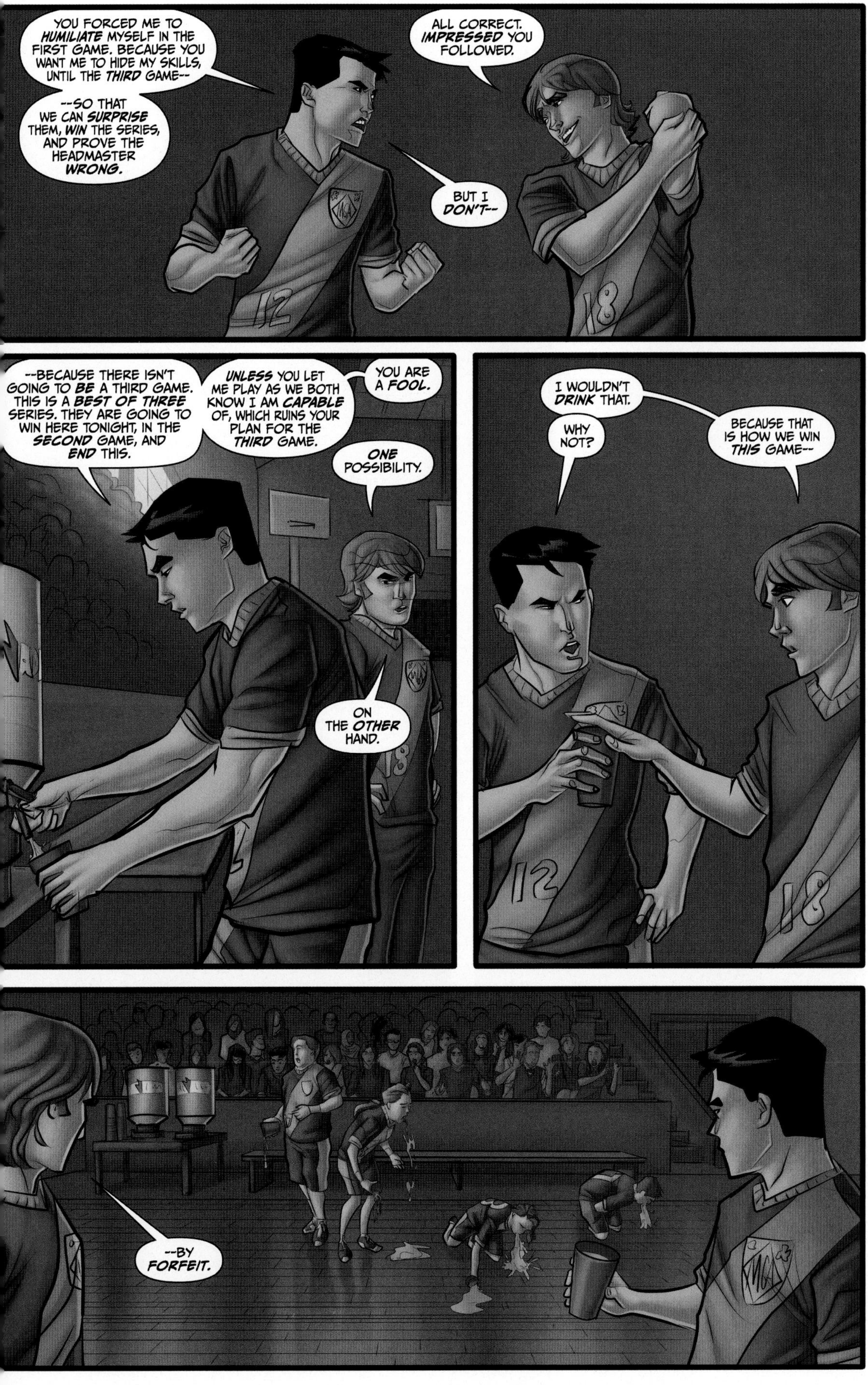
YOU FORCED ME TO HUMILIATE MYSELF IN THE FIRST GAME. BECAUSE YOU WANT ME TO HIDE MY SKILLS, UNTIL THE THIRD GAME--
--SO THAT WE CAN SURPRISE THEM, WIN THE SERIES, AND PROVE THE HEADMASTER WRONG.
ALL CORRECT. IMPRESSED YOU FOLLOWED.
BUT I DON'T--
--BECAUSE THERE ISN'T GOING TO BE A THIRD GAME. THIS IS A BEST OF THREE SERIES. THEY ARE GOING TO WIN HERE TONIGHT, IN THE SECOND GAME, AND END THIS.
UNLESS YOU LET ME PLAY AS WE BOTH KNOW I AM CAPABLE OF, WHICH RUINS YOUR PLAN FOR THE THIRD GAME.
YOU ARE A FOOL.
ONE POSSIBILITY.
ON THE OTHER HAND.
I WOULDN'T DRINK THAT.
WHY NOT?
BECAUSE THAT IS HOW WE WIN THIS GAME--
--BY FORFEIT.

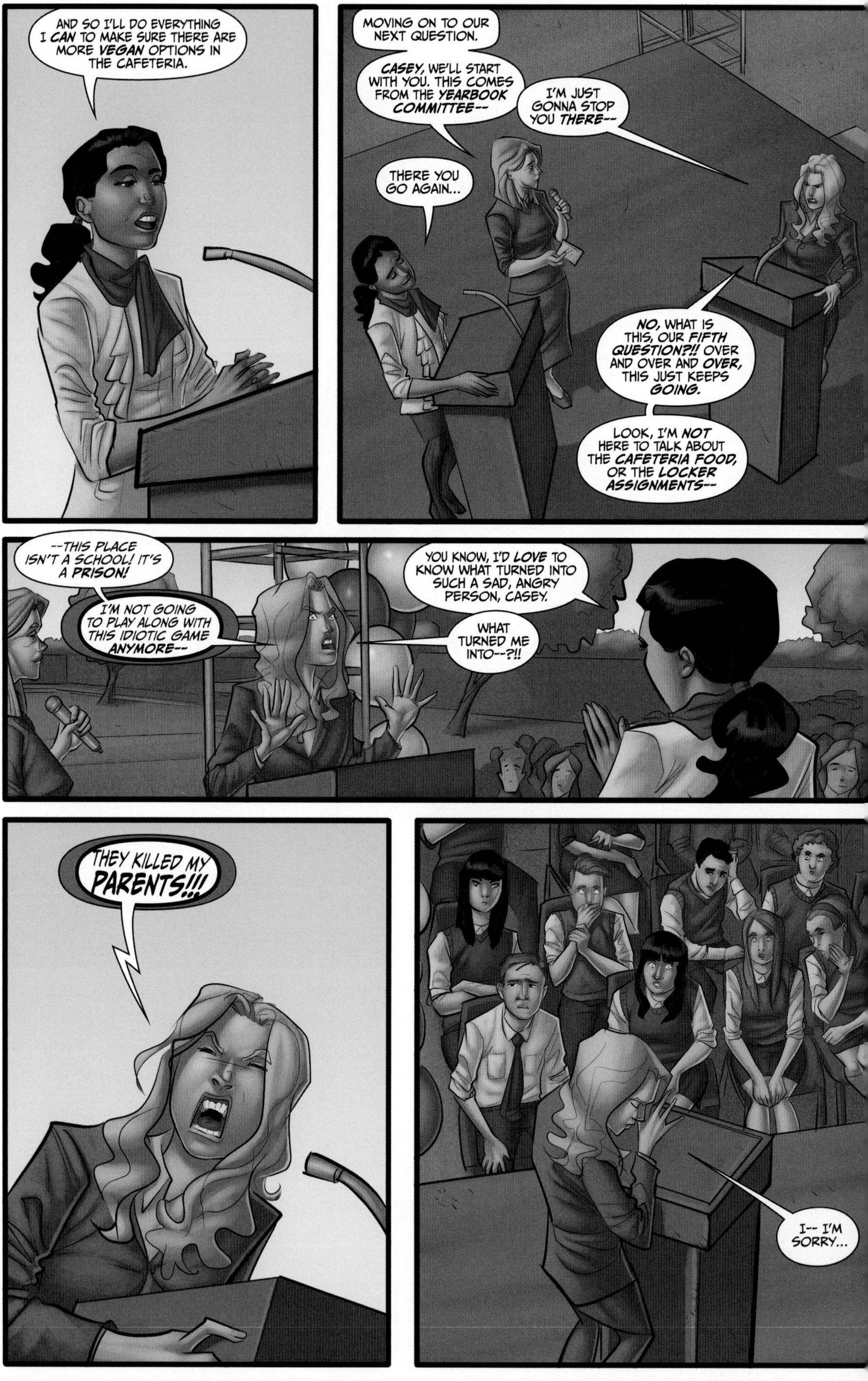
AND SO I'LL DO EVERYTHING I CAN TO MAKE SURE THERE ARE MORE VEGAN OPTIONS IN THE CAFETERIA.
MOVING ON TO OUR NEXT QUESTION.
CASEY, WE'LL START WITH YOU. THIS COMES FROM THE YEARBOOK COMMITTEE--
I'M JUST GONNA STOP YOU THERE--
THERE YOU GO AGAIN...
NO, WHAT IS THIS, OUR FIFTH QUESTION?!! OVER AND OVER AND OVER, THIS JUST KEEPS GOING.
LOOK, I'M NOT HERE TO TALK ABOUT THE CAFETERIA FOOD, OR THE LOCKER ASSIGNMENTS--
--THIS PLACE ISN'T A SCHOOL! IT'S A PRISON!
I'M NOT GOING TO PLAY ALONG WITH THIS IDIOTIC GAME ANYMORE--
YOU KNOW, I'D LOVE TO KNOW WHAT TURNED INTO SUCH A SAD, ANGRY PERSON, CASEY.
WHAT TURNED ME INTO--?!!
THEY KILLED MY PARENTS!!!
I-- I'M SORRY...

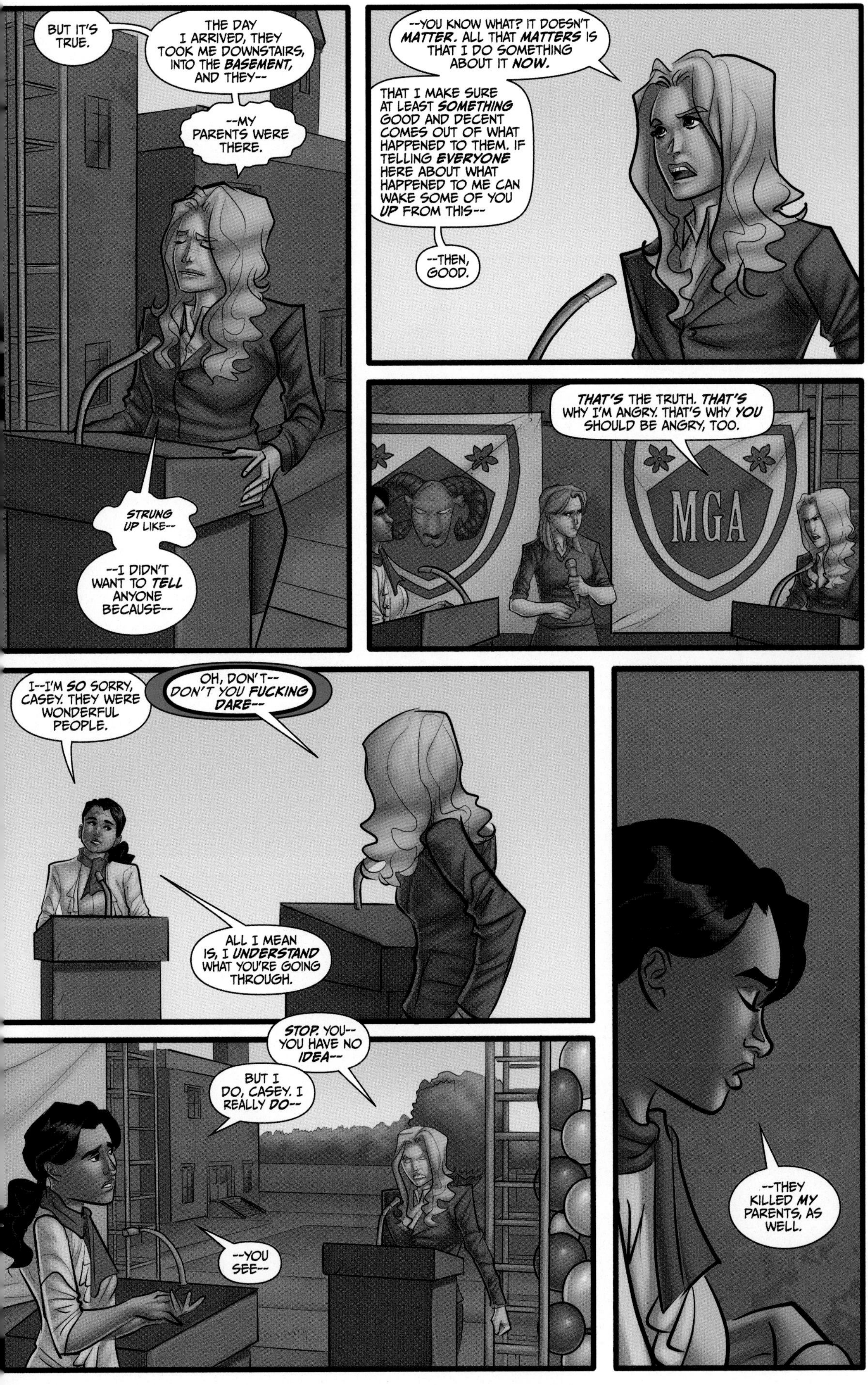
BUT IT'S TRUE.
THE DAY I ARRIVED, THEY TOOK ME DOWNSTAIRS, INTO THE *BASEMENT,* AND THEY--
--MY PARENTS WERE THERE.
STRUNG UP LIKE--
--I DIDN'T WANT TO *TELL* ANYONE BECAUSE--
--YOU KNOW WHAT? IT DOESN'T *MATTER.* ALL THAT *MATTERS* IS THAT I DO SOMETHING ABOUT IT *NOW.*
THAT I MAKE SURE AT LEAST *SOMETHING* GOOD AND DECENT COMES OUT OF WHAT HAPPENED TO THEM. IF TELLING *EVERYONE* HERE ABOUT WHAT HAPPENED TO ME CAN WAKE SOME OF YOU *UP* FROM THIS--
--THEN, GOOD.
THAT'S THE TRUTH. *THAT'S* WHY I'M ANGRY. THAT'S WHY *YOU* SHOULD BE ANGRY, TOO.
MGA
I--I'M *SO* SORRY, CASEY. THEY WERE WONDERFUL PEOPLE.
OH, DON'T-- *DON'T YOU FUCKING DARE--*
ALL I MEAN IS, I *UNDERSTAND* WHAT YOU'RE GOING THROUGH.
STOP. YOU-- YOU HAVE NO *IDEA--*
BUT I DO, CASEY. I REALLY *DO--*
--YOU SEE--
--THEY KILLED *MY* PARENTS, AS WELL.

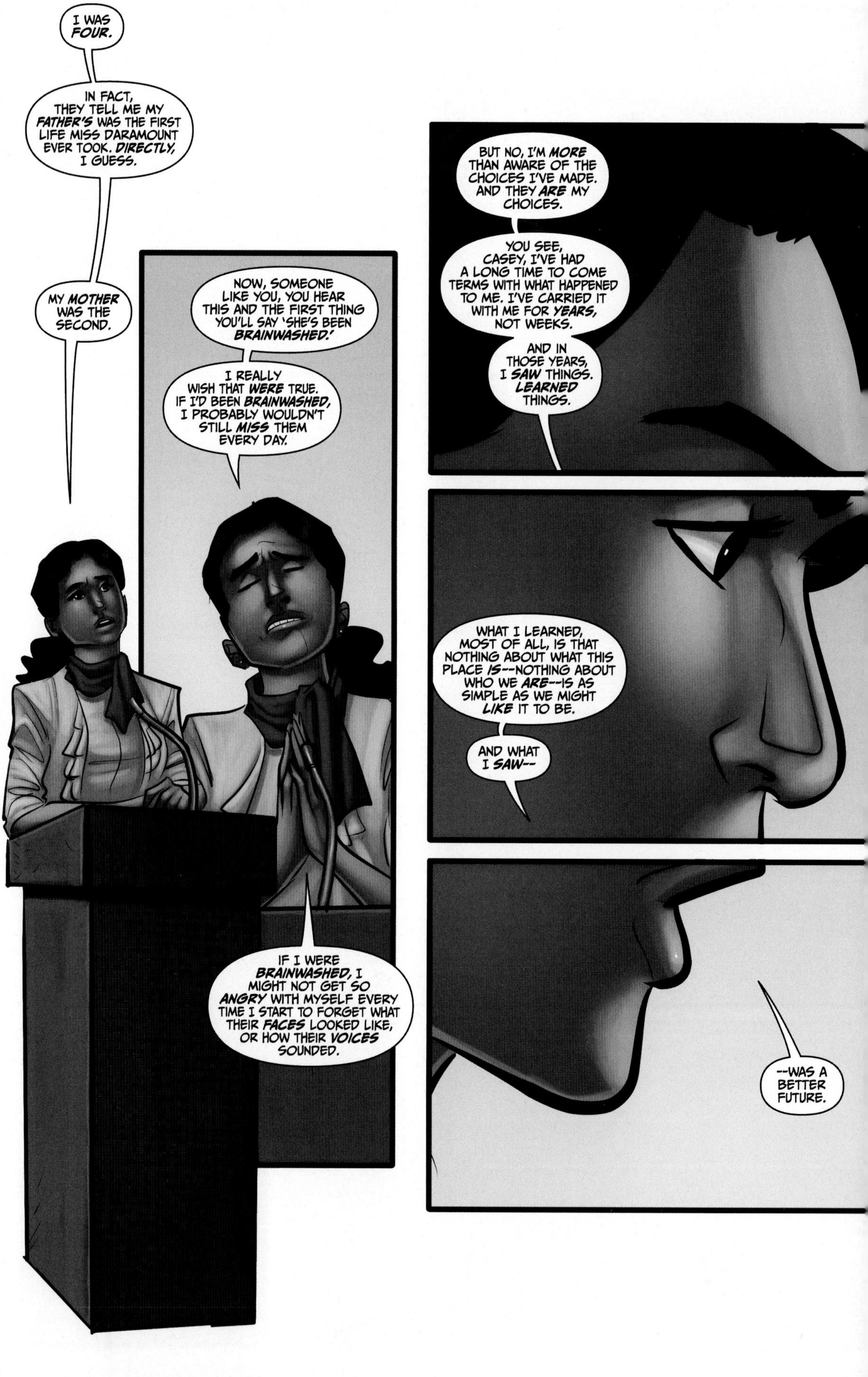
I WAS FOUR.
IN FACT, THEY TELL ME MY FATHER'S WAS THE FIRST LIFE MISS DARAMOUNT EVER TOOK. DIRECTLY, I GUESS.
MY MOTHER WAS THE SECOND.
NOW, SOMEONE LIKE YOU, YOU HEAR THIS AND THE FIRST THING YOU'LL SAY 'SHE'S BEEN BRAINWASHED.'
I REALLY WISH THAT WERE TRUE. IF I'D BEEN BRAINWASHED, I PROBABLY WOULDN'T STILL MISS THEM EVERY DAY.
IF I WERE BRAINWASHED, I MIGHT NOT GET SO ANGRY WITH MYSELF EVERY TIME I START TO FORGET WHAT THEIR FACES LOOKED LIKE, OR HOW THEIR VOICES SOUNDED.
BUT NO, I'M MORE THAN AWARE OF THE CHOICES I'VE MADE. AND THEY ARE MY CHOICES.
YOU SEE, CASEY, I'VE HAD A LONG TIME TO COME TERMS WITH WHAT HAPPENED TO ME. I'VE CARRIED IT WITH ME FOR YEARS, NOT WEEKS.
AND IN THOSE YEARS, I SAW THINGS. LEARNED THINGS.
WHAT I LEARNED, MOST OF ALL, IS THAT NOTHING ABOUT WHAT THIS PLACE IS--NOTHING ABOUT WHO WE ARE--IS AS SIMPLE AS WE MIGHT LIKE IT TO BE.
AND WHAT I SAW--
--WAS A BETTER FUTURE.

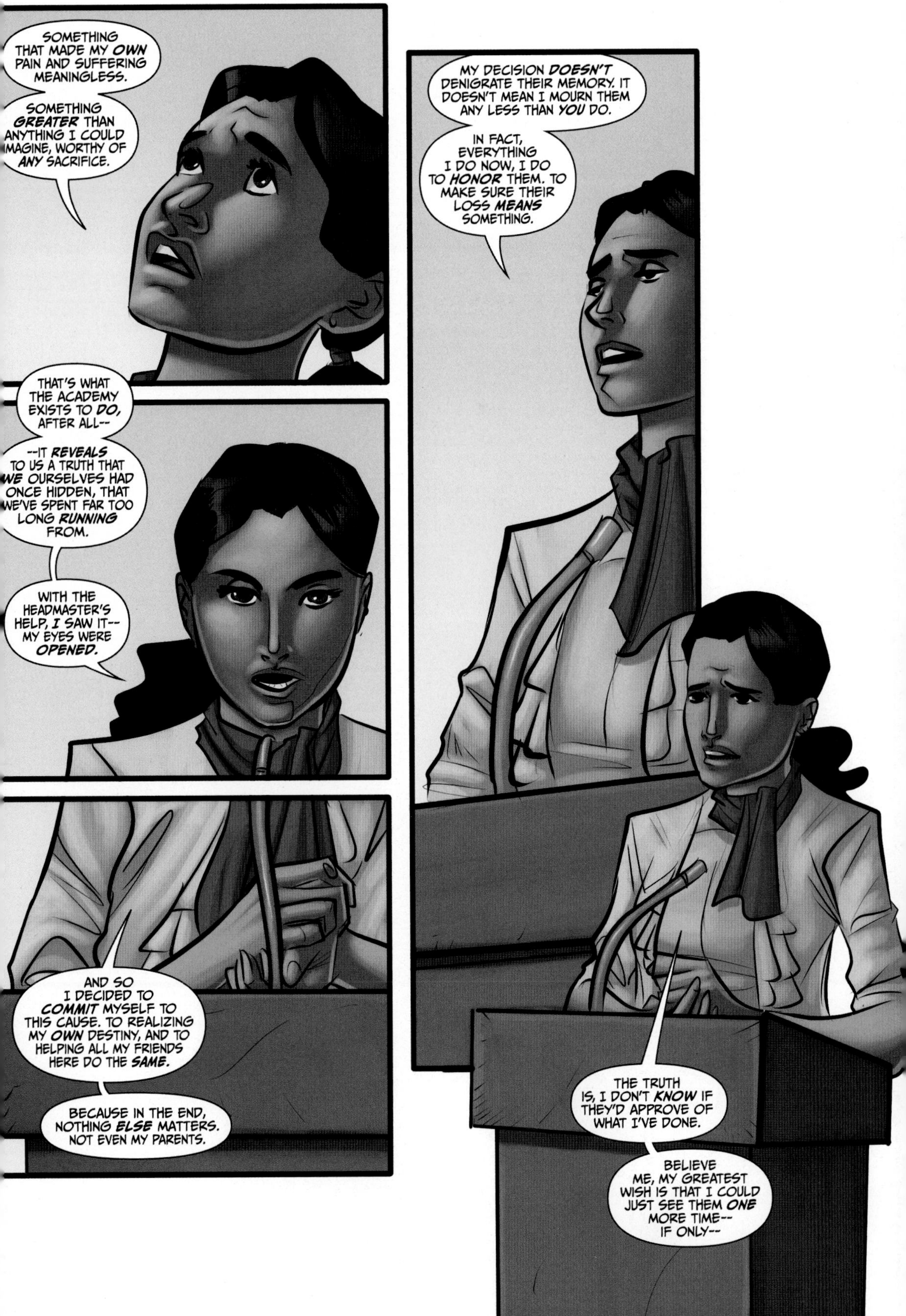
SOMETHING THAT MADE MY OWN PAIN AND SUFFERING MEANINGLESS.
SOMETHING GREATER THAN ANYTHING I COULD IMAGINE, WORTHY OF ANY SACRIFICE.
THAT'S WHAT THE ACADEMY EXISTS TO DO, AFTER ALL--
--IT REVEALS TO US A TRUTH THAT WE OURSELVES HAD ONCE HIDDEN, THAT WE'VE SPENT FAR TOO LONG RUNNING FROM.
WITH THE HEADMASTER'S HELP, I SAW IT-- MY EYES WERE OPENED.
AND SO I DECIDED TO COMMIT MYSELF TO THIS CAUSE. TO REALIZING MY OWN DESTINY, AND TO HELPING ALL MY FRIENDS HERE DO THE SAME.
BECAUSE IN THE END, NOTHING ELSE MATTERS. NOT EVEN MY PARENTS.
MY DECISION DOESN'T DENIGRATE THEIR MEMORY. IT DOESN'T MEAN I MOURN THEM ANY LESS THAN YOU DO.
IN FACT, EVERYTHING I DO NOW, I DO TO HONOR THEM. TO MAKE SURE THEIR LOSS MEANS SOMETHING.
THE TRUTH IS, I DON'T KNOW IF THEY'D APPROVE OF WHAT I'VE DONE.
BELIEVE ME, MY GREATEST WISH IS THAT I COULD JUST SEE THEM ONE MORE TIME-- IF ONLY--

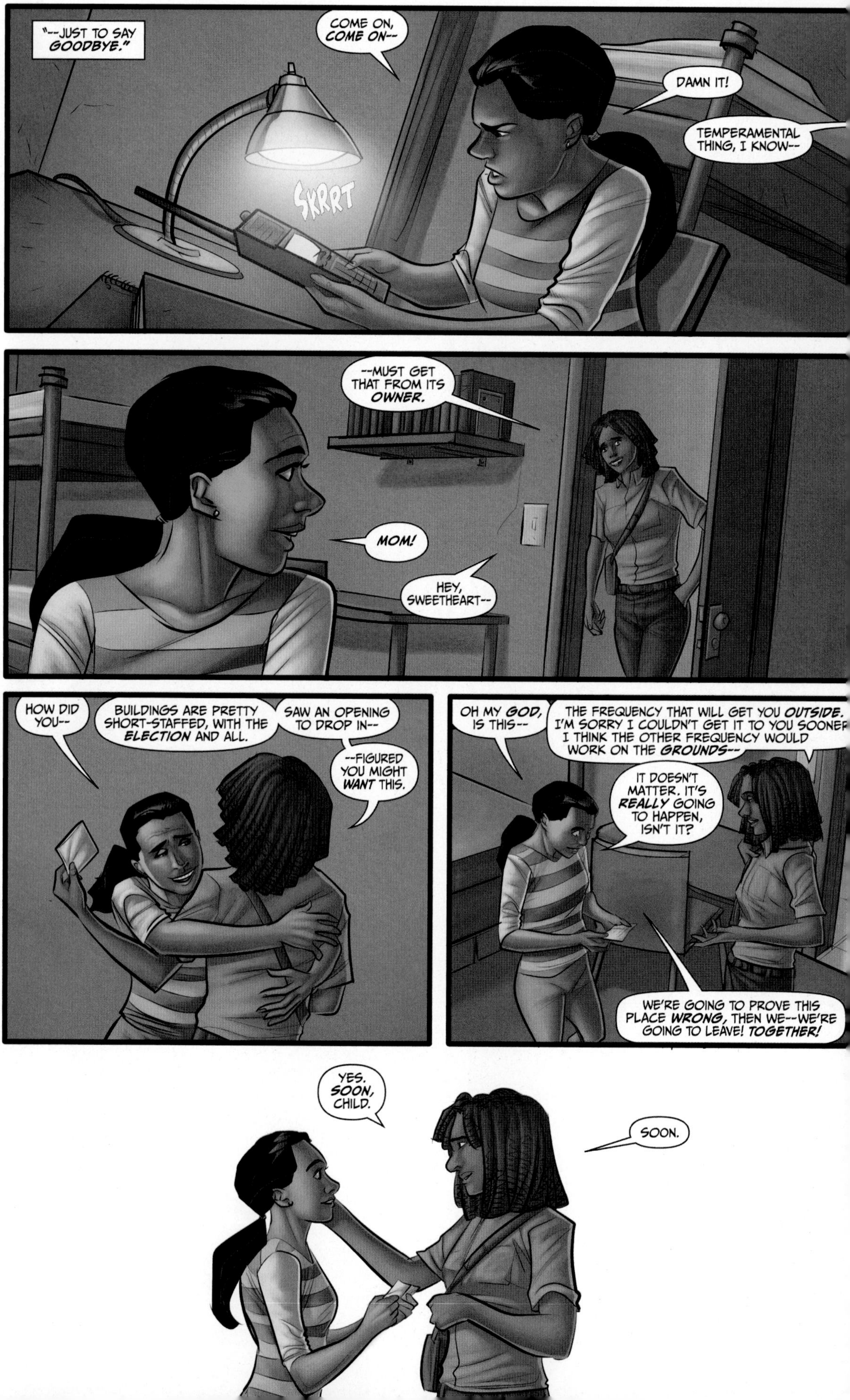
"--JUST TO SAY GOODBYE."
COME ON, COME ON--
SKRRT
DAMN IT!
TEMPERAMENTAL THING, I KNOW--
--MUST GET THAT FROM ITS OWNER.
MOM!
HEY, SWEETHEART--
HOW DID YOU--
BUILDINGS ARE PRETTY SHORT-STAFFED, WITH THE ELECTION AND ALL.
SAW AN OPENING TO DROP IN--
--FIGURED YOU MIGHT WANT THIS.
OH MY GOD, IS THIS--
THE FREQUENCY THAT WILL GET YOU OUTSIDE. I'M SORRY I COULDN'T GET IT TO YOU SOONER. I THINK THE OTHER FREQUENCY WOULD WORK ON THE GROUNDS--
IT DOESN'T MATTER. IT'S REALLY GOING TO HAPPEN, ISN'T IT?
WE'RE GOING TO PROVE THIS PLACE WRONG, THEN WE--WE'RE GOING TO LEAVE! TOGETHER!
YES. SOON, CHILD.
SOON.

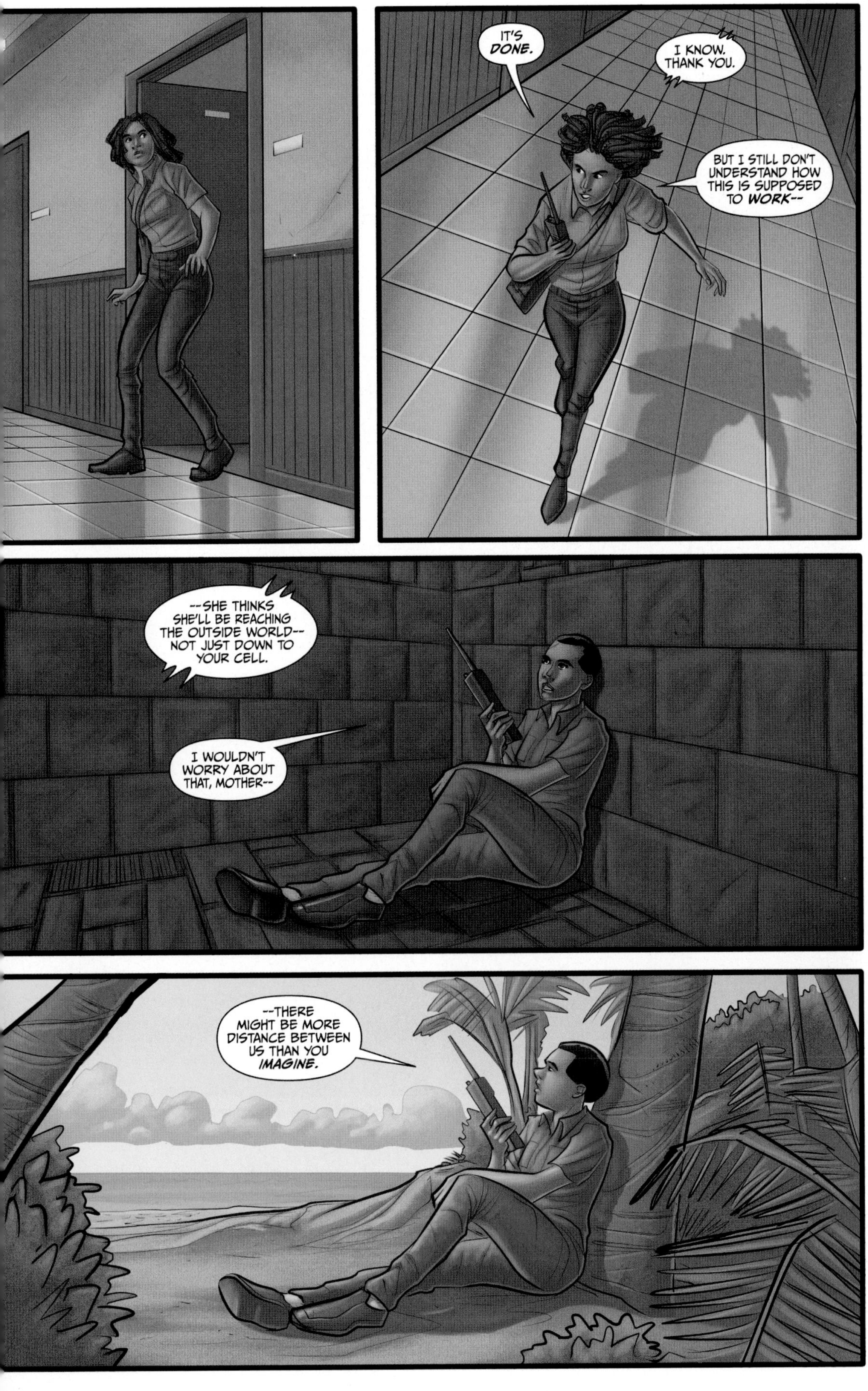
IT'S DONE.
I KNOW. THANK YOU.
BUT I STILL DON'T UNDERSTAND HOW THIS IS SUPPOSED TO WORK--
--SHE THINKS SHE'LL BE REACHING THE OUTSIDE WORLD-- NOT JUST DOWN TO YOUR CELL.
I WOULDN'T WORRY ABOUT THAT, MOTHER--
--THERE MIGHT BE MORE DISTANCE BETWEEN US THAN YOU IMAGINE.

--BUT THAT'S *MY* STORY, NOT YOURS.

MY HOPE FOR YOU, CASEY, IS THAT YOU GET TO SEE WHAT *I'VE* SEEN.

IN FACT, IF I THOUGHT YOU'D APPROACH IT WITH AN OPEN *MIND*, I'D DROP OUT OF THIS ELECTION AND ENDORSE YOU *MYSELF*.

BUT I GOT TO KNOW YOU PRETTY *WELL* BACK IN ILLINOIS, I'D LIKE TO THINK-- AND THERE'S A LOT ABOUT YOU THAT, FRANKLY, REALLY *WORRIES* ME.

YOU'RE ARROGANT. YOU'RE IMPULSIVE. YOU THINK YOU'RE *BETTER* THAN EVERYONE ELSE AROUND YOU, AND YOU THINK THAT MEANS YOU KNOW WHAT'S *BEST* FOR THEM. YOU'RE *ANGRY*, AND *HAVE* BEEN FOR A LONG TIME.

NOW, NORMALLY, I'D SAY THAT DOESN'T NECESSARILY MAKE YOU A BAD PERSON. WE *ALL* HAVE OUR FLAWS, AFTER ALL.

BUT, AGAIN, I KNOW A *LOT* MORE ABOUT THIS PLACE THAN YOU DO. AND ABOUT WHAT *BROUGHT* US HERE. YOU SEE--

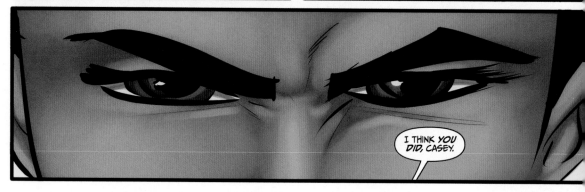

I THINK *YOU* DID, CASEY.

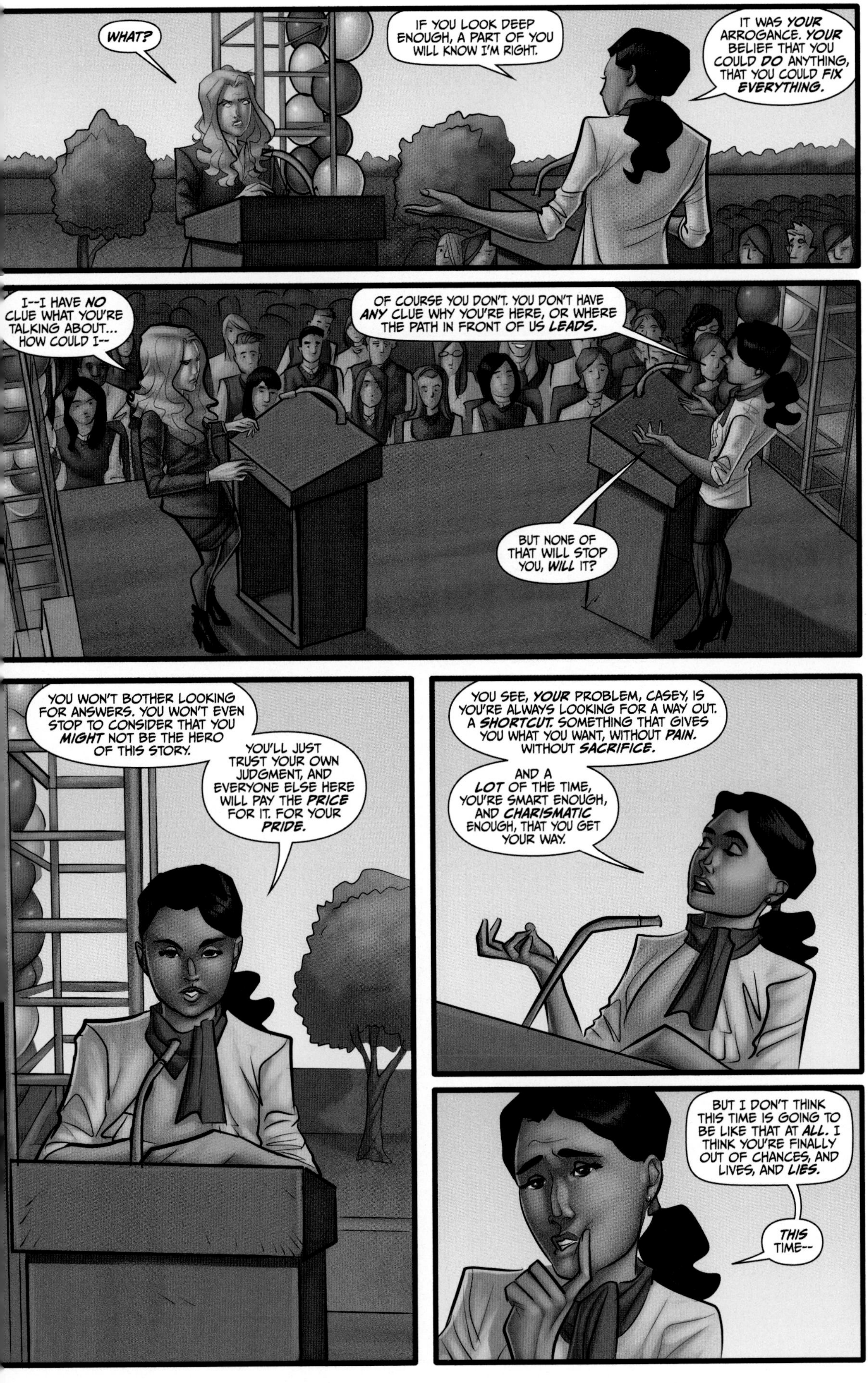
WHAT?
IF YOU LOOK DEEP ENOUGH, A PART OF YOU WILL KNOW I'M RIGHT.
IT WAS YOUR ARROGANCE. YOUR BELIEF THAT YOU COULD DO ANYTHING, THAT YOU COULD FIX EVERYTHING.
I--I HAVE NO CLUE WHAT YOU'RE TALKING ABOUT... HOW COULD I--
OF COURSE YOU DON'T. YOU DON'T HAVE ANY CLUE WHY YOU'RE HERE, OR WHERE THE PATH IN FRONT OF US LEADS.
BUT NONE OF THAT WILL STOP YOU, WILL IT?
YOU WON'T BOTHER LOOKING FOR ANSWERS. YOU WON'T EVEN STOP TO CONSIDER THAT YOU MIGHT NOT BE THE HERO OF THIS STORY.
YOU'LL JUST TRUST YOUR OWN JUDGMENT, AND EVERYONE ELSE HERE WILL PAY THE PRICE FOR IT. FOR YOUR PRIDE.
YOU SEE, YOUR PROBLEM, CASEY, IS YOU'RE ALWAYS LOOKING FOR A WAY OUT. A SHORTCUT. SOMETHING THAT GIVES YOU WHAT YOU WANT, WITHOUT PAIN. WITHOUT SACRIFICE.
AND A LOT OF THE TIME, YOU'RE SMART ENOUGH, AND CHARISMATIC ENOUGH, THAT YOU GET YOUR WAY.
BUT I DON'T THINK THIS TIME IS GOING TO BE LIKE THAT AT ALL. I THINK YOU'RE FINALLY OUT OF CHANCES, AND LIVES, AND LIES.
THIS TIME--

"--YOU WON'T BE *ABLE* TO CHEAT YOUR WAY OUT OF THIS."

I'M *SUPPOSED* TO BE PROVIDING EMOTIONAL SUPPORT AT THE *DEBATE* RIGHT NOW, YOU KNOW.

YES, I'M SURE YOU'RE *SORELY* MISSED. BUT YOU *COULD* IN FACT GIVE ME A *HAND*--

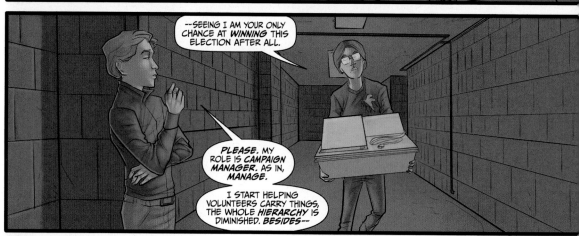

--SEEING I AM YOUR ONLY CHANCE AT *WINNING* THIS ELECTION AFTER ALL.

PLEASE. MY ROLE IS *CAMPAIGN MANAGER.* AS IN, *MANAGE.*

I START HELPING VOLUNTEERS CARRY THINGS, THE WHOLE *HIERARCHY* IS DIMINISHED. *BESIDES*--

--YOU DON'T *KNOW* THAT. THE POWER OF THE *PRESS,* THE INFLUENCE OF *ALCOHOL,* THE NUMBER OF GUYS WHO WILL VOTE FOR CASEY BECAUSE THEY PREFER *BLONDES*...NEVER *UNDERESTIMATE* THE STUPIDITY OF THE AVERAGE VOTER.

SPARE ME. YOU OF *ALL* PEOPLE CAN SEE ISABEL HAS THIS THING LOCKED UP.

YOU WANT TO *BEAT* THE BITCH--

--YOU'RE GOING TO HAVE TO *CHEAT.*

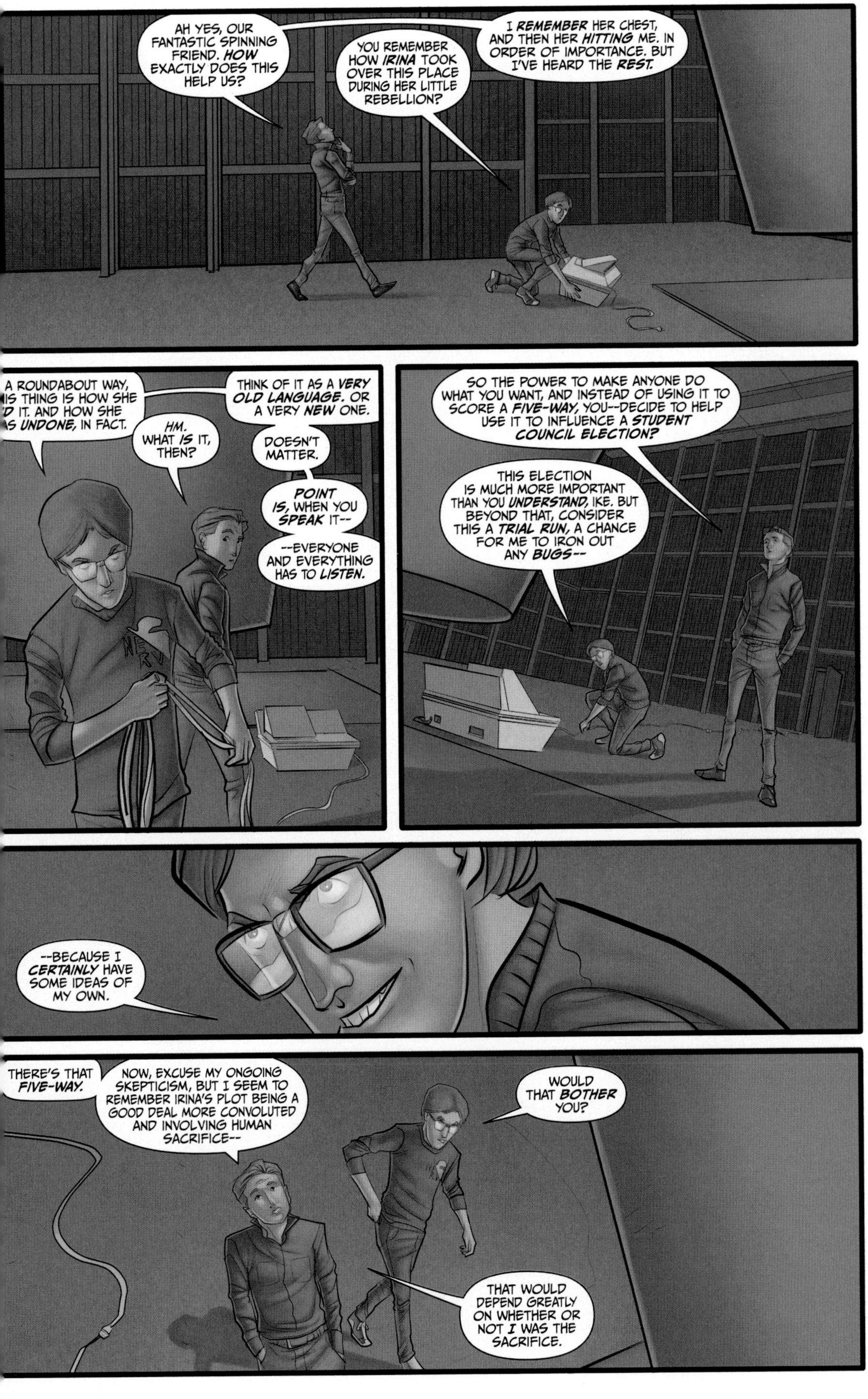
AH YES, OUR FANTASTIC SPINNING FRIEND. HOW EXACTLY DOES THIS HELP US?
YOU REMEMBER HOW IRINA TOOK OVER THIS PLACE DURING HER LITTLE REBELLION?
I REMEMBER HER CHEST, AND THEN HER HITTING ME. IN ORDER OF IMPORTANCE. BUT I'VE HEARD THE REST.
A ROUNDABOUT WAY, IS THING IS HOW SHE 'D IT. AND HOW SHE AS UNDONE, IN FACT.
HM. WHAT IS IT, THEN?
THINK OF IT AS A VERY OLD LANGUAGE. OR A VERY NEW ONE.
DOESN'T MATTER.
POINT IS, WHEN YOU SPEAK IT--
--EVERYONE AND EVERYTHING HAS TO LISTEN.
SO THE POWER TO MAKE ANYONE DO WHAT YOU WANT, AND INSTEAD OF USING IT TO SCORE A FIVE-WAY, YOU--DECIDE TO HELP USE IT TO INFLUENCE A STUDENT COUNCIL ELECTION?
THIS ELECTION IS MUCH MORE IMPORTANT THAN YOU UNDERSTAND, IKE. BUT BEYOND THAT, CONSIDER THIS A TRIAL RUN, A CHANCE FOR ME TO IRON OUT ANY BUGS--
--BECAUSE I CERTAINLY HAVE SOME IDEAS OF MY OWN.
THERE'S THAT FIVE-WAY.
NOW, EXCUSE MY ONGOING SKEPTICISM, BUT I SEEM TO REMEMBER IRINA'S PLOT BEING A GOOD DEAL MORE CONVOLUTED AND INVOLVING HUMAN SACRIFICE--
WOULD THAT BOTHER YOU?
THAT WOULD DEPEND GREATLY ON WHETHER OR NOT I WAS THE SACRIFICE.

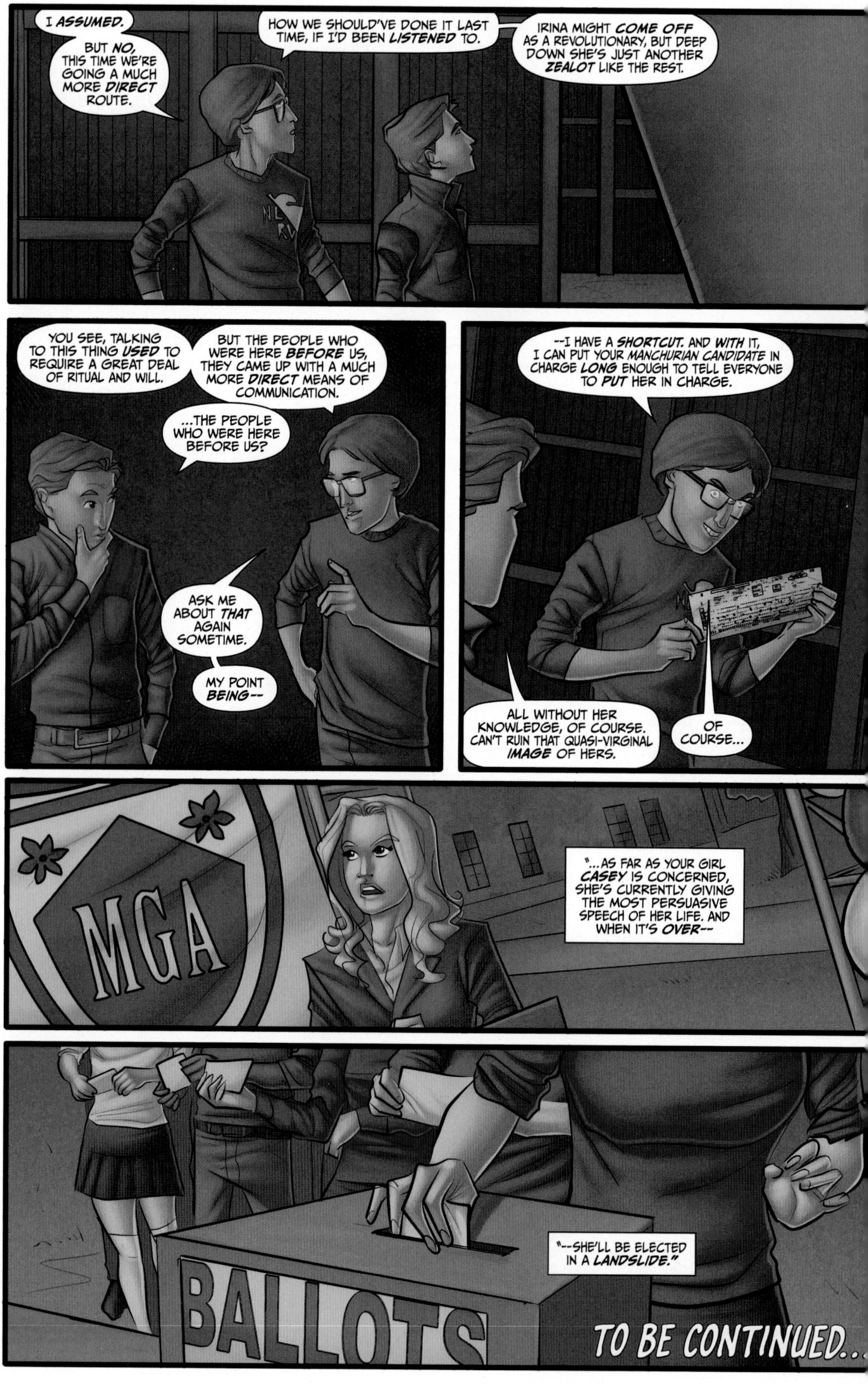

I ASSUMED.
BUT NO, THIS TIME WE'RE GOING A MUCH MORE DIRECT ROUTE.
HOW WE SHOULD'VE DONE IT LAST TIME, IF I'D BEEN LISTENED TO.
IRINA MIGHT COME OFF AS A REVOLUTIONARY, BUT DEEP DOWN SHE'S JUST ANOTHER ZEALOT LIKE THE REST.
YOU SEE, TALKING TO THIS THING USED TO REQUIRE A GREAT DEAL OF RITUAL AND WILL.
BUT THE PEOPLE WHO WERE HERE BEFORE US, THEY CAME UP WITH A MUCH MORE DIRECT MEANS OF COMMUNICATION.
...THE PEOPLE WHO WERE HERE BEFORE US?
ASK ME ABOUT THAT AGAIN SOMETIME.
MY POINT BEING--
--I HAVE A SHORTCUT. AND WITH IT, I CAN PUT YOUR MANCHURIAN CANDIDATE IN CHARGE LONG ENOUGH TO TELL EVERYONE TO PUT HER IN CHARGE.
ALL WITHOUT HER KNOWLEDGE, OF COURSE. CAN'T RUIN THAT QUASI-VIRGINAL IMAGE OF HERS.
OF COURSE...
MGA
"...AS FAR AS YOUR GIRL CASEY IS CONCERNED, SHE'S CURRENTLY GIVING THE MOST PERSUASIVE SPEECH OF HER LIFE. AND WHEN IT'S OVER--
"--SHE'LL BE ELECTED IN A LANDSLIDE."
BALLOTS
TO BE CONTINUED...

fortynine

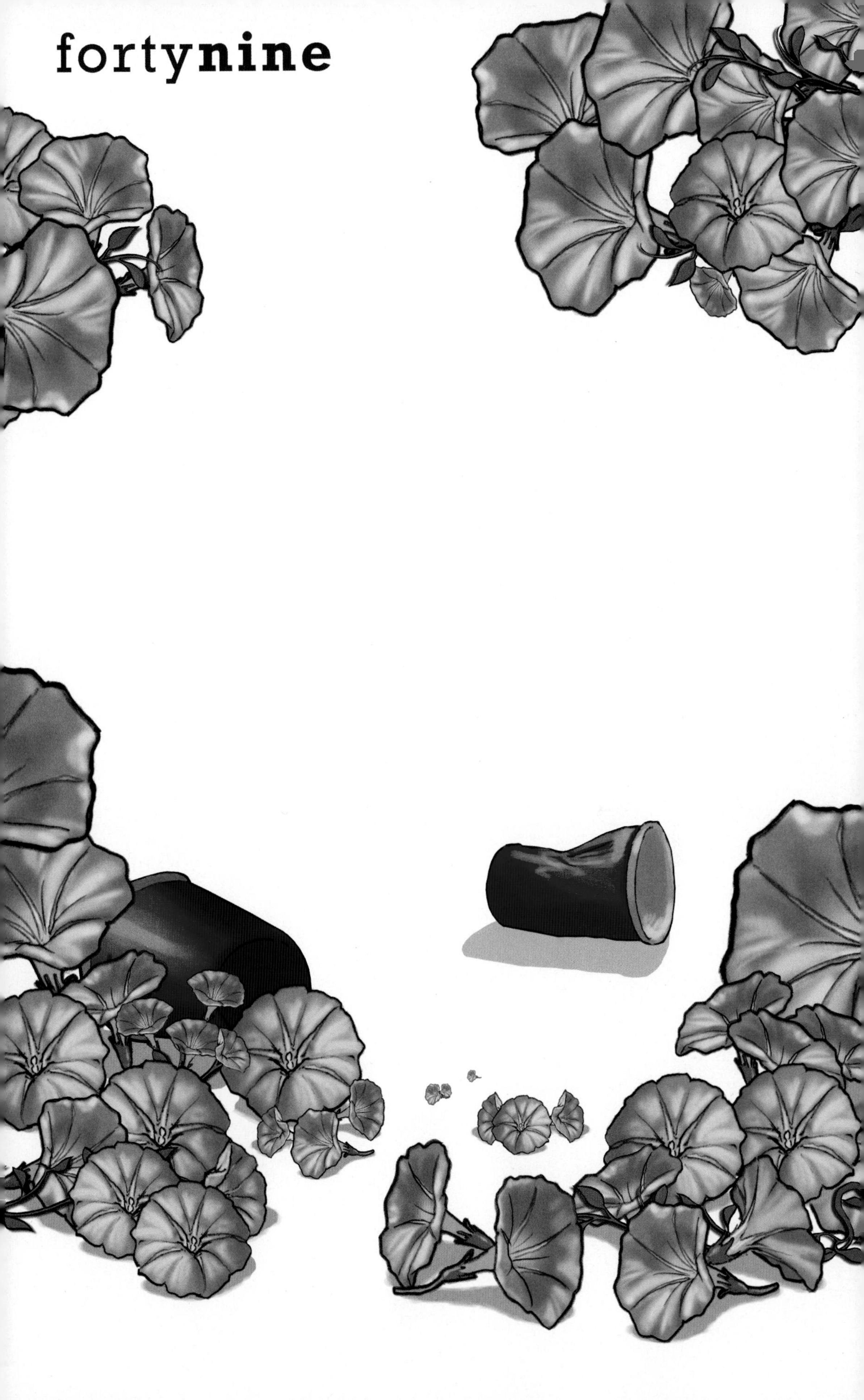

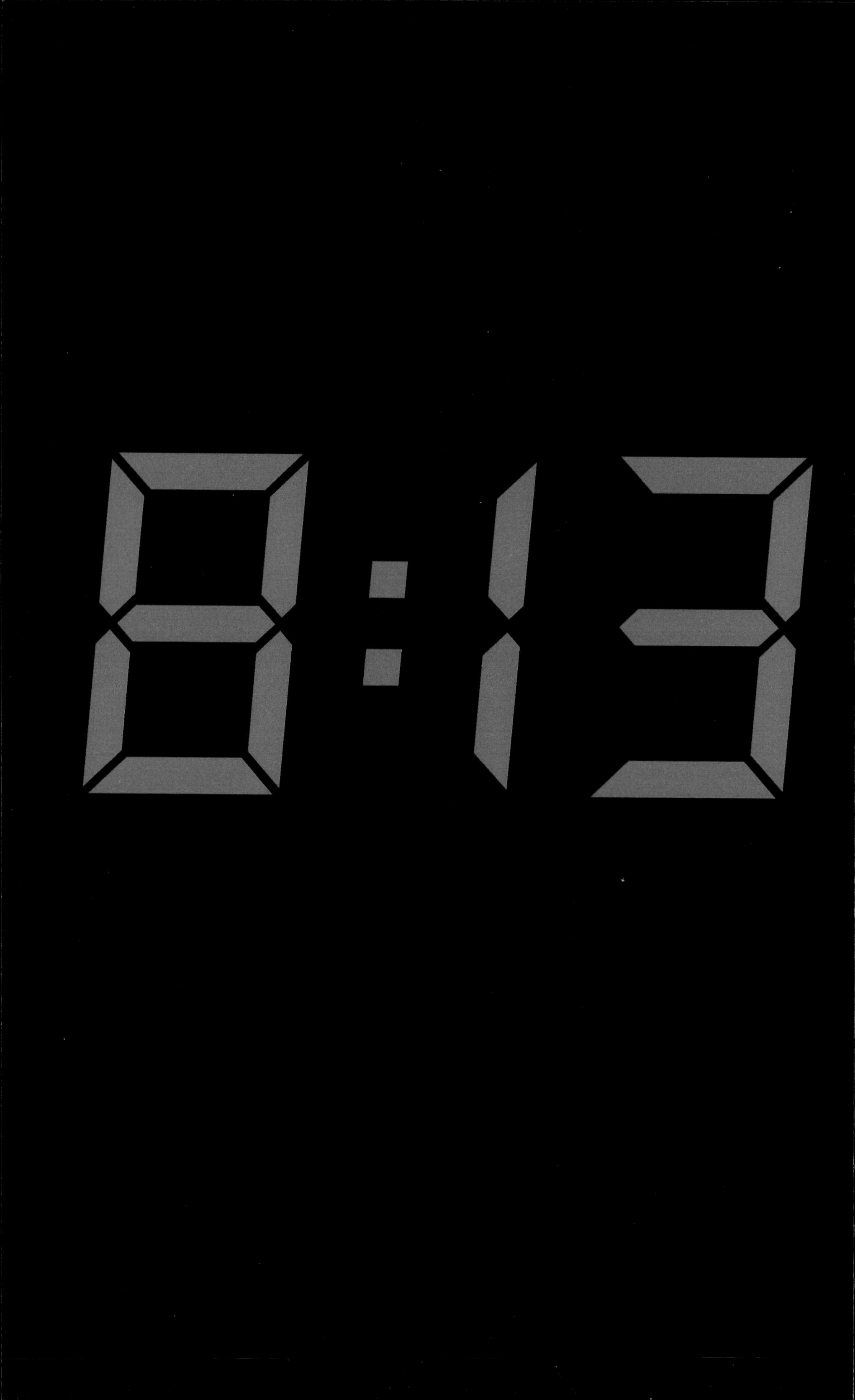
8:13

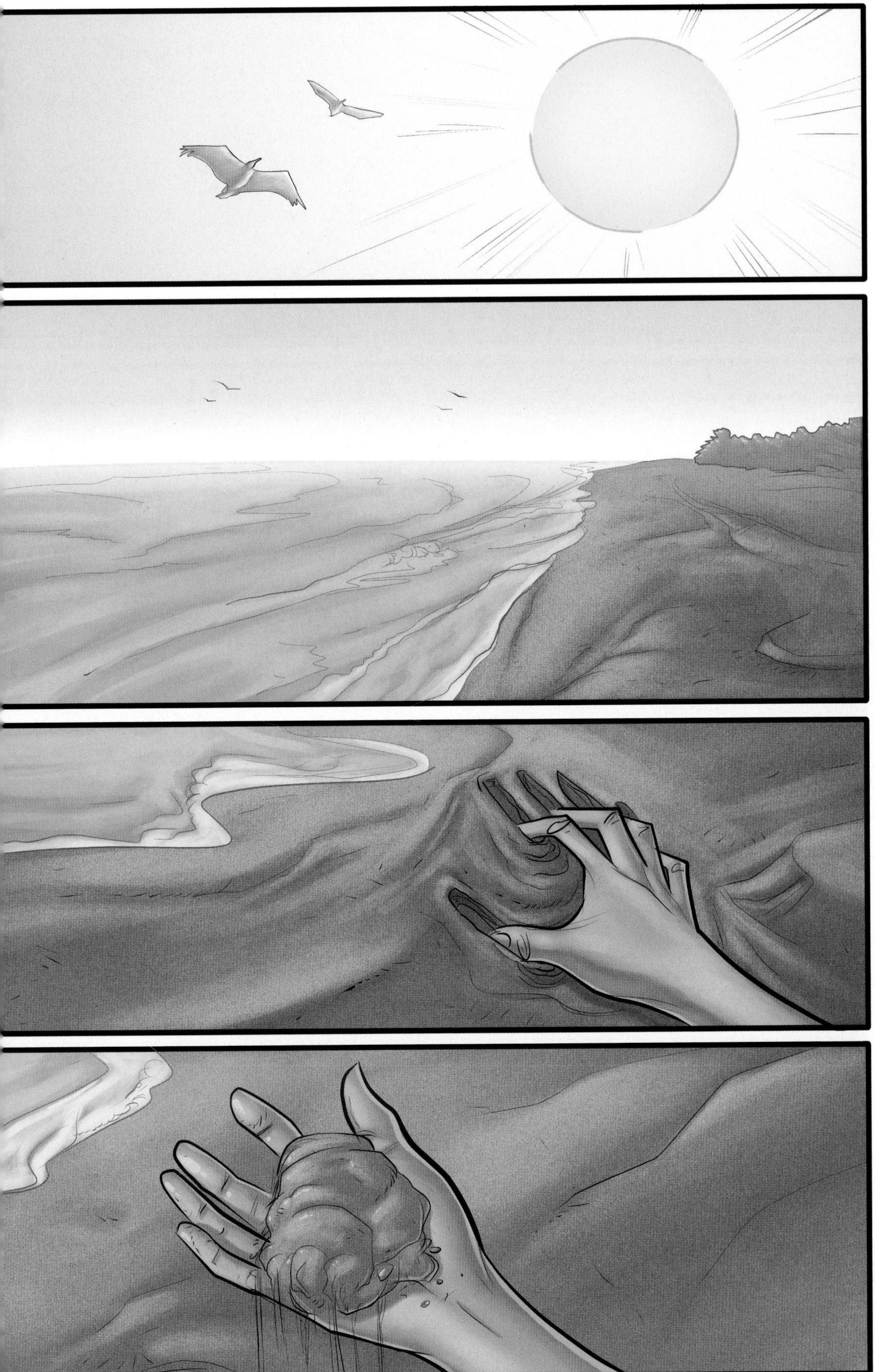

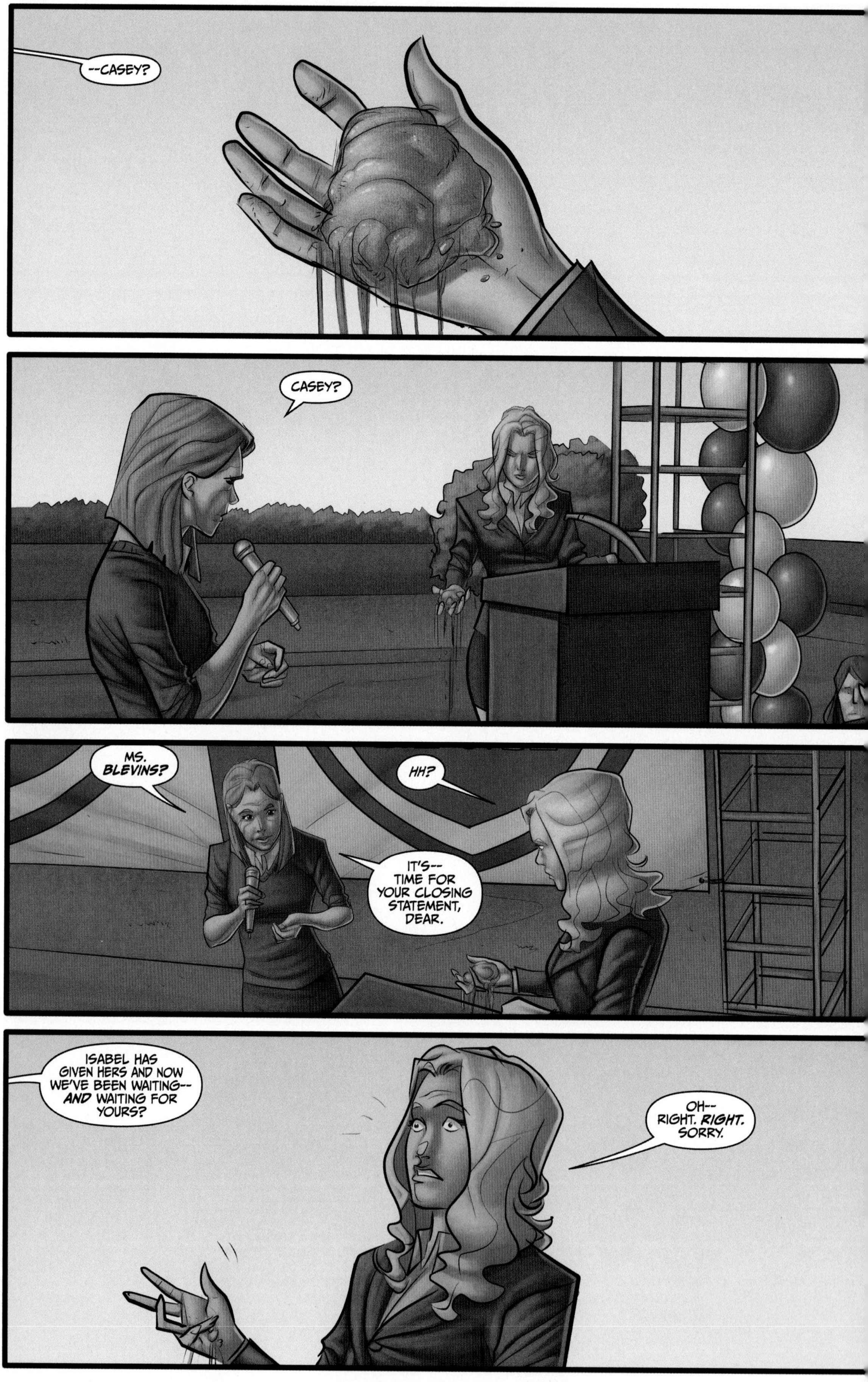
--CASEY?
CASEY?
MS. BLEVINS?
HH?
IT'S-- TIME FOR YOUR CLOSING STATEMENT, DEAR.
ISABEL HAS GIVEN HERS AND NOW WE'VE BEEN WAITING-- AND WAITING FOR YOURS?
OH-- RIGHT. RIGHT. SORRY.

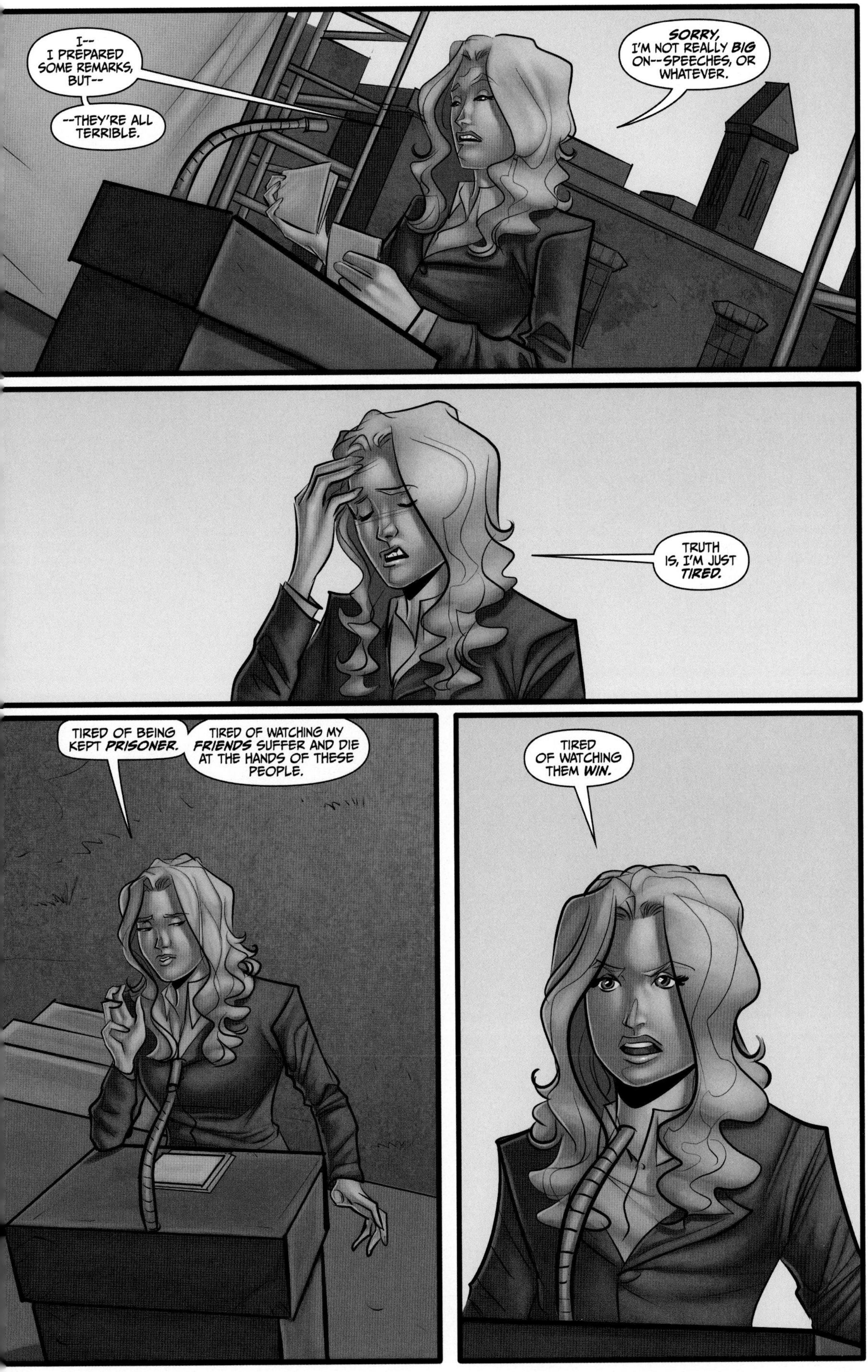
I--
I PREPARED SOME REMARKS, BUT--
--THEY'RE ALL TERRIBLE.
SORRY, I'M NOT REALLY BIG ON--SPEECHES, OR WHATEVER.
TRUTH IS, I'M JUST TIRED.
TIRED OF BEING KEPT PRISONER.
TIRED OF WATCHING MY FRIENDS SUFFER AND DIE AT THE HANDS OF THESE PEOPLE.
TIRED OF WATCHING THEM WIN.

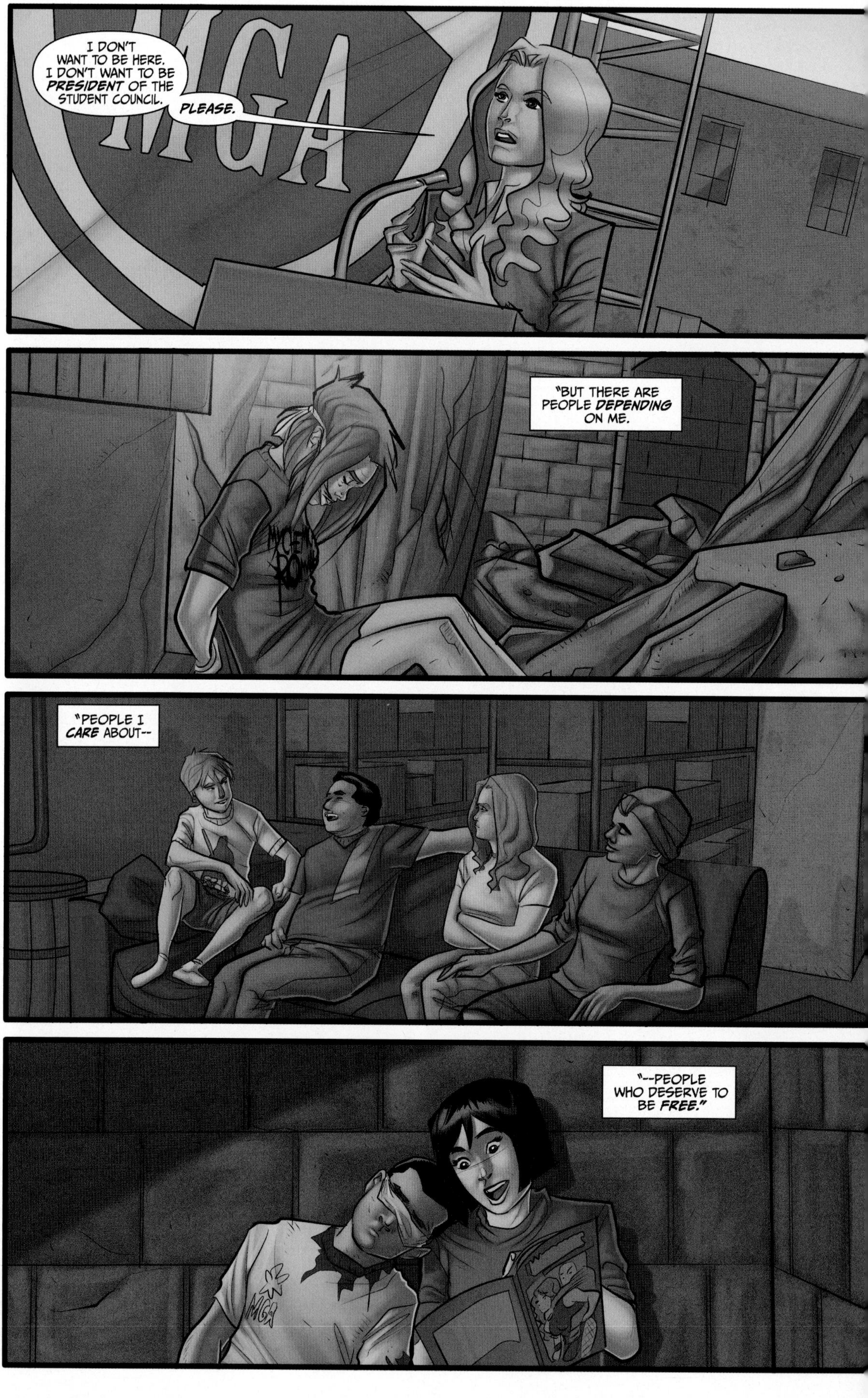
I DON'T WANT TO BE HERE. I DON'T WANT TO BE *PRESIDENT* OF THE STUDENT COUNCIL.
PLEASE.
"BUT THERE ARE PEOPLE *DEPENDING* ON ME.
"PEOPLE I *CARE* ABOUT--
"--PEOPLE WHO DESERVE TO BE *FREE.*"

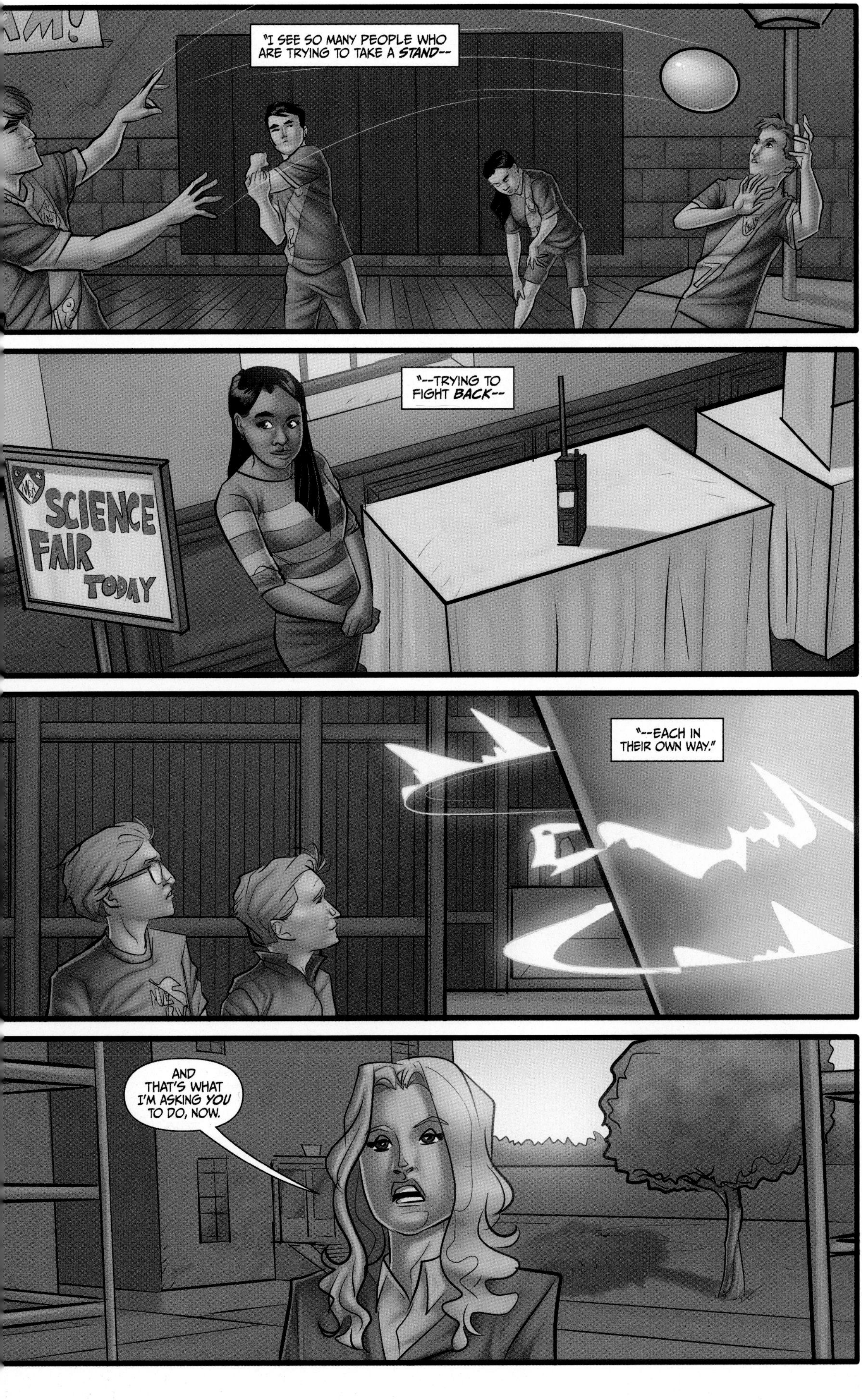
"I SEE SO MANY PEOPLE WHO ARE TRYING TO TAKE A STAND--
"--TRYING TO FIGHT BACK--
SCIENCE FAIR TODAY
"--EACH IN THEIR OWN WAY."
AND THAT'S WHAT I'M ASKING YOU TO DO, NOW.

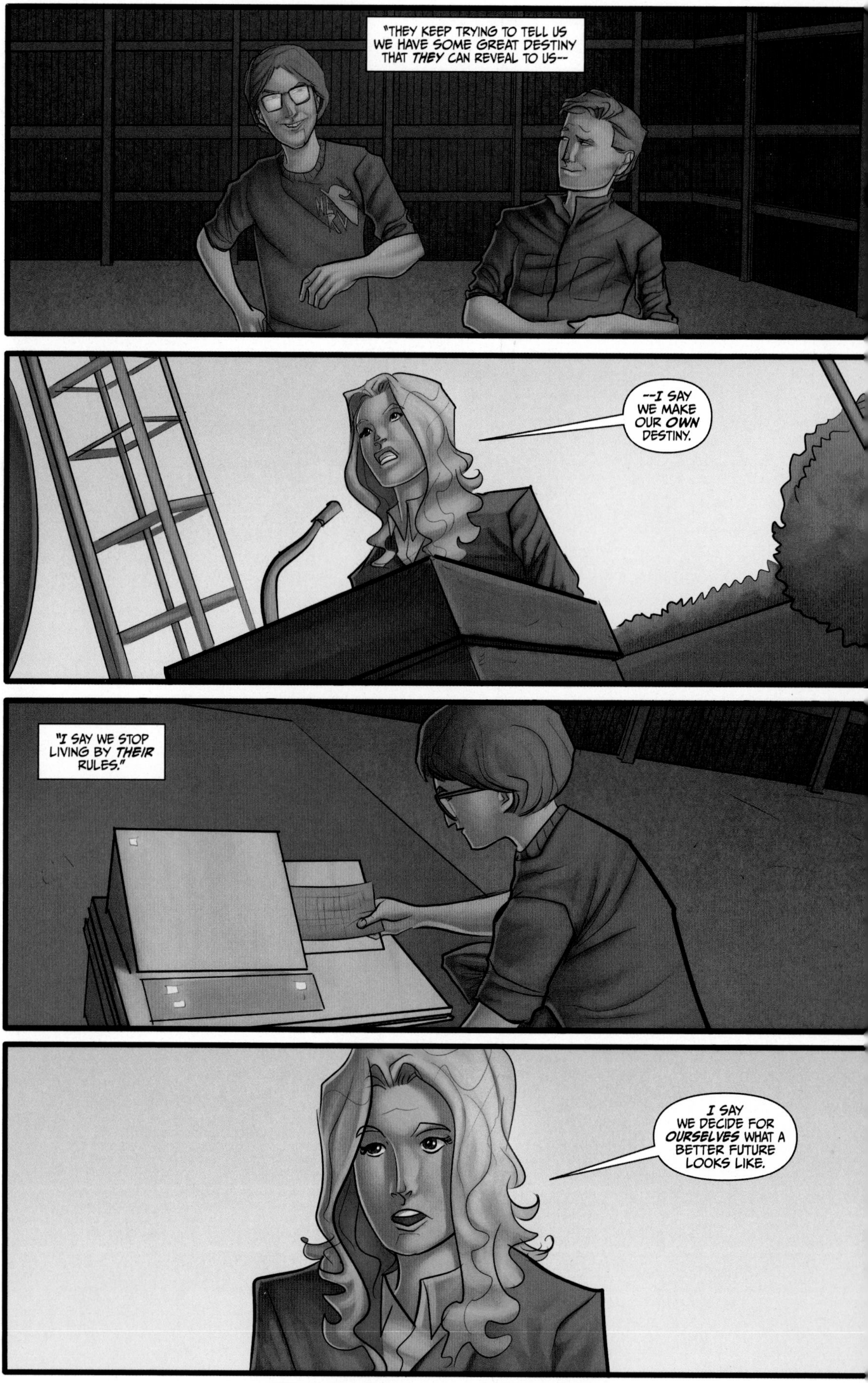
"THEY KEEP TRYING TO TELL US WE HAVE SOME GREAT DESTINY THAT *THEY* CAN REVEAL TO US--
--I SAY WE MAKE OUR *OWN* DESTINY.
"I SAY WE STOP LIVING BY *THEIR* RULES."
I SAY WE DECIDE FOR *OURSELVES* WHAT A BETTER FUTURE LOOKS LIKE.

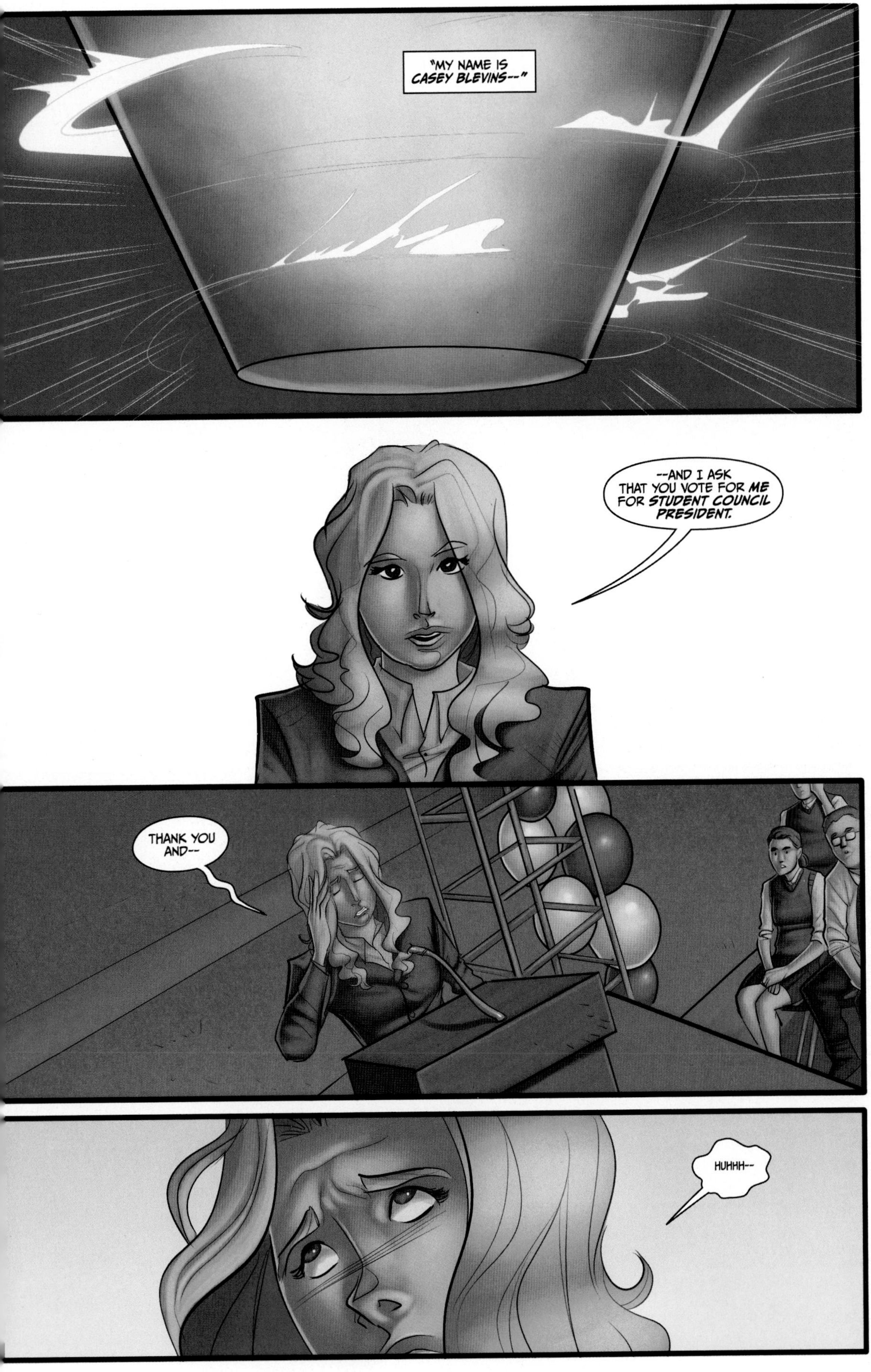
"MY NAME IS CASEY BLEVINS--"
--AND I ASK THAT YOU VOTE FOR ME FOR STUDENT COUNCIL PRESIDENT.
THANK YOU AND--
HUHHH--

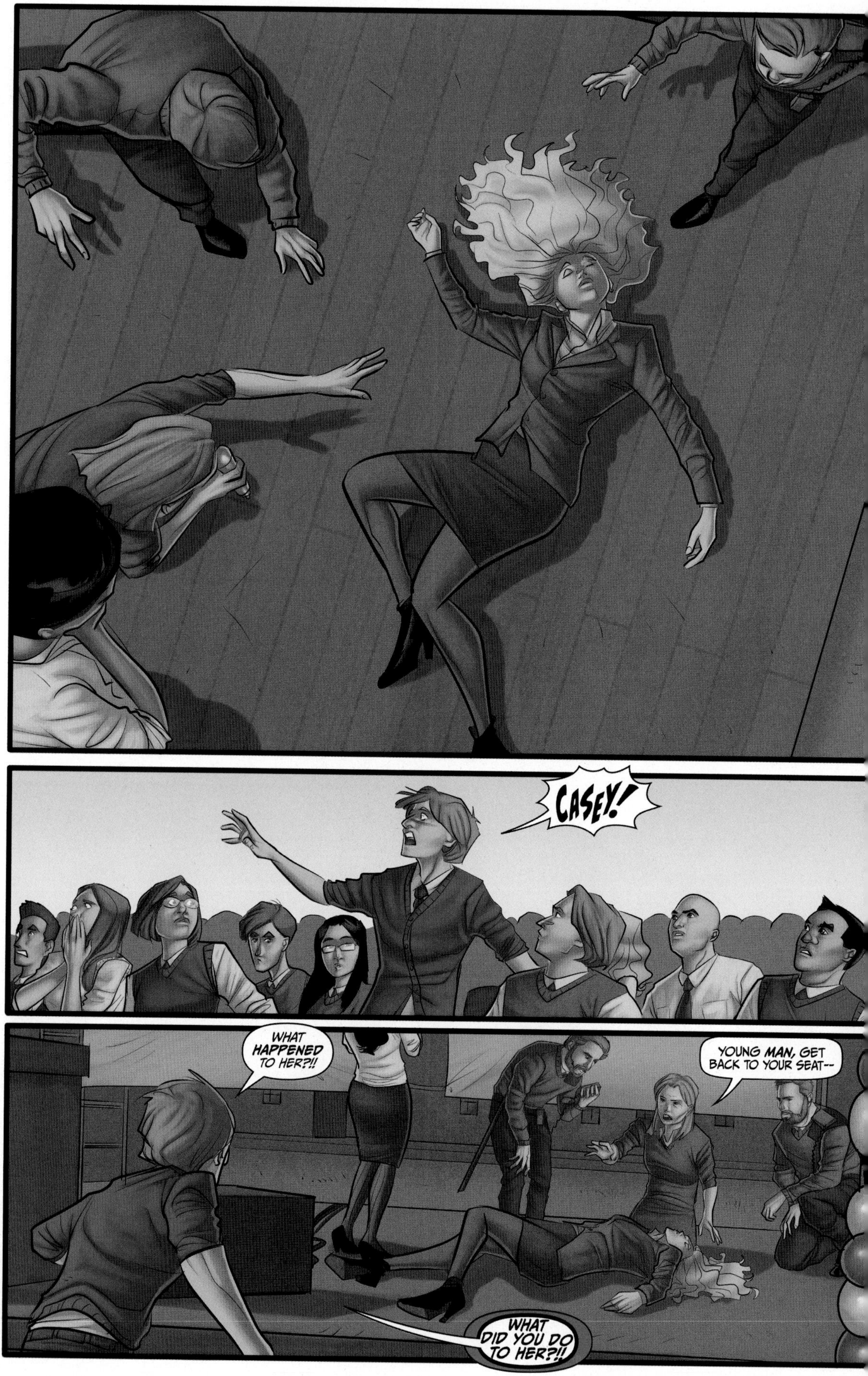
CASEY!
WHAT HAPPENED TO HER?!!
YOUNG MAN, GET BACK TO YOUR SEAT--
WHAT DID YOU DO TO HER?!!

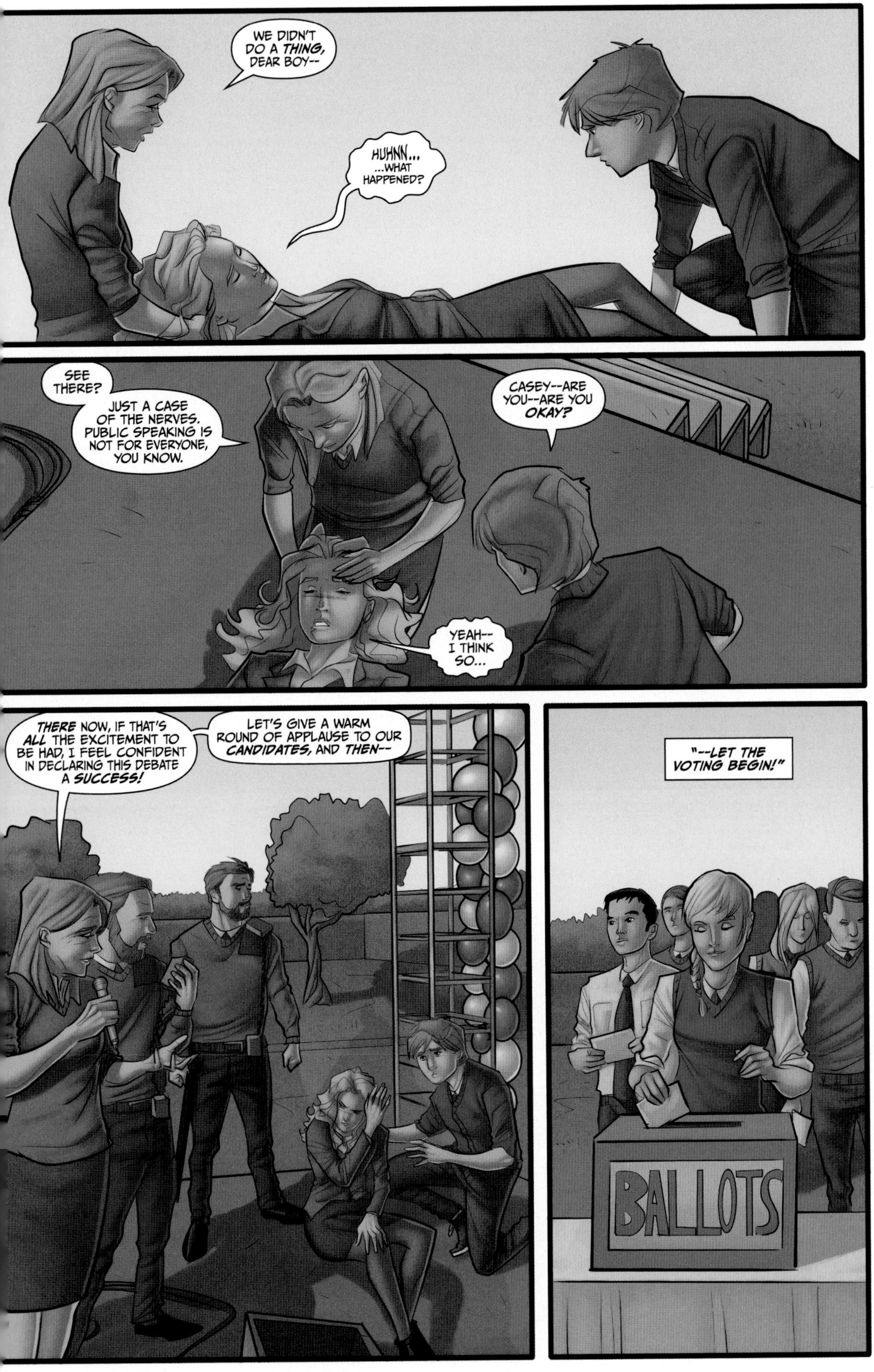
WE DIDN'T DO A *THING,* DEAR BOY--
HUHNN... ...WHAT HAPPENED?
SEE THERE?
JUST A CASE OF THE NERVES. PUBLIC SPEAKING IS NOT FOR EVERYONE, YOU KNOW.
CASEY--ARE YOU--ARE YOU *OKAY?*
YEAH-- I THINK SO...
THERE NOW, IF THAT'S *ALL* THE EXCITEMENT TO BE HAD, I FEEL CONFIDENT IN DECLARING THIS DEBATE A *SUCCESS!*
LET'S GIVE A WARM ROUND OF APPLAUSE TO OUR *CANDIDATES,* AND *THEN--*
"--LET THE VOTING BEGIN!"
BALLOTS

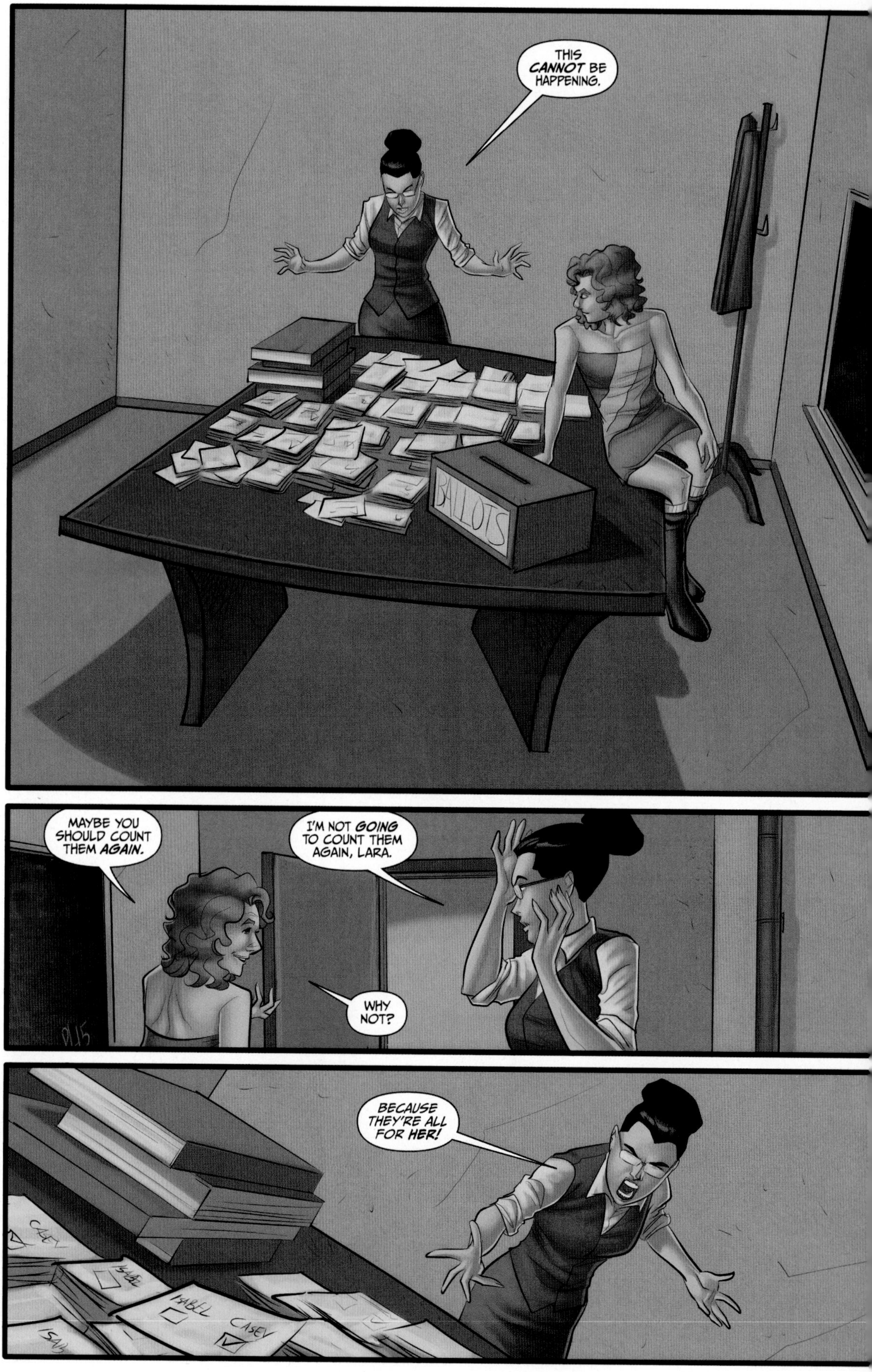
THIS CANNOT BE HAPPENING.
BALLOTS
MAYBE YOU SHOULD COUNT THEM AGAIN.
I'M NOT GOING TO COUNT THEM AGAIN, LARA.
WHY NOT?
BECAUSE THEY'RE ALL FOR HER!
CASEY
ISABEL
ISABEL
CASEY

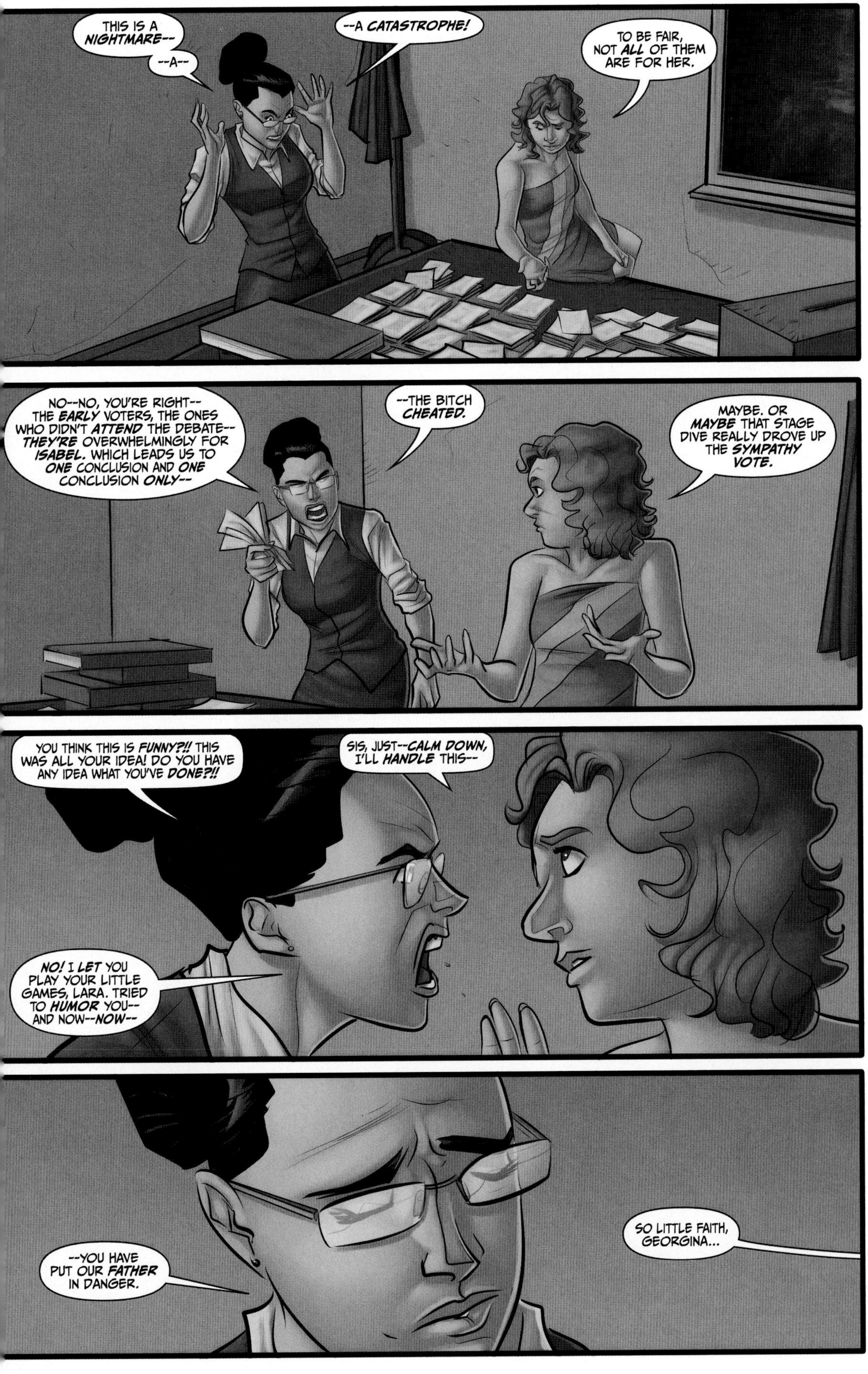
THIS IS A NIGHTMARE--
--A--
--A CATASTROPHE!
TO BE FAIR, NOT ALL OF THEM ARE FOR HER.
NO--NO, YOU'RE RIGHT-- THE EARLY VOTERS, THE ONES WHO DIDN'T ATTEND THE DEBATE-- THEY'RE OVERWHELMINGLY FOR ISABEL. WHICH LEADS US TO ONE CONCLUSION AND ONE CONCLUSION ONLY--
--THE BITCH CHEATED.
MAYBE. OR MAYBE THAT STAGE DIVE REALLY DROVE UP THE SYMPATHY VOTE.
YOU THINK THIS IS FUNNY?!! THIS WAS ALL YOUR IDEA! DO YOU HAVE ANY IDEA WHAT YOU'VE DONE?!!
SIS, JUST--CALM DOWN, I'LL HANDLE THIS--
NO! I LET YOU PLAY YOUR LITTLE GAMES, LARA. TRIED TO HUMOR YOU-- AND NOW--NOW--
--YOU HAVE PUT OUR FATHER IN DANGER.
SO LITTLE FAITH, GEORGINA...

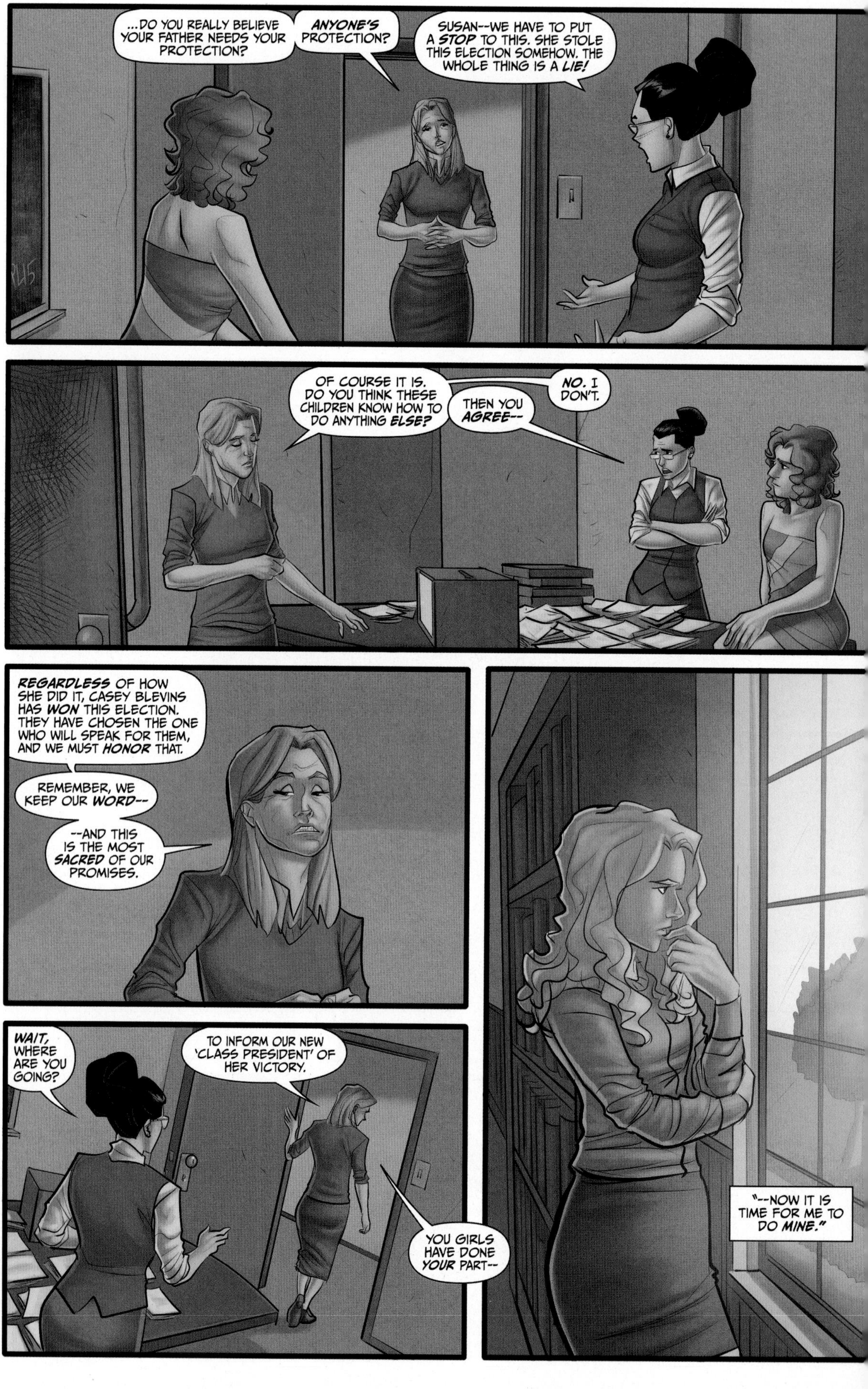
...DO YOU REALLY BELIEVE YOUR FATHER NEEDS YOUR PROTECTION?
ANYONE'S PROTECTION?
SUSAN--WE HAVE TO PUT A STOP TO THIS. SHE STOLE THIS ELECTION SOMEHOW. THE WHOLE THING IS A LIE!
OF COURSE IT IS. DO YOU THINK THESE CHILDREN KNOW HOW TO DO ANYTHING ELSE?
THEN YOU AGREE--
NO. I DON'T.
REGARDLESS OF HOW SHE DID IT, CASEY BLEVINS HAS WON THIS ELECTION. THEY HAVE CHOSEN THE ONE WHO WILL SPEAK FOR THEM, AND WE MUST HONOR THAT.
REMEMBER, WE KEEP OUR WORD--
--AND THIS IS THE MOST SACRED OF OUR PROMISES.
WAIT, WHERE ARE YOU GOING?
TO INFORM OUR NEW 'CLASS PRESIDENT' OF HER VICTORY.
YOU GIRLS HAVE DONE YOUR PART--
"--NOW IT IS TIME FOR ME TO DO MINE."

AFTERNOON, CAMPERS! IT'S A **BIG NIGHT** HERE AT MORNING GLORY ACADEMY--

--STARTING WITH THE **SCIENCE FAIR COMPETITION**--

--AND THE FINALS OF THIS YEAR'S **TOWERBALL TOURNAMENT!**

AND ALL *THAT* LEADS TO THE **MAIN EVENT,** A LITTLE AFTER *EIGHT*--

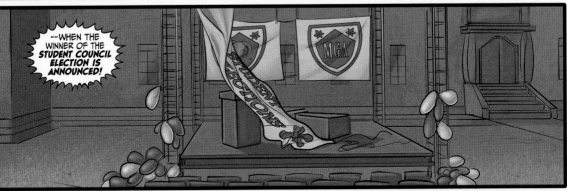

--WHEN THE WINNER OF THE **STUDENT COUNCIL ELECTION** IS ANNOUNCED!

YES SIR, I DON'T KNOW *HOW* WE'RE GONNA HANDLE ALL THIS *EXCITEMENT*--

--MAYBE IT'LL KILL US *ALL!*

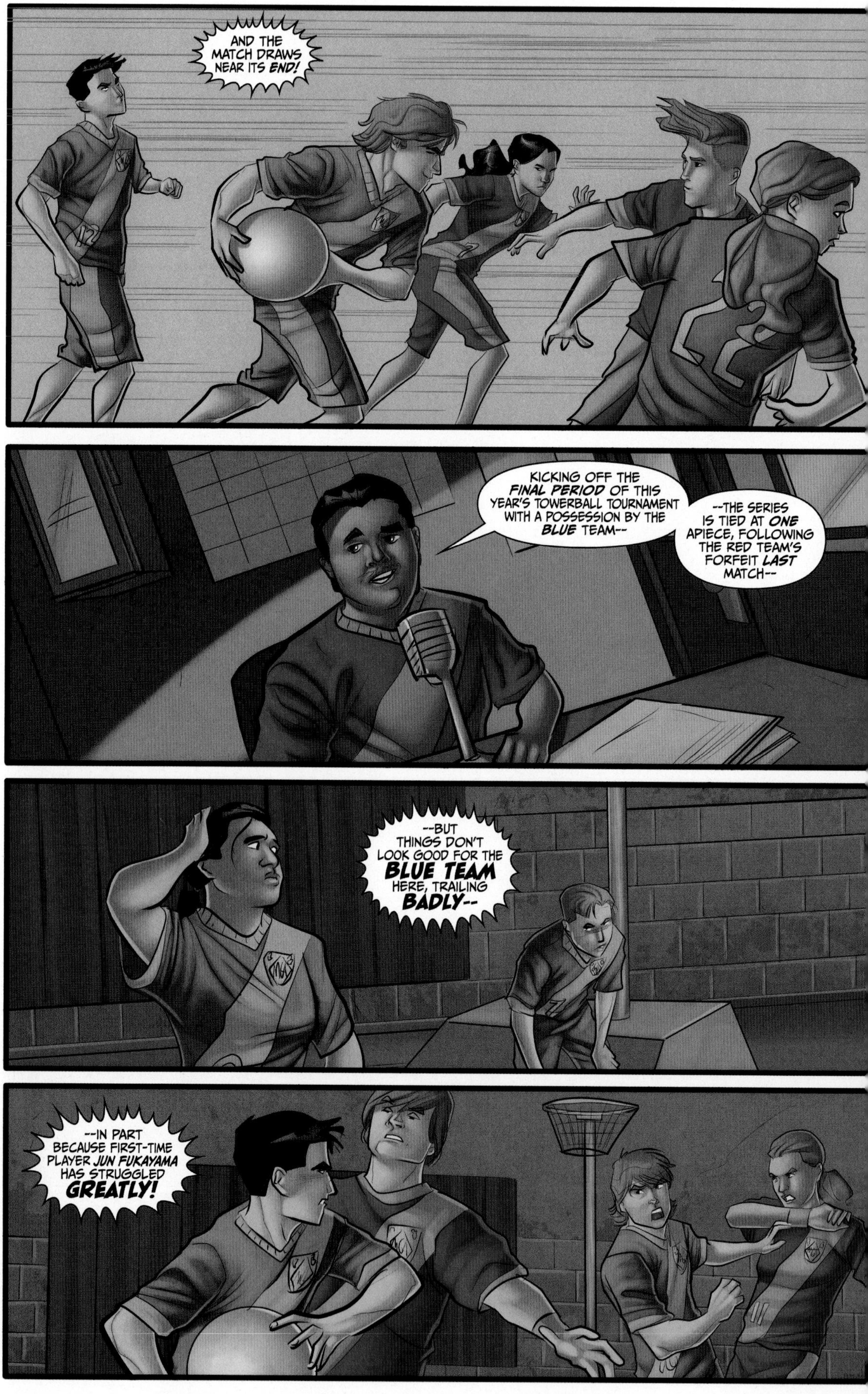
AND THE MATCH DRAWS NEAR ITS END!
KICKING OFF THE FINAL PERIOD OF THIS YEAR'S TOWERBALL TOURNAMENT WITH A POSSESSION BY THE BLUE TEAM--
--THE SERIES IS TIED AT ONE APIECE, FOLLOWING THE RED TEAM'S FORFEIT LAST MATCH--
--BUT THINGS DON'T LOOK GOOD FOR THE BLUE TEAM HERE, TRAILING BADLY--
--IN PART BECAUSE FIRST-TIME PLAYER JUN FUKAYAMA HAS STRUGGLED GREATLY!

TIME IS RUNNING OUT FOR THE PERENNIAL UNDERDOGS--
TIME
12:00
0
HOME
PERIOD 4
24
GUEST
--AND FUKAYAMA TURNS THE BALL OVER AGAIN!
THIS TEAM JUST CANNOT CATCH A BREAK!
5
AND THE RED TEAM SCORE AGAIN!
OOF!

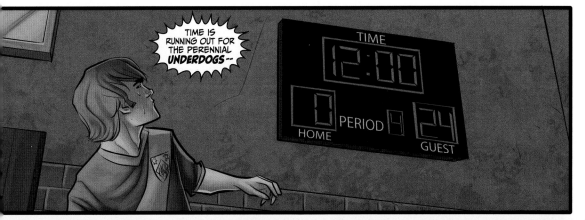

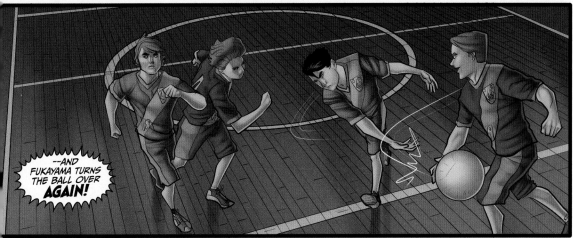

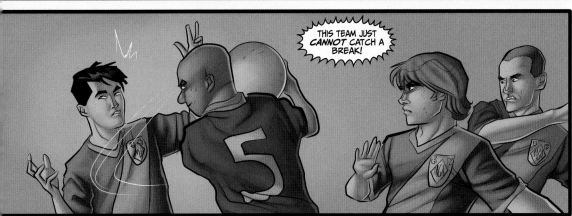

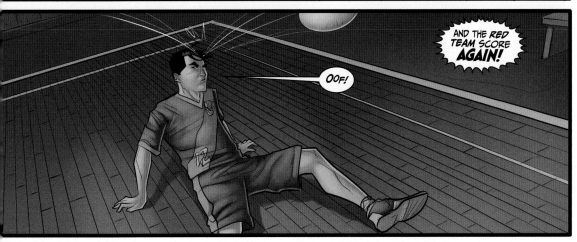

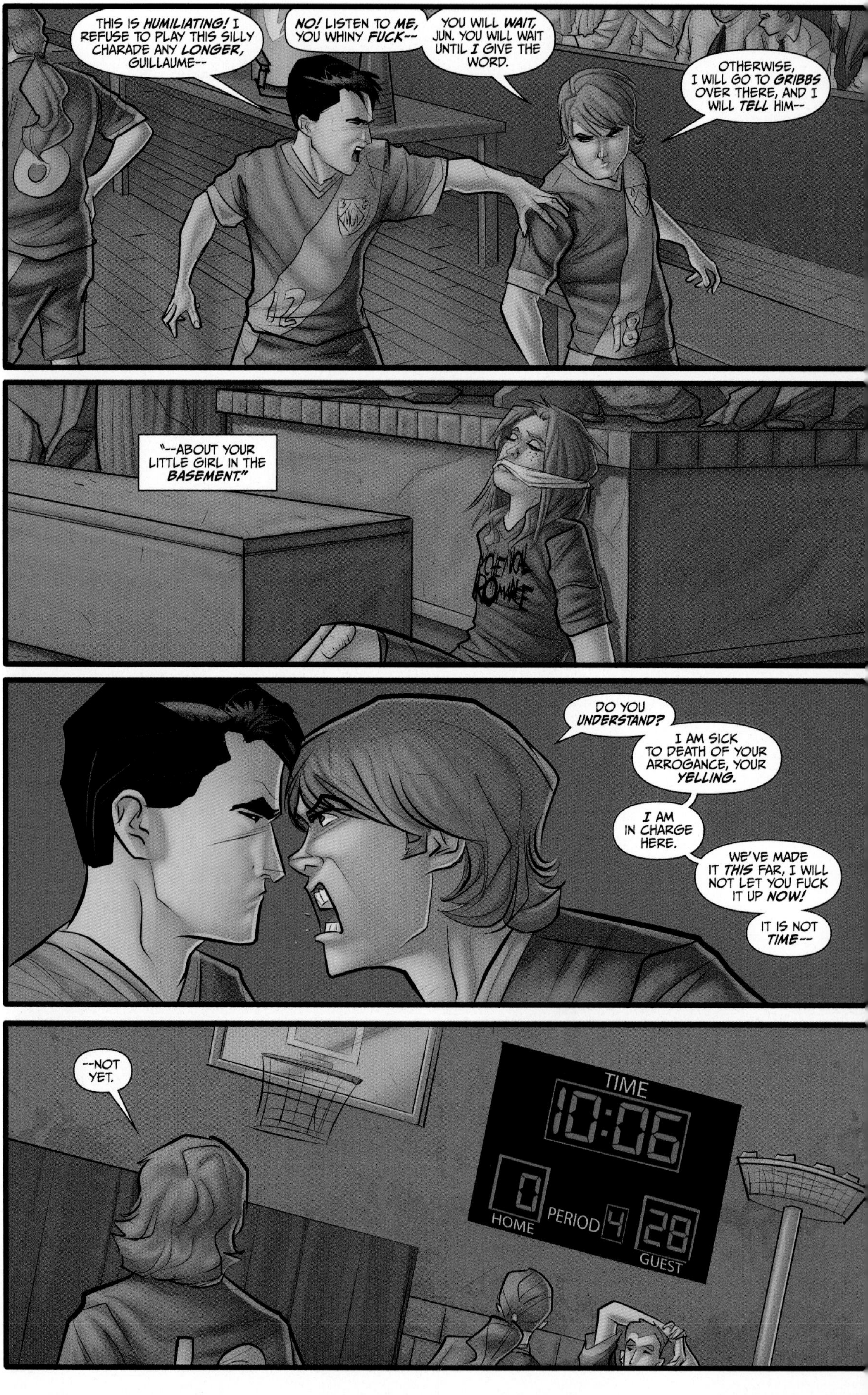
THIS IS HUMILIATING! I REFUSE TO PLAY THIS SILLY CHARADE ANY LONGER, GUILLAUME--
NO! LISTEN TO ME, YOU WHINY FUCK--
YOU WILL WAIT, JUN. YOU WILL WAIT UNTIL I GIVE THE WORD.
OTHERWISE, I WILL GO TO GRIBBS OVER THERE, AND I WILL TELL HIM--
"--ABOUT YOUR LITTLE GIRL IN THE BASEMENT."
DO YOU UNDERSTAND?
I AM SICK TO DEATH OF YOUR ARROGANCE, YOUR YELLING.
I AM IN CHARGE HERE.
WE'VE MADE IT THIS FAR, I WILL NOT LET YOU FUCK IT UP NOW!
IT IS NOT TIME--
--NOT YET.
TIME
10:06
0
HOME
PERIOD 4
28
GUEST

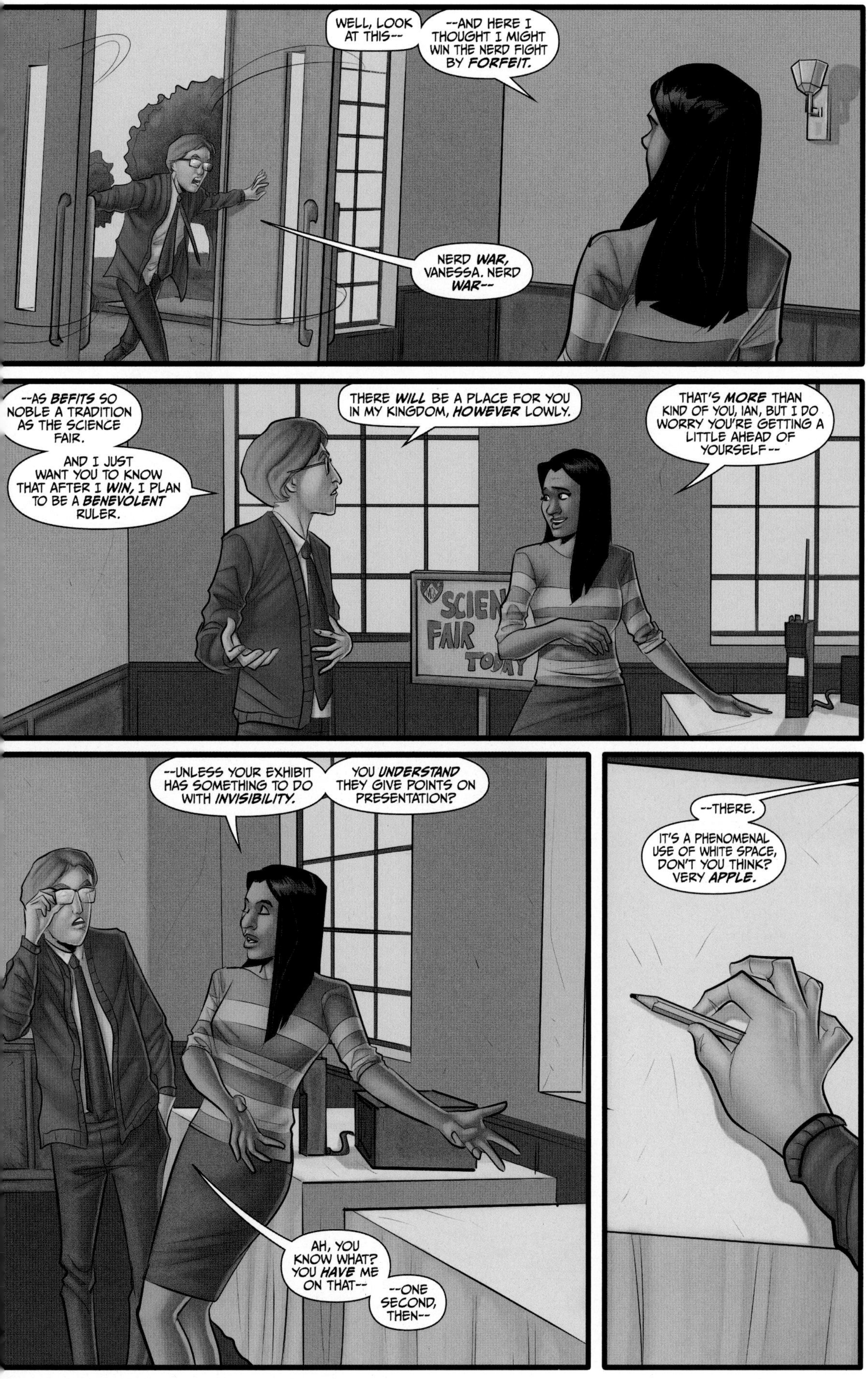
WELL, LOOK AT THIS--
--AND HERE I THOUGHT I MIGHT WIN THE NERD FIGHT BY FORFEIT.
NERD WAR, VANESSA. NERD WAR--
--AS BEFITS SO NOBLE A TRADITION AS THE SCIENCE FAIR.
AND I JUST WANT YOU TO KNOW THAT AFTER I WIN, I PLAN TO BE A BENEVOLENT RULER.
THERE WILL BE A PLACE FOR YOU IN MY KINGDOM, HOWEVER LOWLY.
THAT'S MORE THAN KIND OF YOU, IAN, BUT I DO WORRY YOU'RE GETTING A LITTLE AHEAD OF YOURSELF--
SCIENCE FAIR TODAY
--UNLESS YOUR EXHIBIT HAS SOMETHING TO DO WITH INVISIBILITY.
YOU UNDERSTAND THEY GIVE POINTS ON PRESENTATION?
AH, YOU KNOW WHAT? YOU HAVE ME ON THAT--
--ONE SECOND, THEN--
--THERE.
IT'S A PHENOMENAL USE OF WHITE SPACE, DON'T YOU THINK? VERY APPLE.

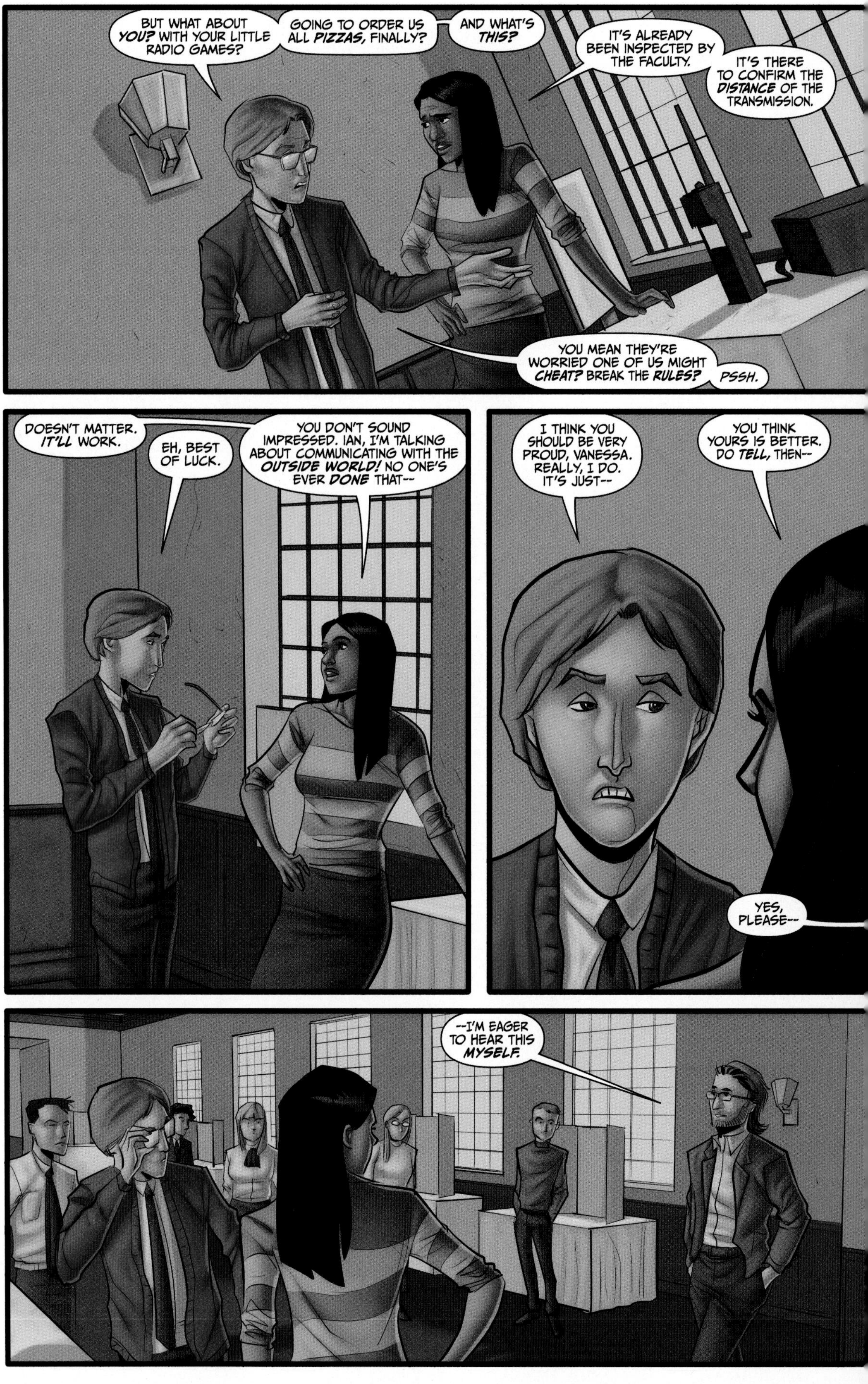
BUT WHAT ABOUT *YOU?* WITH YOUR LITTLE RADIO GAMES?
GOING TO ORDER US ALL *PIZZAS,* FINALLY?
AND WHAT'S *THIS?*
IT'S ALREADY BEEN INSPECTED BY THE FACULTY.
IT'S THERE TO CONFIRM THE *DISTANCE* OF THE TRANSMISSION.
YOU MEAN THEY'RE WORRIED ONE OF US MIGHT *CHEAT?* BREAK THE *RULES?*
PSSH.
DOESN'T MATTER. *IT'LL* WORK.
EH, BEST OF LUCK.
YOU DON'T SOUND IMPRESSED. IAN, I'M TALKING ABOUT COMMUNICATING WITH THE *OUTSIDE WORLD!* NO ONE'S EVER *DONE* THAT--
I THINK YOU SHOULD BE VERY PROUD, VANESSA. REALLY, I DO. IT'S JUST--
YOU THINK YOURS IS BETTER. DO *TELL,* THEN--
YES, PLEASE--
--I'M EAGER TO HEAR THIS *MYSELF.*

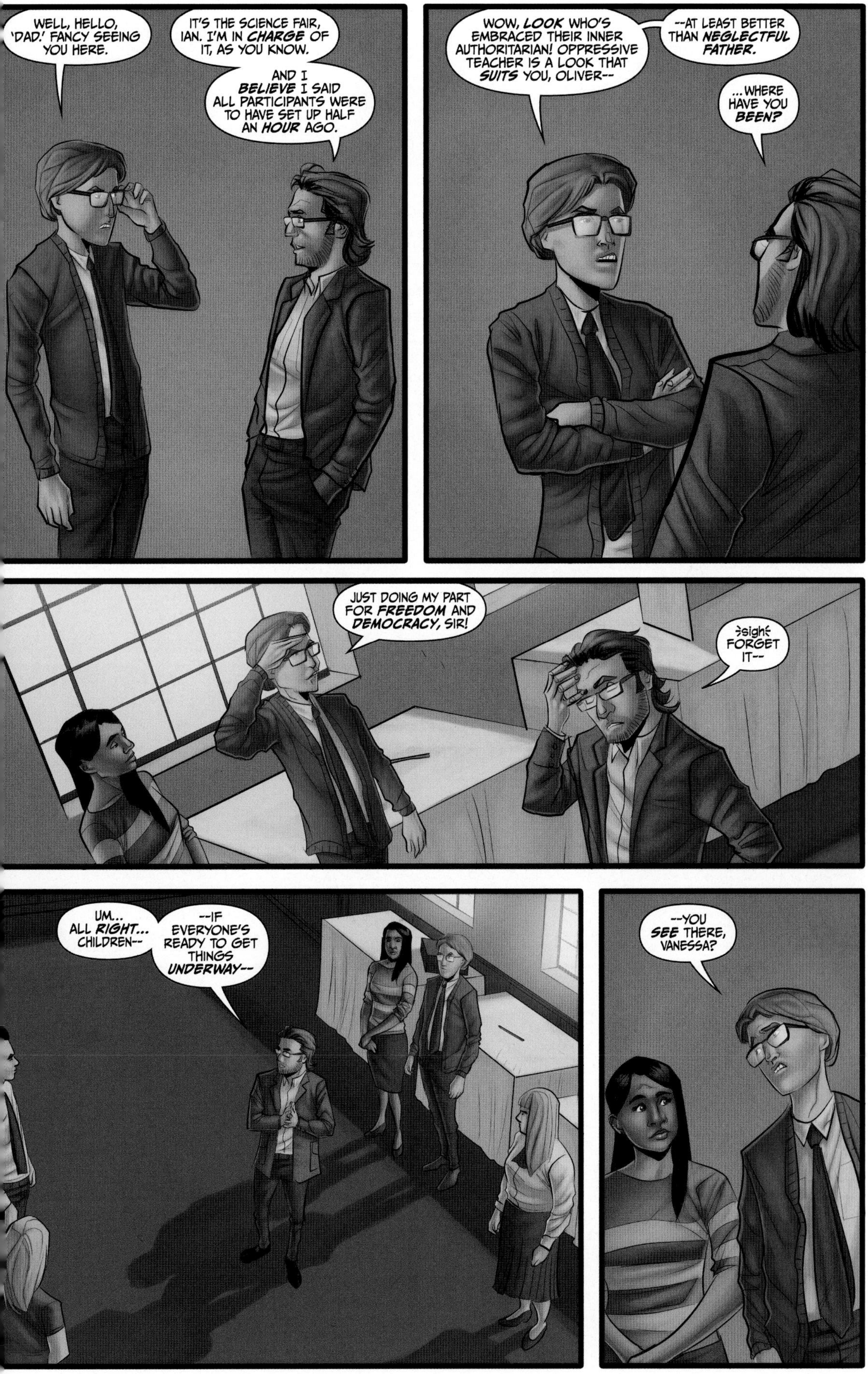
WELL, HELLO, 'DAD.' FANCY SEEING YOU HERE.
IT'S THE SCIENCE FAIR, IAN. I'M IN CHARGE OF IT, AS YOU KNOW.
AND I BELIEVE I SAID ALL PARTICIPANTS WERE TO HAVE SET UP HALF AN HOUR AGO.
WOW, LOOK WHO'S EMBRACED THEIR INNER AUTHORITARIAN! OPPRESSIVE TEACHER IS A LOOK THAT SUITS YOU, OLIVER--
--AT LEAST BETTER THAN NEGLECTFUL FATHER.
...WHERE HAVE YOU BEEN?
JUST DOING MY PART FOR FREEDOM AND DEMOCRACY, SIR!
sigh FORGET IT--
UM... ALL RIGHT... CHILDREN--
--IF EVERYONE'S READY TO GET THINGS UNDERWAY--
--YOU SEE THERE, VANESSA?

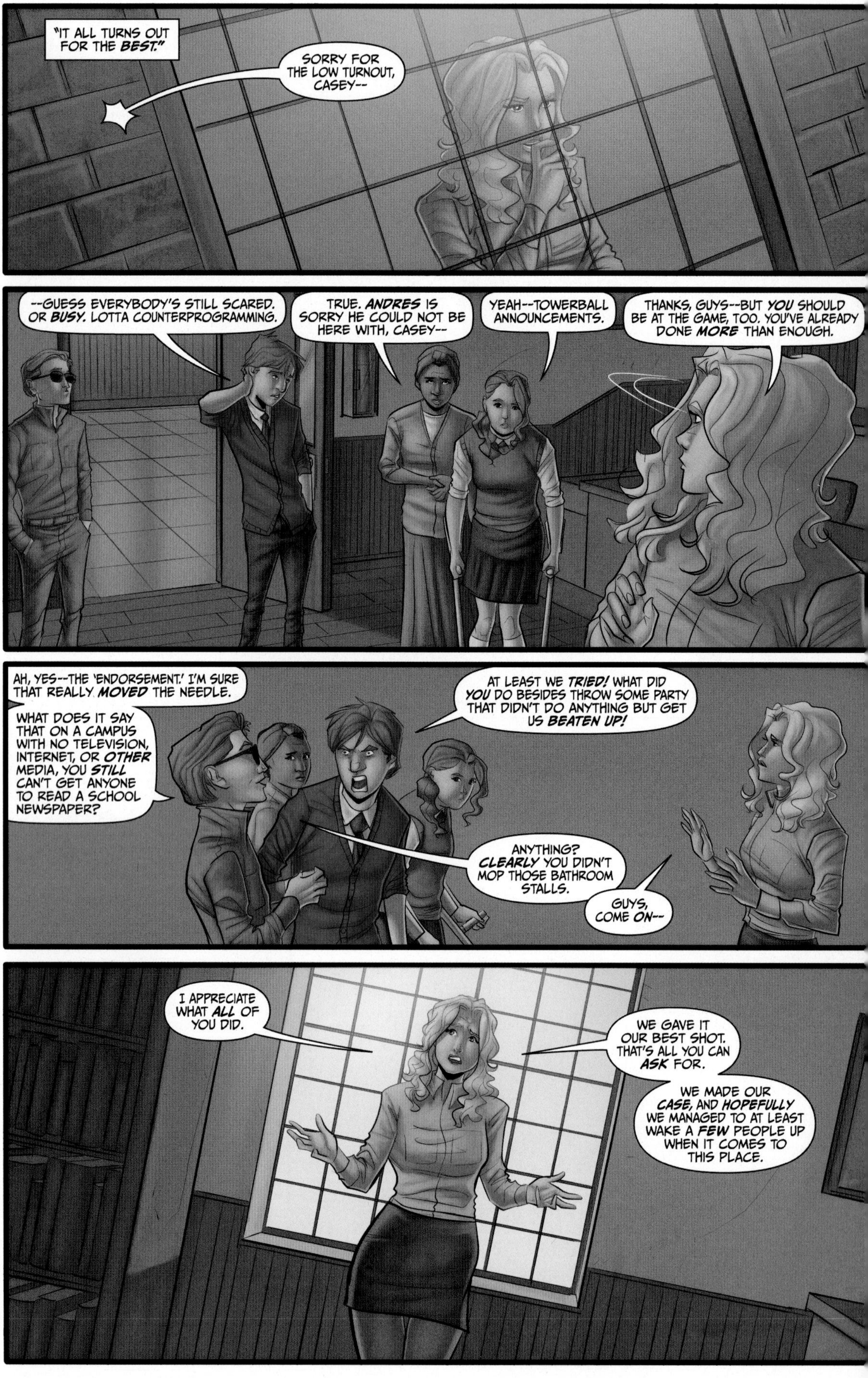
"IT ALL TURNS OUT FOR THE BEST."
SORRY FOR THE LOW TURNOUT, CASEY--
--GUESS EVERYBODY'S STILL SCARED. OR BUSY. LOTTA COUNTERPROGRAMMING.
TRUE. ANDRES IS SORRY HE COULD NOT BE HERE WITH, CASEY--
YEAH--TOWERBALL ANNOUNCEMENTS.
THANKS, GUYS--BUT YOU SHOULD BE AT THE GAME, TOO. YOU'VE ALREADY DONE MORE THAN ENOUGH.
AH, YES--THE 'ENDORSEMENT.' I'M SURE THAT REALLY MOVED THE NEEDLE.
WHAT DOES IT SAY THAT ON A CAMPUS WITH NO TELEVISION, INTERNET, OR OTHER MEDIA, YOU STILL CAN'T GET ANYONE TO READ A SCHOOL NEWSPAPER?
AT LEAST WE TRIED! WHAT DID YOU DO BESIDES THROW SOME PARTY THAT DIDN'T DO ANYTHING BUT GET US BEATEN UP!
ANYTHING? CLEARLY YOU DIDN'T MOP THOSE BATHROOM STALLS.
GUYS, COME ON--
I APPRECIATE WHAT ALL OF YOU DID.
WE GAVE IT OUR BEST SHOT. THAT'S ALL YOU CAN ASK FOR.
WE MADE OUR CASE, AND HOPEFULLY WE MANAGED TO AT LEAST WAKE A FEW PEOPLE UP WHEN IT COMES TO THIS PLACE.

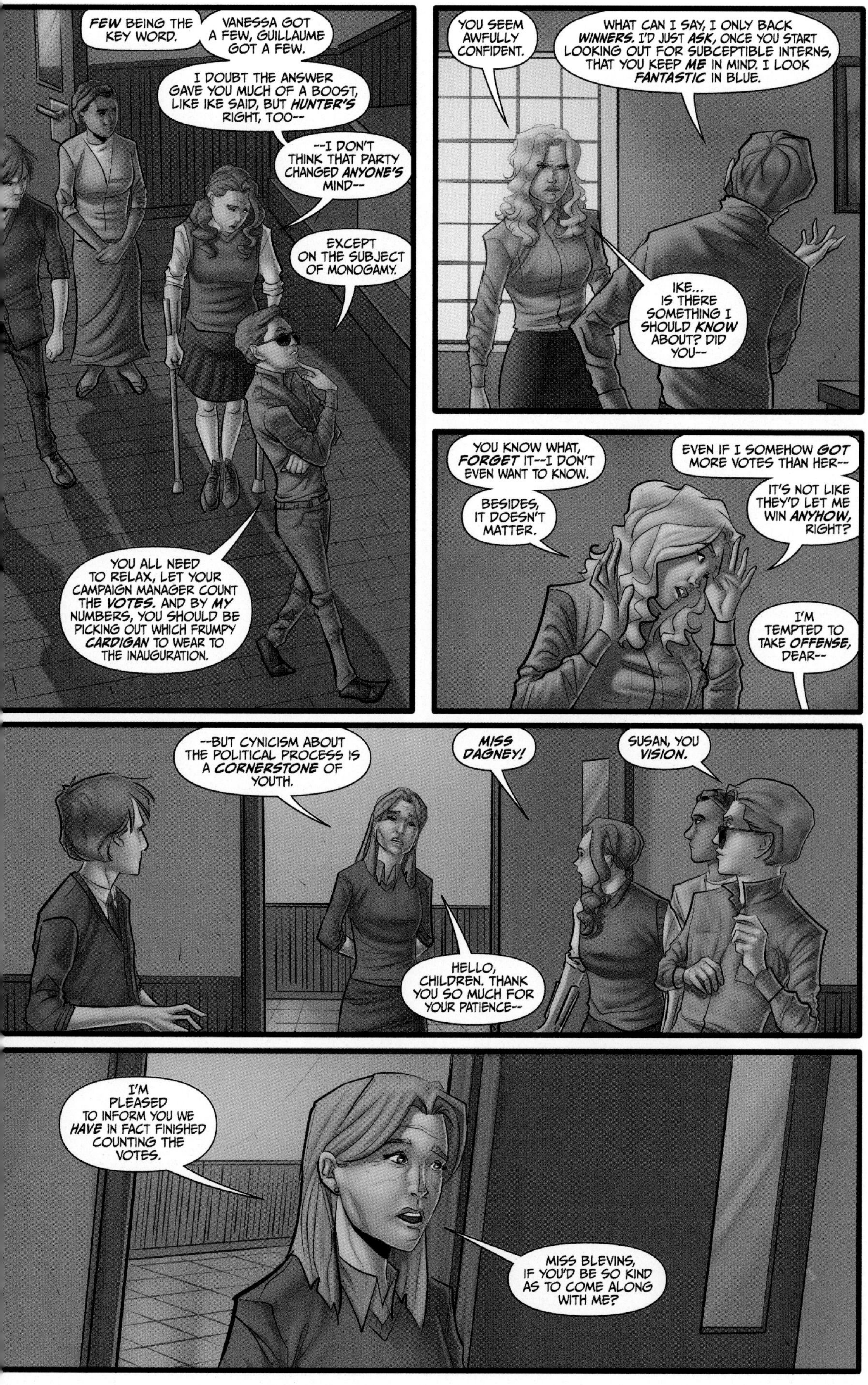
FEW BEING THE KEY WORD.
VANESSA GOT A FEW, GUILLAUME GOT A FEW.
I DOUBT THE ANSWER GAVE YOU MUCH OF A BOOST, LIKE IKE SAID, BUT HUNTER'S RIGHT, TOO--
--I DON'T THINK THAT PARTY CHANGED ANYONE'S MIND--
EXCEPT ON THE SUBJECT OF MONOGAMY.
YOU ALL NEED TO RELAX, LET YOUR CAMPAIGN MANAGER COUNT THE VOTES. AND BY MY NUMBERS, YOU SHOULD BE PICKING OUT WHICH FRUMPY CARDIGAN TO WEAR TO THE INAUGURATION.
YOU SEEM AWFULLY CONFIDENT.
WHAT CAN I SAY, I ONLY BACK WINNERS. I'D JUST ASK, ONCE YOU START LOOKING OUT FOR SUBCEPTIBLE INTERNS, THAT YOU KEEP ME IN MIND. I LOOK FANTASTIC IN BLUE.
IKE... IS THERE SOMETHING I SHOULD KNOW ABOUT? DID YOU--
YOU KNOW WHAT, FORGET IT--I DON'T EVEN WANT TO KNOW.
BESIDES, IT DOESN'T MATTER.
EVEN IF I SOMEHOW GOT MORE VOTES THAN HER--
IT'S NOT LIKE THEY'D LET ME WIN ANYHOW, RIGHT?
I'M TEMPTED TO TAKE OFFENSE, DEAR--
--BUT CYNICISM ABOUT THE POLITICAL PROCESS IS A CORNERSTONE OF YOUTH.
MISS DAGNEY!
SUSAN, YOU VISION.
HELLO, CHILDREN. THANK YOU SO MUCH FOR YOUR PATIENCE--
I'M PLEASED TO INFORM YOU WE HAVE IN FACT FINISHED COUNTING THE VOTES.
MISS BLEVINS, IF YOU'D BE SO KIND AS TO COME ALONG WITH ME?

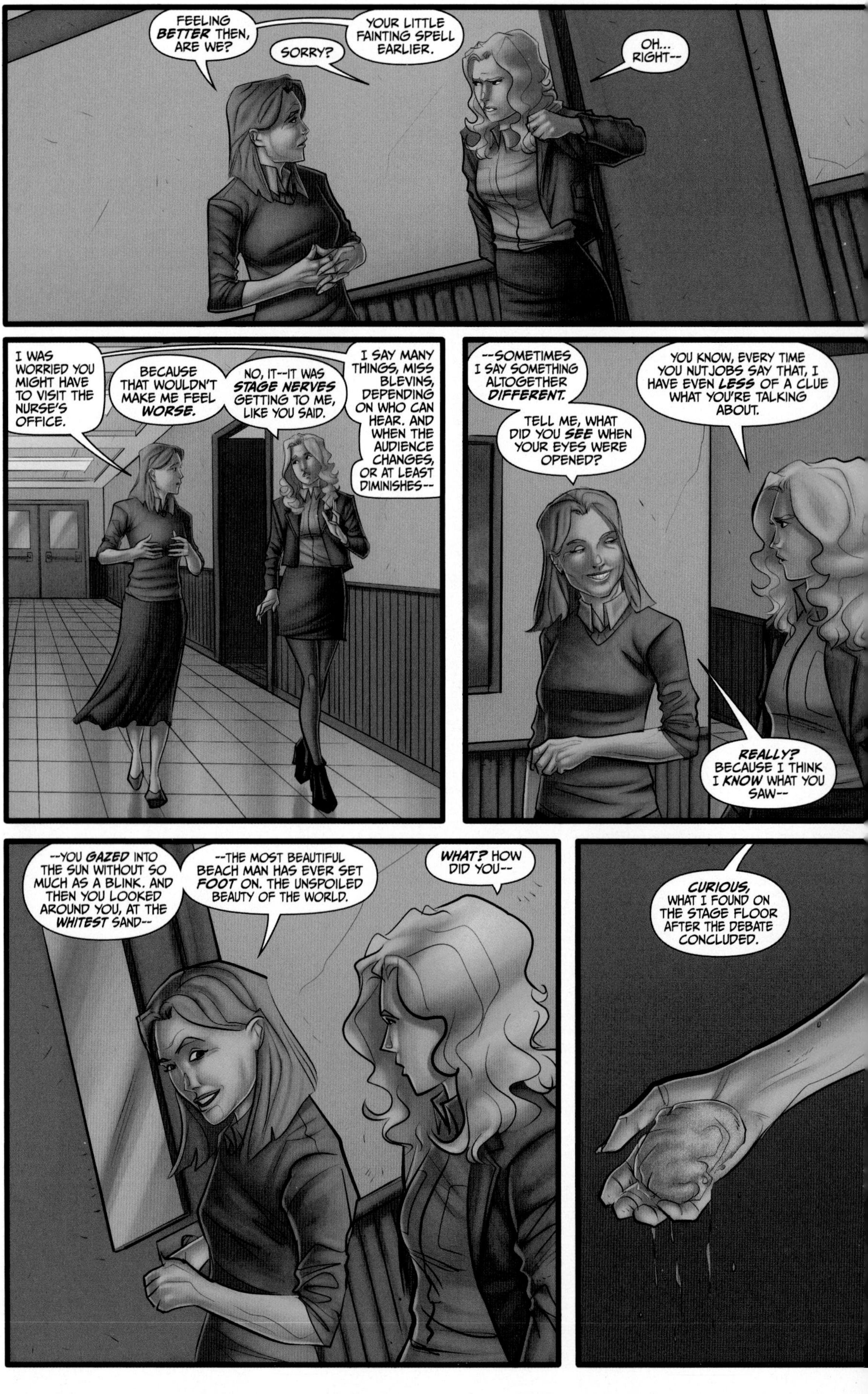
FEELING BETTER THEN, ARE WE?
SORRY?
YOUR LITTLE FAINTING SPELL EARLIER.
OH... RIGHT--
I WAS WORRIED YOU MIGHT HAVE TO VISIT THE NURSE'S OFFICE.
BECAUSE THAT WOULDN'T MAKE ME FEEL WORSE.
NO, IT--IT WAS STAGE NERVES GETTING TO ME, LIKE YOU SAID.
I SAY MANY THINGS, MISS BLEVINS, DEPENDING ON WHO CAN HEAR. AND WHEN THE AUDIENCE CHANGES, OR AT LEAST DIMINISHES--
--SOMETIMES I SAY SOMETHING ALTOGETHER DIFFERENT.
TELL ME, WHAT DID YOU SEE WHEN YOUR EYES WERE OPENED?
YOU KNOW, EVERY TIME YOU NUTJOBS SAY THAT, I HAVE EVEN LESS OF A CLUE WHAT YOU'RE TALKING ABOUT.
REALLY? BECAUSE I THINK I KNOW WHAT YOU SAW--
--YOU GAZED INTO THE SUN WITHOUT SO MUCH AS A BLINK. AND THEN YOU LOOKED AROUND YOU, AT THE WHITEST SAND--
--THE MOST BEAUTIFUL BEACH MAN HAS EVER SET FOOT ON. THE UNSPOILED BEAUTY OF THE WORLD.
WHAT? HOW DID YOU--
CURIOUS, WHAT I FOUND ON THE STAGE FLOOR AFTER THE DEBATE CONCLUDED.

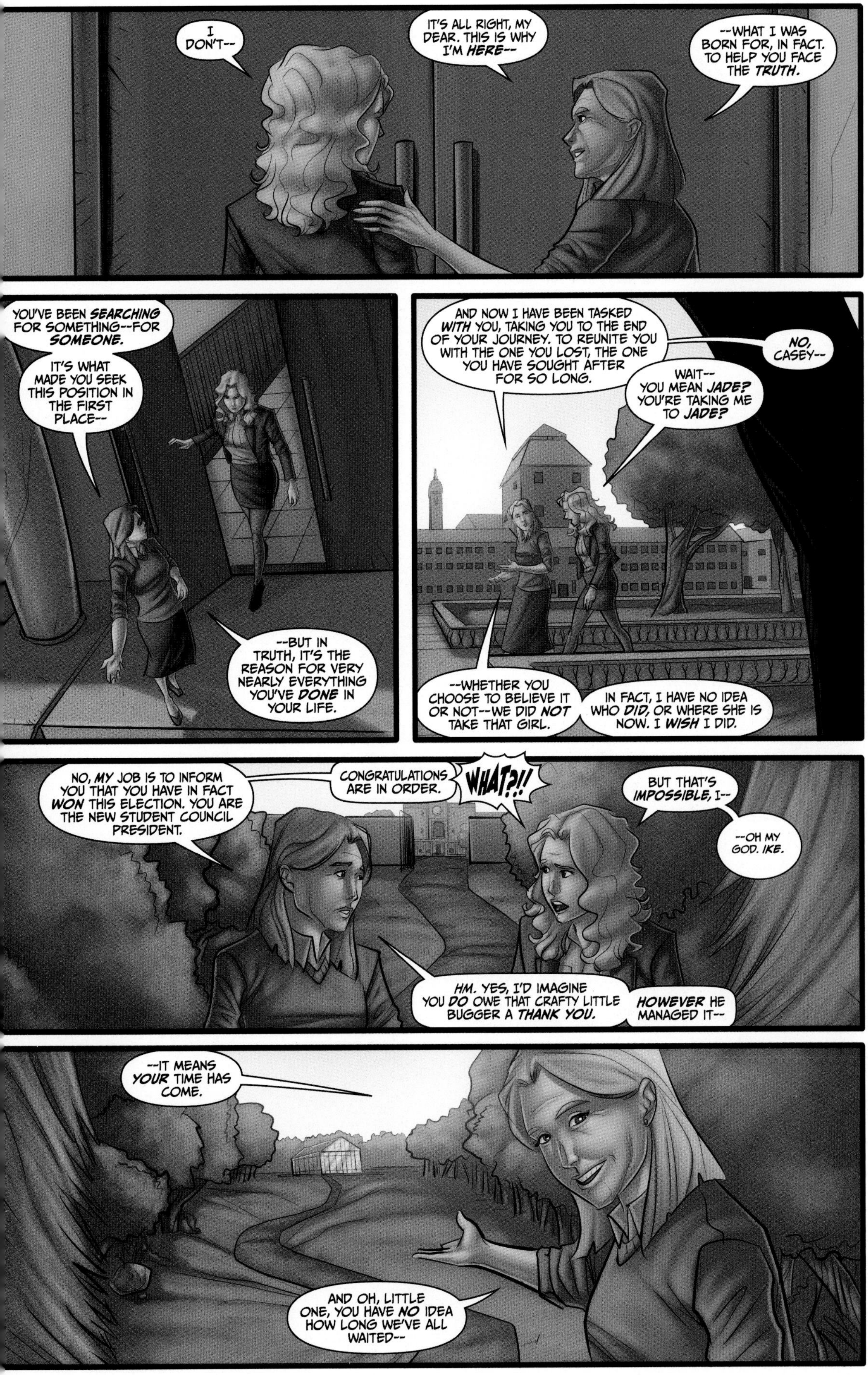
I DON'T--
IT'S ALL RIGHT, MY DEAR. THIS IS WHY I'M *HERE*--
--WHAT I WAS BORN FOR, IN FACT. TO HELP YOU FACE THE *TRUTH.*
YOU'VE BEEN *SEARCHING* FOR SOMETHING--FOR *SOMEONE.*
IT'S WHAT MADE YOU SEEK THIS POSITION IN THE FIRST PLACE--
--BUT IN TRUTH, IT'S THE REASON FOR VERY NEARLY EVERYTHING YOU'VE *DONE* IN YOUR LIFE.
AND NOW I HAVE BEEN TASKED *WITH* YOU, TAKING YOU TO THE END OF YOUR JOURNEY. TO REUNITE YOU WITH THE ONE YOU LOST, THE ONE YOU HAVE SOUGHT AFTER FOR SO LONG.
WAIT-- YOU MEAN *JADE?* YOU'RE TAKING ME TO *JADE?*
NO, CASEY--
--WHETHER YOU CHOOSE TO BELIEVE IT OR NOT--WE DID *NOT* TAKE THAT GIRL.
IN FACT, I HAVE NO IDEA WHO *DID,* OR WHERE SHE IS NOW. I *WISH* I DID.
NO, *MY* JOB IS TO INFORM YOU THAT YOU HAVE IN FACT *WON* THIS ELECTION. YOU ARE THE NEW STUDENT COUNCIL PRESIDENT.
CONGRATULATIONS ARE IN ORDER.
WHAT?!!
BUT THAT'S *IMPOSSIBLE,* I--
--OH MY GOD. *IKE.*
HM. YES, I'D IMAGINE YOU *DO* OWE THAT CRAFTY LITTLE BUGGER A *THANK YOU.*
HOWEVER HE MANAGED IT--
--IT MEANS *YOUR* TIME HAS COME.
AND OH, LITTLE ONE, YOU HAVE *NO* IDEA HOW LONG WE'VE ALL WAITED--

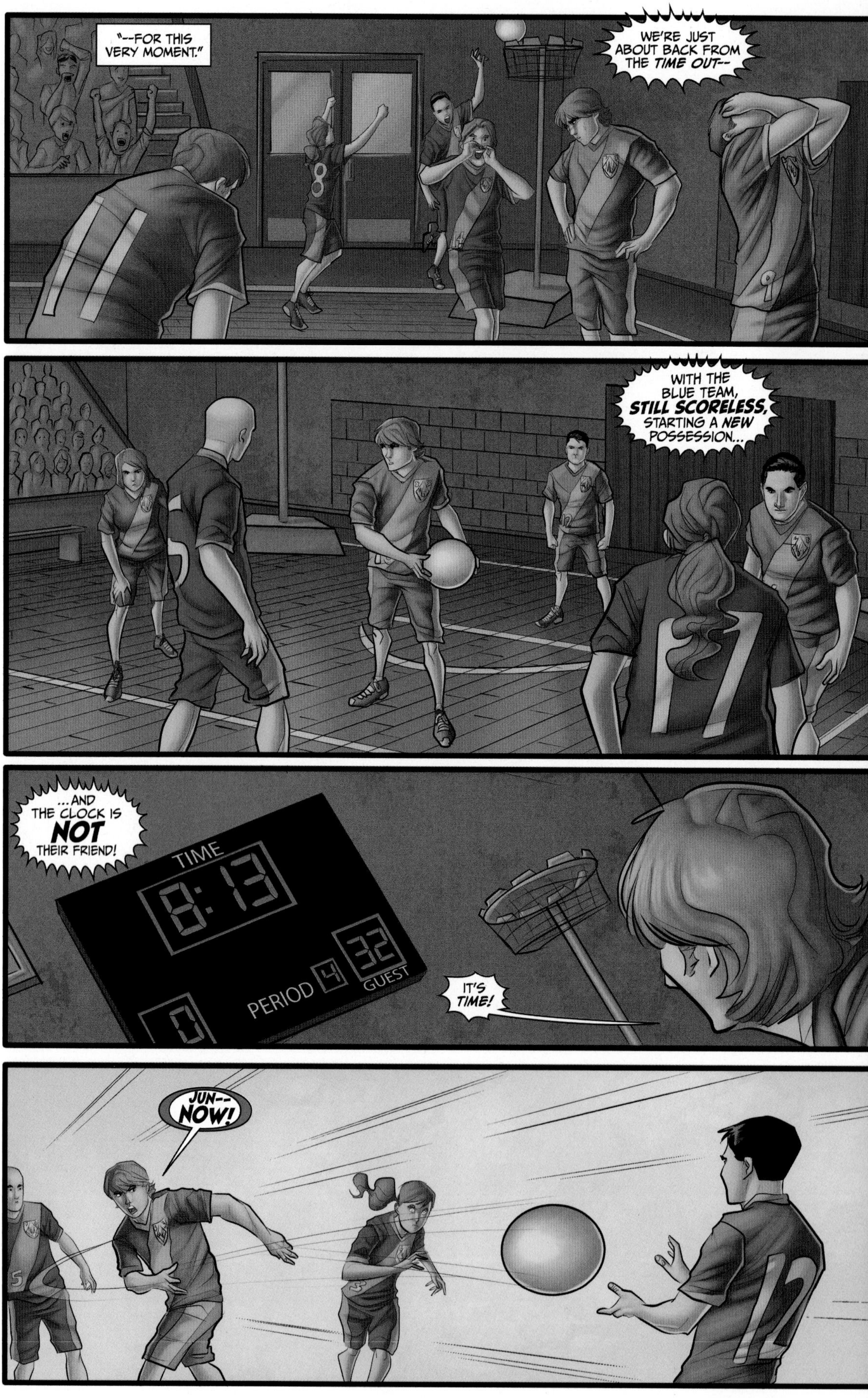
"--FOR THIS VERY MOMENT."
WE'RE JUST ABOUT BACK FROM THE *TIME OUT*--
WITH THE BLUE TEAM, **STILL SCORELESS,** STARTING A *NEW* POSSESSION...
...AND THE CLOCK IS **NOT** THEIR FRIEND!
TIME
8:13
PERIOD 4
32
GUEST
0
IT'S *TIME!*
JUN-- NOW!

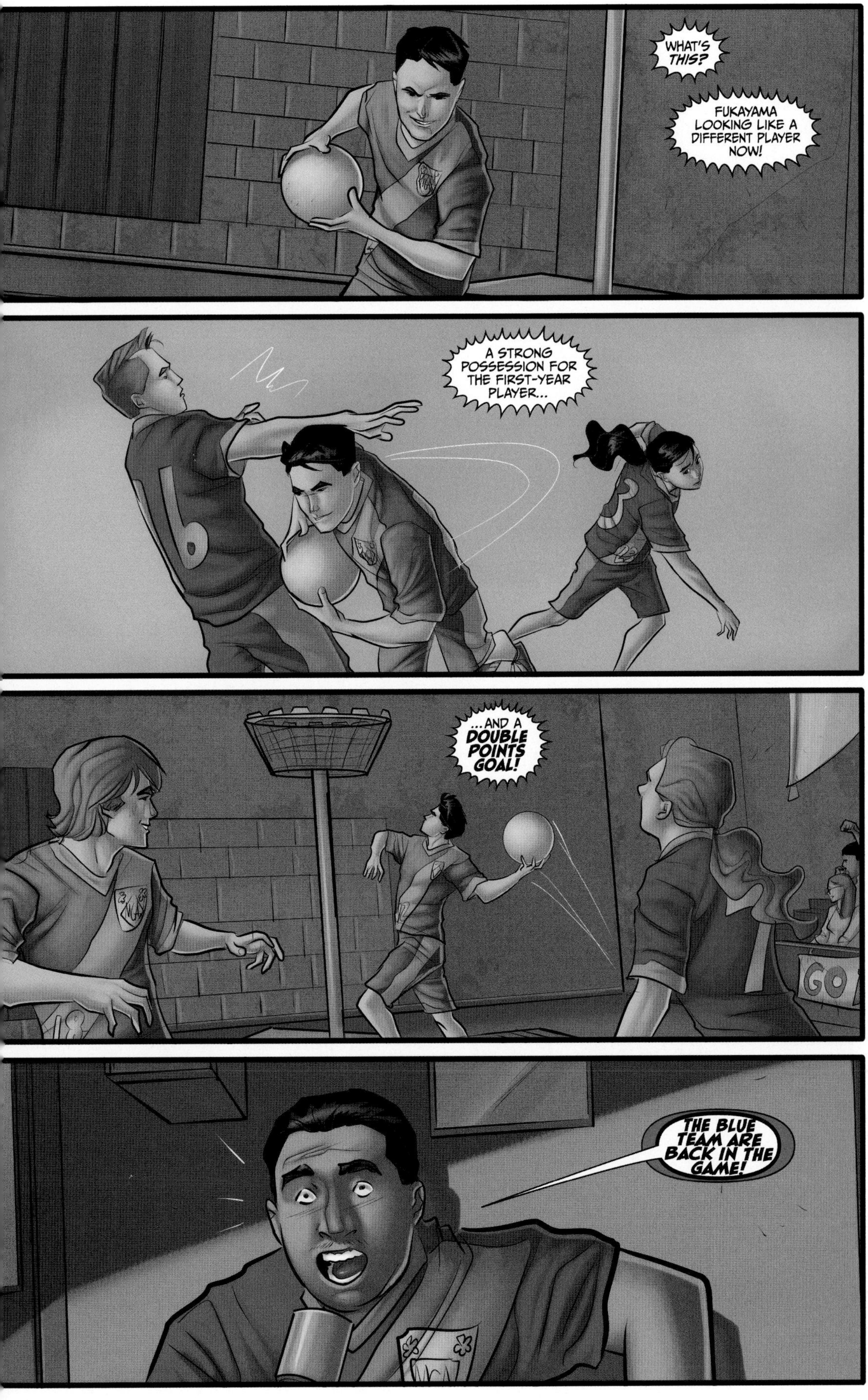
WHAT'S *THIS?*
FUKAYAMA LOOKING LIKE A DIFFERENT PLAYER NOW!
A STRONG POSSESSION FOR THE FIRST-YEAR PLAYER...
...AND A **DOUBLE POINTS GOAL!**
GO
THE BLUE TEAM ARE BACK IN THE GAME!

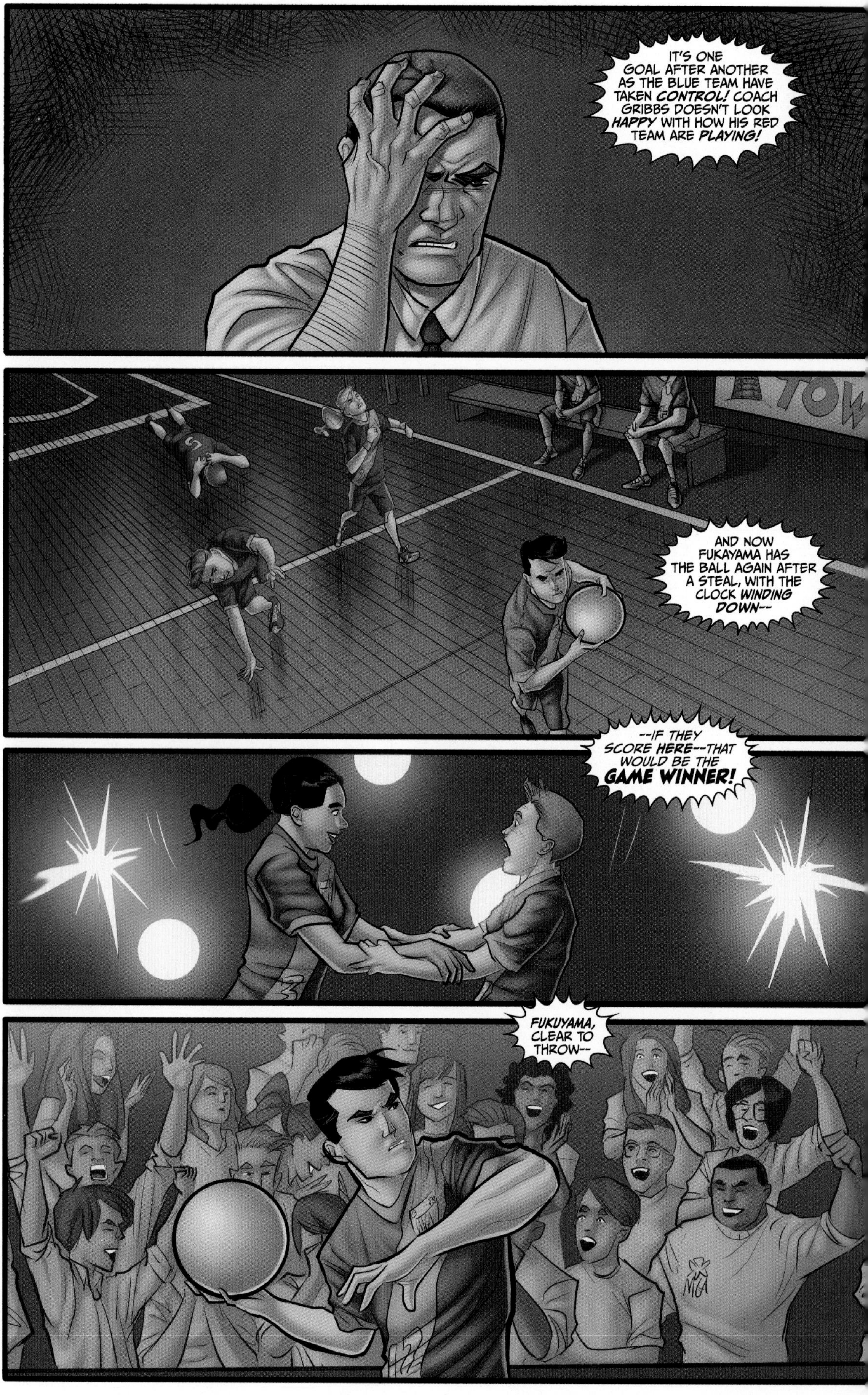
IT'S ONE GOAL AFTER ANOTHER AS THE BLUE TEAM HAVE TAKEN CONTROL! COACH GRIBBS DOESN'T LOOK HAPPY WITH HOW HIS RED TEAM ARE PLAYING!
AND NOW FUKAYAMA HAS THE BALL AGAIN AFTER A STEAL, WITH THE CLOCK WINDING DOWN--
--IF THEY SCORE HERE--THAT WOULD BE THE GAME WINNER!
FUKUYAMA, CLEAR TO THROW--

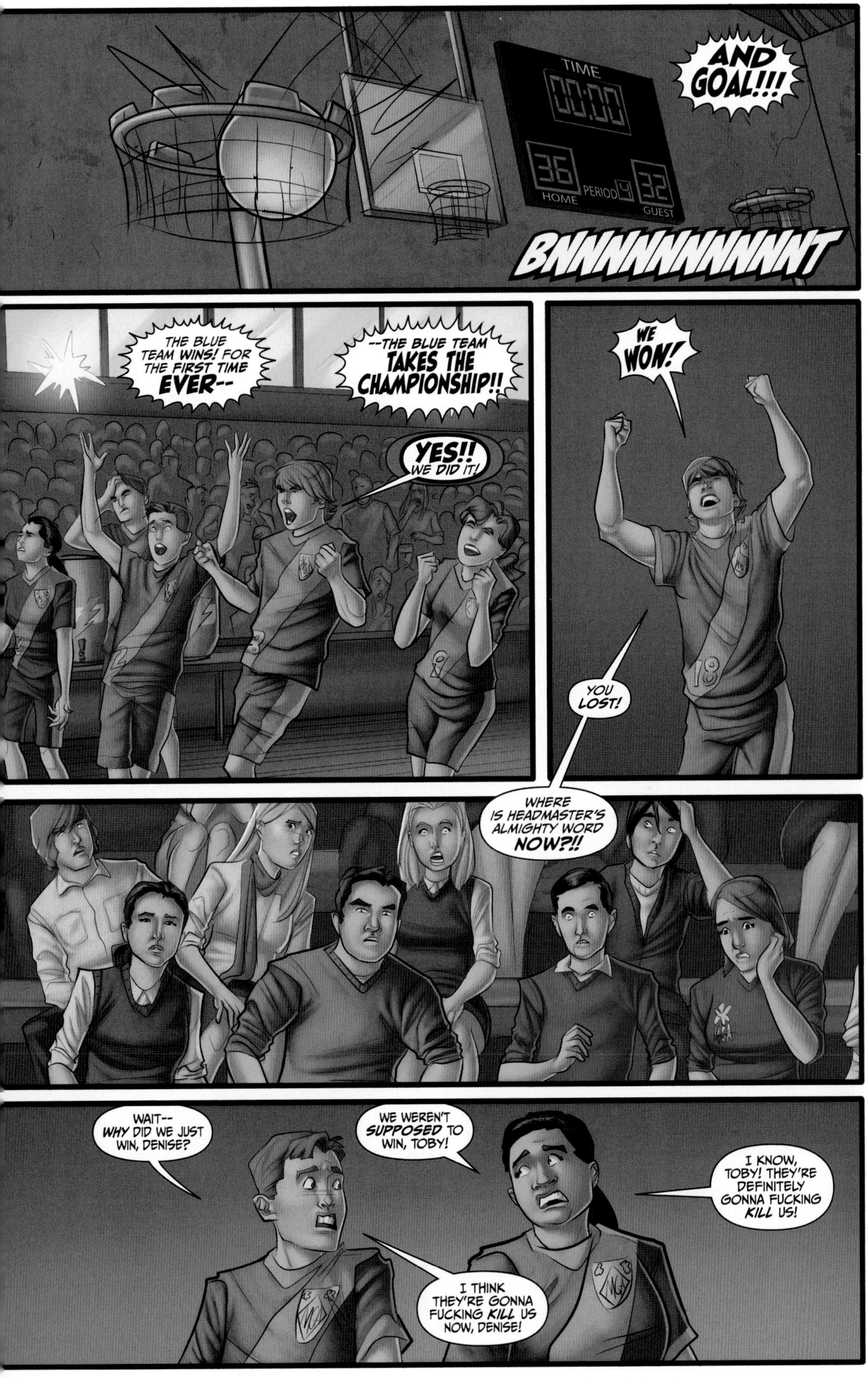

TIME
00:00
36
HOME
PERIOD 4
32
GUEST
AND GOAL!!!
BNNNNNNNNNNNT
THE BLUE TEAM WINS! FOR THE FIRST TIME EVER--
--THE BLUE TEAM TAKES THE CHAMPIONSHIP!!
YES!! WE DID IT!
WE WON!
YOU LOST!
WHERE IS HEADMASTER'S ALMIGHTY WORD NOW?!!
WAIT-- WHY DID WE JUST WIN, DENISE?
WE WEREN'T SUPPOSED TO WIN, TOBY!
I KNOW, TOBY! THEY'RE DEFINITELY GONNA FUCKING KILL US!
I THINK THEY'RE GONNA FUCKING KILL US NOW, DENISE!

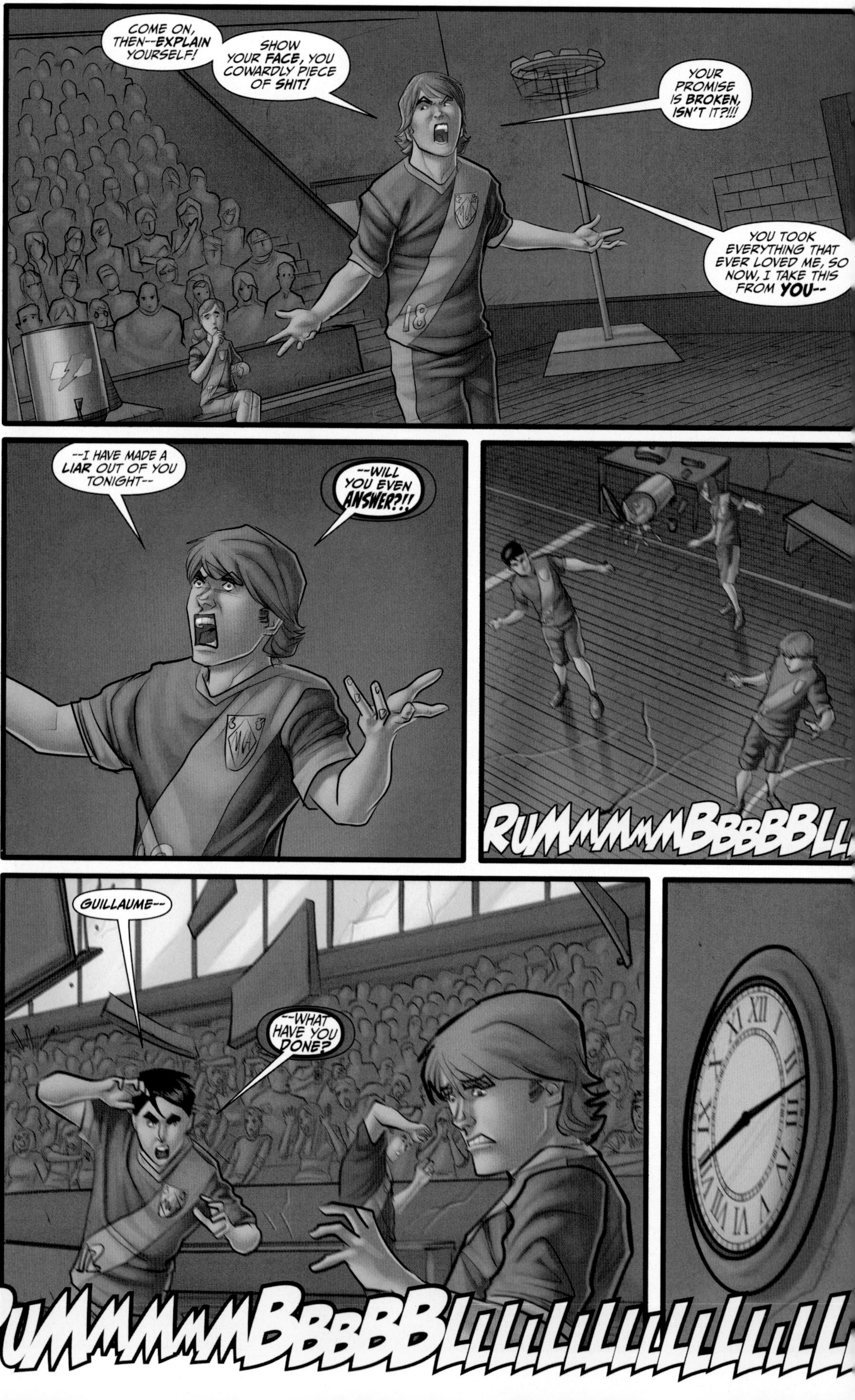
COME ON, THEN--EXPLAIN YOURSELF!
SHOW YOUR FACE, YOU COWARDLY PIECE OF SHIT!
YOUR PROMISE IS BROKEN, ISN'T IT?!!!
YOU TOOK EVERYTHING THAT EVER LOVED ME, SO NOW, I TAKE THIS FROM YOU--
--I HAVE MADE A LIAR OUT OF YOU TONIGHT--
--WILL YOU EVEN ANSWER?!!
RUMMMMMBBBBBLL
GUILLAUME--
--WHAT HAVE YOU DONE?
RUMMMMMBBBBBLLLLLLLLLLLLLL

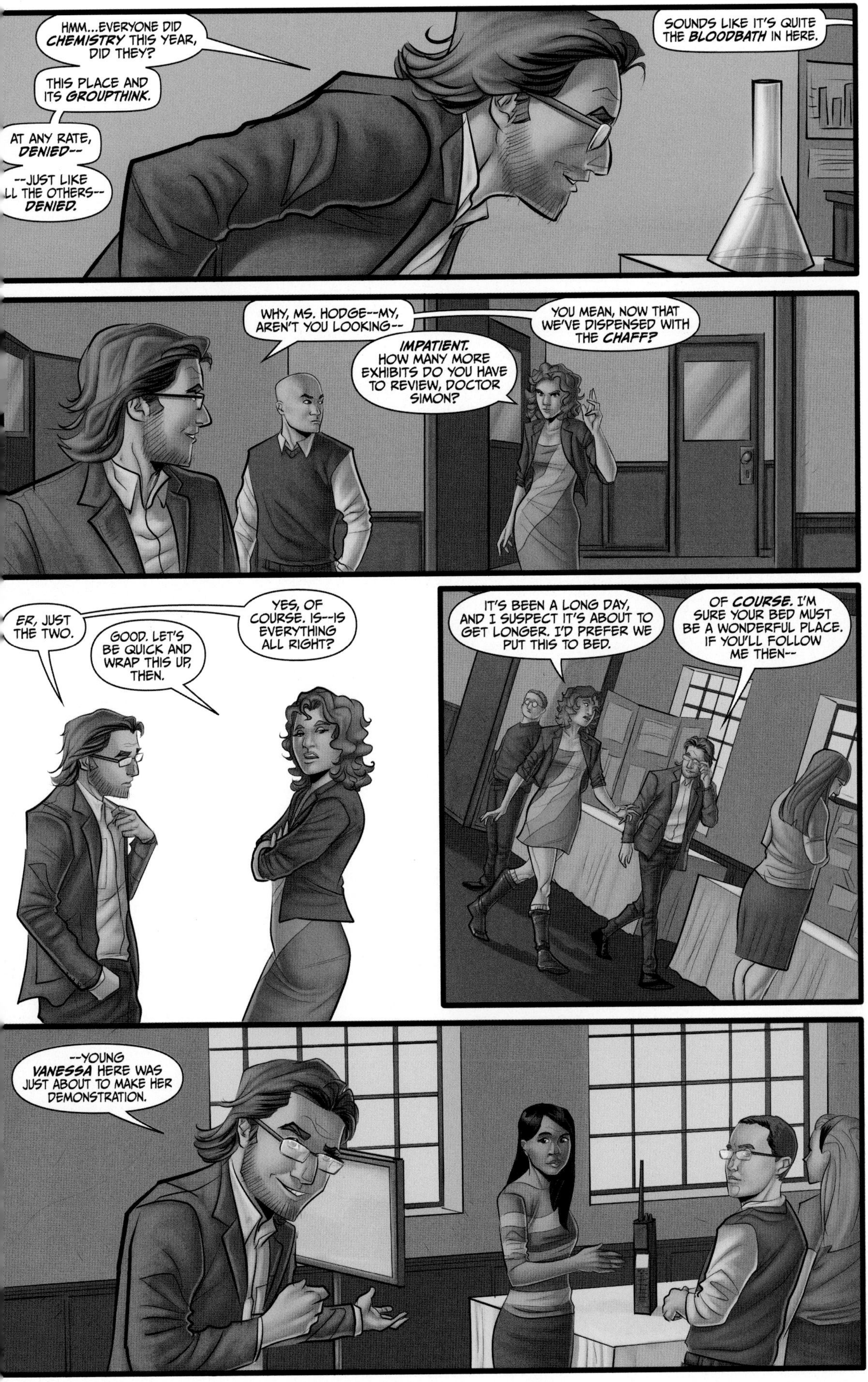
HMM...EVERYONE DID CHEMISTRY THIS YEAR, DID THEY?
THIS PLACE AND ITS GROUPTHINK.
AT ANY RATE, DENIED--
--JUST LIKE LL THE OTHERS-- DENIED.
SOUNDS LIKE IT'S QUITE THE BLOODBATH IN HERE.
WHY, MS. HODGE--MY, AREN'T YOU LOOKING--
IMPATIENT. HOW MANY MORE EXHIBITS DO YOU HAVE TO REVIEW, DOCTOR SIMON?
YOU MEAN, NOW THAT WE'VE DISPENSED WITH THE CHAFF?
ER, JUST THE TWO.
YES, OF COURSE. IS--IS EVERYTHING ALL RIGHT?
GOOD. LET'S BE QUICK AND WRAP THIS UP, THEN.
IT'S BEEN A LONG DAY, AND I SUSPECT IT'S ABOUT TO GET LONGER. I'D PREFER WE PUT THIS TO BED.
OF COURSE. I'M SURE YOUR BED MUST BE A WONDERFUL PLACE. IF YOU'LL FOLLOW ME THEN--
--YOUNG VANESSA HERE WAS JUST ABOUT TO MAKE HER DEMONSTRATION.

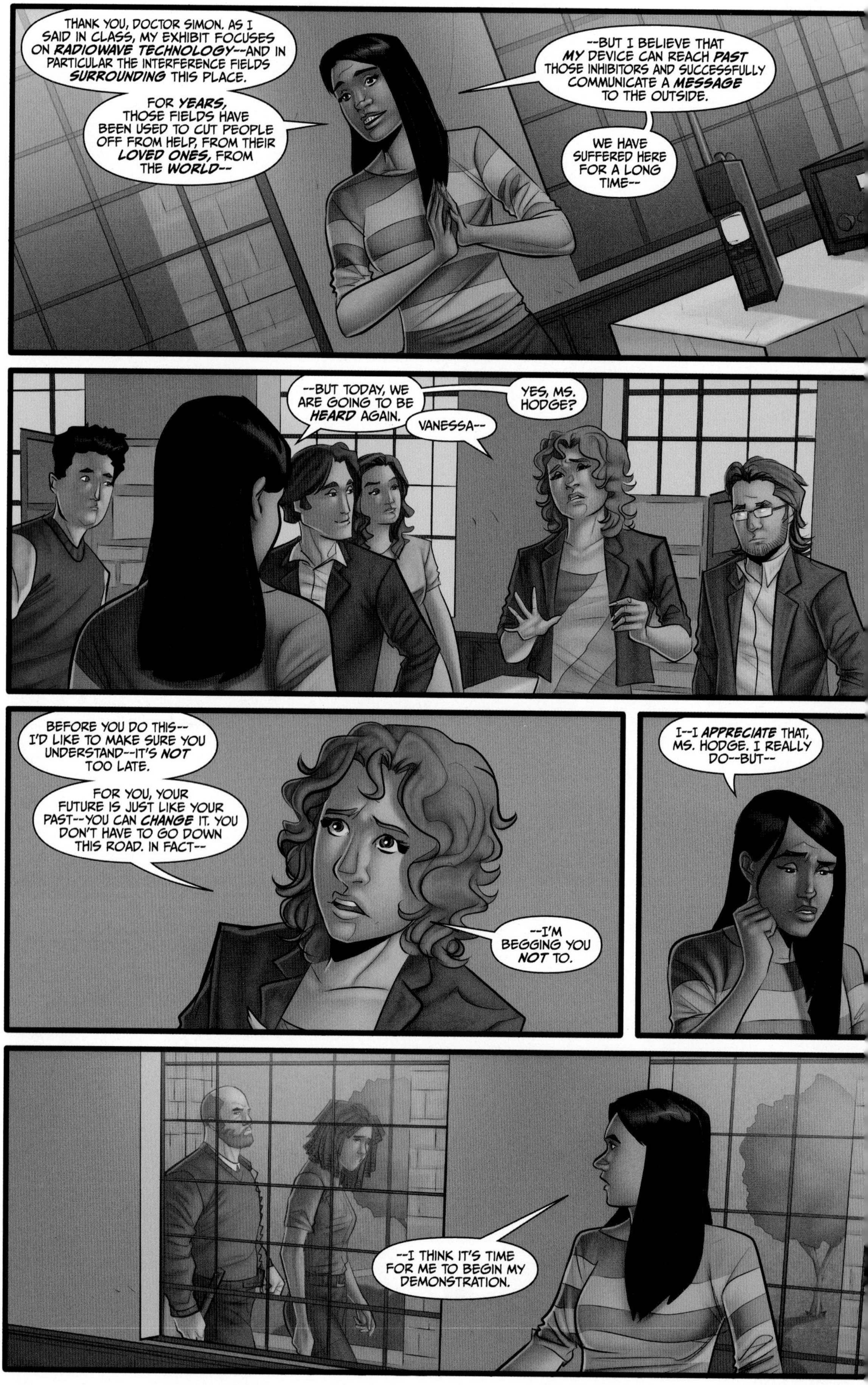
THANK YOU, DOCTOR SIMON. AS I SAID IN CLASS, MY EXHIBIT FOCUSES ON RADIOWAVE TECHNOLOGY--AND IN PARTICULAR THE INTERFERENCE FIELDS SURROUNDING THIS PLACE.
FOR YEARS, THOSE FIELDS HAVE BEEN USED TO CUT PEOPLE OFF FROM HELP, FROM THEIR LOVED ONES, FROM THE WORLD--
--BUT I BELIEVE THAT MY DEVICE CAN REACH PAST THOSE INHIBITORS AND SUCCESSFULLY COMMUNICATE A MESSAGE TO THE OUTSIDE.
WE HAVE SUFFERED HERE FOR A LONG TIME--
--BUT TODAY, WE ARE GOING TO BE HEARD AGAIN.
VANESSA--
YES, MS. HODGE?
BEFORE YOU DO THIS-- I'D LIKE TO MAKE SURE YOU UNDERSTAND--IT'S NOT TOO LATE.
FOR YOU, YOUR FUTURE IS JUST LIKE YOUR PAST--YOU CAN CHANGE IT. YOU DON'T HAVE TO GO DOWN THIS ROAD. IN FACT--
--I'M BEGGING YOU NOT TO.
I--I APPRECIATE THAT, MS. HODGE. I REALLY DO--BUT--
--I THINK IT'S TIME FOR ME TO BEGIN MY DEMONSTRATION.

HELLO? IS ANYONE THERE?

MY NAME IS VANESSA RICHMOND-- I'M BEING HELD PRISONER AT A PLACE CALLED MORNING GLORY ACADEMY.

DO YOU COPY?

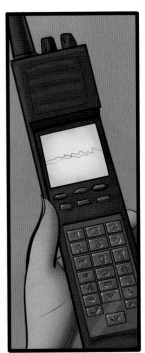

HELLO? HELLO?

I REPEAT-- MY NAME IS VANESSA RICHMOND.

I'M BEING HELD PRISONER AT A PLACE CALLED MORNING GLORY ACADEMY.

PLEASE-- DO YOU COPY?

WELL, THAT WAS ANTI-CLIMATIC.

NO...PLEASE... THIS WAS SUPPOSED TO WORK...

SHE SAID IT WOULD WORK...

IT'S ALL RIGHT, VANESSA--

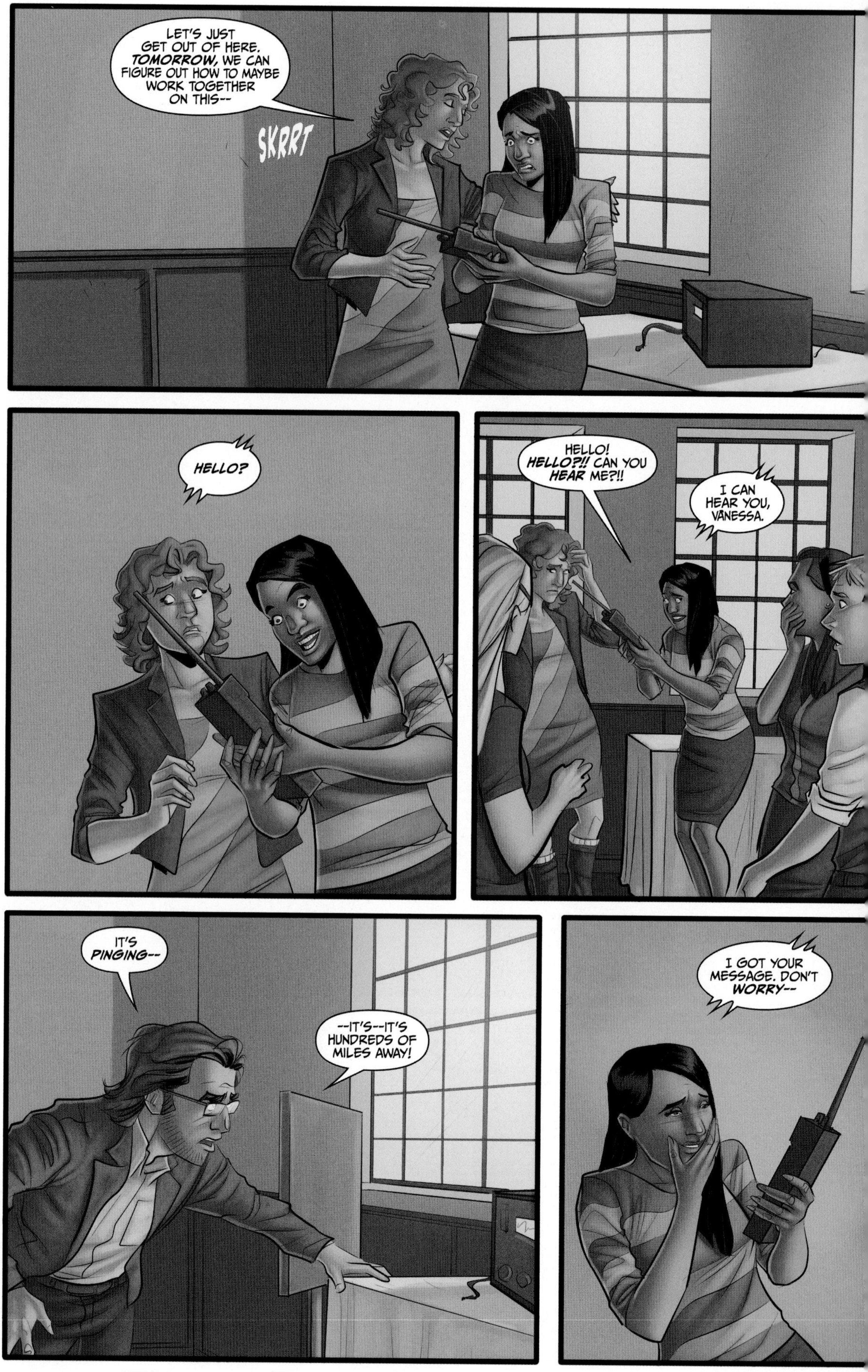
LET'S JUST GET OUT OF HERE. TOMORROW, WE CAN FIGURE OUT HOW TO MAYBE WORK TOGETHER ON THIS--
SKRRT
HELLO?
HELLO! HELLO?!! CAN YOU HEAR ME?!!
I CAN HEAR YOU, VANESSA.
IT'S PINGING--
--IT'S--IT'S HUNDREDS OF MILES AWAY!
I GOT YOUR MESSAGE. DON'T WORRY--

--HELP IS ON THE WAY.

--WORKED.

IT WORKED! IT--

VANESSA--

I'M SO SORRY.

RUMMMMMBBBBLLLLLL

8:13

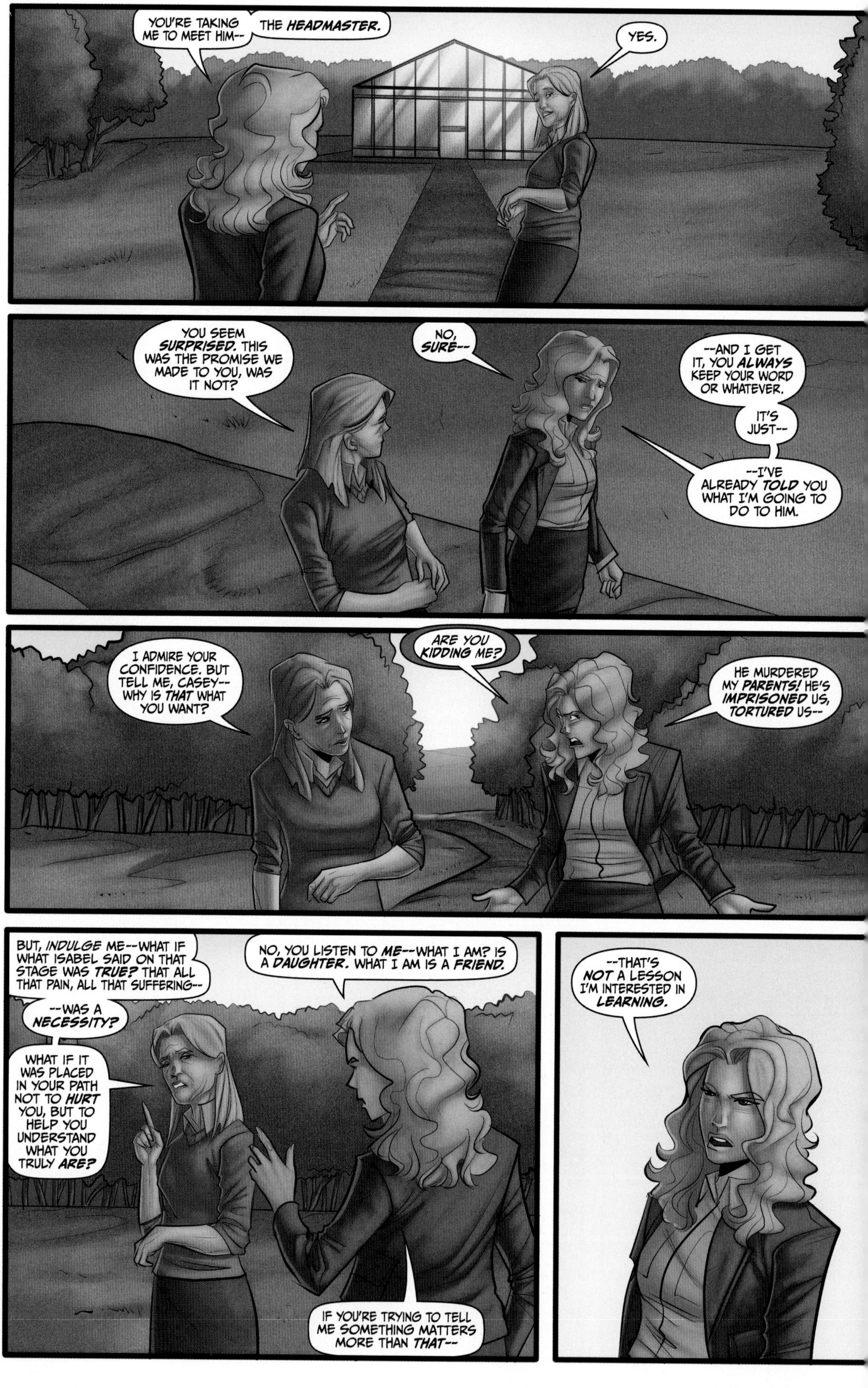
YOU'RE TAKING ME TO MEET HIM--
THE HEADMASTER.
YES.
YOU SEEM SURPRISED. THIS WAS THE PROMISE WE MADE TO YOU, WAS IT NOT?
NO, SURE--
--AND I GET IT, YOU ALWAYS KEEP YOUR WORD OR WHATEVER.
IT'S JUST--
--I'VE ALREADY TOLD YOU WHAT I'M GOING TO DO TO HIM.
I ADMIRE YOUR CONFIDENCE. BUT TELL ME, CASEY-- WHY IS THAT WHAT YOU WANT?
ARE YOU KIDDING ME?
HE MURDERED MY PARENTS! HE'S IMPRISONED US, TORTURED US--
BUT, INDULGE ME--WHAT IF WHAT ISABEL SAID ON THAT STAGE WAS TRUE? THAT ALL THAT PAIN, ALL THAT SUFFERING--
--WAS A NECESSITY?
WHAT IF IT WAS PLACED IN YOUR PATH NOT TO HURT YOU, BUT TO HELP YOU UNDERSTAND WHAT YOU TRULY ARE?
NO, YOU LISTEN TO ME--WHAT I AM? IS A DAUGHTER. WHAT I AM IS A FRIEND.
IF YOU'RE TRYING TO TELL ME SOMETHING MATTERS MORE THAN THAT--
--THAT'S NOT A LESSON I'M INTERESTED IN LEARNING.

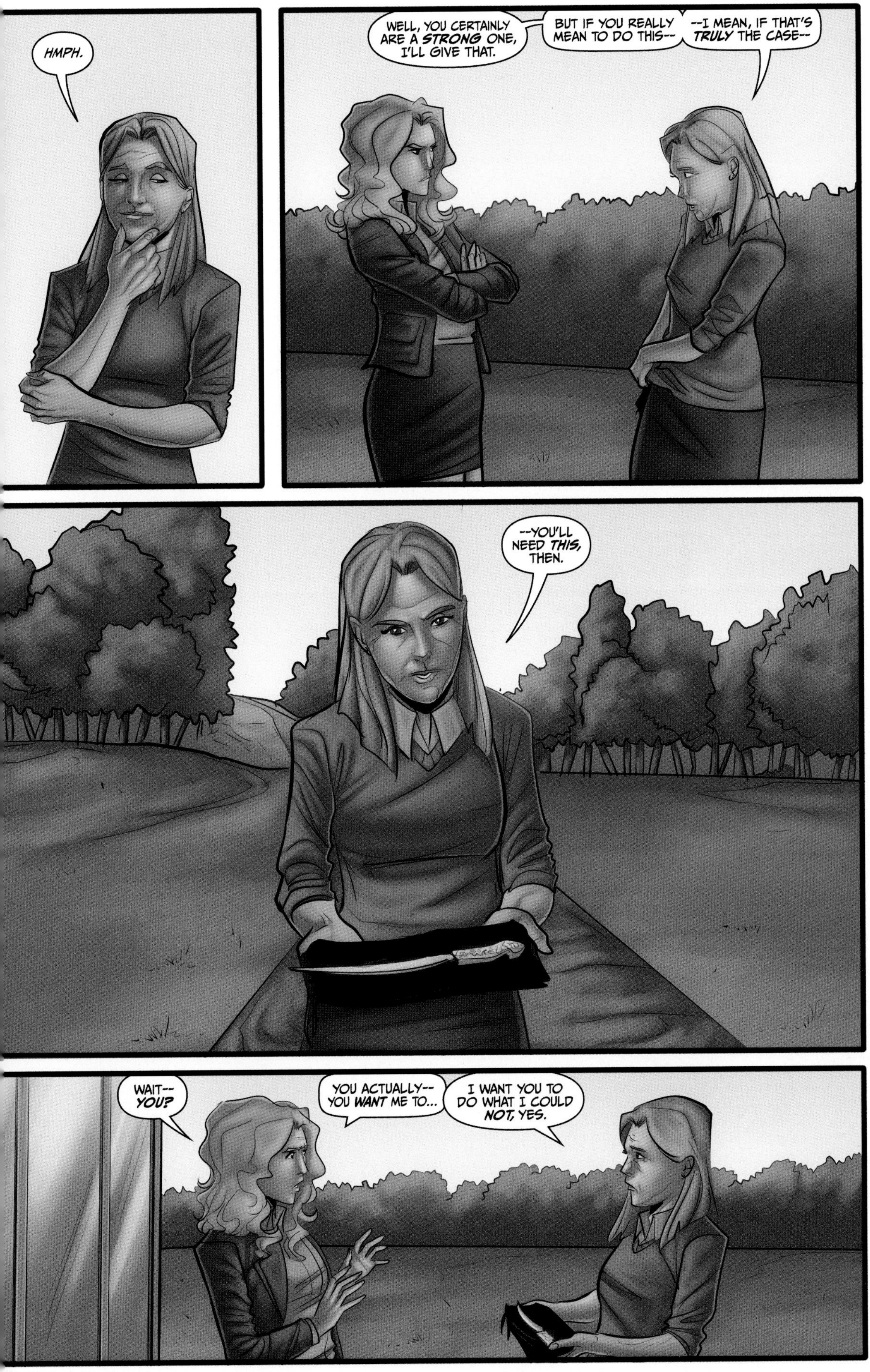
HMPH.
WELL, YOU CERTAINLY ARE A STRONG ONE, I'LL GIVE THAT.
BUT IF YOU REALLY MEAN TO DO THIS--
--I MEAN, IF THAT'S TRULY THE CASE--
--YOU'LL NEED THIS, THEN.
WAIT-- YOU?
YOU ACTUALLY-- YOU WANT ME TO...
I WANT YOU TO DO WHAT I COULD NOT, YES.

I HELD THE BLADE TO HIS LITTLE THROAT AND I KNEW--I *KNEW* WHAT I WAS SUPPOSED TO DO, BUT--

--I HAVE *HATED* MYSELF EVER SINCE.

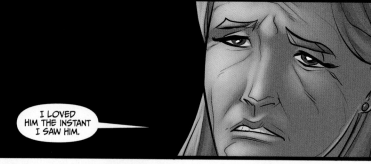

I LOVED HIM THE INSTANT I SAW HIM.

EVEN THOUGH I *KNEW* WHAT HE WAS.

WHAT HE WOULD *DO* TO US.

SO WHAT WILL *YOU* DO NOW, DEAR?

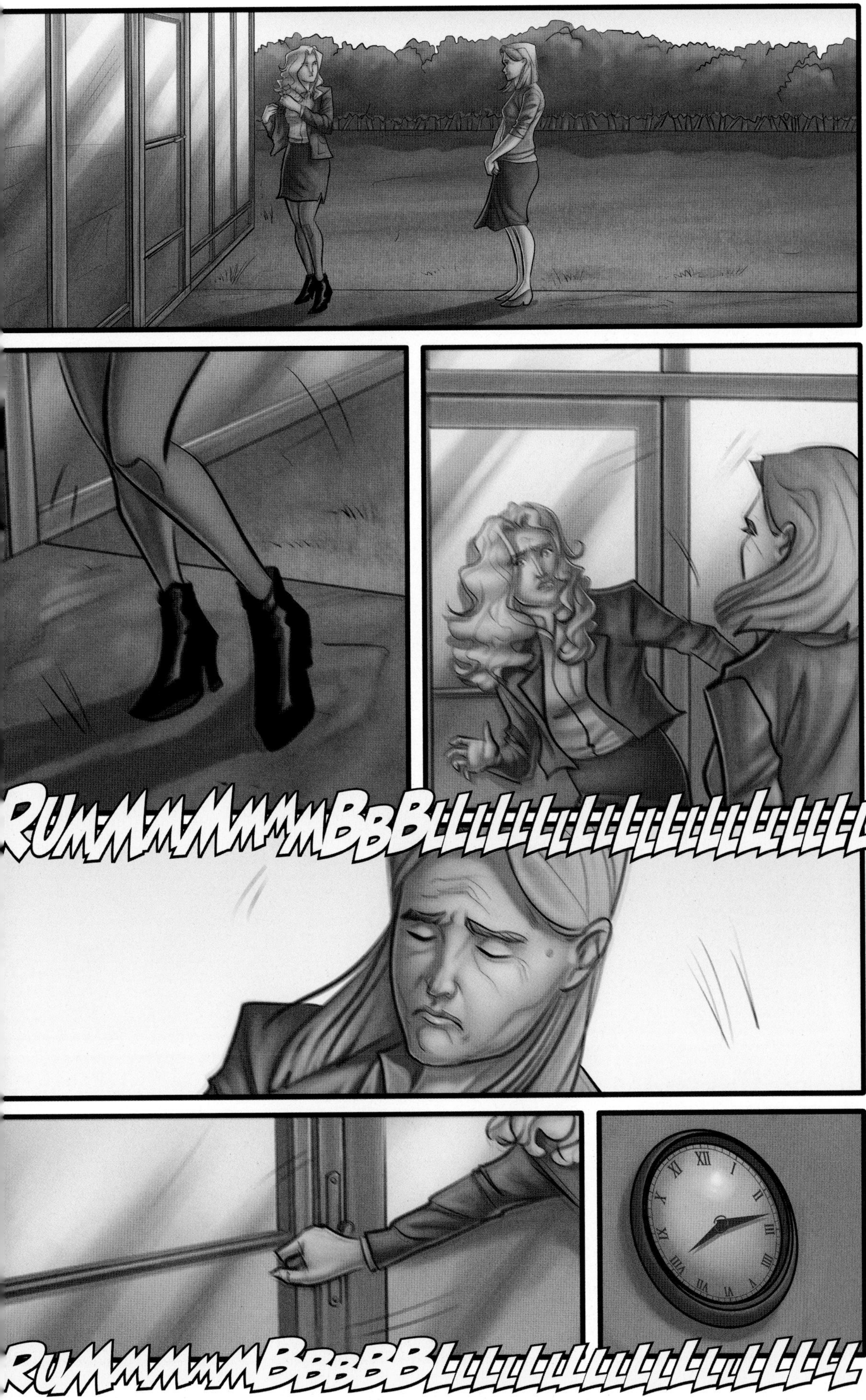
RUMMMMMMMBBBLLLLLLLLLLLLLLLLLLLLLLL
RUMMMMMMBBBBBLLLLLLLLLLLLLLLLLLLLLLL

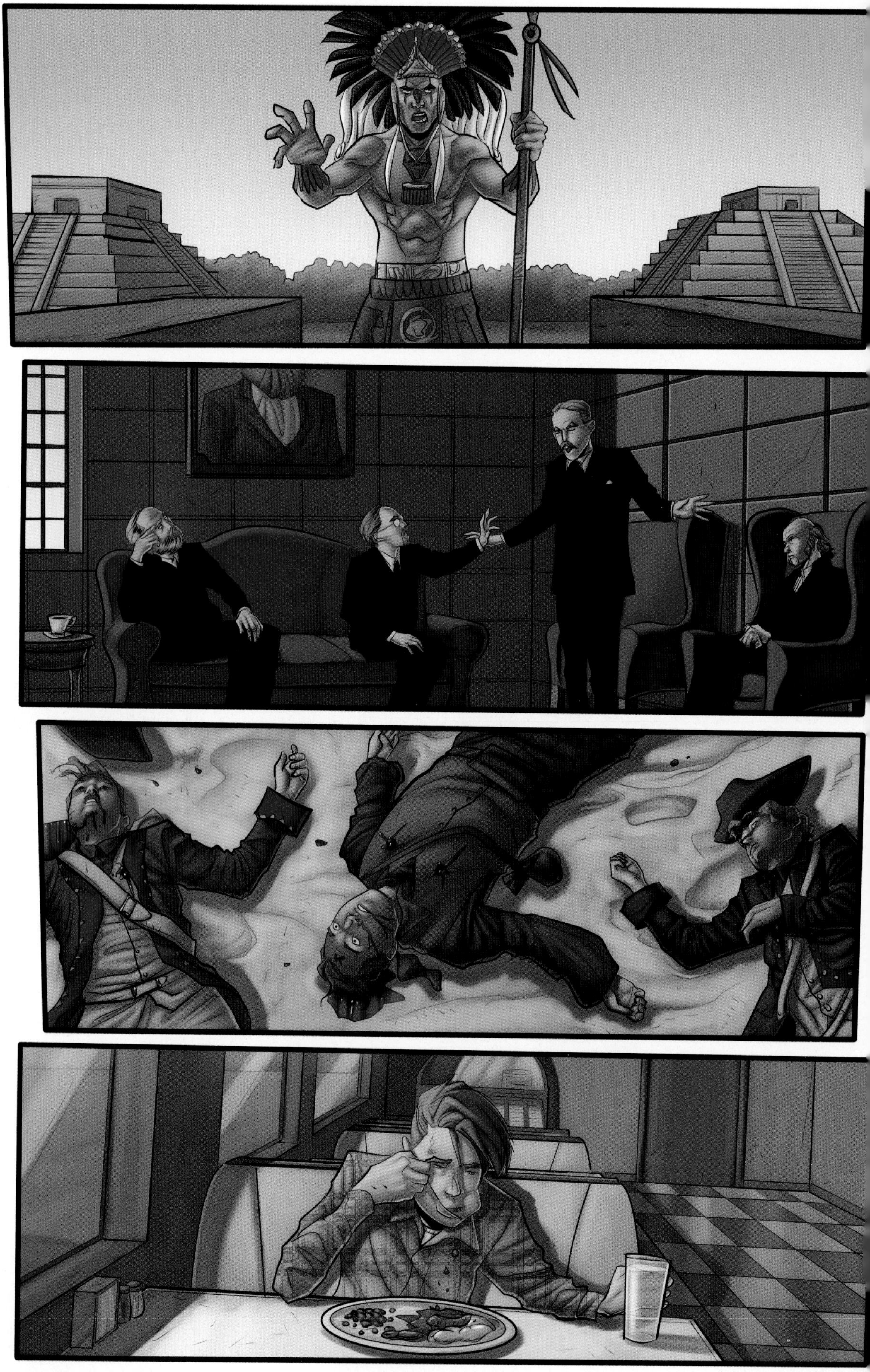

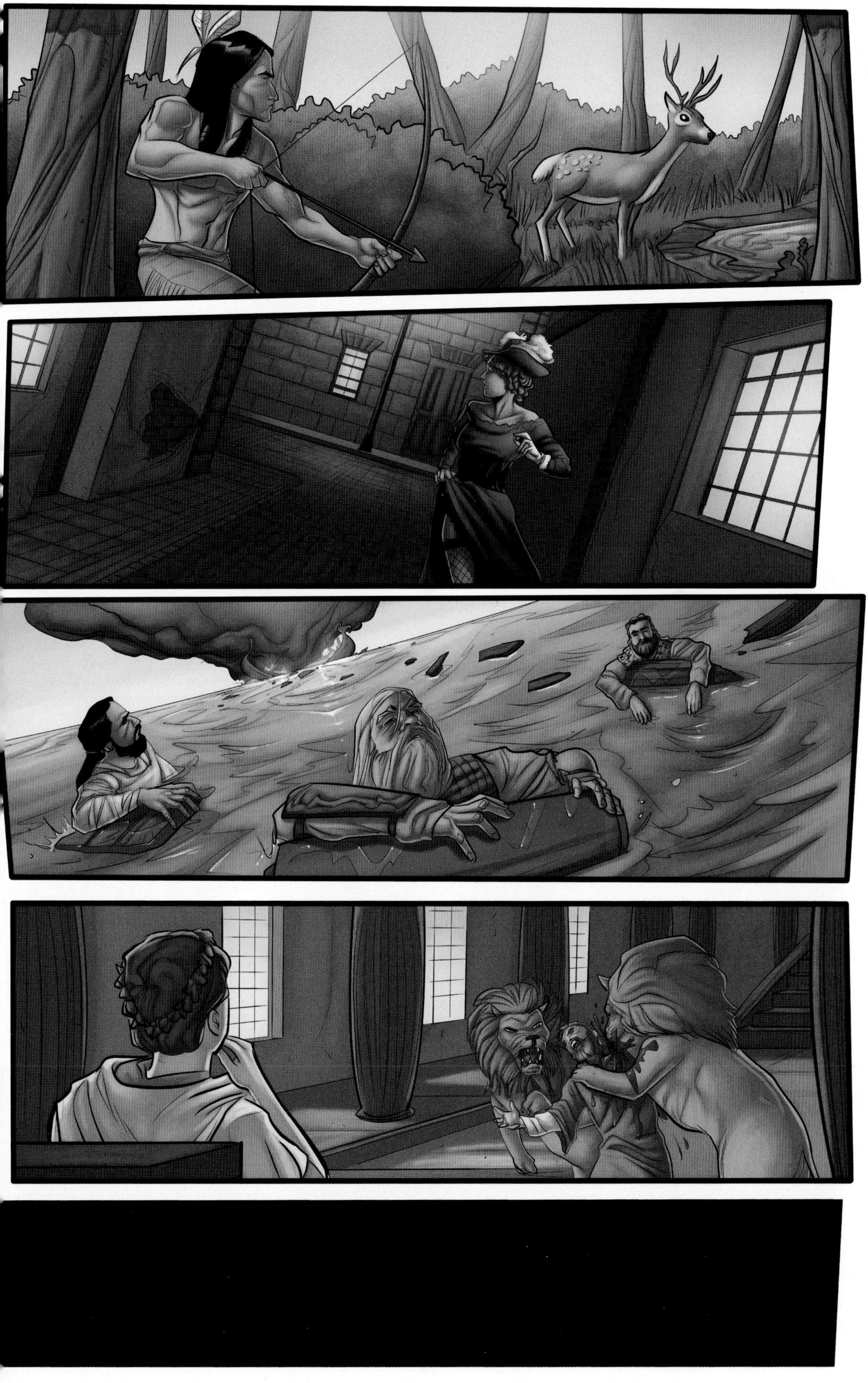

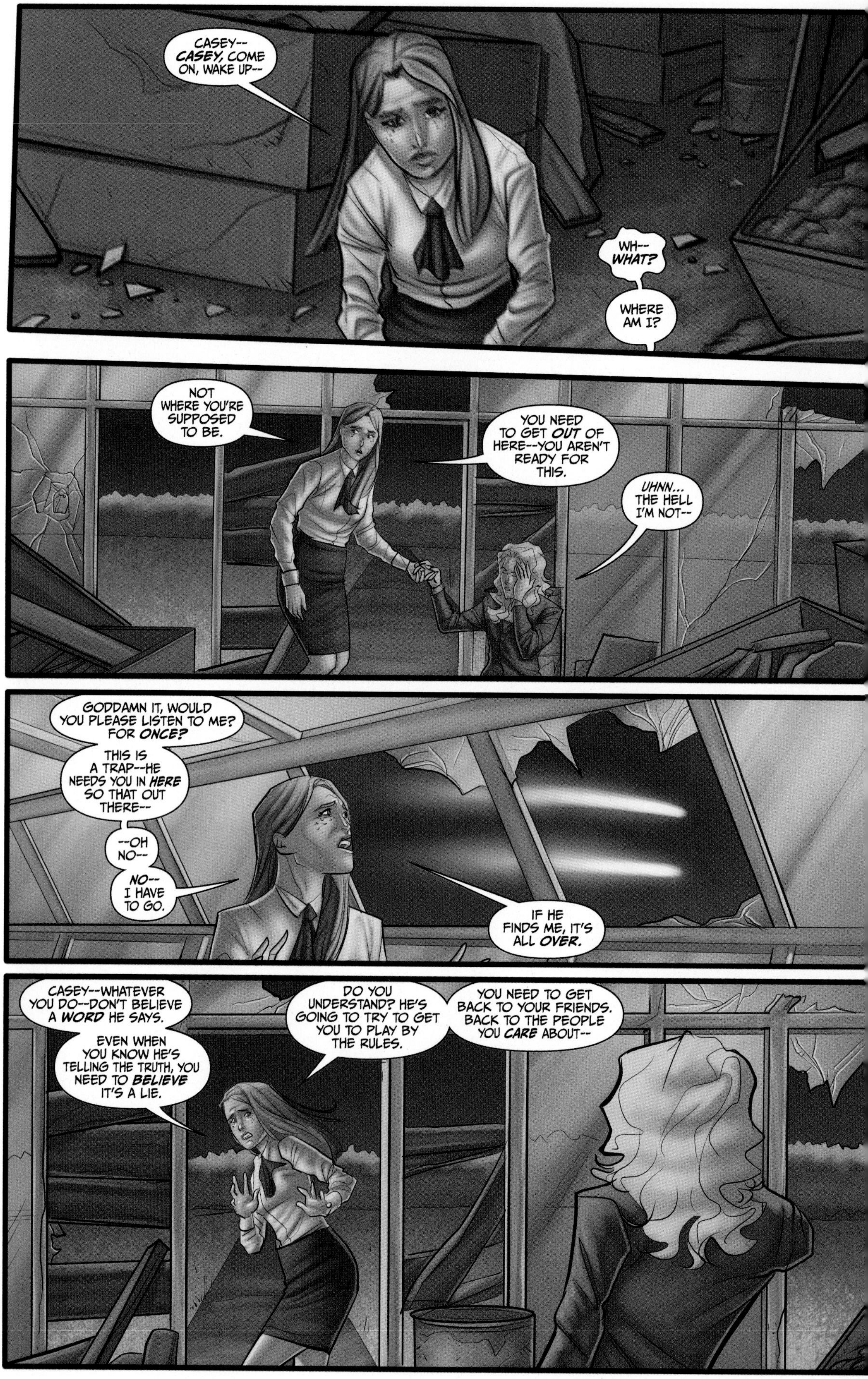

CASEY-- *CASEY,* COME ON, WAKE UP--
WH-- *WHAT?*
WHERE AM I?
NOT WHERE YOU'RE SUPPOSED TO BE.
YOU NEED TO GET *OUT* OF HERE--YOU AREN'T READY FOR THIS.
UHNN... THE HELL I'M NOT--
GODDAMN IT, WOULD YOU PLEASE LISTEN TO ME? FOR *ONCE?*
THIS IS A TRAP--HE NEEDS YOU IN *HERE* SO THAT OUT THERE--
--OH NO--
NO-- I HAVE TO GO.
IF HE FINDS ME, IT'S ALL *OVER.*
CASEY--WHATEVER YOU DO--DON'T BELIEVE A *WORD* HE SAYS.
EVEN WHEN YOU KNOW HE'S TELLING THE TRUTH, YOU NEED TO *BELIEVE* IT'S A LIE.
DO YOU UNDERSTAND? HE'S GOING TO TRY TO GET YOU TO PLAY BY THE RULES.
YOU NEED TO GET BACK TO YOUR FRIENDS. BACK TO THE PEOPLE YOU *CARE* ABOUT--

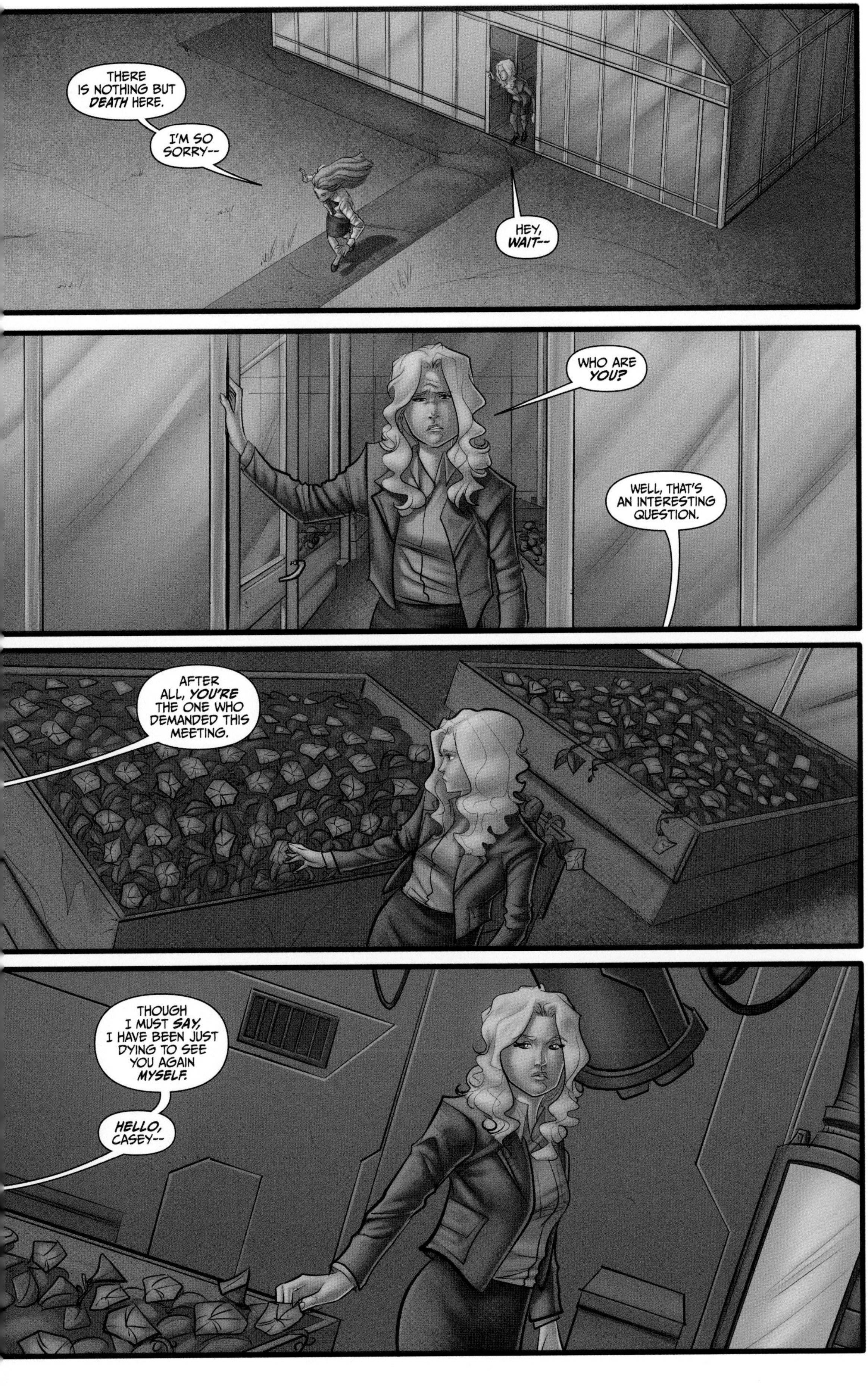
THERE IS NOTHING BUT *DEATH* HERE.
I'M SO SORRY--
HEY, *WAIT*--
WHO ARE *YOU?*
WELL, THAT'S AN INTERESTING QUESTION.
AFTER ALL, *YOU'RE* THE ONE WHO DEMANDED THIS MEETING.
THOUGH I MUST *SAY,* I HAVE BEEN JUST DYING TO SEE YOU AGAIN *MYSELF.*
HELLO, CASEY--

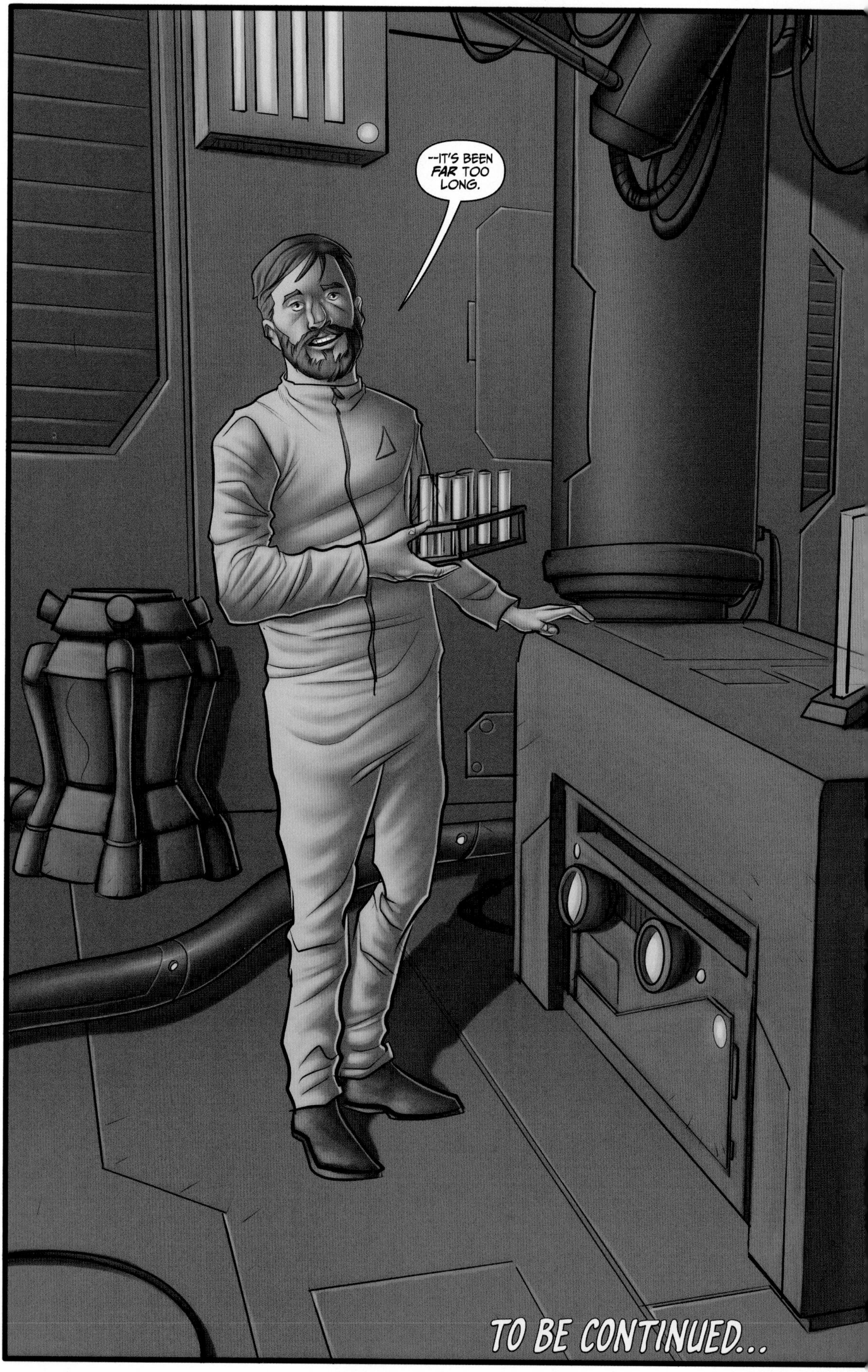
--IT'S BEEN FAR TOO LONG.
TO BE CONTINUED...

fifty

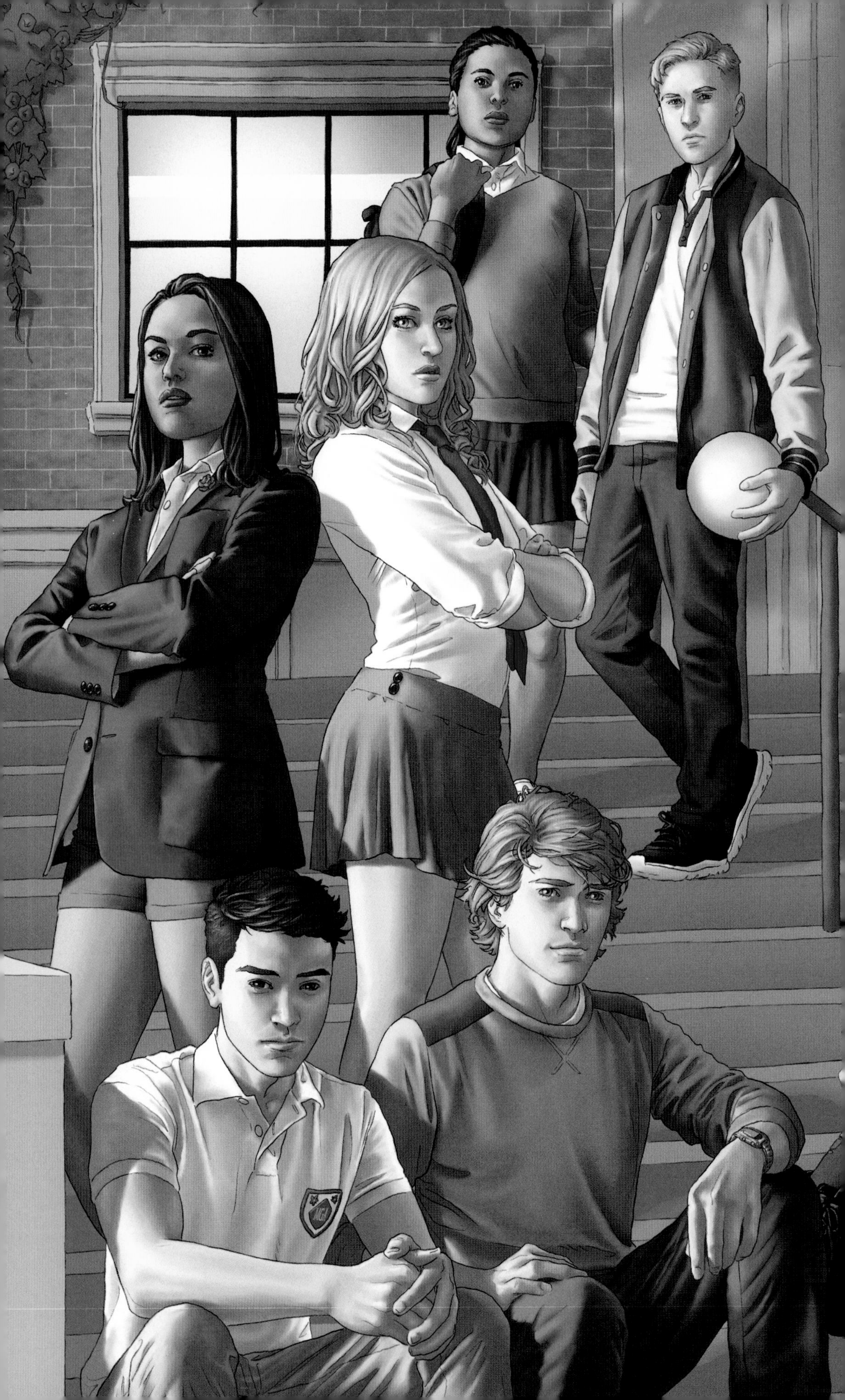

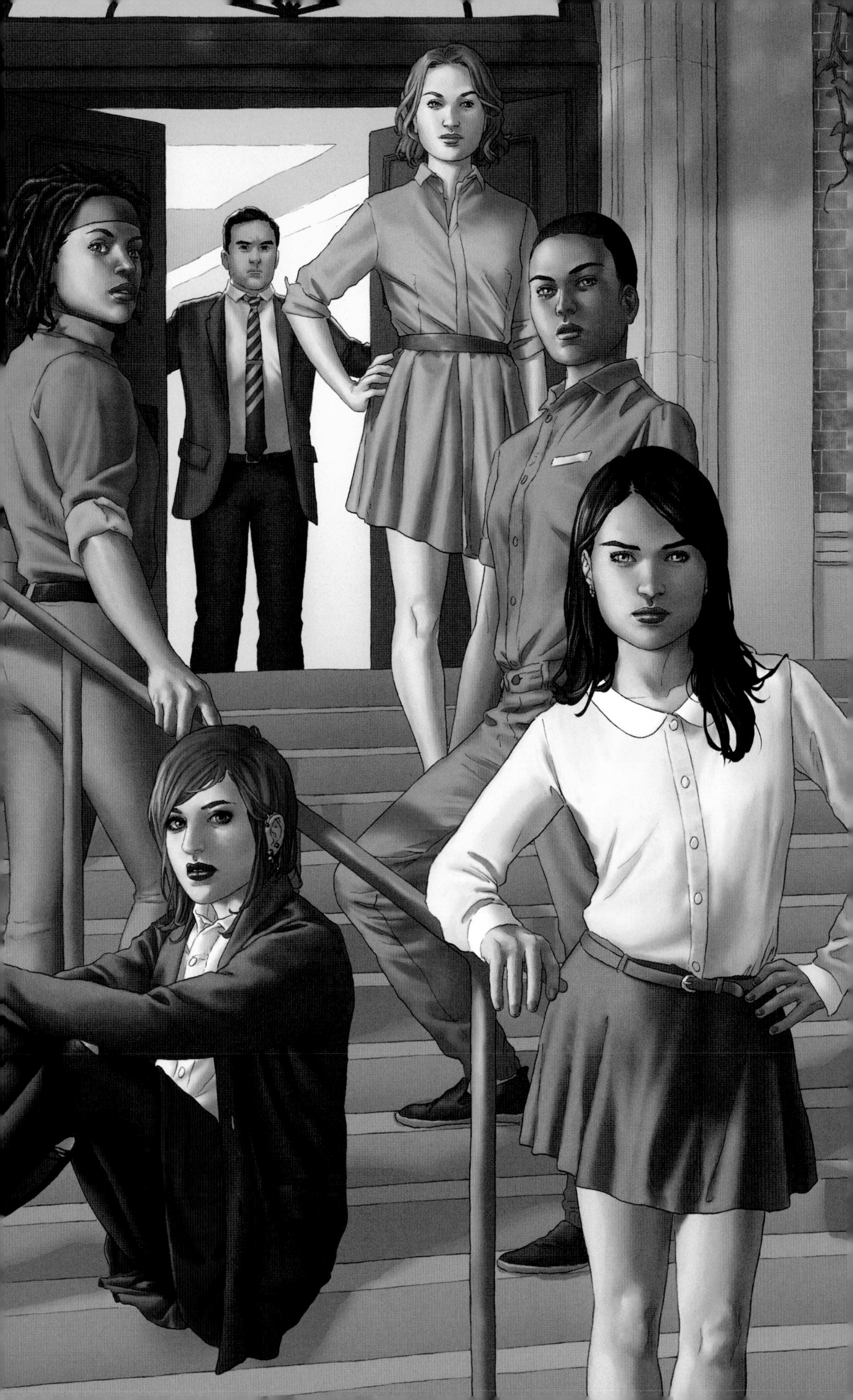

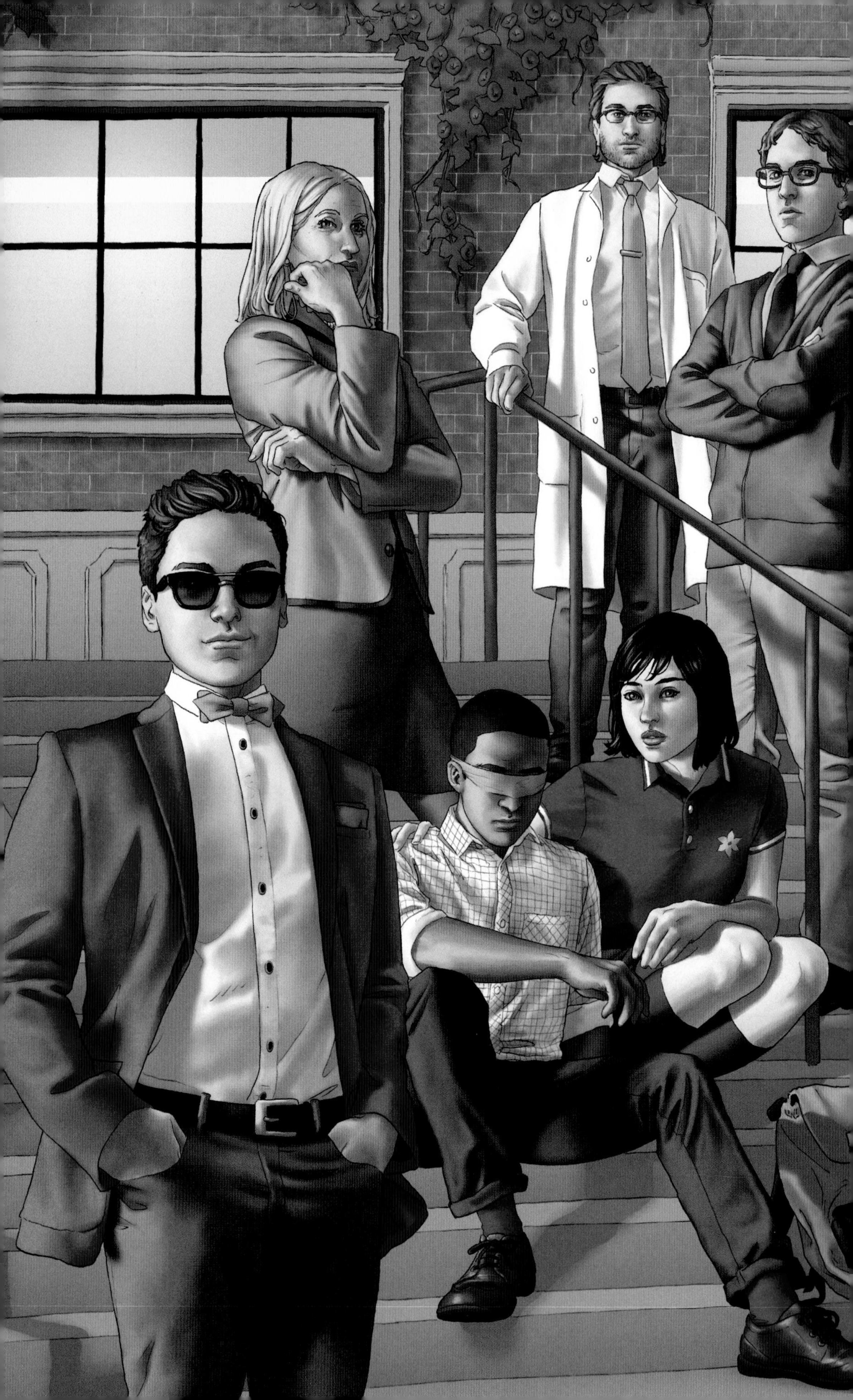

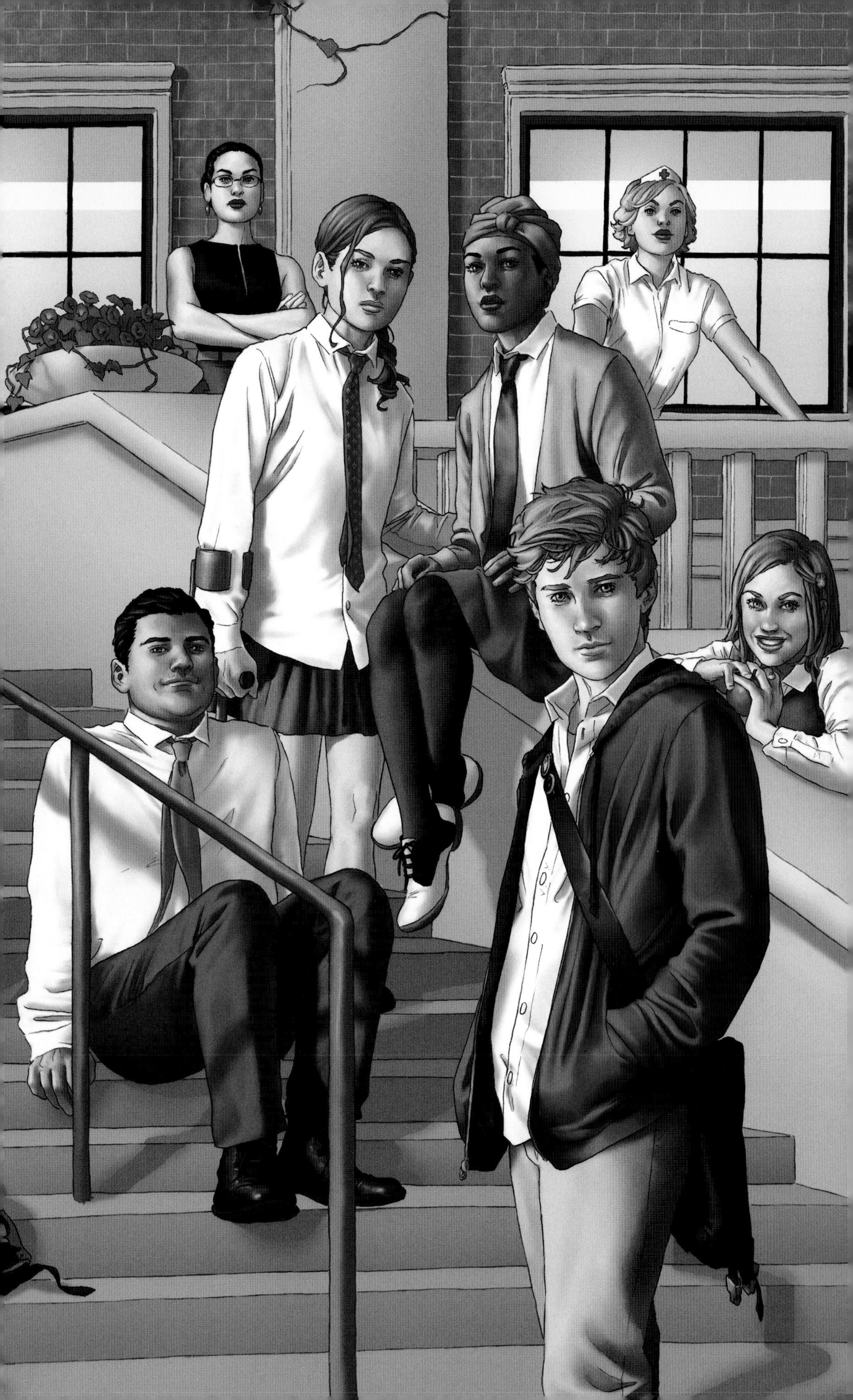

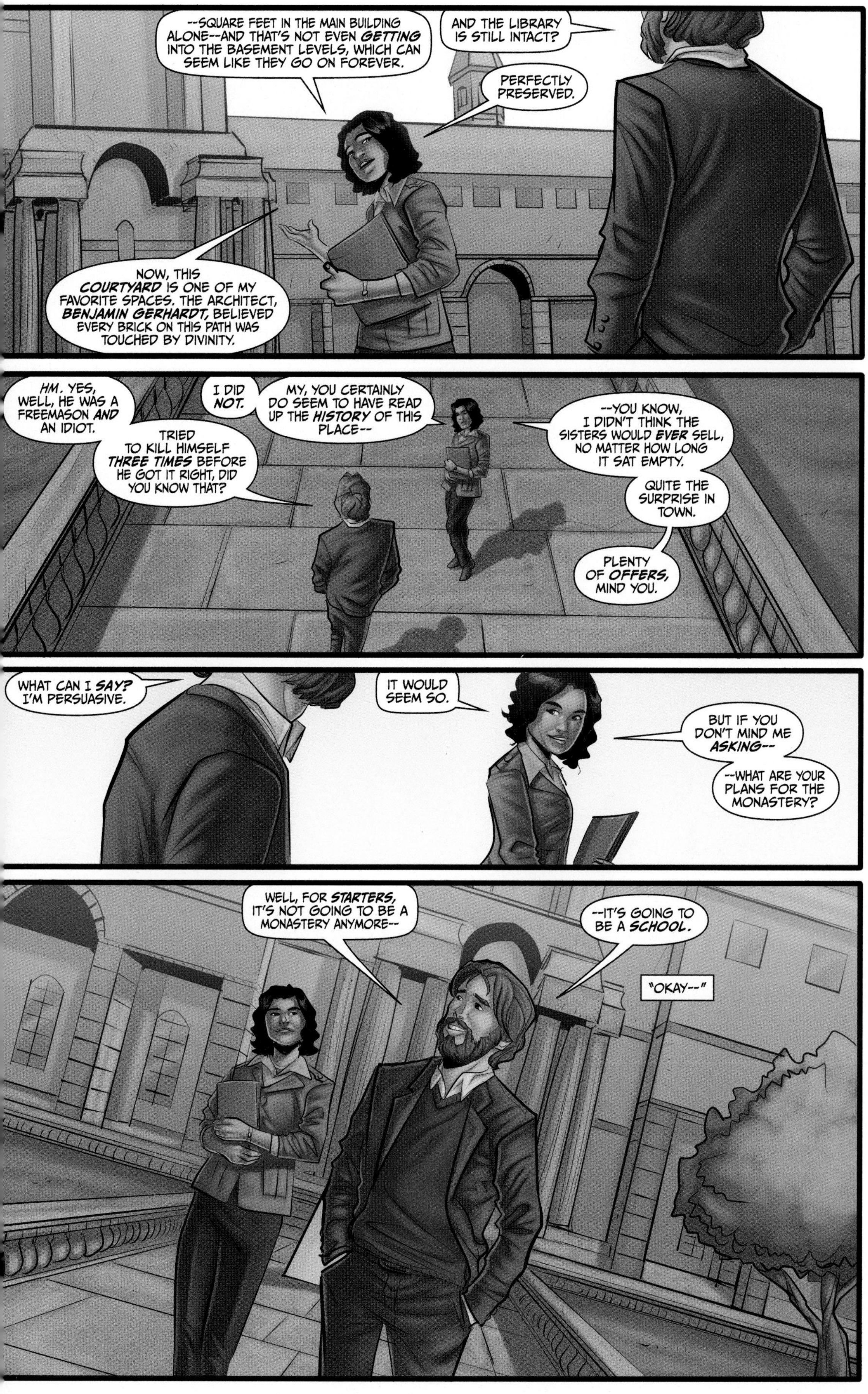
--SQUARE FEET IN THE MAIN BUILDING ALONE--AND THAT'S NOT EVEN GETTING INTO THE BASEMENT LEVELS, WHICH CAN SEEM LIKE THEY GO ON FOREVER.
AND THE LIBRARY IS STILL INTACT?
PERFECTLY PRESERVED.
NOW, THIS COURTYARD IS ONE OF MY FAVORITE SPACES. THE ARCHITECT, BENJAMIN GERHARDT, BELIEVED EVERY BRICK ON THIS PATH WAS TOUCHED BY DIVINITY.
HM. YES, WELL, HE WAS A FREEMASON AND AN IDIOT.
TRIED TO KILL HIMSELF THREE TIMES BEFORE HE GOT IT RIGHT, DID YOU KNOW THAT?
I DID NOT.
MY, YOU CERTAINLY DO SEEM TO HAVE READ UP THE HISTORY OF THIS PLACE--
--YOU KNOW, I DIDN'T THINK THE SISTERS WOULD EVER SELL, NO MATTER HOW LONG IT SAT EMPTY.
QUITE THE SURPRISE IN TOWN.
PLENTY OF OFFERS, MIND YOU.
WHAT CAN I SAY? I'M PERSUASIVE.
IT WOULD SEEM SO.
BUT IF YOU DON'T MIND ME ASKING--
--WHAT ARE YOUR PLANS FOR THE MONASTERY?
WELL, FOR STARTERS, IT'S NOT GOING TO BE A MONASTERY ANYMORE--
--IT'S GOING TO BE A SCHOOL.
"OKAY--"

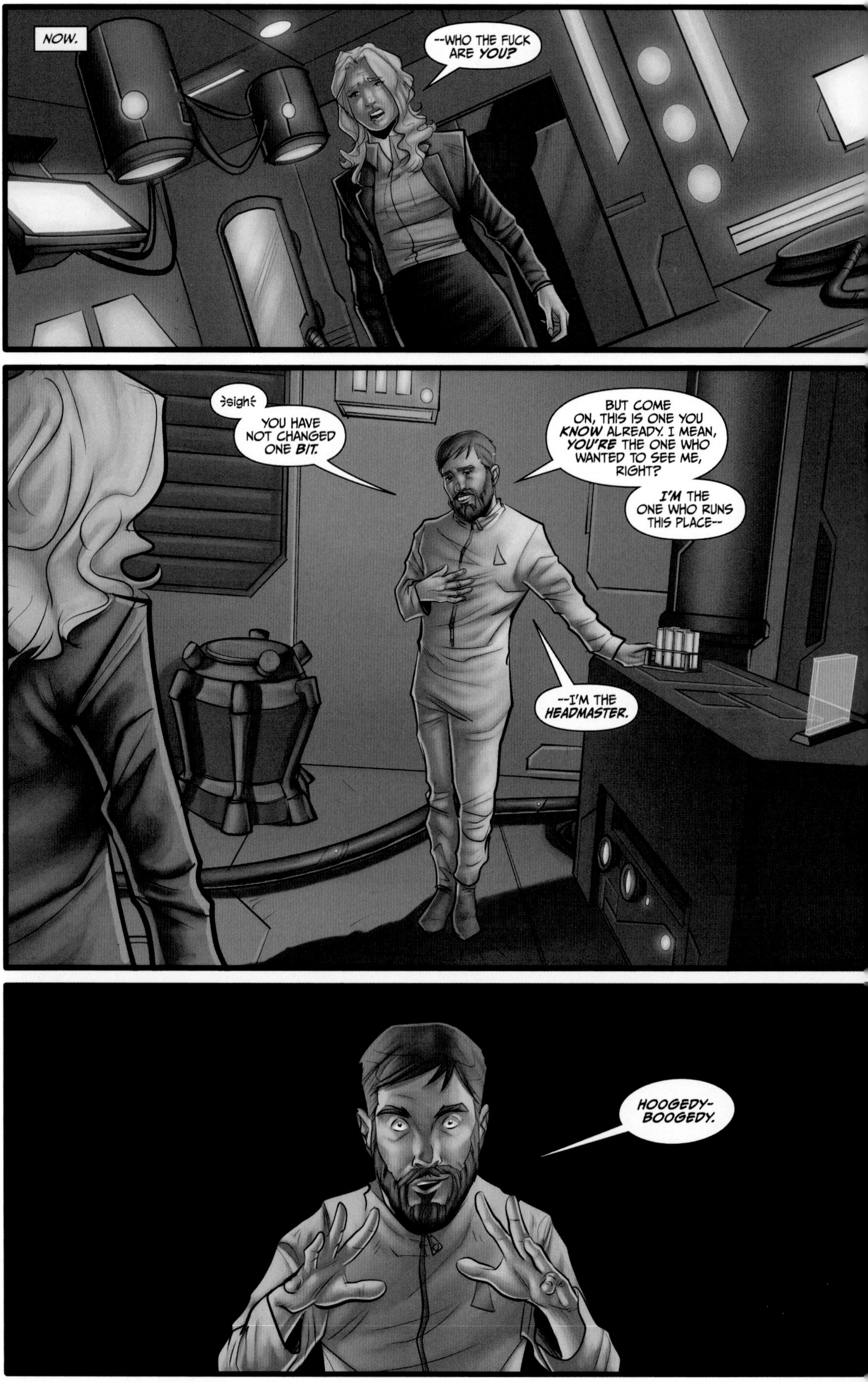
NOW.
--WHO THE FUCK ARE *YOU?*
ꟷsighꟷ
YOU HAVE NOT CHANGED ONE *BIT.*
BUT COME ON, THIS IS ONE YOU *KNOW* ALREADY. I MEAN, *YOU'RE* THE ONE WHO WANTED TO SEE ME, RIGHT?
I'M THE ONE WHO RUNS THIS PLACE--
--I'M THE *HEADMASTER.*
HOOGEDY-BOOGEDY.

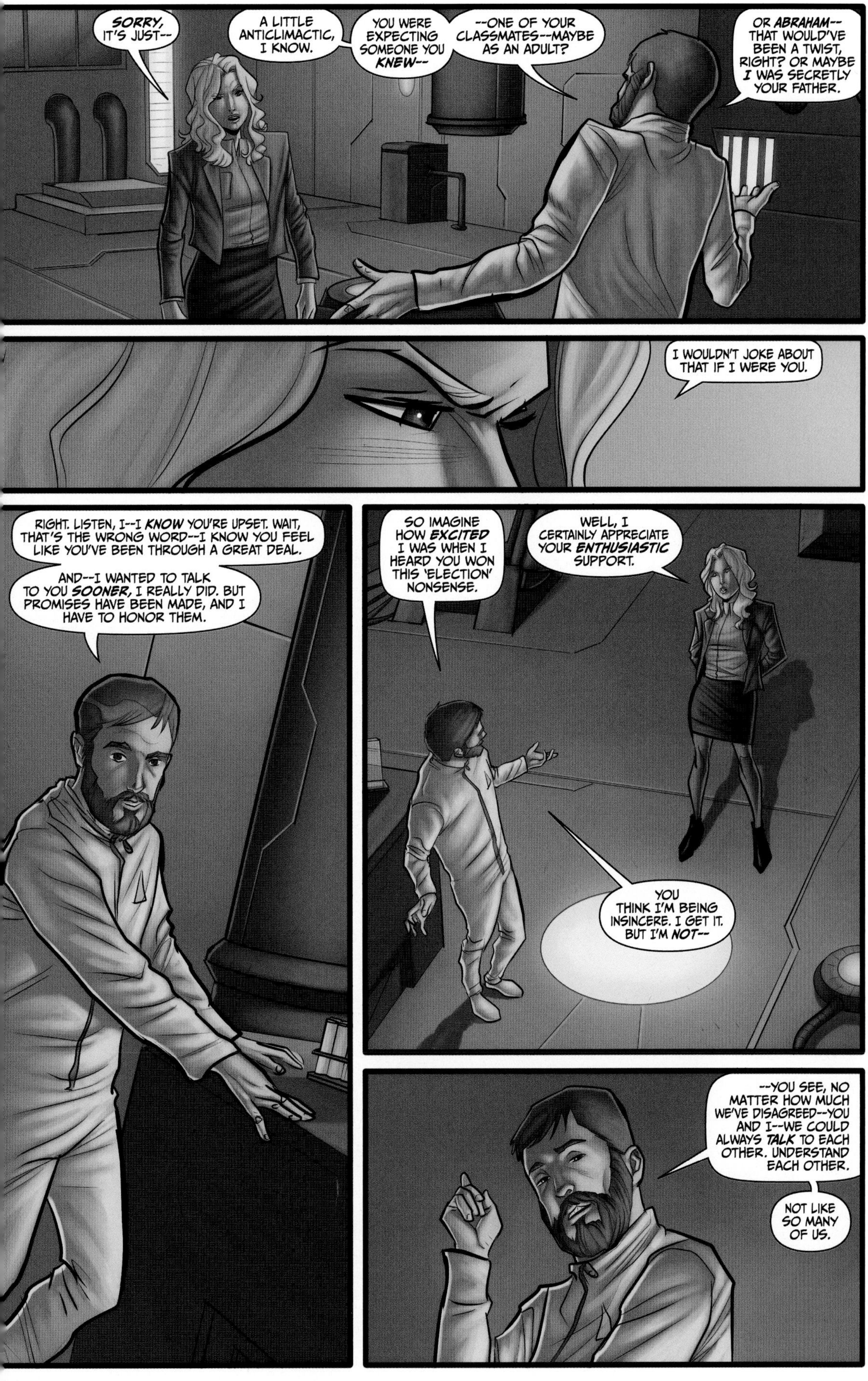
SORRY, IT'S JUST--
A LITTLE ANTICLIMACTIC, I KNOW.
YOU WERE EXPECTING SOMEONE YOU KNEW--
--ONE OF YOUR CLASSMATES--MAYBE AS AN ADULT?
OR ABRAHAM--THAT WOULD'VE BEEN A TWIST, RIGHT? OR MAYBE I WAS SECRETLY YOUR FATHER.
I WOULDN'T JOKE ABOUT THAT IF I WERE YOU.
RIGHT. LISTEN, I--I KNOW YOU'RE UPSET. WAIT, THAT'S THE WRONG WORD--I KNOW YOU FEEL LIKE YOU'VE BEEN THROUGH A GREAT DEAL.
AND--I WANTED TO TALK TO YOU SOONER, I REALLY DID. BUT PROMISES HAVE BEEN MADE, AND I HAVE TO HONOR THEM.
SO IMAGINE HOW EXCITED I WAS WHEN I HEARD YOU WON THIS 'ELECTION' NONSENSE.
WELL, I CERTAINLY APPRECIATE YOUR ENTHUSIASTIC SUPPORT.
YOU THINK I'M BEING INSINCERE. I GET IT. BUT I'M NOT--
--YOU SEE, NO MATTER HOW MUCH WE'VE DISAGREED--YOU AND I--WE COULD ALWAYS TALK TO EACH OTHER. UNDERSTAND EACH OTHER.
NOT LIKE SO MANY OF US.

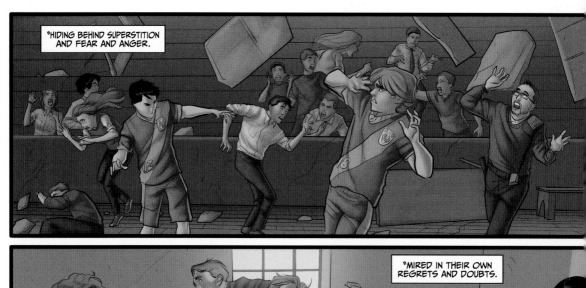

"HIDING BEHIND SUPERSTITION AND FEAR AND ANGER.

"MIRED IN THEIR OWN REGRETS AND DOUBTS.

"TOO WEAK AND SELFISH TO BECOME WHAT THEY ARE MEANT TO BE.

"UNWILLING TO EMBRACE THE TRUTH."

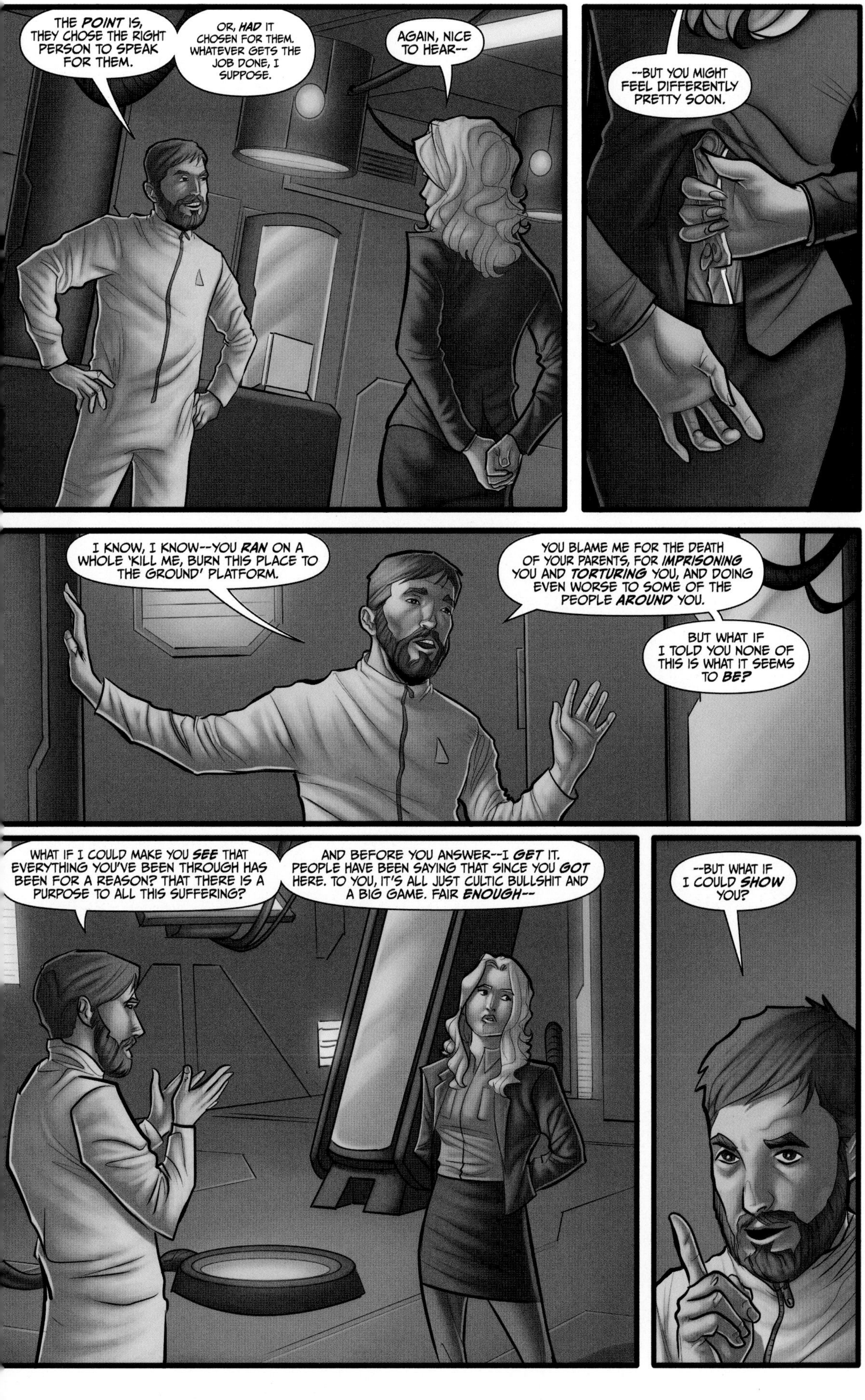
THE POINT IS, THEY CHOSE THE RIGHT PERSON TO SPEAK FOR THEM.
OR, HAD IT CHOSEN FOR THEM. WHATEVER GETS THE JOB DONE, I SUPPOSE.
AGAIN, NICE TO HEAR--
--BUT YOU MIGHT FEEL DIFFERENTLY PRETTY SOON.
I KNOW, I KNOW--YOU RAN ON A WHOLE 'KILL ME, BURN THIS PLACE TO THE GROUND' PLATFORM.
YOU BLAME ME FOR THE DEATH OF YOUR PARENTS, FOR IMPRISONING YOU AND TORTURING YOU, AND DOING EVEN WORSE TO SOME OF THE PEOPLE AROUND YOU.
BUT WHAT IF I TOLD YOU NONE OF THIS IS WHAT IT SEEMS TO BE?
WHAT IF I COULD MAKE YOU SEE THAT EVERYTHING YOU'VE BEEN THROUGH HAS BEEN FOR A REASON? THAT THERE IS A PURPOSE TO ALL THIS SUFFERING?
AND BEFORE YOU ANSWER--I GET IT. PEOPLE HAVE BEEN SAYING THAT SINCE YOU GOT HERE. TO YOU, IT'S ALL JUST CULTIC BULLSHIT AND A BIG GAME. FAIR ENOUGH--
--BUT WHAT IF I COULD SHOW YOU?

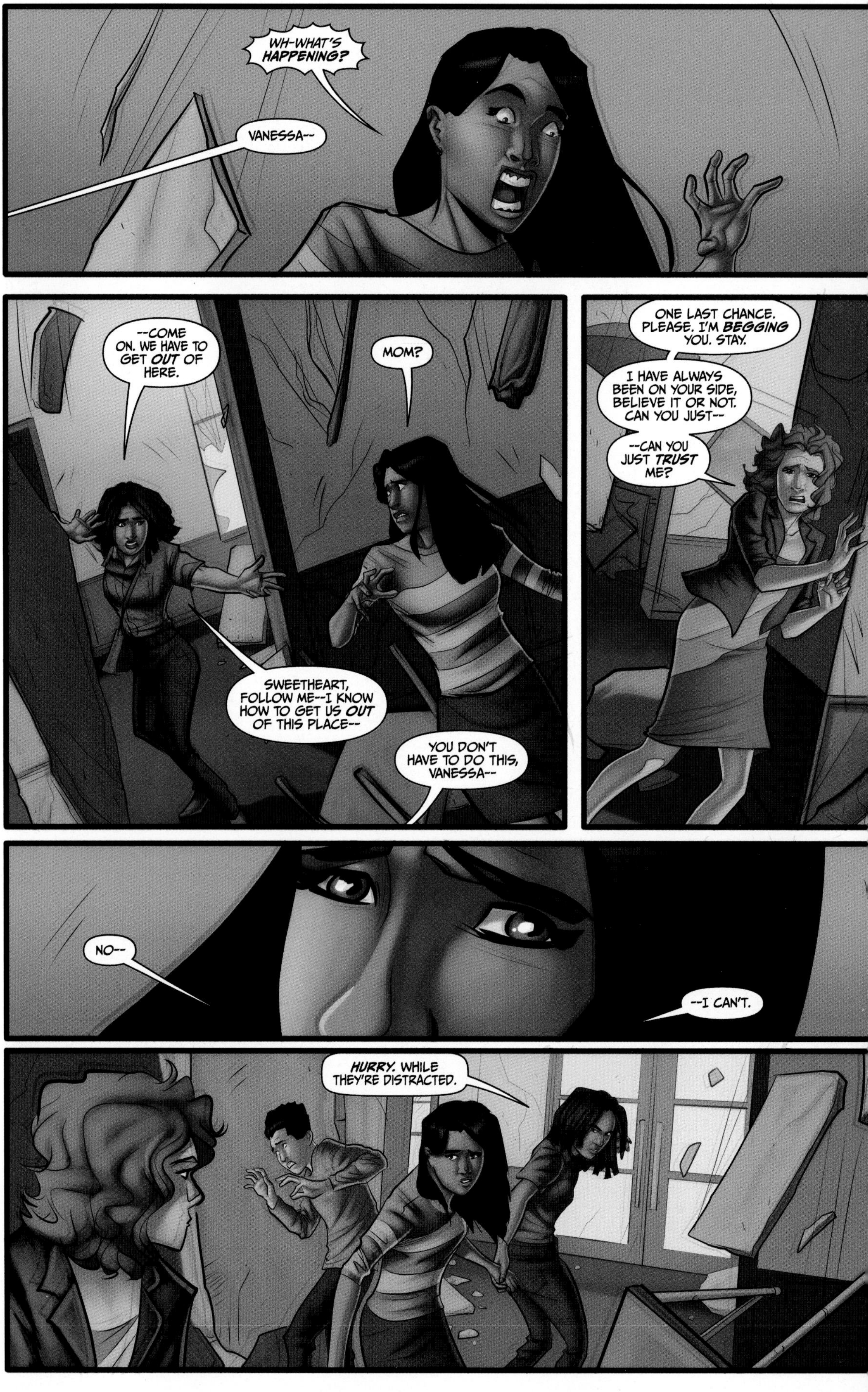
WH-WHAT'S HAPPENING?
VANESSA--
--COME ON. WE HAVE TO GET OUT OF HERE.
MOM?
SWEETHEART, FOLLOW ME--I KNOW HOW TO GET US OUT OF THIS PLACE--
YOU DON'T HAVE TO DO THIS, VANESSA--
ONE LAST CHANCE. PLEASE. I'M BEGGING YOU. STAY.
I HAVE ALWAYS BEEN ON YOUR SIDE, BELIEVE IT OR NOT. CAN YOU JUST--
--CAN YOU JUST TRUST ME?
NO--
--I CAN'T.
HURRY. WHILE THEY'RE DISTRACTED.

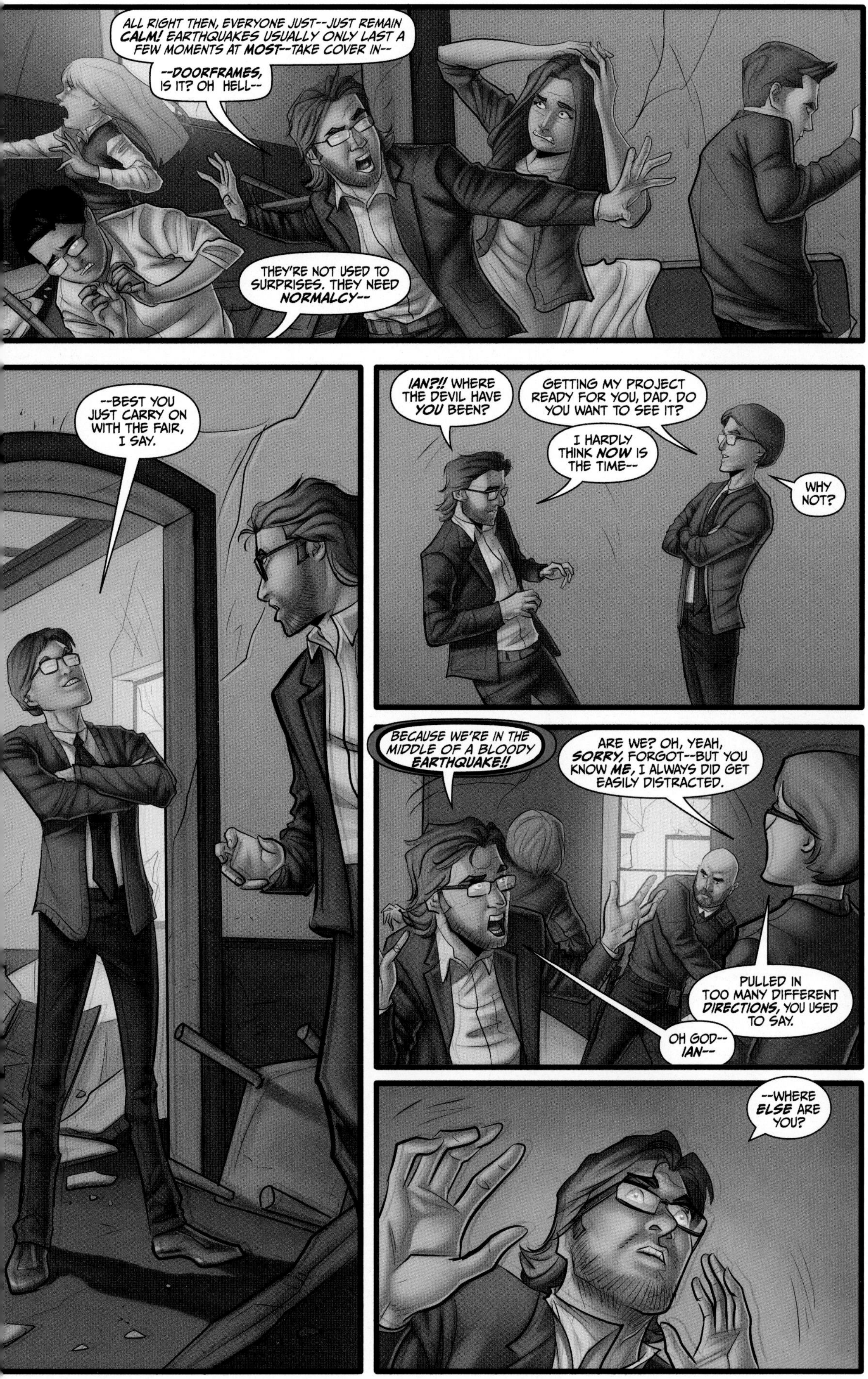
ALL RIGHT THEN, EVERYONE JUST--JUST REMAIN CALM! EARTHQUAKES USUALLY ONLY LAST A FEW MOMENTS AT MOST--TAKE COVER IN--
--DOORFRAMES, IS IT? OH HELL--
THEY'RE NOT USED TO SURPRISES. THEY NEED NORMALCY--
--BEST YOU JUST CARRY ON WITH THE FAIR, I SAY.
IAN?!! WHERE THE DEVIL HAVE YOU BEEN?
GETTING MY PROJECT READY FOR YOU, DAD. DO YOU WANT TO SEE IT?
I HARDLY THINK NOW IS THE TIME--
WHY NOT?
BECAUSE WE'RE IN THE MIDDLE OF A BLOODY EARTHQUAKE!!
ARE WE? OH, YEAH, SORRY, FORGOT--BUT YOU KNOW ME, I ALWAYS DID GET EASILY DISTRACTED.
PULLED IN TOO MANY DIFFERENT DIRECTIONS, YOU USED TO SAY.
OH GOD-- IAN--
--WHERE ELSE ARE YOU?

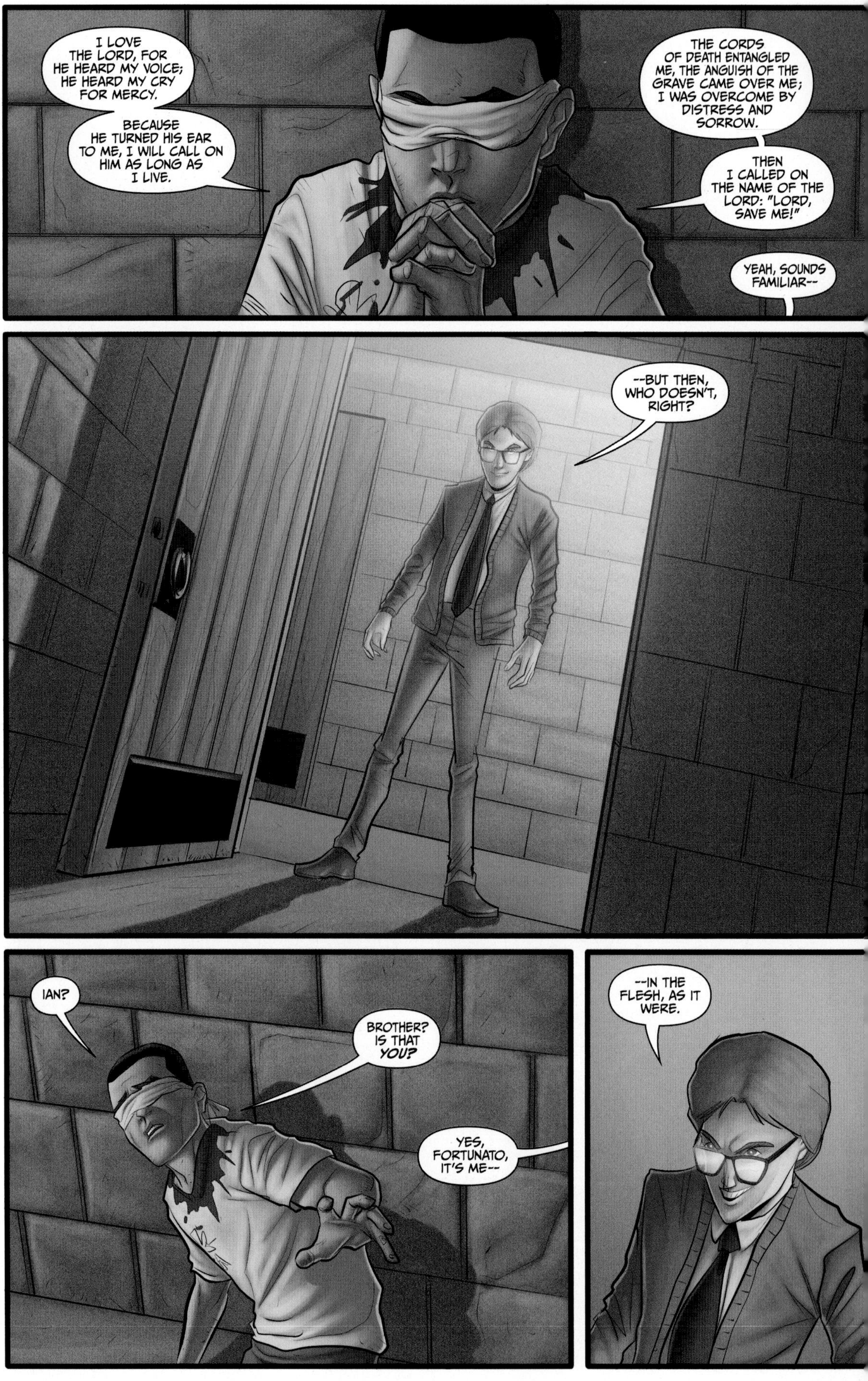
I LOVE THE LORD, FOR HE HEARD MY VOICE; HE HEARD MY CRY FOR MERCY.
BECAUSE HE TURNED HIS EAR TO ME, I WILL CALL ON HIM AS LONG AS I LIVE.
THE CORDS OF DEATH ENTANGLED ME, THE ANGUISH OF THE GRAVE CAME OVER ME; I WAS OVERCOME BY DISTRESS AND SORROW.
THEN I CALLED ON THE NAME OF THE LORD: "LORD, SAVE ME!"
YEAH, SOUNDS FAMILIAR--
--BUT THEN, WHO DOESN'T, RIGHT?
IAN?
BROTHER? IS THAT *YOU?*
YES, FORTUNATO, IT'S ME--
--IN THE FLESH, AS IT WERE.

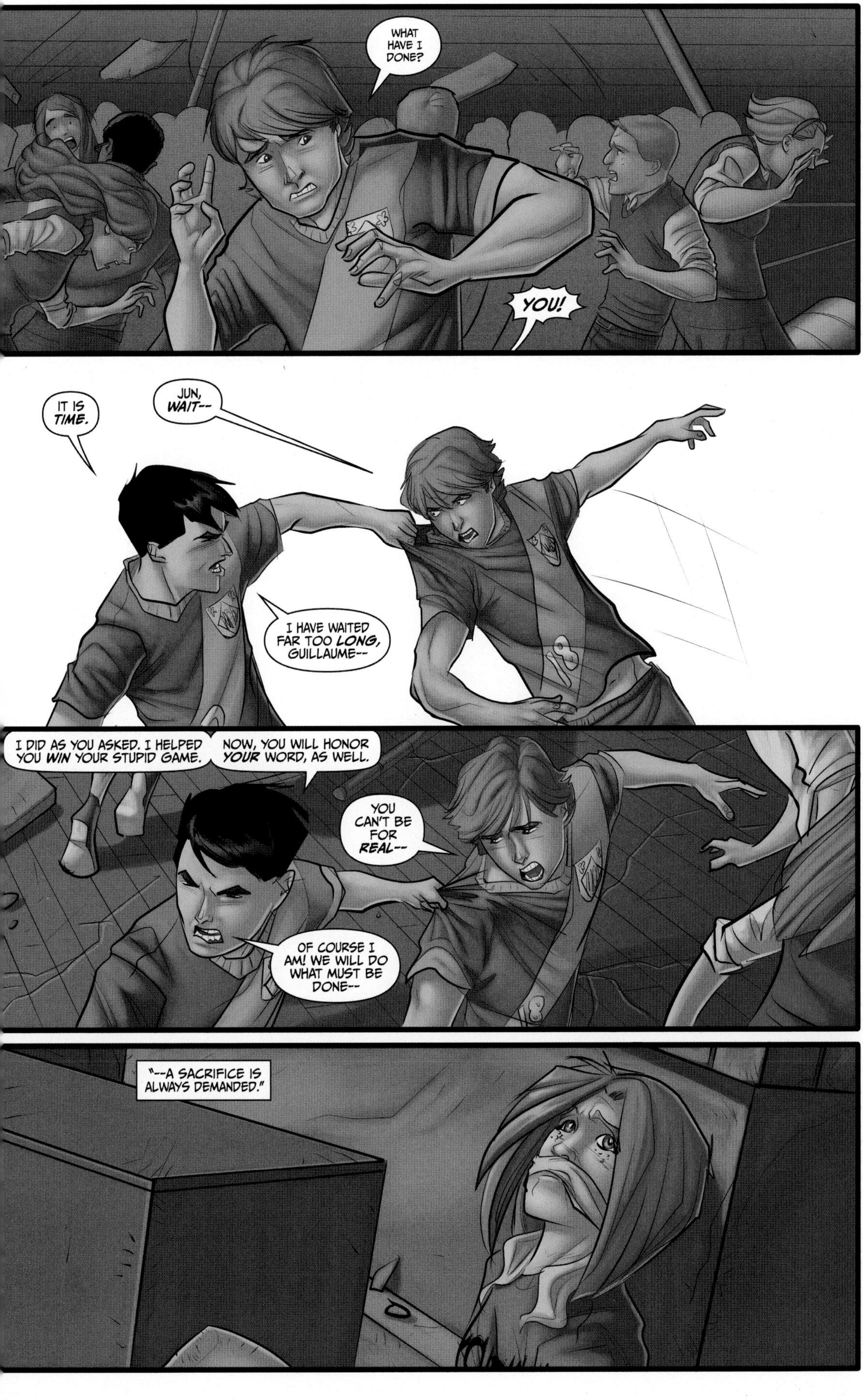
WHAT HAVE I DONE?
YOU!
IT IS TIME.
JUN, WAIT--
I HAVE WAITED FAR TOO LONG, GUILLAUME--
I DID AS YOU ASKED. I HELPED YOU WIN YOUR STUPID GAME.
NOW, YOU WILL HONOR YOUR WORD, AS WELL.
YOU CAN'T BE FOR REAL--
OF COURSE I AM! WE WILL DO WHAT MUST BE DONE--
"--A SACRIFICE IS ALWAYS DEMANDED."

CAN I JUST *SAY*--

--IT IS *AMAZING* THE TROUBLE YOU KIDS GET YOURSELF INTO.

I MEAN, I *THOUGHT* AN ENVIRONMENT WITH SOME STRUCTURE, SOME CLEAR GROUND RULES FROM AN EARLY AGE MIGHT ENCOURAGE SOME *STABILITY*.

I GUESS THAT'S ON *ME*, THOUGH.

UNREALISTIC EXPECTATIONS AND A WILLFUL DISREGARD FOR PAST HISTORY.

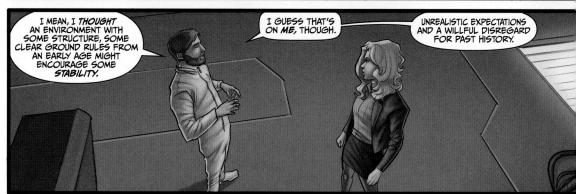

STILL--I HAVEN'T GIVEN UP HOPE. I BELIEVE, ONE WAY OR ANOTHER, I *CAN* GET THROUGH TO YOU. THAT FOR ONCE, THIS DOESN'T END WITH YOU GETTING BURNED AT A *STAKE* OR WHAT HAVE YOU.

SO WITH THAT IN *MIND*--I'D LIKE TO PULL BACK THE CURTAIN A LITTLE. TRY A MORE *HONEST* APPROACH.

HERE WE GO--

--MAY I DIRECT YOUR ATTENTION TO MONITOR *2*.

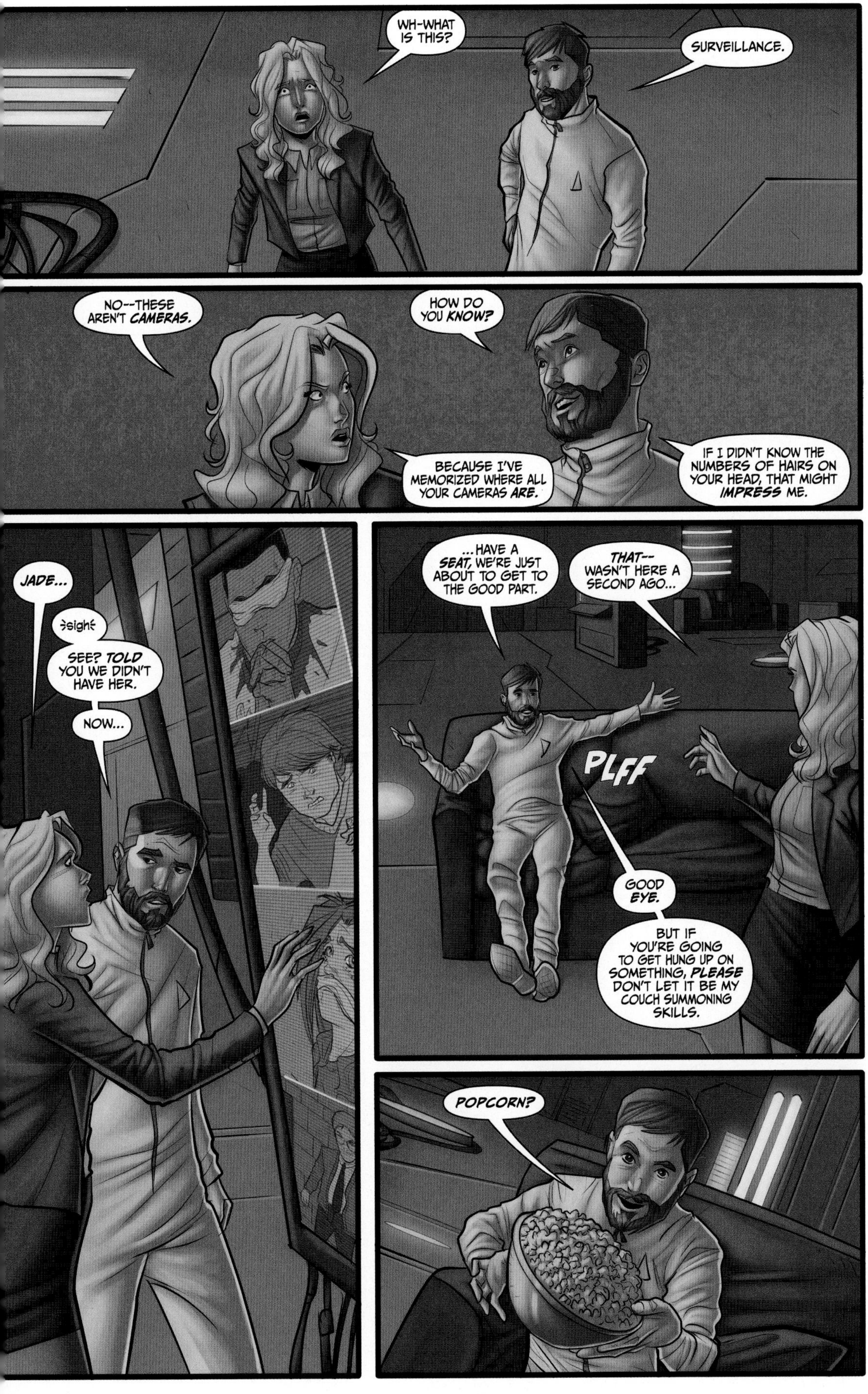
WH--WHAT IS THIS?
SURVEILLANCE.
NO--THESE AREN'T *CAMERAS.*
HOW DO YOU *KNOW?*
BECAUSE I'VE MEMORIZED WHERE ALL YOUR CAMERAS *ARE.*
IF I DIDN'T KNOW THE NUMBERS OF HAIRS ON YOUR HEAD, THAT MIGHT *IMPRESS* ME.
JADE...
sigh
SEE? *TOLD* YOU WE DIDN'T HAVE HER.
NOW...
...HAVE A *SEAT,* WE'RE JUST ABOUT TO GET TO THE GOOD PART.
THAT-- WASN'T HERE A SECOND AGO...
PLFF
GOOD *EYE.*
BUT IF YOU'RE GOING TO GET HUNG UP ON SOMETHING, *PLEASE* DON'T LET IT BE MY COUCH SUMMONING SKILLS.
POPCORN?

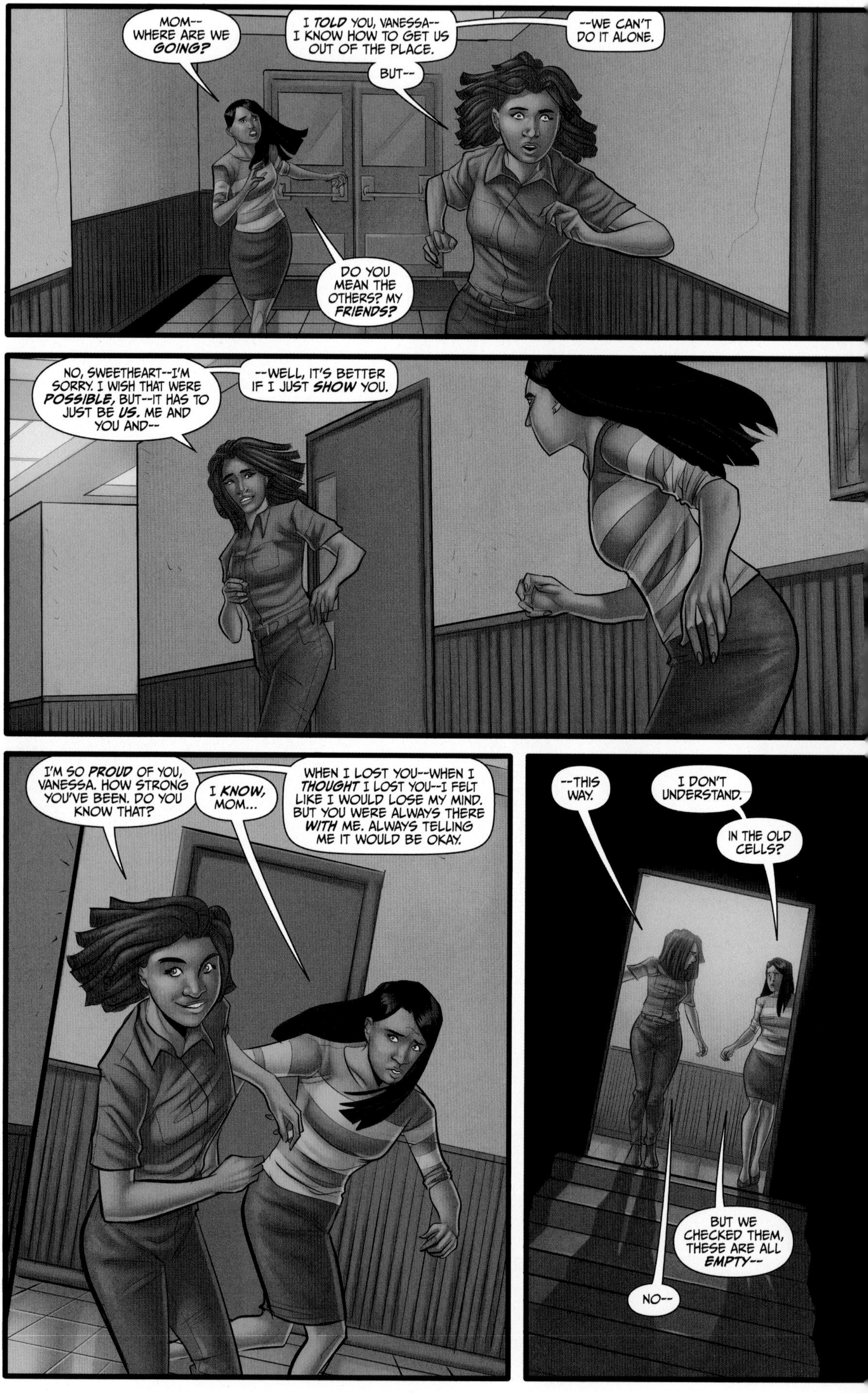
MOM-- WHERE ARE WE GOING?
I TOLD YOU, VANESSA-- I KNOW HOW TO GET US OUT OF THE PLACE.
--WE CAN'T DO IT ALONE.
BUT--
DO YOU MEAN THE OTHERS? MY FRIENDS?
NO, SWEETHEART--I'M SORRY. I WISH THAT WERE POSSIBLE, BUT--IT HAS TO JUST BE US. ME AND YOU AND--
--WELL, IT'S BETTER IF I JUST SHOW YOU.
I'M SO PROUD OF YOU, VANESSA. HOW STRONG YOU'VE BEEN. DO YOU KNOW THAT?
I KNOW, MOM...
WHEN I LOST YOU--WHEN I THOUGHT I LOST YOU--I FELT LIKE I WOULD LOSE MY MIND. BUT YOU WERE ALWAYS THERE WITH ME. ALWAYS TELLING ME IT WOULD BE OKAY.
--THIS WAY.
I DON'T UNDERSTAND.
IN THE OLD CELLS?
BUT WE CHECKED THEM, THESE ARE ALL EMPTY--
NO--

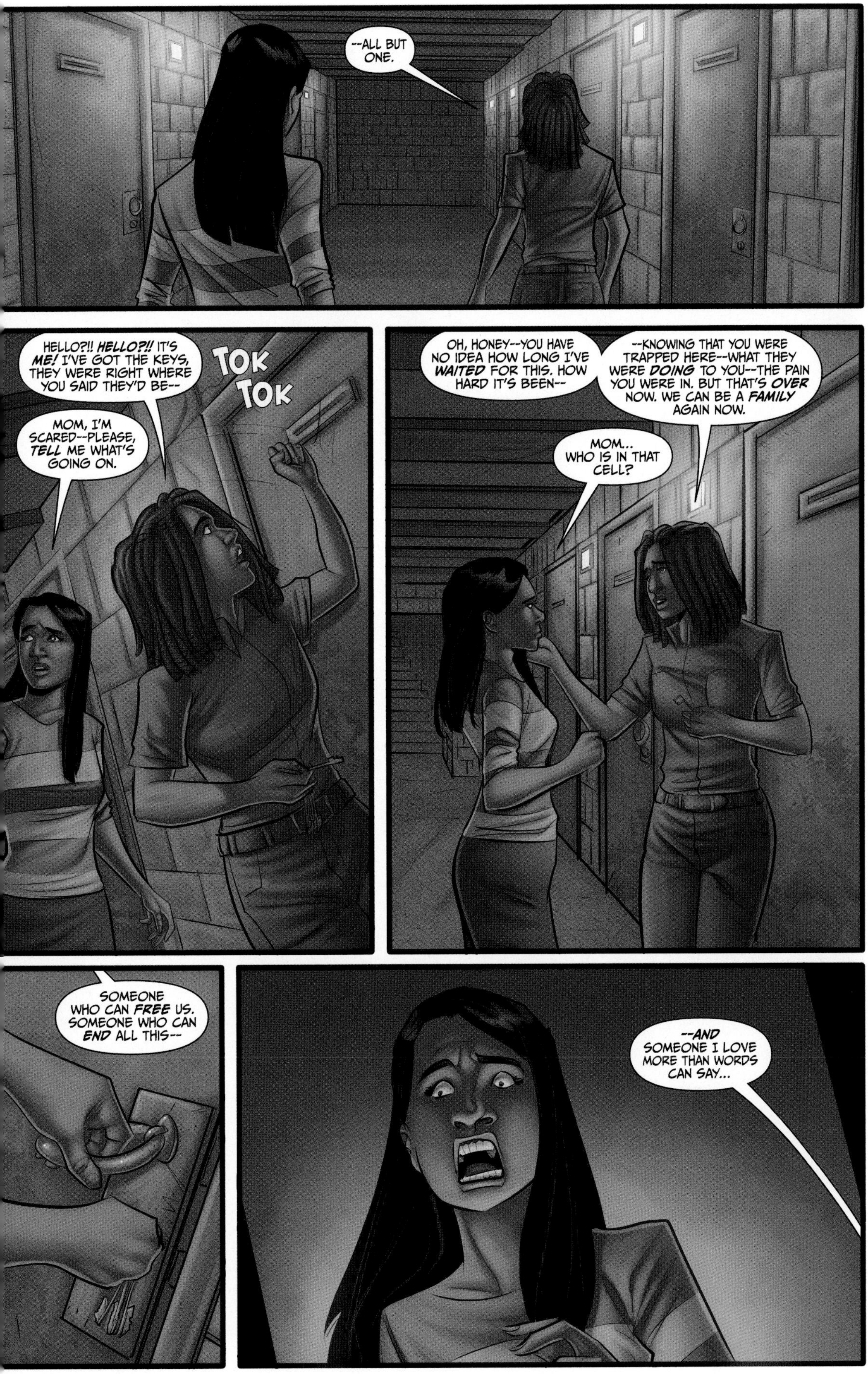
--ALL BUT ONE.
HELLO?!! HELLO?!! IT'S ME! I'VE GOT THE KEYS, THEY WERE RIGHT WHERE YOU SAID THEY'D BE--
TOK TOK
MOM, I'M SCARED--PLEASE, TELL ME WHAT'S GOING ON.
OH, HONEY--YOU HAVE NO IDEA HOW LONG I'VE WAITED FOR THIS. HOW HARD IT'S BEEN--
--KNOWING THAT YOU WERE TRAPPED HERE--WHAT THEY WERE DOING TO YOU--THE PAIN YOU WERE IN. BUT THAT'S OVER NOW. WE CAN BE A FAMILY AGAIN NOW.
MOM... WHO IS IN THAT CELL?
SOMEONE WHO CAN FREE US. SOMEONE WHO CAN END ALL THIS--
--AND SOMEONE I LOVE MORE THAN WORDS CAN SAY...

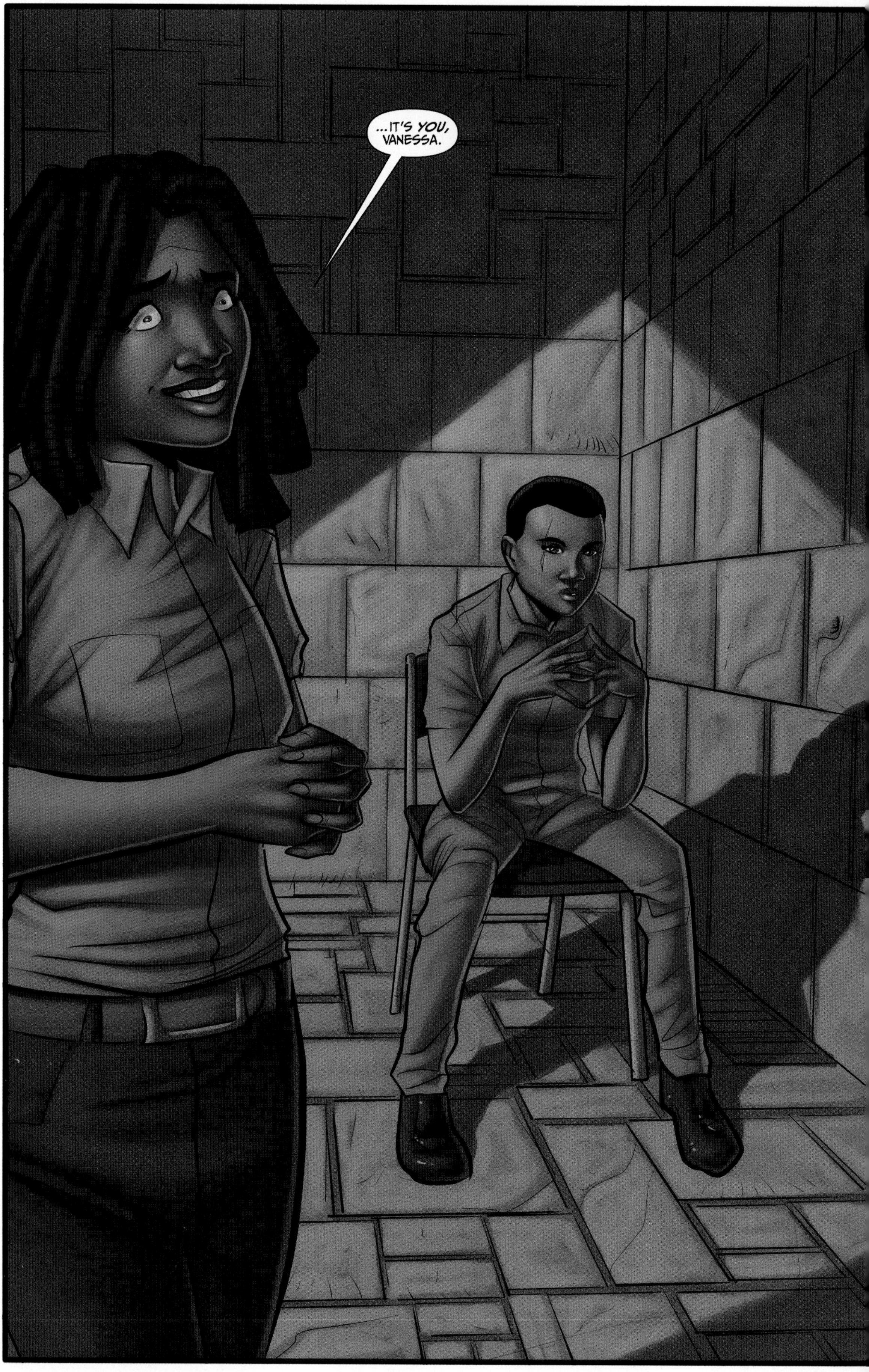
...IT'S *YOU*, VANESSA.

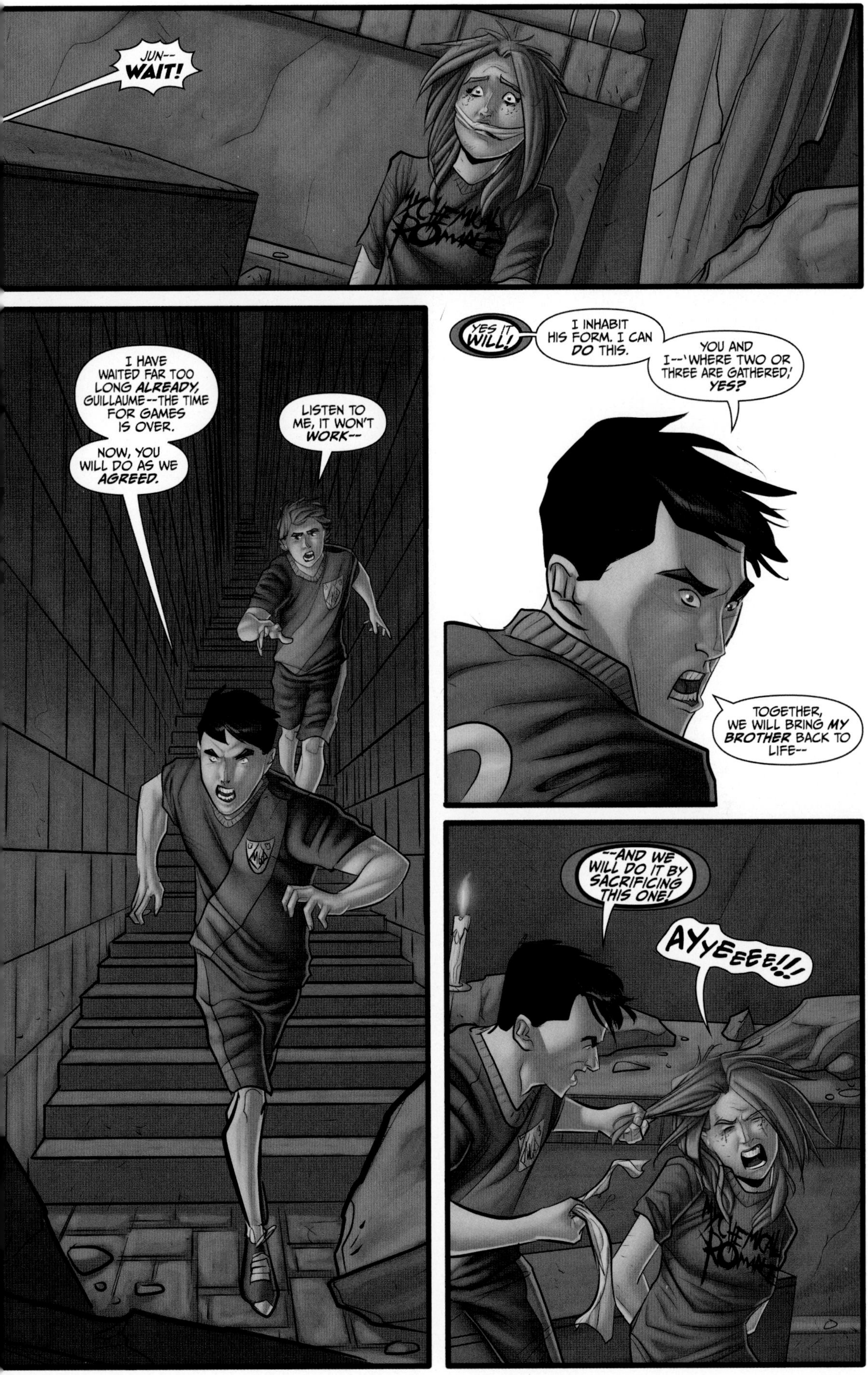
JUN--
WAIT!
I HAVE WAITED FAR TOO LONG ALREADY, GUILLAUME--THE TIME FOR GAMES IS OVER.
NOW, YOU WILL DO AS WE AGREED.
LISTEN TO ME, IT WON'T WORK--
YES IT WILL!
I INHABIT HIS FORM. I CAN DO THIS.
YOU AND I--'WHERE TWO OR THREE ARE GATHERED,' YES?
TOGETHER, WE WILL BRING MY BROTHER BACK TO LIFE--
--AND WE WILL DO IT BY SACRIFICING THIS ONE!
AYYEEEEE!!!

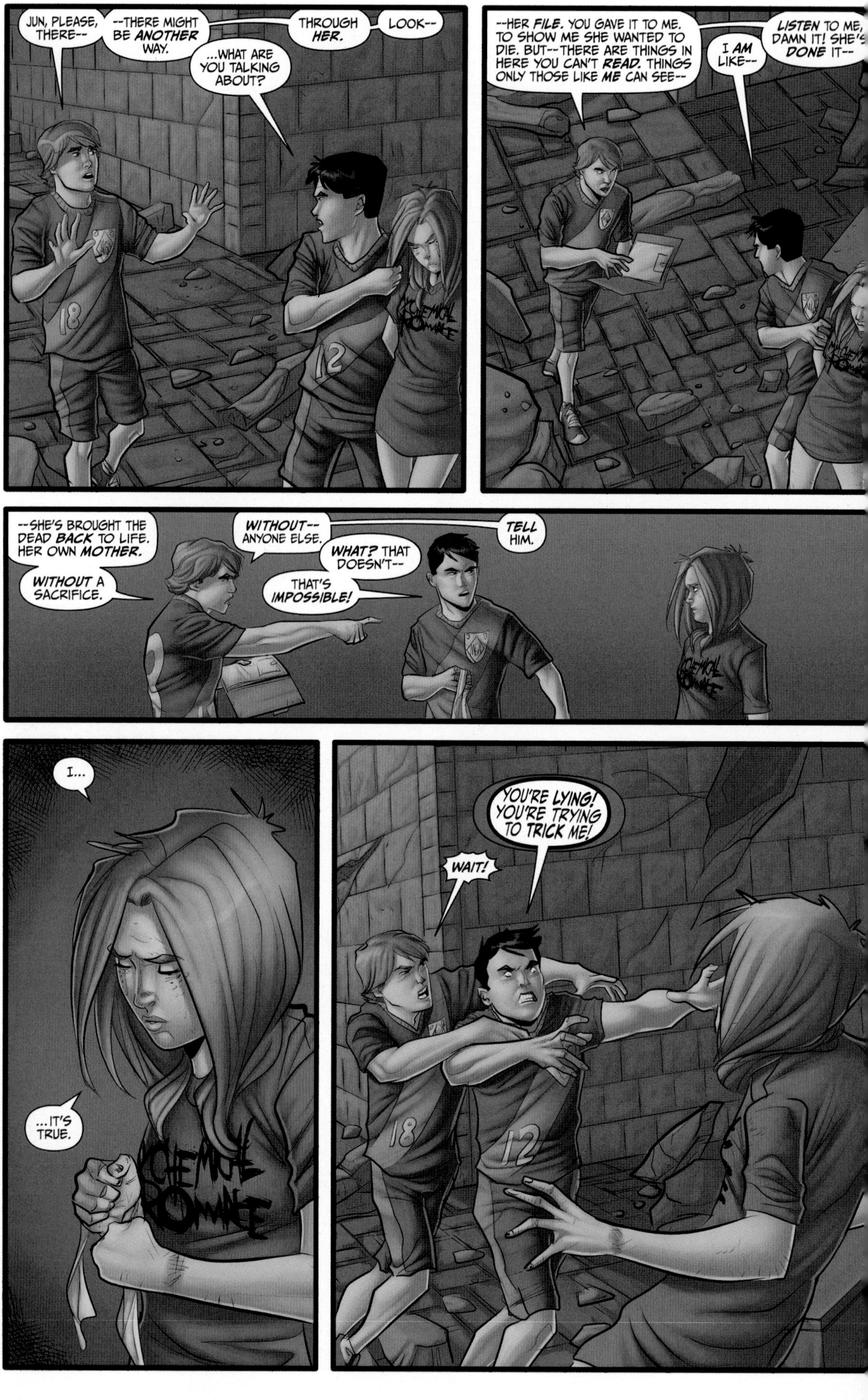
JUN, PLEASE, THERE--
--THERE MIGHT BE ANOTHER WAY.
...WHAT ARE YOU TALKING ABOUT?
THROUGH HER.
LOOK--
--HER FILE. YOU GAVE IT TO ME. TO SHOW ME SHE WANTED TO DIE. BUT--THERE ARE THINGS IN HERE YOU CAN'T READ. THINGS ONLY THOSE LIKE ME CAN SEE--
I AM LIKE--
LISTEN TO ME, DAMN IT! SHE'S DONE IT--
--SHE'S BROUGHT THE DEAD BACK TO LIFE. HER OWN MOTHER.
WITHOUT A SACRIFICE.
WITHOUT-- ANYONE ELSE.
WHAT? THAT DOESN'T--
THAT'S IMPOSSIBLE!
TELL HIM.
I...
...IT'S TRUE.
YOU'RE LYING! YOU'RE TRYING TO TRICK ME!
WAIT!

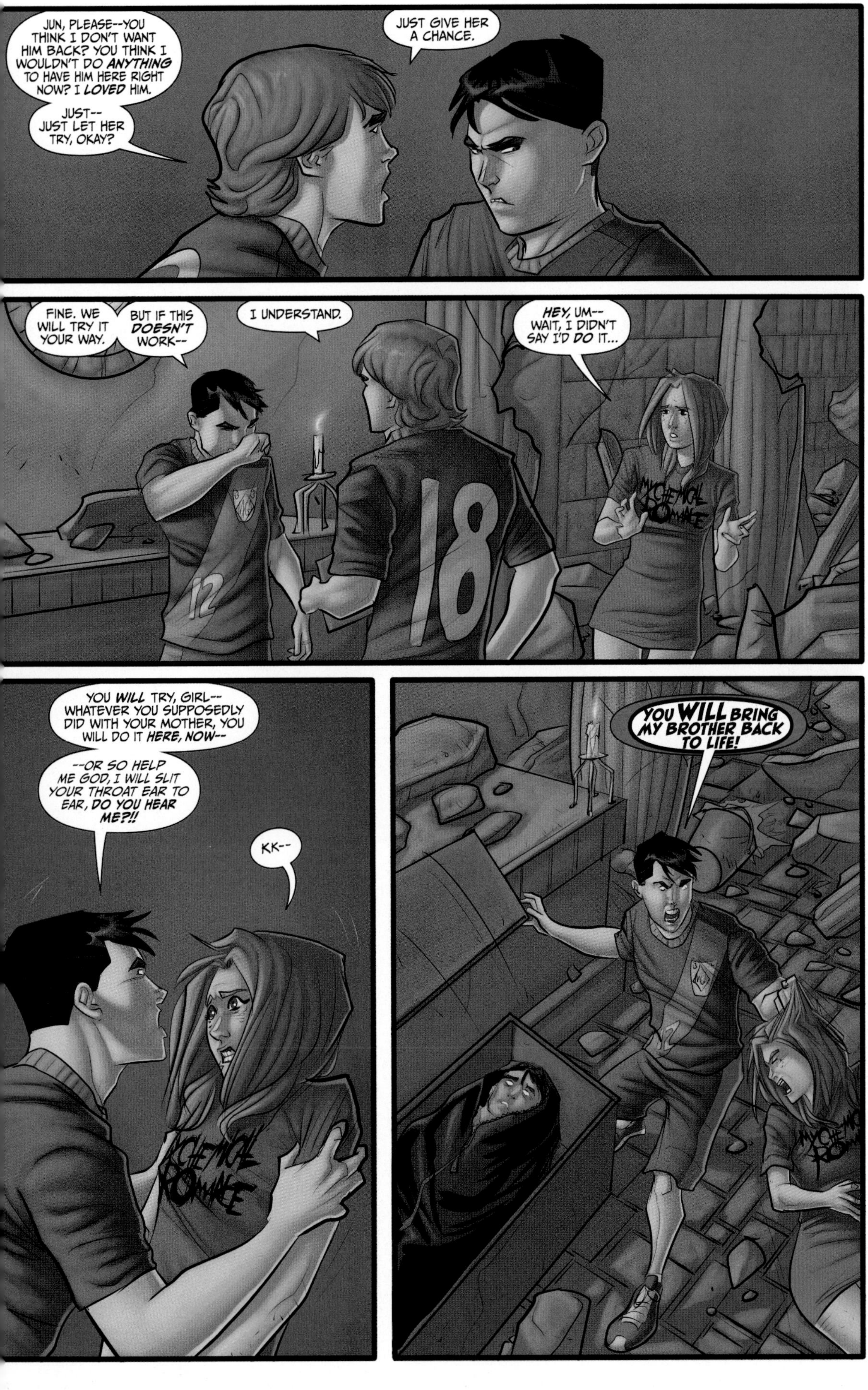
JUN, PLEASE--YOU THINK I DON'T WANT HIM BACK? YOU THINK I WOULDN'T DO ANYTHING TO HAVE HIM HERE RIGHT NOW? I LOVED HIM.
JUST-- JUST LET HER TRY, OKAY?
JUST GIVE HER A CHANCE.
FINE. WE WILL TRY IT YOUR WAY.
BUT IF THIS DOESN'T WORK--
I UNDERSTAND.
HEY, UM-- WAIT, I DIDN'T SAY I'D DO IT...
YOU WILL TRY, GIRL-- WHATEVER YOU SUPPOSEDLY DID WITH YOUR MOTHER, YOU WILL DO IT HERE, NOW--
--OR SO HELP ME GOD, I WILL SLIT YOUR THROAT EAR TO EAR, DO YOU HEAR ME?!!
KK--
YOU WILL BRING MY BROTHER BACK TO LIFE!

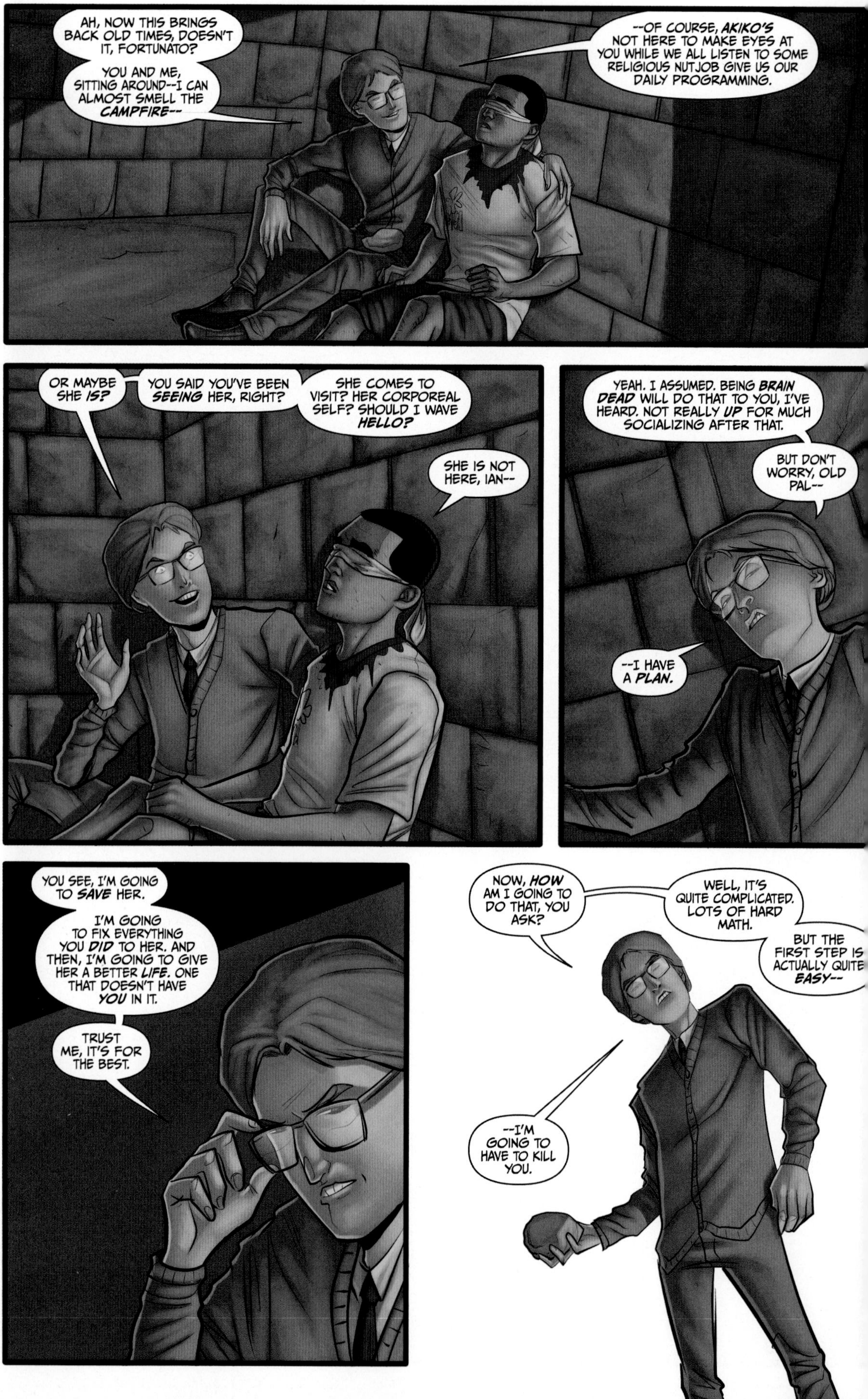
AH, NOW THIS BRINGS BACK OLD TIMES, DOESN'T IT, FORTUNATO?
YOU AND ME, SITTING AROUND--I CAN ALMOST SMELL THE CAMPFIRE--
--OF COURSE, AKIKO'S NOT HERE TO MAKE EYES AT YOU WHILE WE ALL LISTEN TO SOME RELIGIOUS NUTJOB GIVE US OUR DAILY PROGRAMMING.
OR MAYBE SHE IS?
YOU SAID YOU'VE BEEN SEEING HER, RIGHT?
SHE COMES TO VISIT? HER CORPOREAL SELF? SHOULD I WAVE HELLO?
SHE IS NOT HERE, IAN--
YEAH. I ASSUMED. BEING BRAIN DEAD WILL DO THAT TO YOU, I'VE HEARD. NOT REALLY UP FOR MUCH SOCIALIZING AFTER THAT.
BUT DON'T WORRY, OLD PAL--
--I HAVE A PLAN.
YOU SEE, I'M GOING TO SAVE HER.
I'M GOING TO FIX EVERYTHING YOU DID TO HER. AND THEN, I'M GOING TO GIVE HER A BETTER LIFE. ONE THAT DOESN'T HAVE YOU IN IT.
TRUST ME, IT'S FOR THE BEST.
NOW, HOW AM I GOING TO DO THAT, YOU ASK?
WELL, IT'S QUITE COMPLICATED. LOTS OF HARD MATH.
BUT THE FIRST STEP IS ACTUALLY QUITE EASY--
--I'M GOING TO HAVE TO KILL YOU.

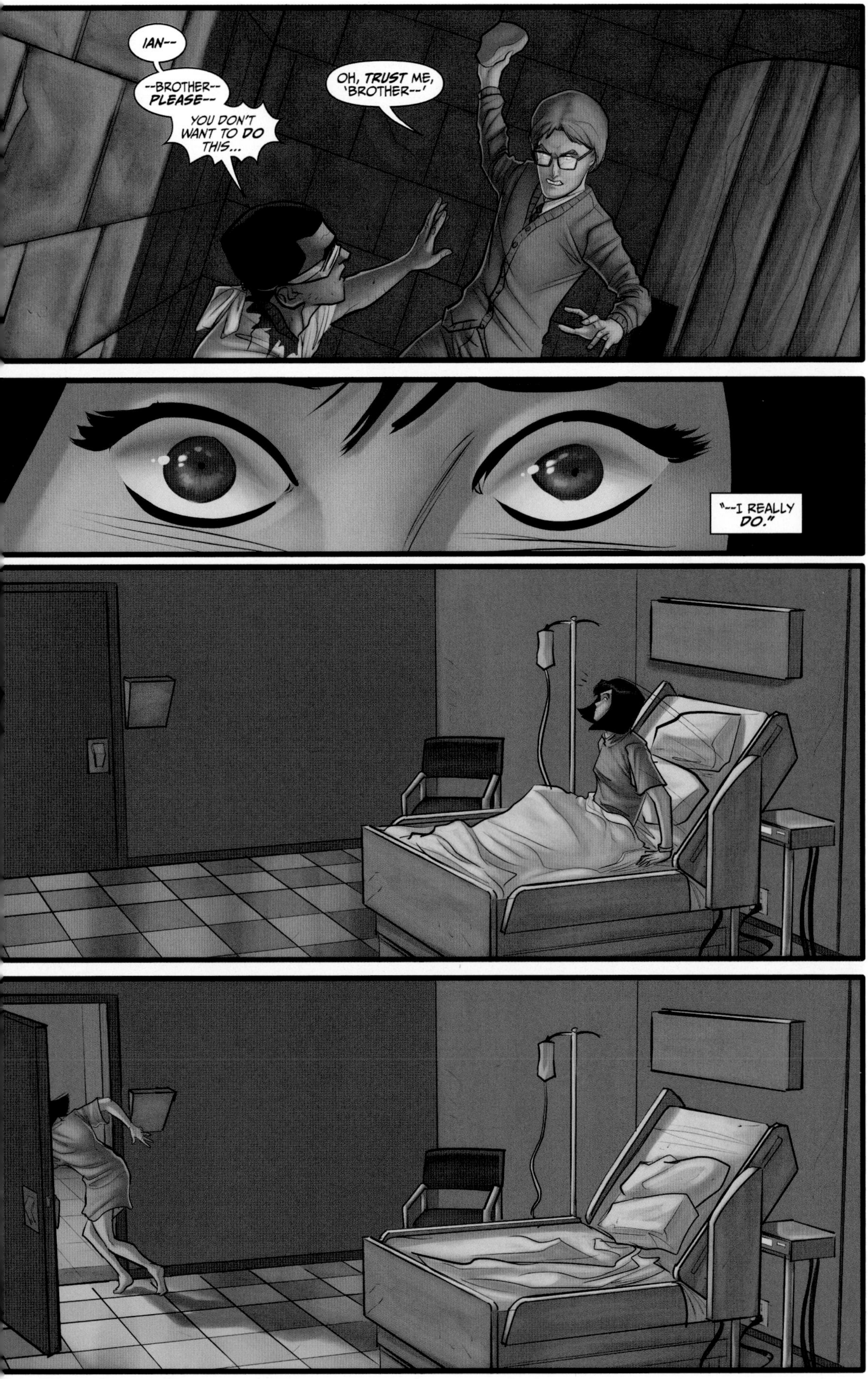
IAN--
--BROTHER--
PLEASE--
YOU DON'T WANT TO DO THIS...
OH, TRUST ME, 'BROTHER--'
"--I REALLY DO."

STOP THIS, ALL RIGHT? STOP IT *NOW.*

YOU MEAN YOU DON'T WANT TO SEE HOW IT ENDS?

YOU HAVE TO LET ME HELP THEM. AND YOU--YOU HAVE TO LET US GO.

OKAY, WELL *NOW* I FEEL LIKE YOU'RE BACKTRACKING A BIT. I MEAN YOU *CAME* HERE PROMISING VIOLENT INSURRECTION.

NOW YOU'RE BASICALLY ASKING FOR MY *HELP.* BUT THEN--

--KIND OF INCREDIBLE WHAT A LITTLE EXTRA *INSIGHT* CAN DO TO YOUR PERSPECTIVE, RIGHT?

IT'S ALMOST LIKE YOU DON'T *KNOW* EVERYTHING.

MAYBE NOT. BUT ONE THING I *DO* KNOW--

--YOU'RE A SICK FUCKING *MONSTER.* AND YOU'D HAVE KILLED *ME* AND EVERYONE *ELSE* THE SECOND YOU LAID EYES ON US IF YOU DIDN'T NEED SOMETHING FROM US.

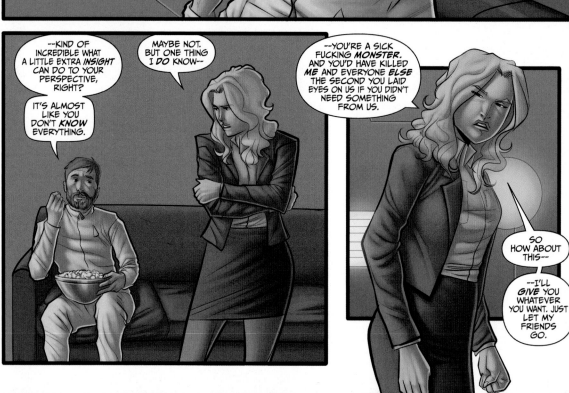

SO HOW ABOUT THIS--

--I'LL *GIVE* YOU WHATEVER YOU WANT. JUST LET MY FRIENDS GO.

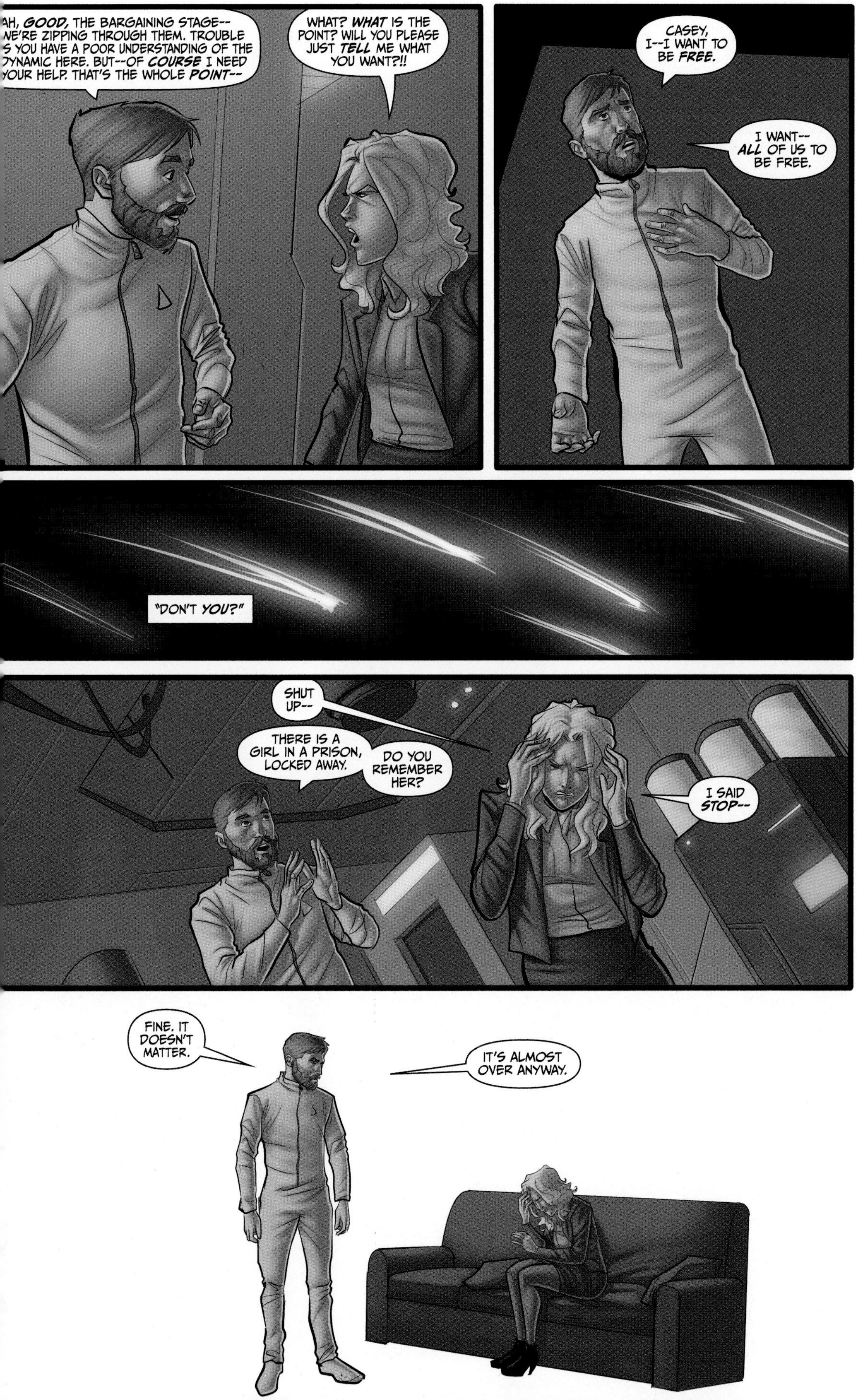
AH, GOOD, THE BARGAINING STAGE-- WE'RE ZIPPING THROUGH THEM. TROUBLE IS YOU HAVE A POOR UNDERSTANDING OF THE DYNAMIC HERE. BUT--OF COURSE I NEED YOUR HELP. THAT'S THE WHOLE POINT--
WHAT? WHAT IS THE POINT? WILL YOU PLEASE JUST TELL ME WHAT YOU WANT?!!
CASEY, I--I WANT TO BE FREE.
I WANT-- ALL OF US TO BE FREE.
"DON'T YOU?"
SHUT UP--
THERE IS A GIRL IN A PRISON, LOCKED AWAY.
DO YOU REMEMBER HER?
I SAID STOP--
FINE. IT DOESN'T MATTER.
IT'S ALMOST OVER ANYWAY.

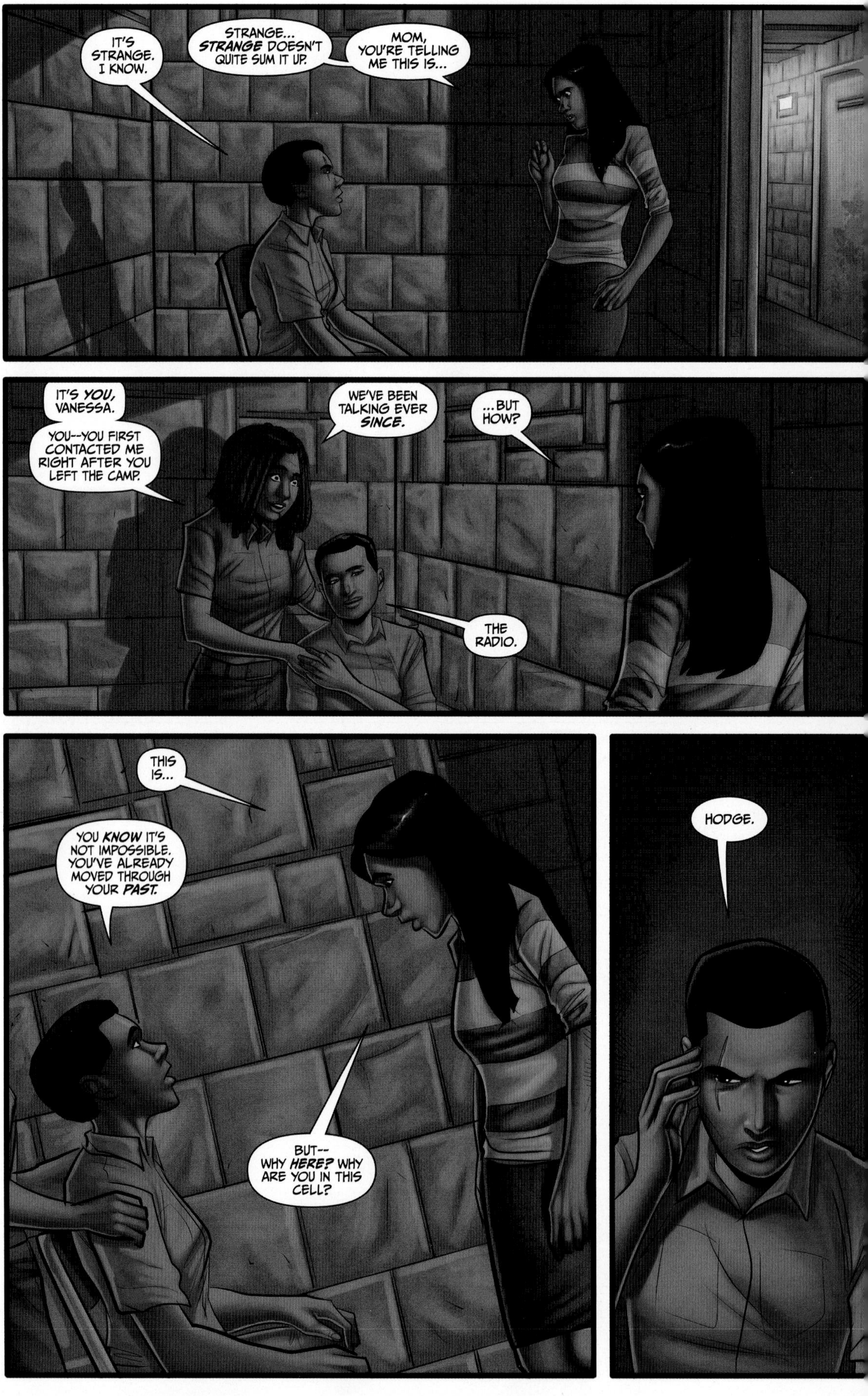
IT'S STRANGE. I KNOW.
STRANGE... STRANGE DOESN'T QUITE SUM IT UP.
MOM, YOU'RE TELLING ME THIS IS...
IT'S YOU, VANESSA.
YOU--YOU FIRST CONTACTED ME RIGHT AFTER YOU LEFT THE CAMP.
WE'VE BEEN TALKING EVER SINCE.
...BUT HOW?
THE RADIO.
THIS IS...
YOU KNOW IT'S NOT IMPOSSIBLE. YOU'VE ALREADY MOVED THROUGH YOUR PAST.
BUT-- WHY HERE? WHY ARE YOU IN THIS CELL?
HODGE.

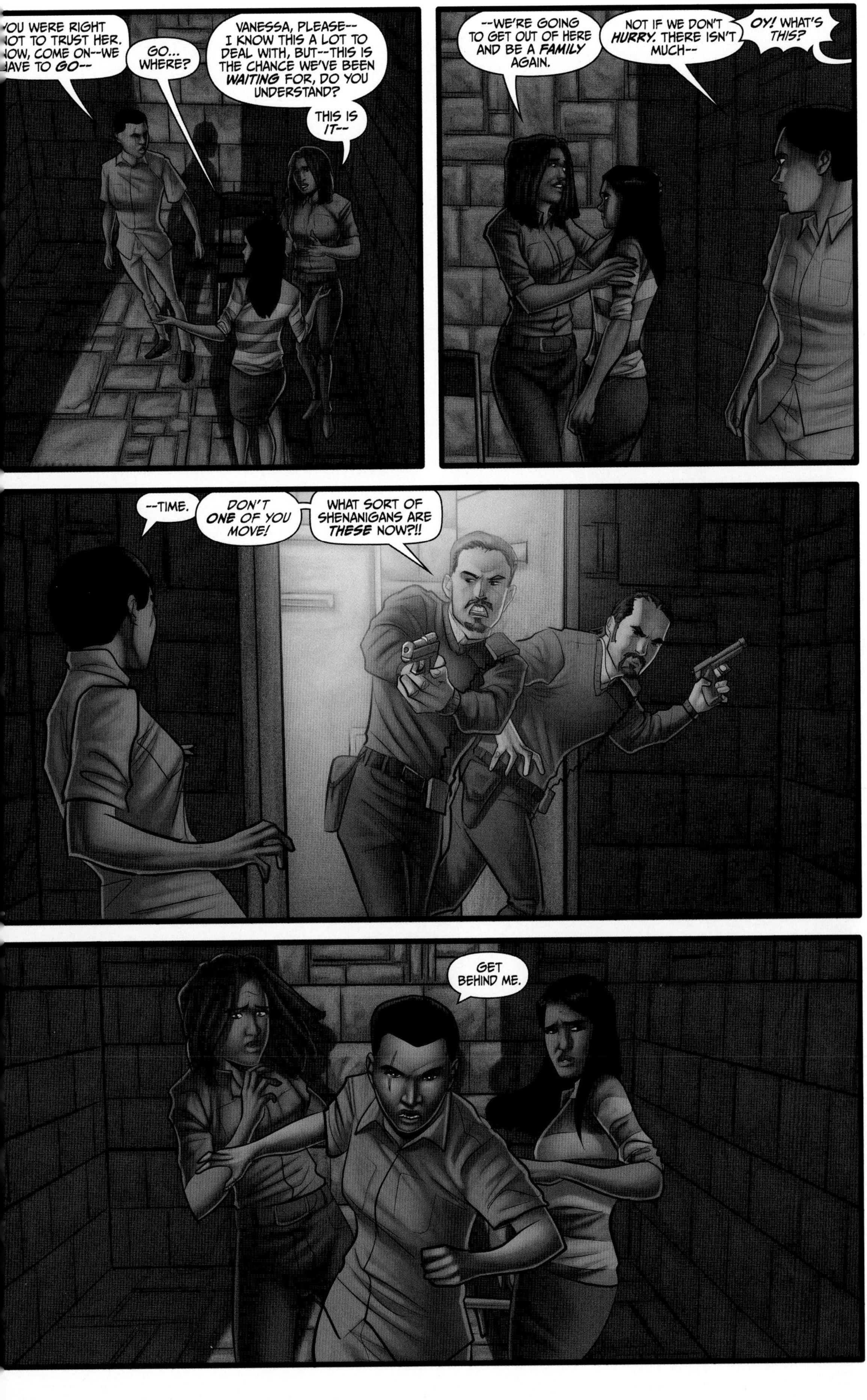
YOU WERE RIGHT NOT TO TRUST HER. NOW, COME ON--WE HAVE TO GO--
GO... WHERE?
VANESSA, PLEASE-- I KNOW THIS A LOT TO DEAL WITH, BUT--THIS IS THE CHANCE WE'VE BEEN WAITING FOR, DO YOU UNDERSTAND?
THIS IS IT--
--WE'RE GOING TO GET OUT OF HERE AND BE A FAMILY AGAIN.
NOT IF WE DON'T HURRY. THERE ISN'T MUCH--
OY! WHAT'S THIS?
--TIME.
DON'T ONE OF YOU MOVE!
WHAT SORT OF SHENANIGANS ARE THESE NOW?!!
GET BEHIND ME.

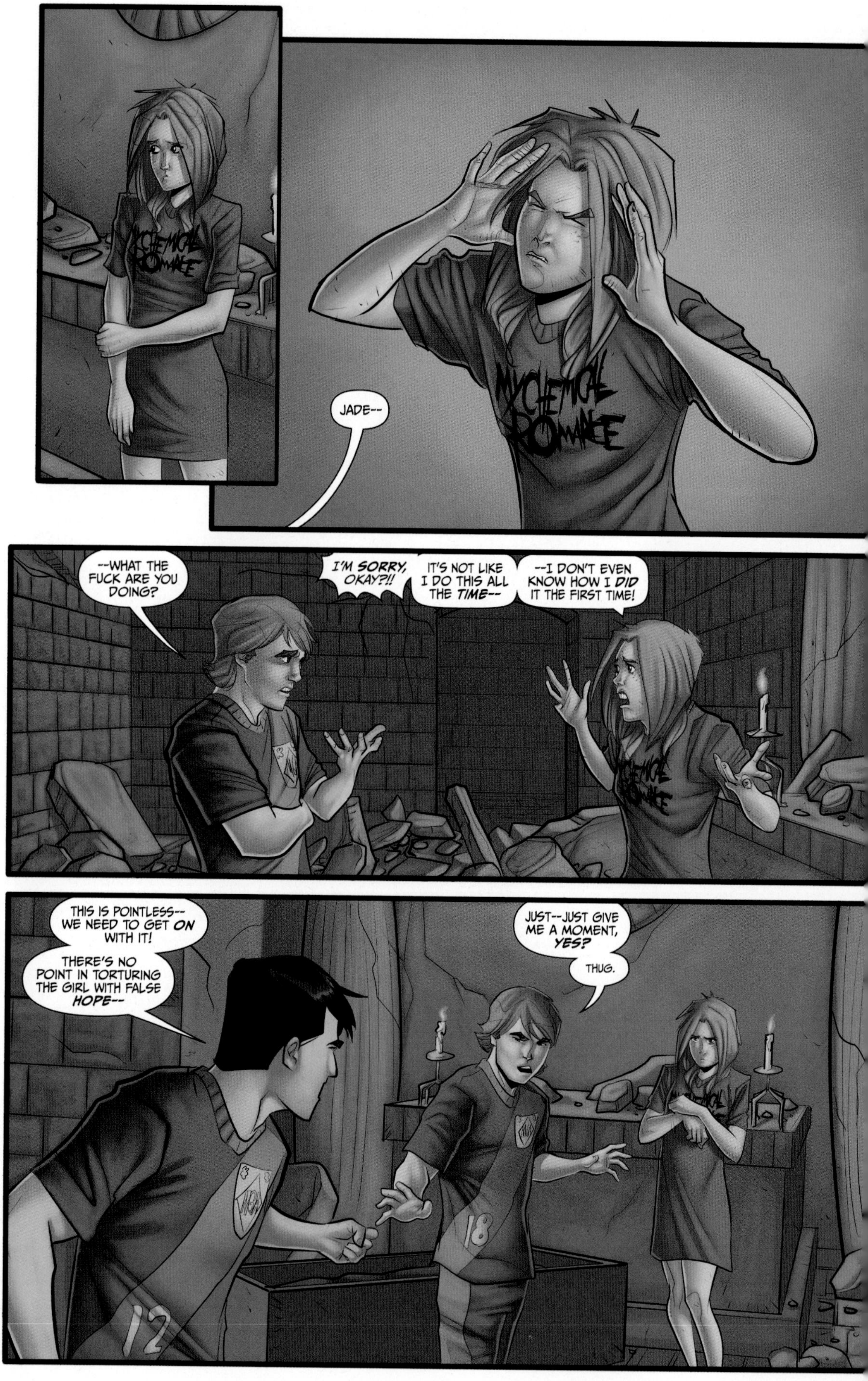

JADE--
--WHAT THE FUCK ARE YOU DOING?
I'M *SORRY,* OKAY?!!
IT'S NOT LIKE I DO THIS ALL THE *TIME*--
--I DON'T EVEN KNOW HOW I *DID* IT THE FIRST TIME!
THIS IS POINTLESS-- WE NEED TO GET *ON* WITH IT!
THERE'S NO POINT IN TORTURING THE GIRL WITH FALSE *HOPE*--
JUST--JUST GIVE ME A MOMENT, *YES?*
THUG.

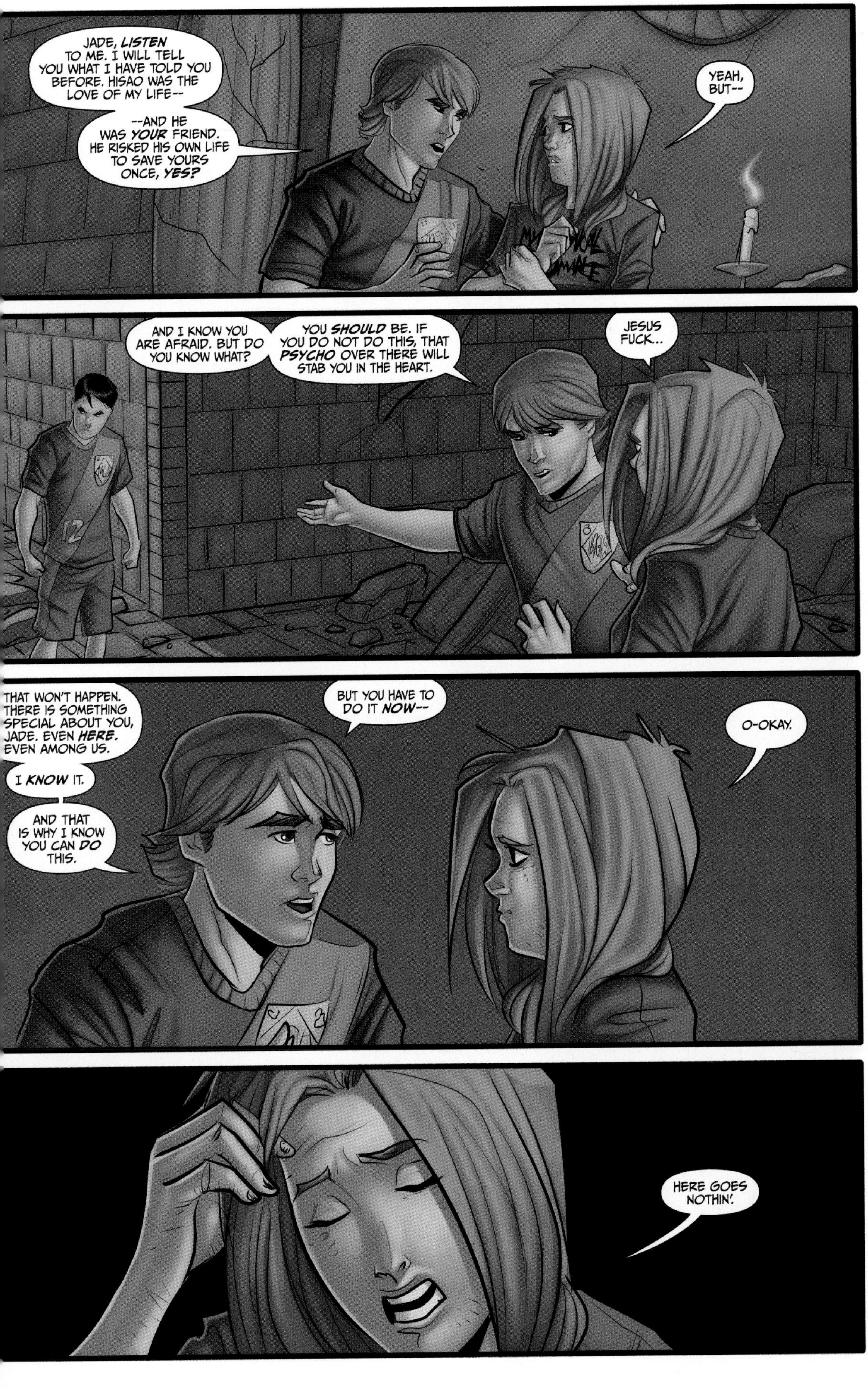

JADE, LISTEN TO ME. I WILL TELL YOU WHAT I HAVE TOLD YOU BEFORE. HISAO WAS THE LOVE OF MY LIFE--
--AND HE WAS YOUR FRIEND. HE RISKED HIS OWN LIFE TO SAVE YOURS ONCE, YES?
YEAH, BUT--
AND I KNOW YOU ARE AFRAID. BUT DO YOU KNOW WHAT?
YOU SHOULD BE. IF YOU DO NOT DO THIS, THAT PSYCHO OVER THERE WILL STAB YOU IN THE HEART.
JESUS FUCK...
THAT WON'T HAPPEN. THERE IS SOMETHING SPECIAL ABOUT YOU, JADE. EVEN HERE. EVEN AMONG US.
I KNOW IT.
AND THAT IS WHY I KNOW YOU CAN DO THIS.
BUT YOU HAVE TO DO IT NOW--
O-OKAY.
HERE GOES NOTHIN'.

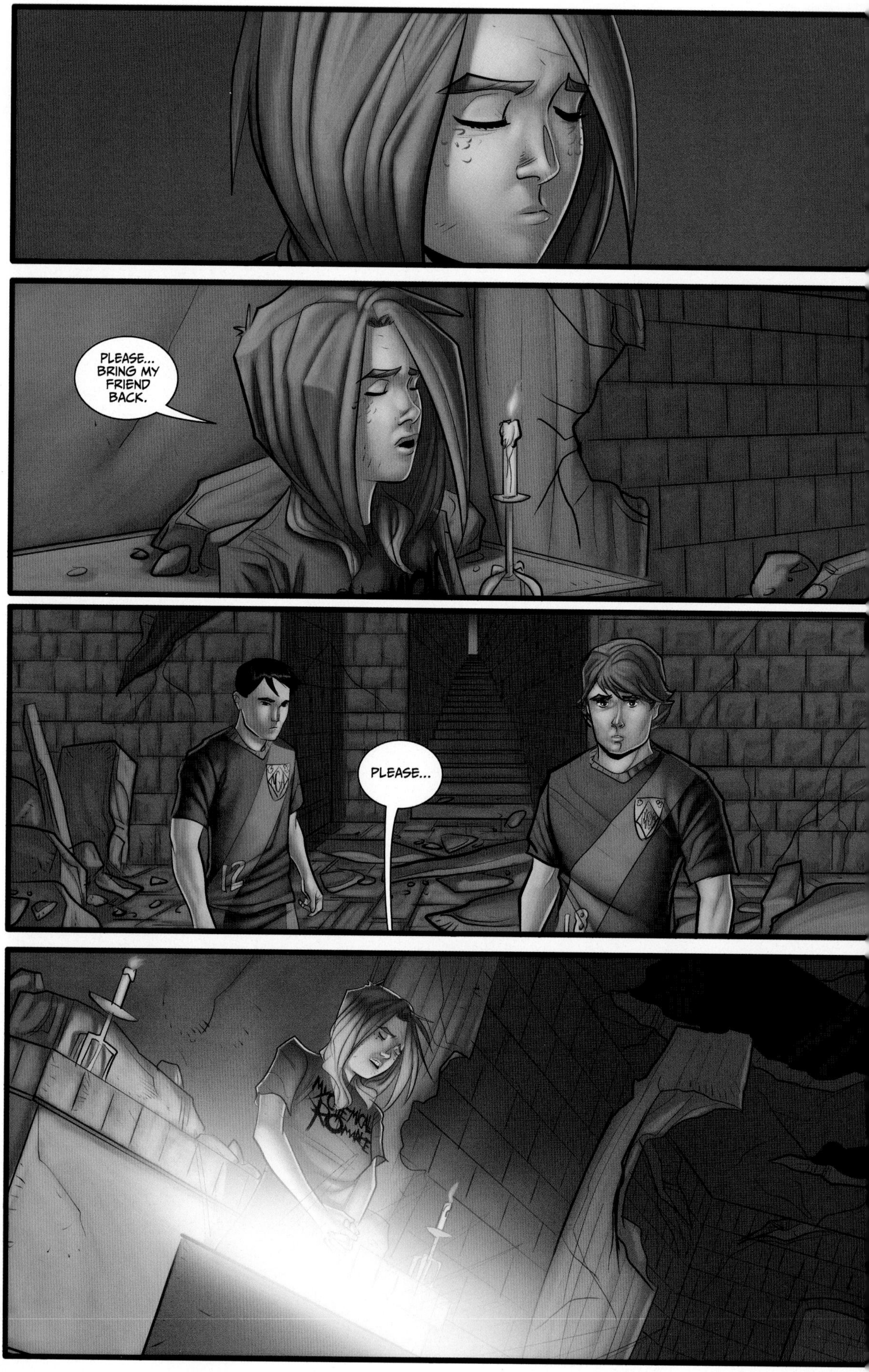
PLEASE... BRING MY FRIEND BACK.
PLEASE...

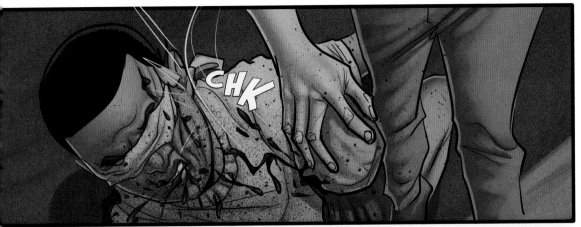

CHK

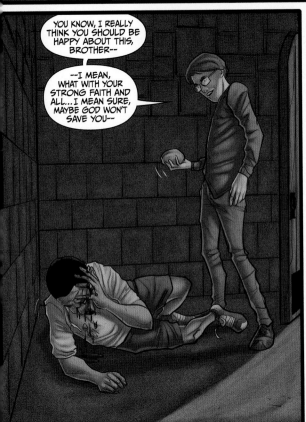

YOU KNOW, I REALLY THINK YOU SHOULD BE HAPPY ABOUT THIS, BROTHER--

--I MEAN, WHAT WITH YOUR STRONG FAITH AND ALL...I MEAN SURE, MAYBE GOD WON'T SAVE YOU--

TOK

--WELL, *DEFINITELY* WON'T SAVE YOU, SEEING AS WE KNOW HOW *THAT* WORKS.

BUT YOU DO GET THE NEXT BEST THING--

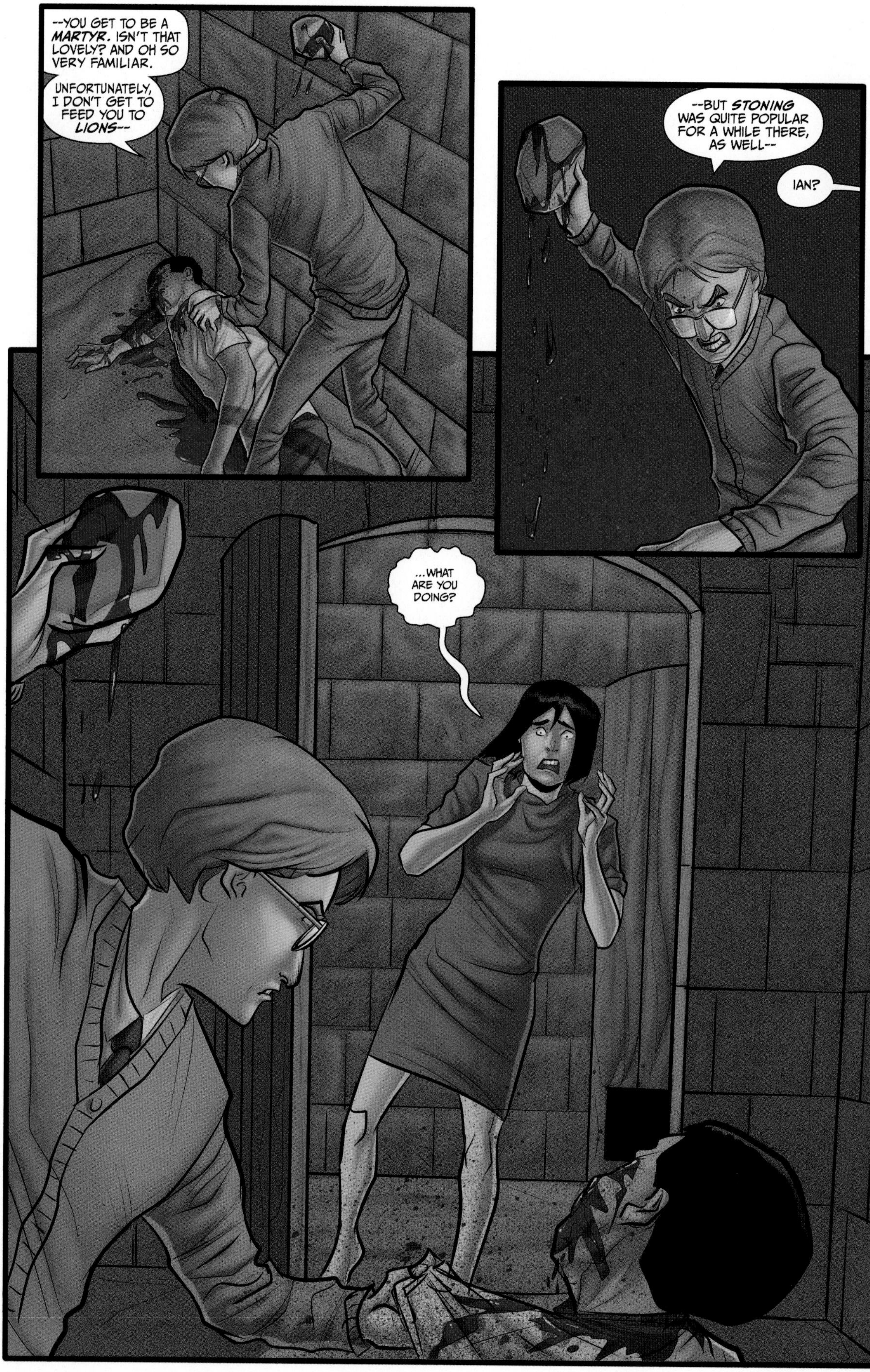
--YOU GET TO BE A MARTYR. ISN'T THAT LOVELY? AND OH SO VERY FAMILIAR.
UNFORTUNATELY, I DON'T GET TO FEED YOU TO LIONS--
--BUT STONING WAS QUITE POPULAR FOR A WHILE THERE, AS WELL--
IAN?
...WHAT ARE YOU DOING?

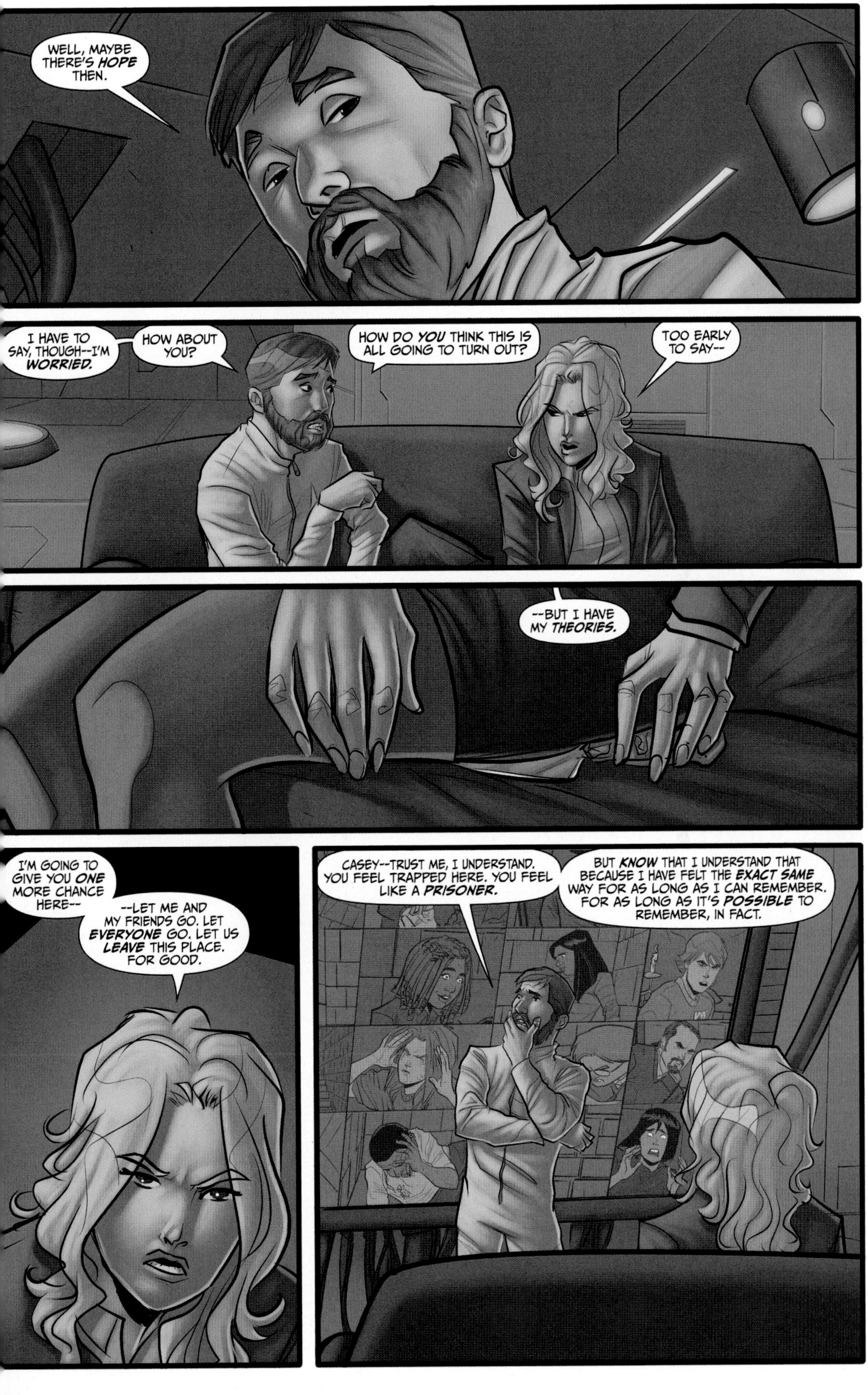
WELL, MAYBE THERE'S *HOPE* THEN.
I HAVE TO SAY, THOUGH--I'M *WORRIED.*
HOW ABOUT YOU?
HOW DO *YOU* THINK THIS IS ALL GOING TO TURN OUT?
TOO EARLY TO SAY--
--BUT I HAVE MY *THEORIES.*
I'M GOING TO GIVE YOU *ONE* MORE CHANCE HERE--
--LET ME AND MY FRIENDS GO. LET *EVERYONE* GO. LET US *LEAVE* THIS PLACE. FOR GOOD.
CASEY--TRUST ME, I UNDERSTAND. YOU FEEL TRAPPED HERE. YOU FEEL LIKE A *PRISONER.*
BUT *KNOW* THAT I UNDERSTAND THAT BECAUSE I HAVE FELT THE *EXACT SAME* WAY FOR AS LONG AS I CAN REMEMBER. FOR AS LONG AS IT'S *POSSIBLE* TO REMEMBER, IN FACT.

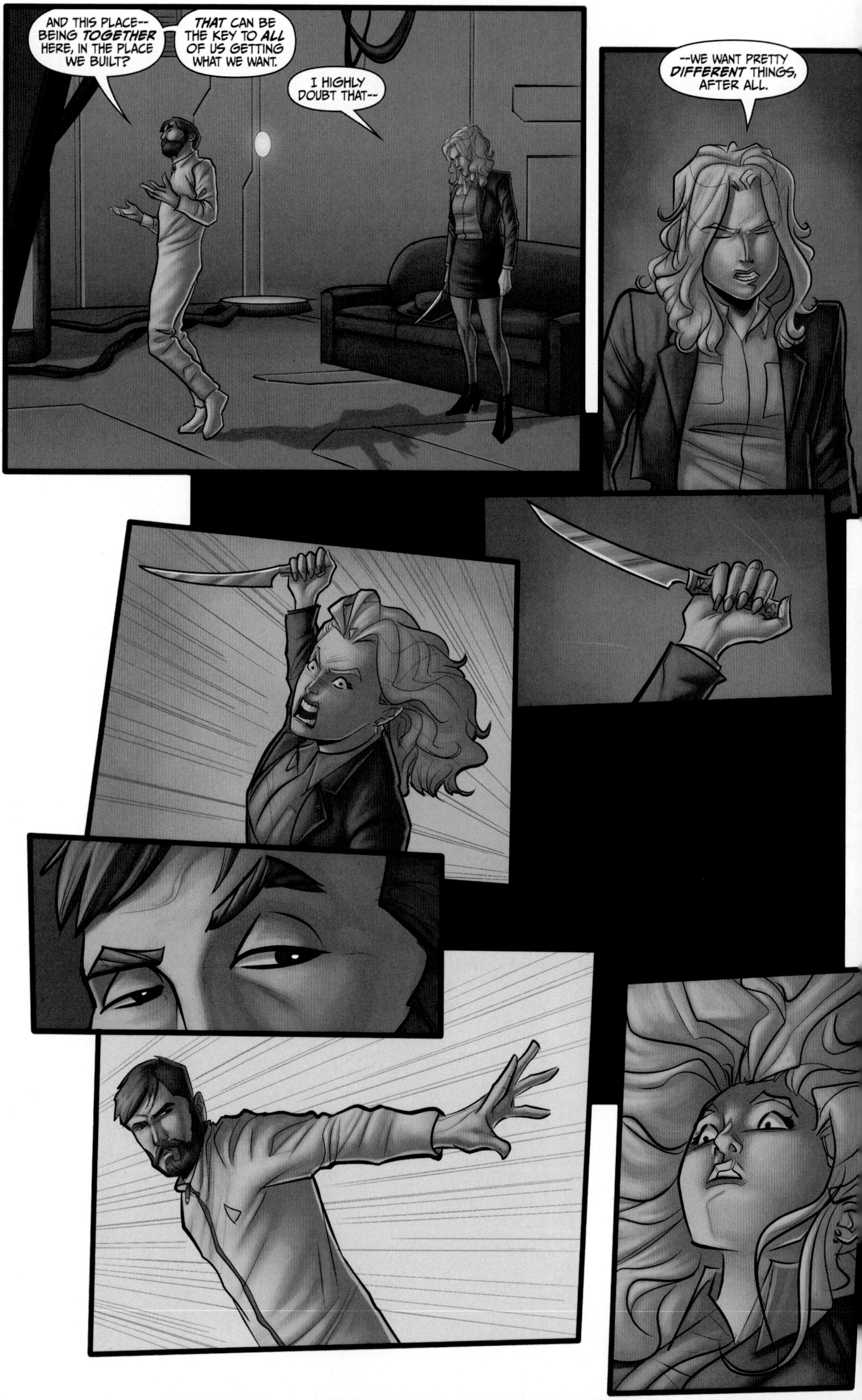
AND THIS PLACE-- BEING TOGETHER HERE, IN THE PLACE WE BUILT?
THAT CAN BE THE KEY TO ALL OF US GETTING WHAT WE WANT.
I HIGHLY DOUBT THAT--
--WE WANT PRETTY DIFFERENT THINGS, AFTER ALL.

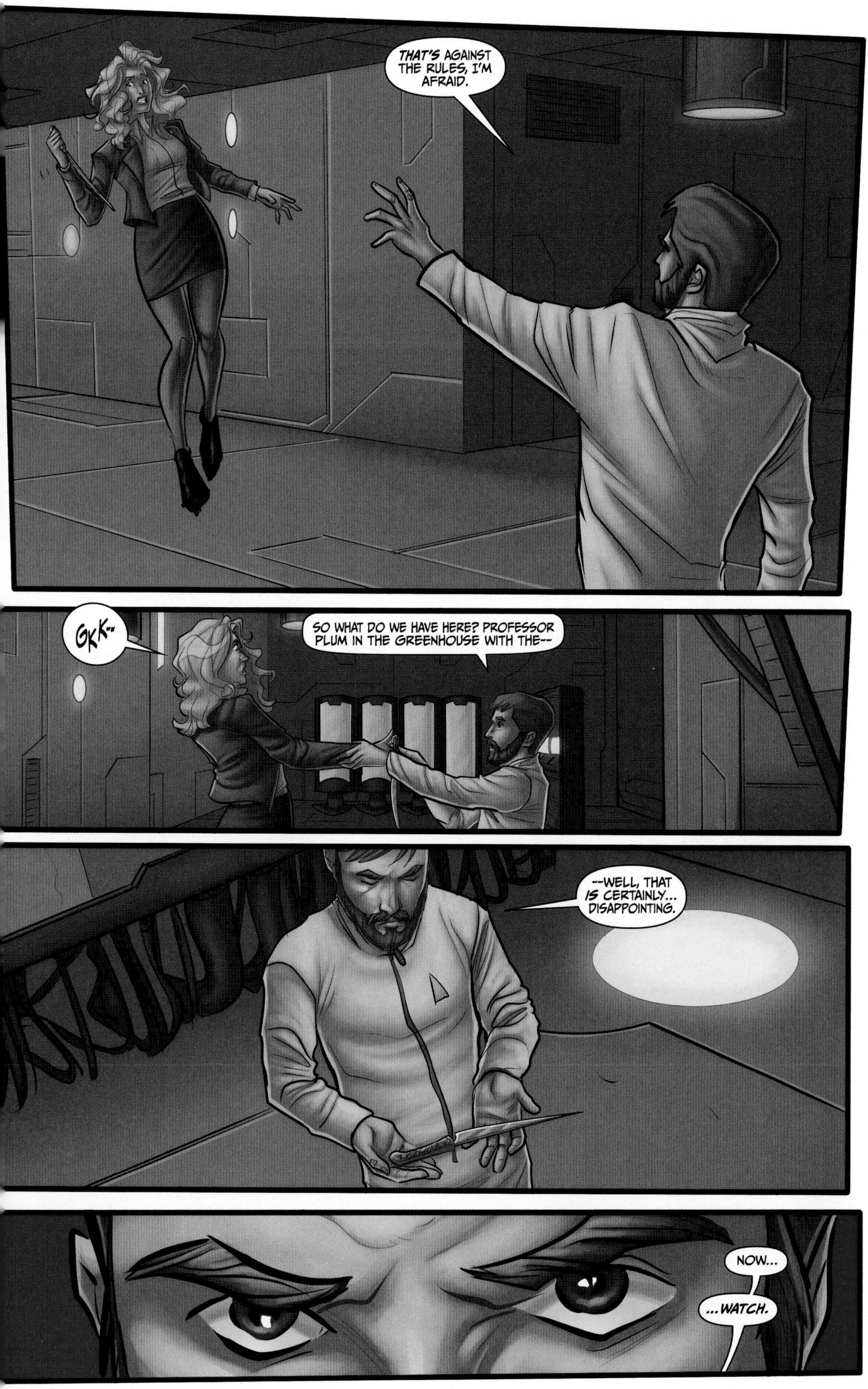
THAT'S AGAINST THE RULES, I'M AFRAID.
GKK--
SO WHAT DO WE HAVE HERE? PROFESSOR PLUM IN THE GREENHOUSE WITH THE--
--WELL, THAT IS CERTAINLY... DISAPPOINTING.
NOW...
...WATCH.

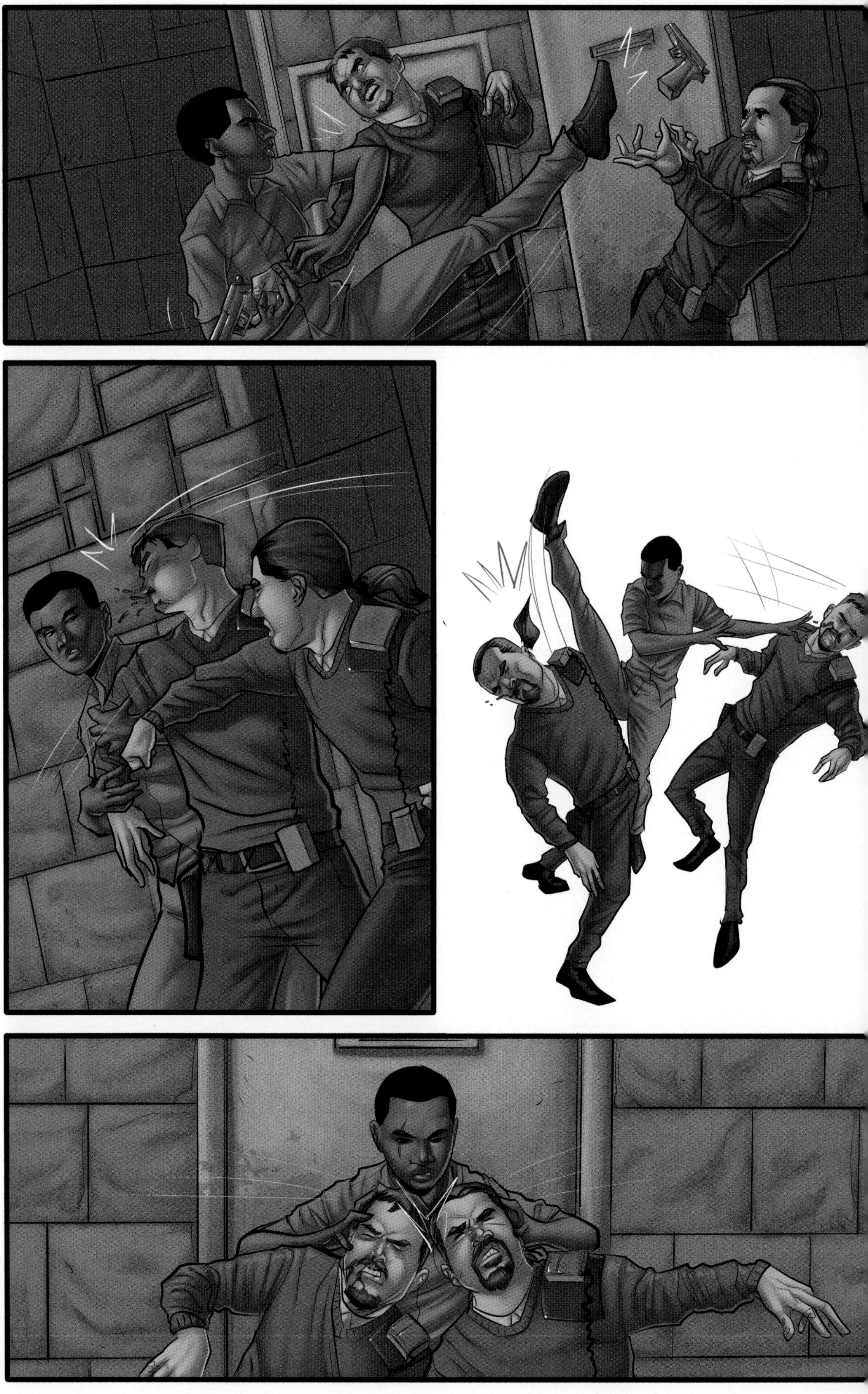

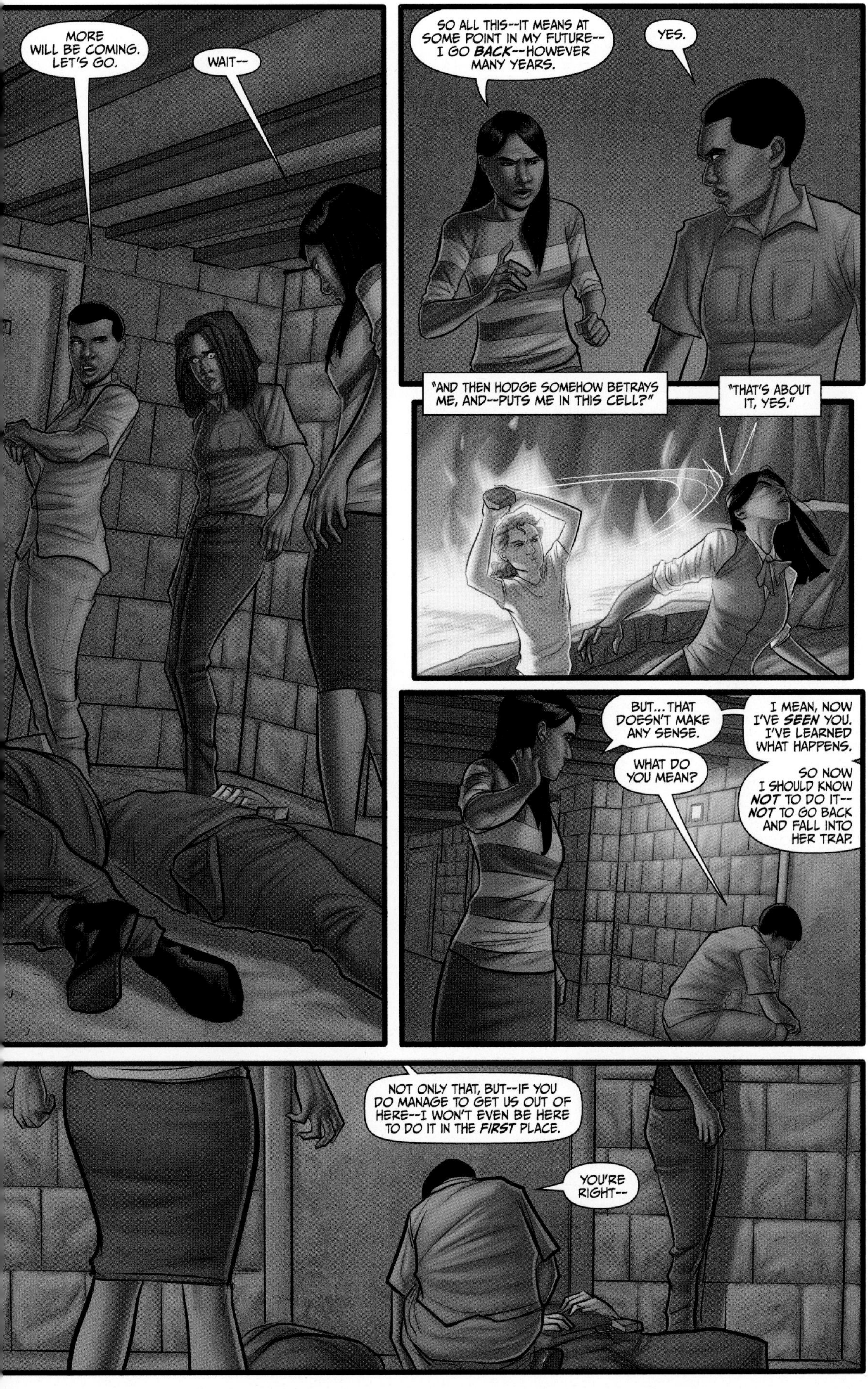
MORE WILL BE COMING. LET'S GO.
WAIT--
SO ALL THIS--IT MEANS AT SOME POINT IN MY FUTURE--I GO BACK--HOWEVER MANY YEARS.
YES.
"AND THEN HODGE SOMEHOW BETRAYS ME, AND--PUTS ME IN THIS CELL?"
"THAT'S ABOUT IT, YES."
BUT... THAT DOESN'T MAKE ANY SENSE.
I MEAN, NOW I'VE SEEN YOU. I'VE LEARNED WHAT HAPPENS.
SO NOW I SHOULD KNOW NOT TO DO IT--NOT TO GO BACK AND FALL INTO HER TRAP.
WHAT DO YOU MEAN?
NOT ONLY THAT, BUT--IF YOU DO MANAGE TO GET US OUT OF HERE--I WON'T EVEN BE HERE TO DO IT IN THE FIRST PLACE.
YOU'RE RIGHT--

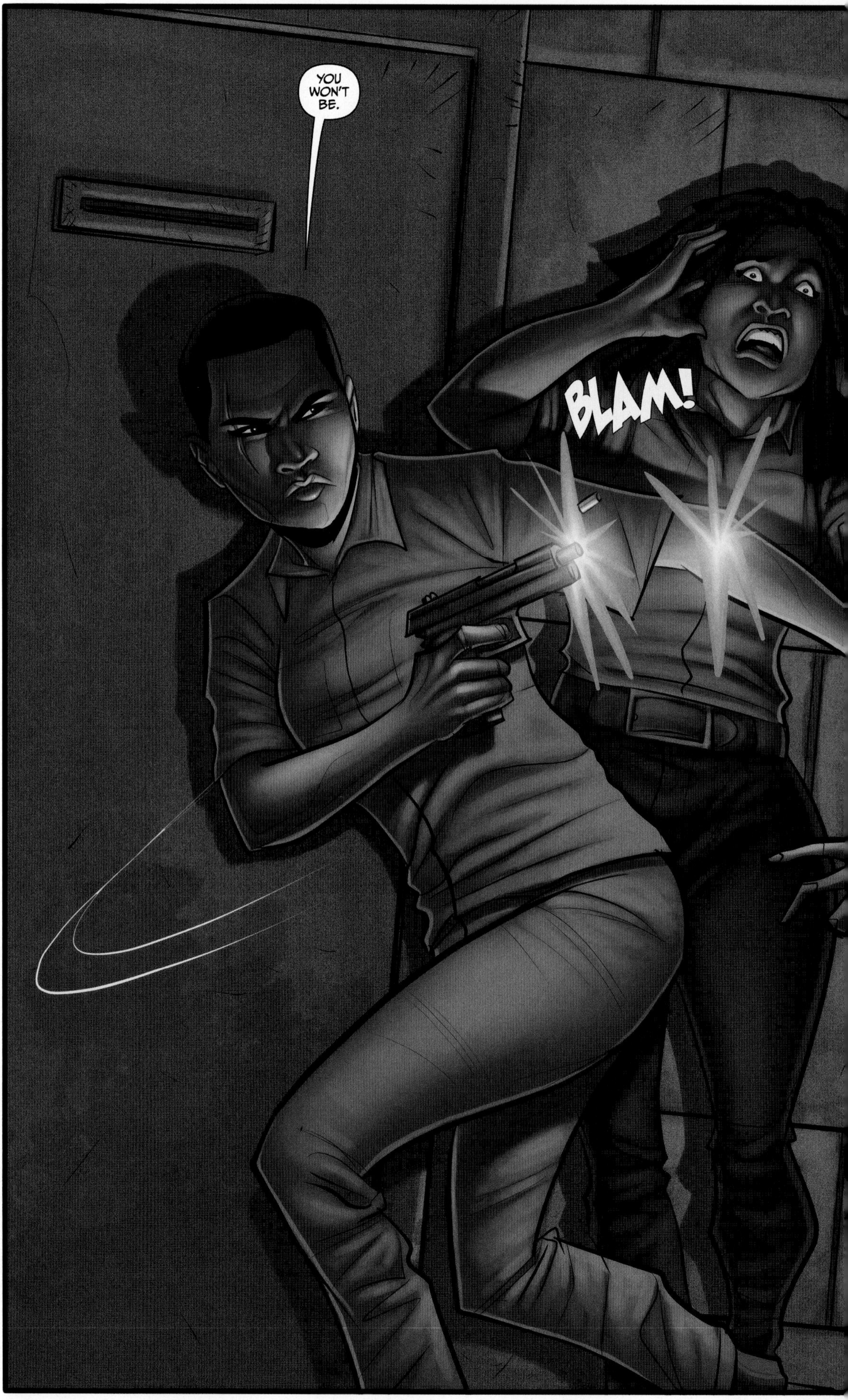
YOU WON'T BE.
BLAM!

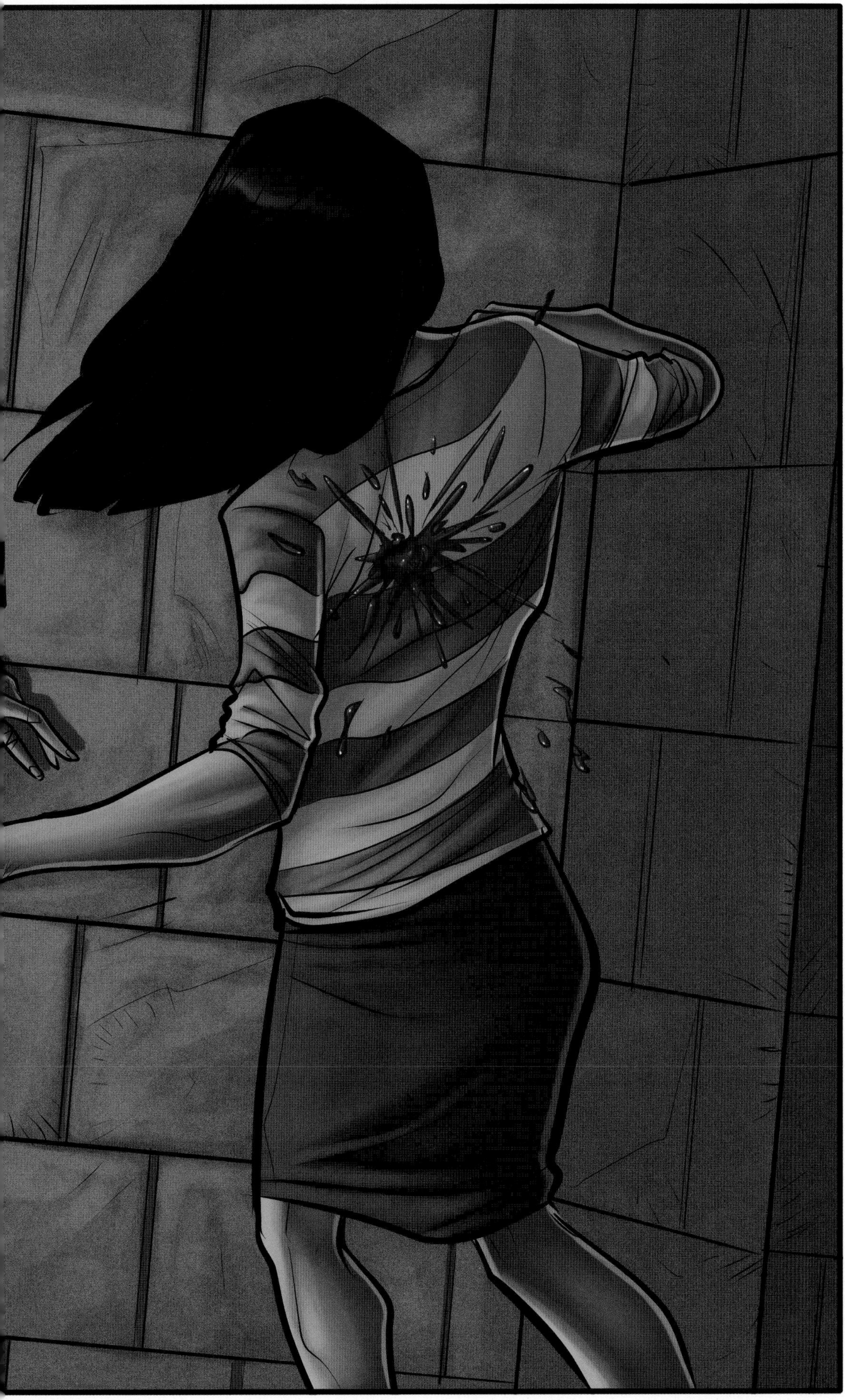

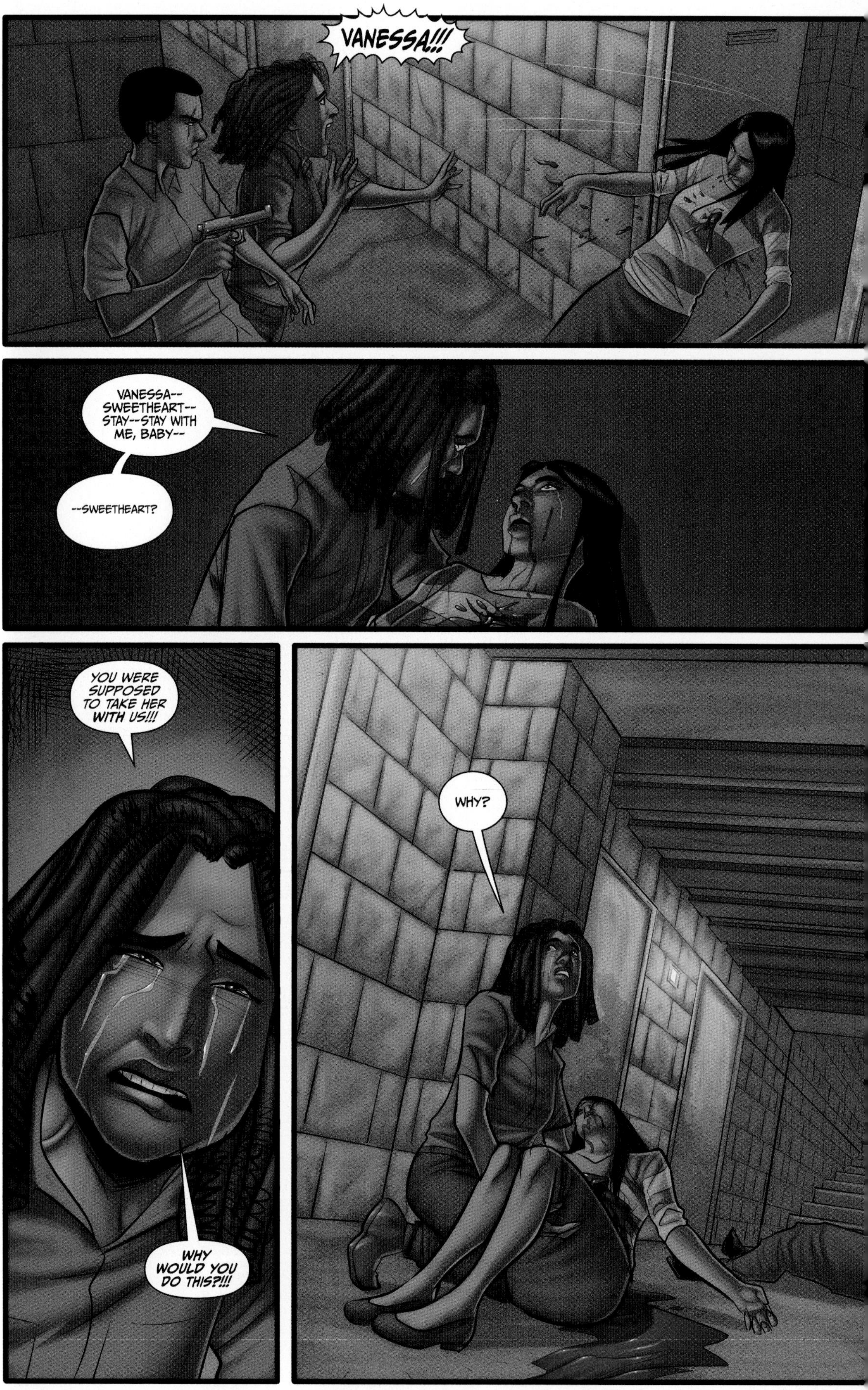
VANESSA!!!
VANESSA-- SWEETHEART-- STAY--STAY WITH ME, BABY--
--SWEETHEART?
YOU WERE SUPPOSED TO TAKE HER WITH US!!!
WHY WOULD YOU DO THIS?!!!
WHY?

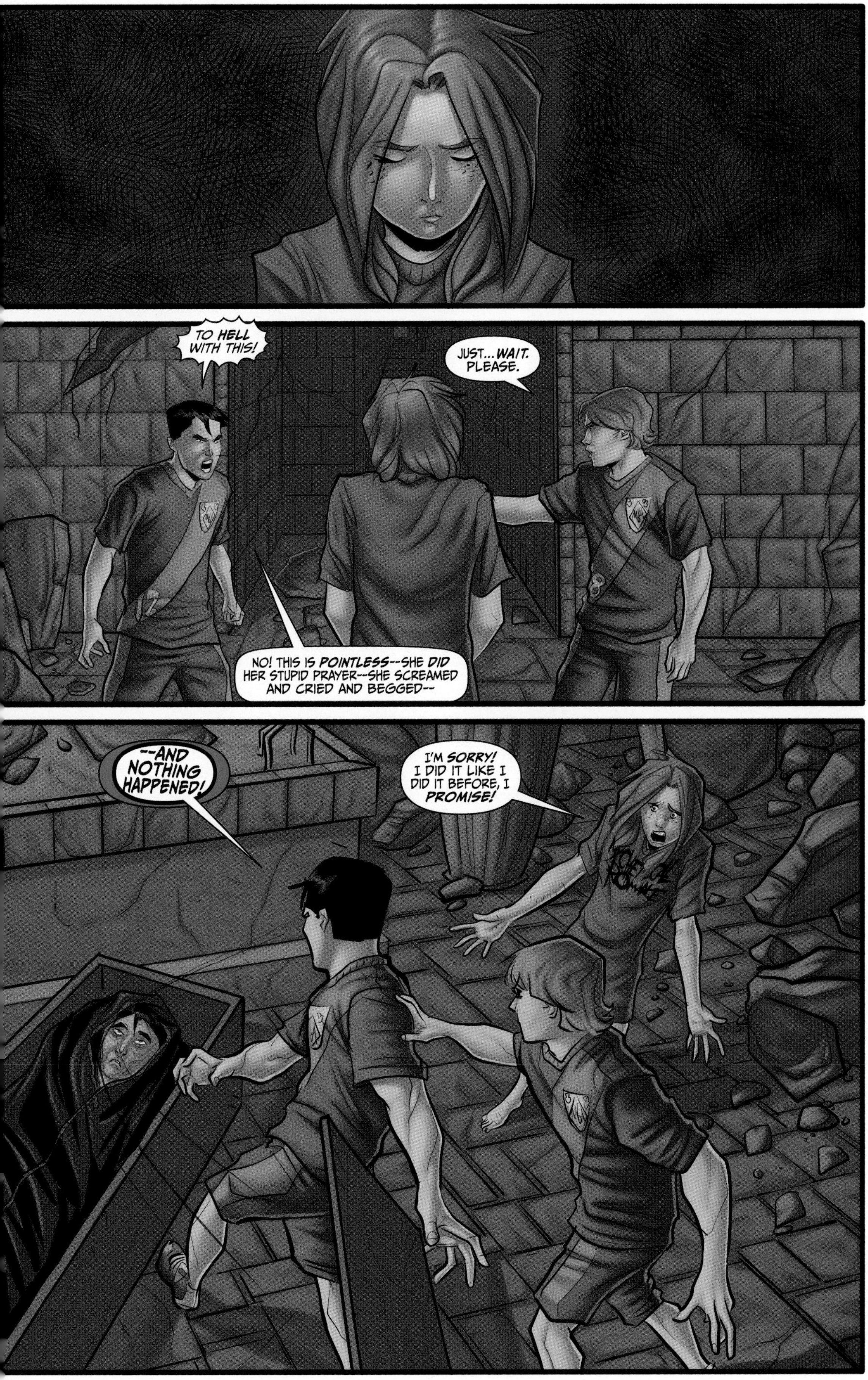

TO HELL WITH THIS!
JUST... WAIT. PLEASE.
NO! THIS IS POINTLESS--SHE DID HER STUPID PRAYER--SHE SCREAMED AND CRIED AND BEGGED--
--AND NOTHING HAPPENED!
I'M SORRY! I DID IT LIKE I DID IT BEFORE, I PROMISE!

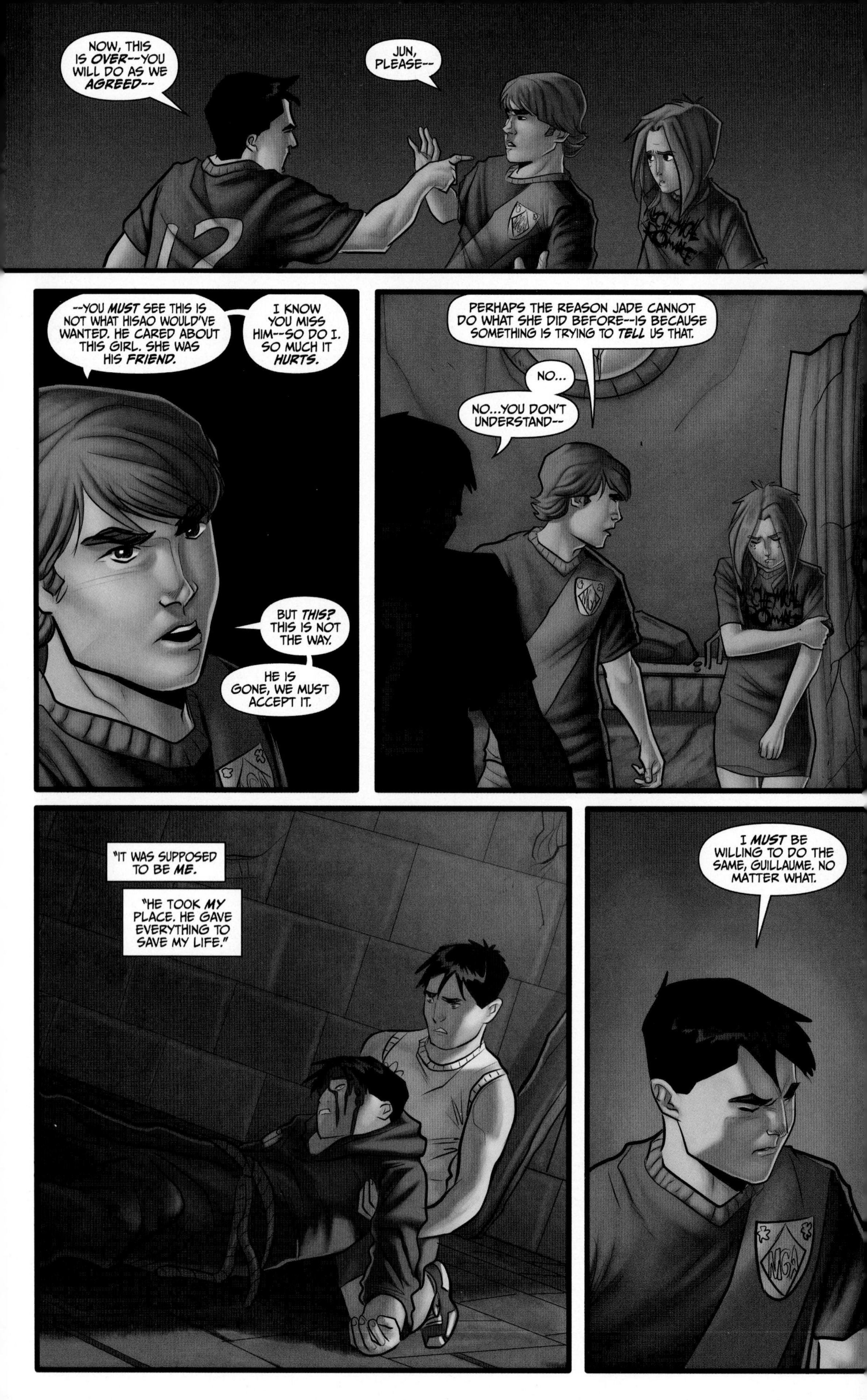
NOW, THIS IS OVER--YOU WILL DO AS WE AGREED--
JUN, PLEASE--
--YOU MUST SEE THIS IS NOT WHAT HISAO WOULD'VE WANTED. HE CARED ABOUT THIS GIRL. SHE WAS HIS FRIEND.
I KNOW YOU MISS HIM--SO DO I. SO MUCH IT HURTS.
BUT THIS? THIS IS NOT THE WAY.
HE IS GONE, WE MUST ACCEPT IT.
PERHAPS THE REASON JADE CANNOT DO WHAT SHE DID BEFORE--IS BECAUSE SOMETHING IS TRYING TO TELL US THAT.
NO...
NO...YOU DON'T UNDERSTAND--
"IT WAS SUPPOSED TO BE ME.
"HE TOOK MY PLACE. HE GAVE EVERYTHING TO SAVE MY LIFE."
I MUST BE WILLING TO DO THE SAME, GUILLAUME. NO MATTER WHAT.

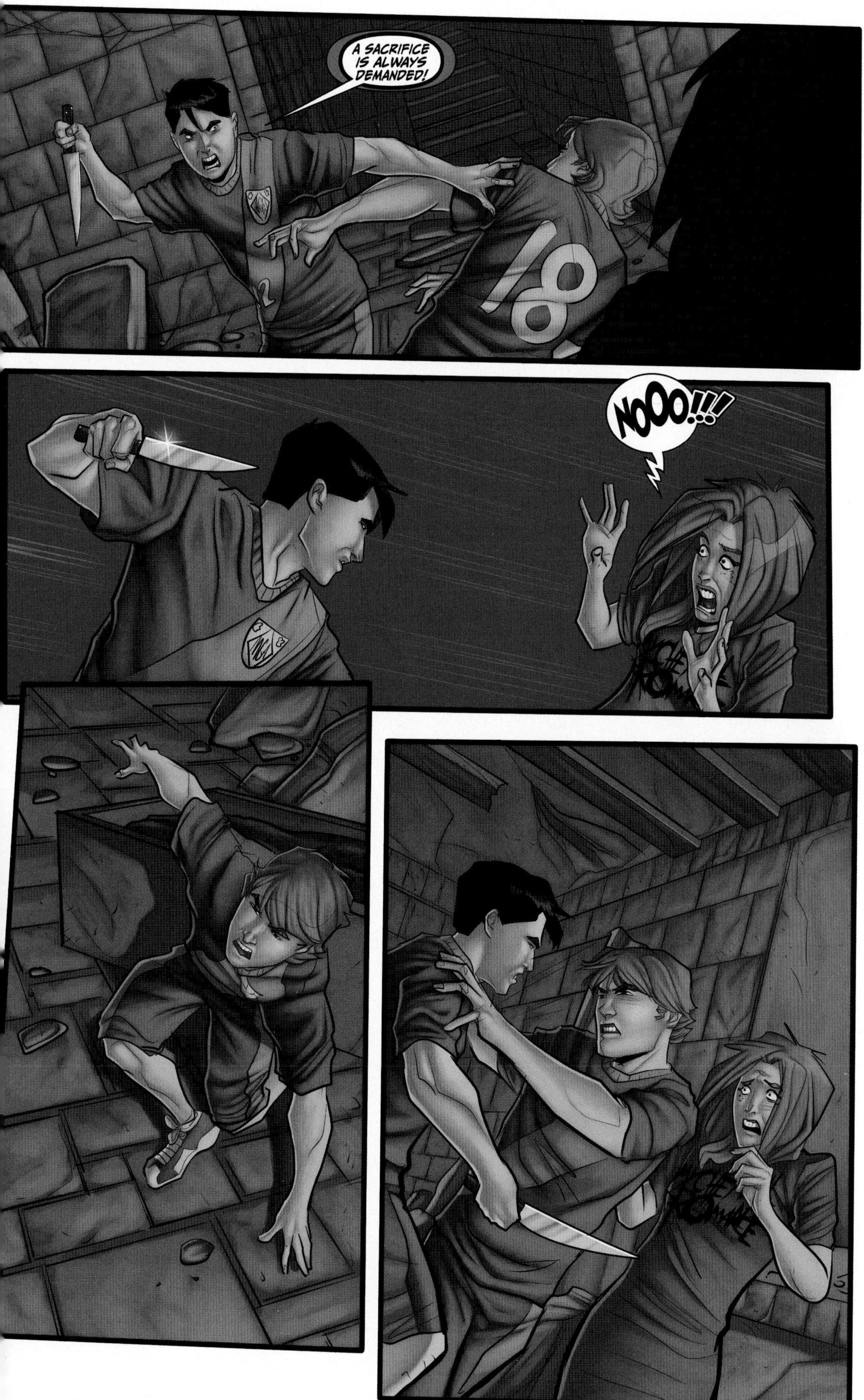
A SACRIFICE IS ALWAYS DEMANDED!
NOOO!!!

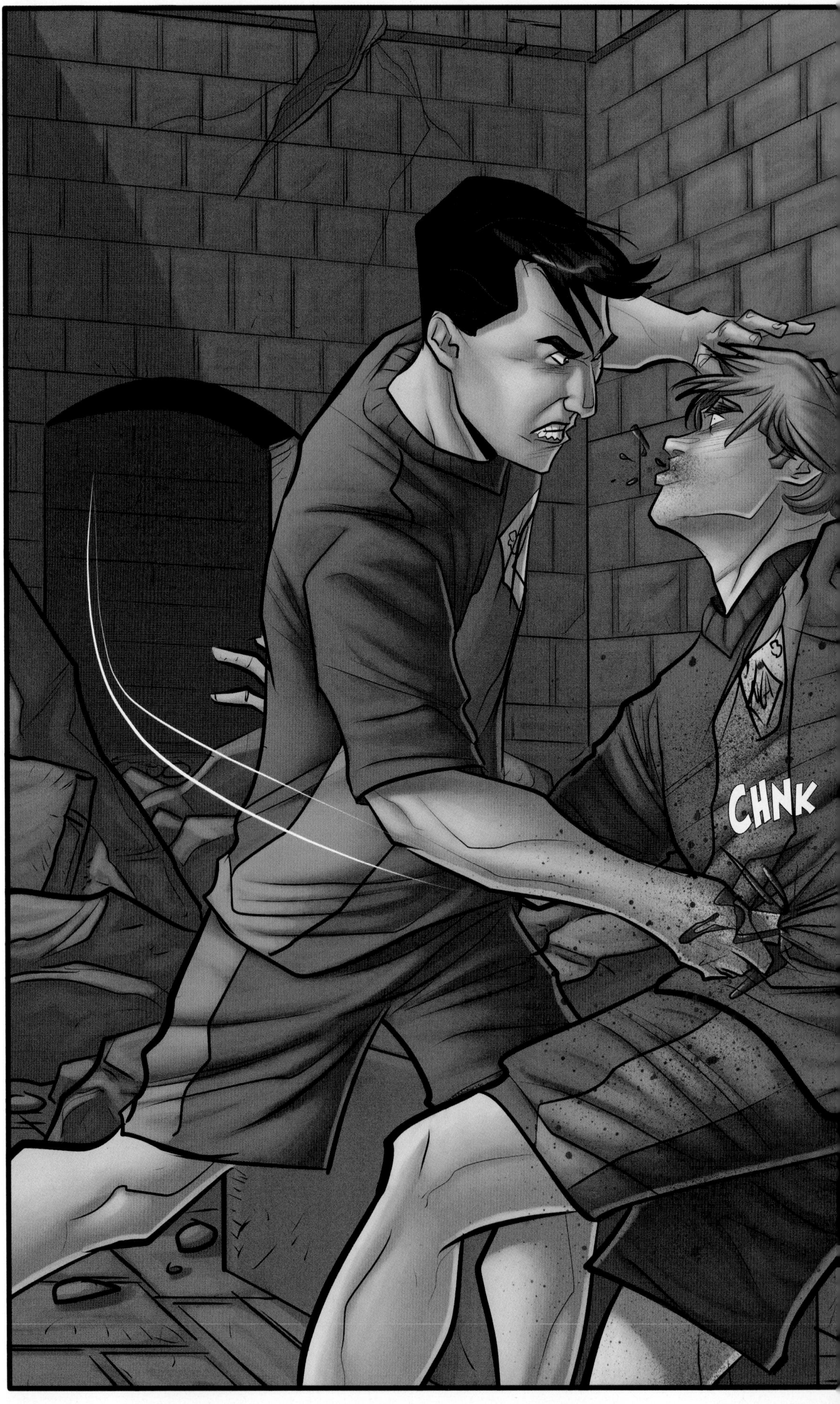
CHNK

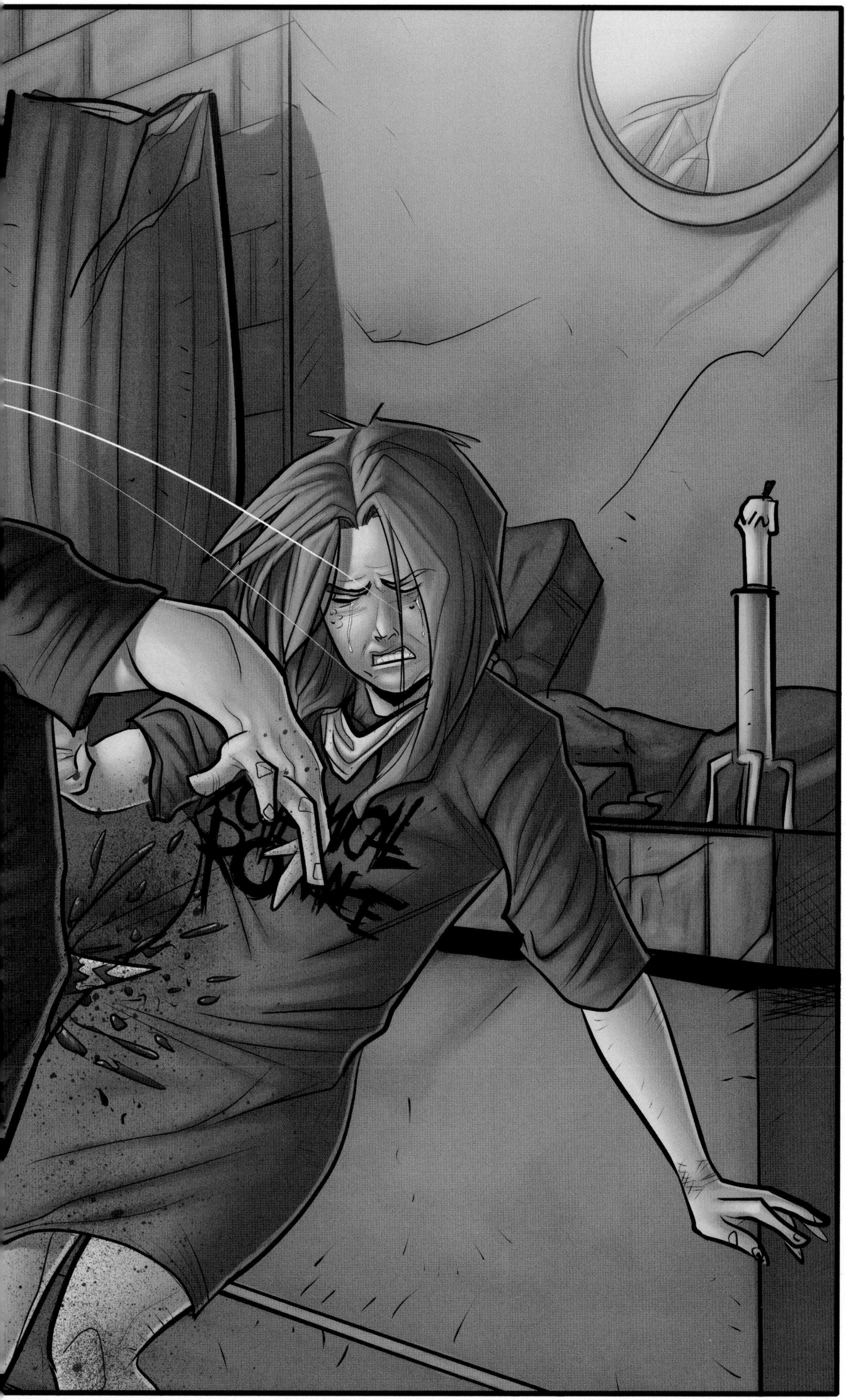

WH-- WHAT HAVE I DONE?

WHAT HAVE I DONE?!!

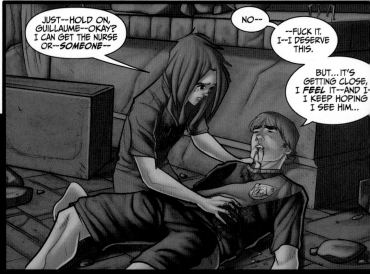

JUST--HOLD ON, GUILLAUME--OKAY? I CAN GET THE NURSE OR--SOMEONE--

NO--

--FUCK IT. I--I DESERVE THIS.

BUT...IT'S GETTING CLOSE, I FEEL IT--AND I KEEP HOPING I SEE HIM...

WHY DON'T I SEE HI--

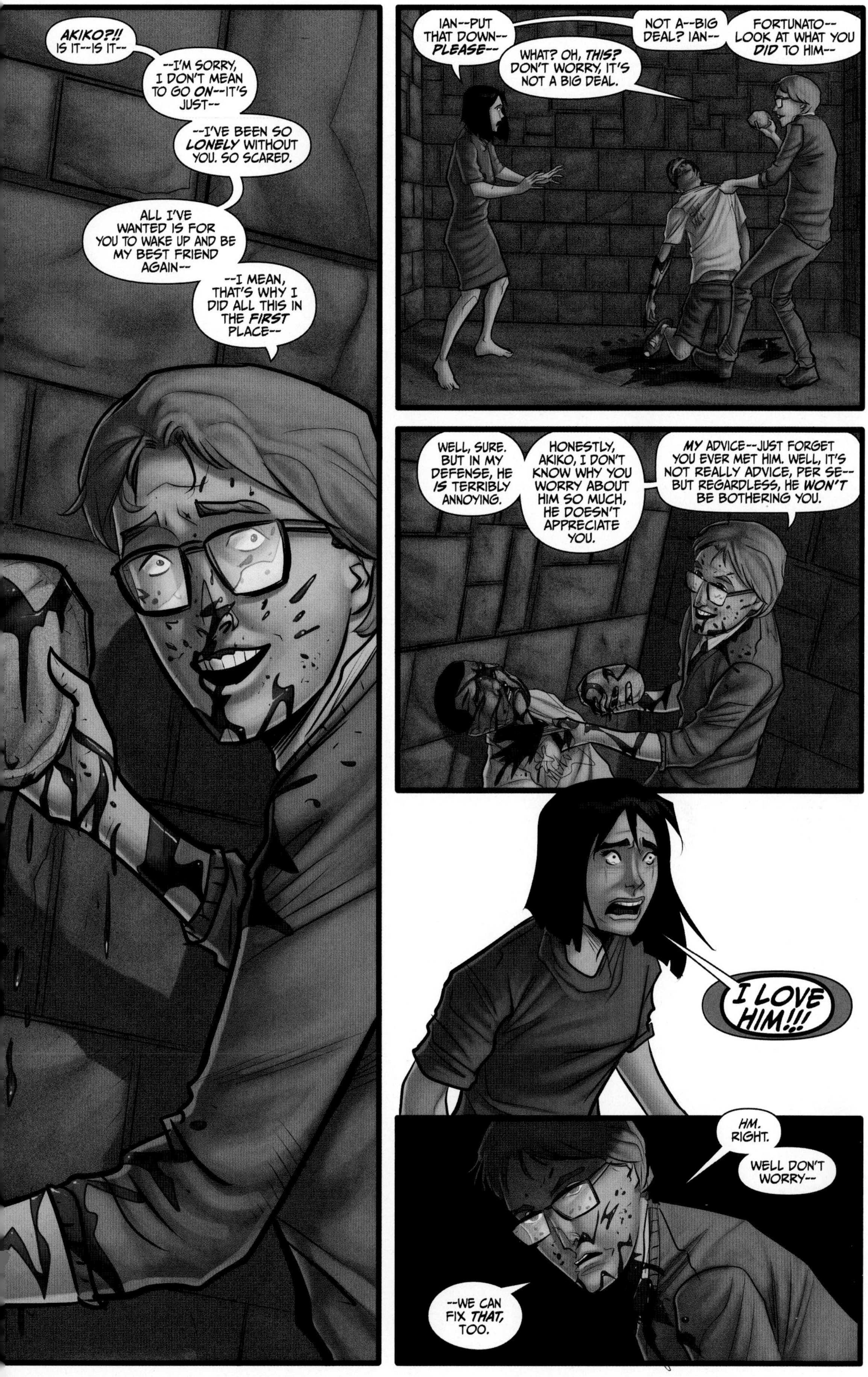
AKIKO?!! IS IT--IS IT--
--I'M SORRY, I DON'T MEAN TO GO ON--IT'S JUST--
--I'VE BEEN SO LONELY WITHOUT YOU. SO SCARED.
ALL I'VE WANTED IS FOR YOU TO WAKE UP AND BE MY BEST FRIEND AGAIN--
--I MEAN, THAT'S WHY I DID ALL THIS IN THE FIRST PLACE--
IAN--PUT THAT DOWN--PLEASE--
WHAT? OH, THIS? DON'T WORRY, IT'S NOT A BIG DEAL.
NOT A--BIG DEAL? IAN--
FORTUNATO--LOOK AT WHAT YOU DID TO HIM--
WELL, SURE. BUT IN MY DEFENSE, HE IS TERRIBLY ANNOYING.
HONESTLY, AKIKO, I DON'T KNOW WHY YOU WORRY ABOUT HIM SO MUCH, HE DOESN'T APPRECIATE YOU.
MY ADVICE--JUST FORGET YOU EVER MET HIM. WELL, IT'S NOT REALLY ADVICE, PER SE--BUT REGARDLESS, HE WON'T BE BOTHERING YOU.
I LOVE HIM!!!
HM. RIGHT.
WELL DON'T WORRY--
--WE CAN FIX THAT, TOO.

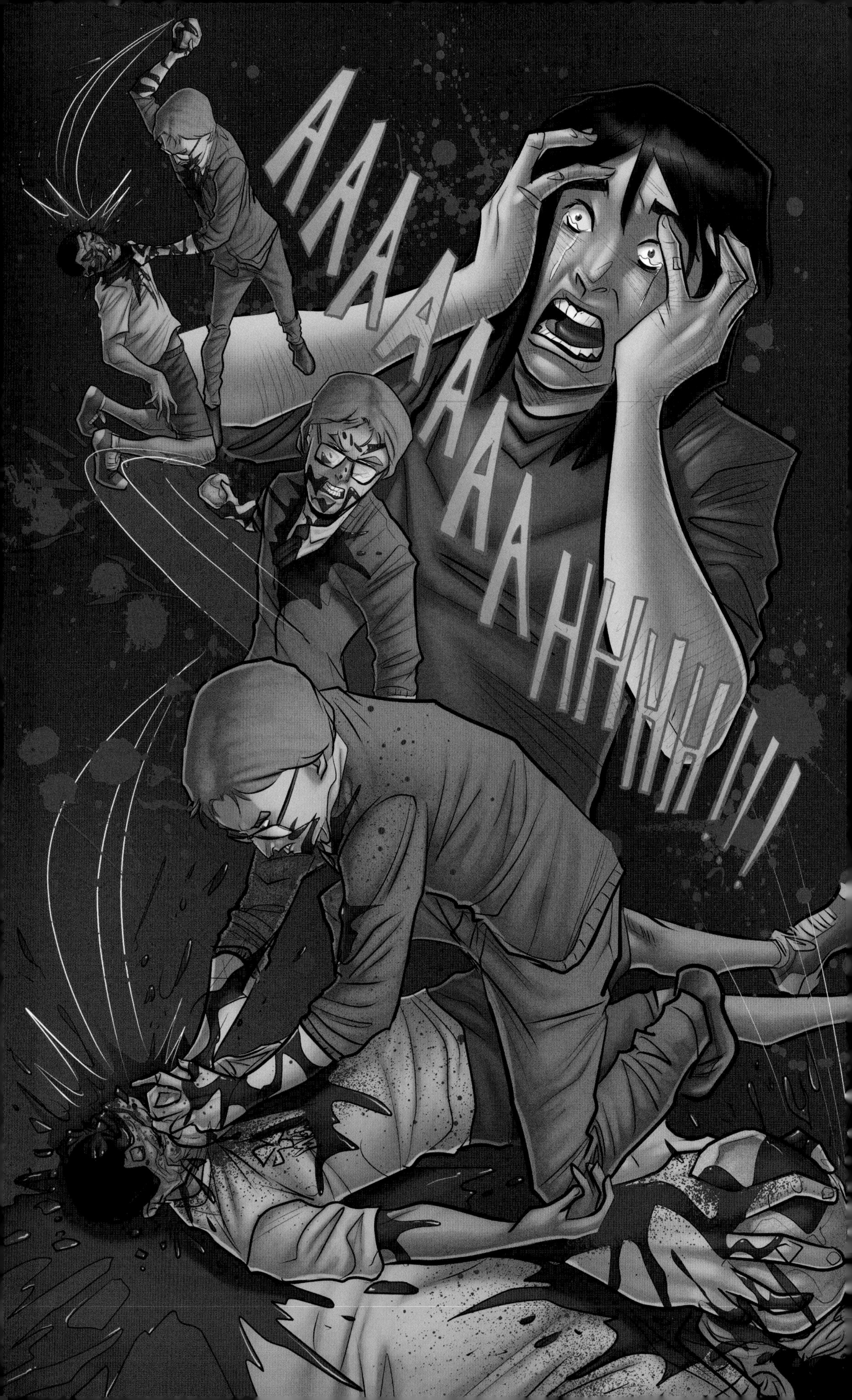
AAAAAAAAAHHHHH!!!

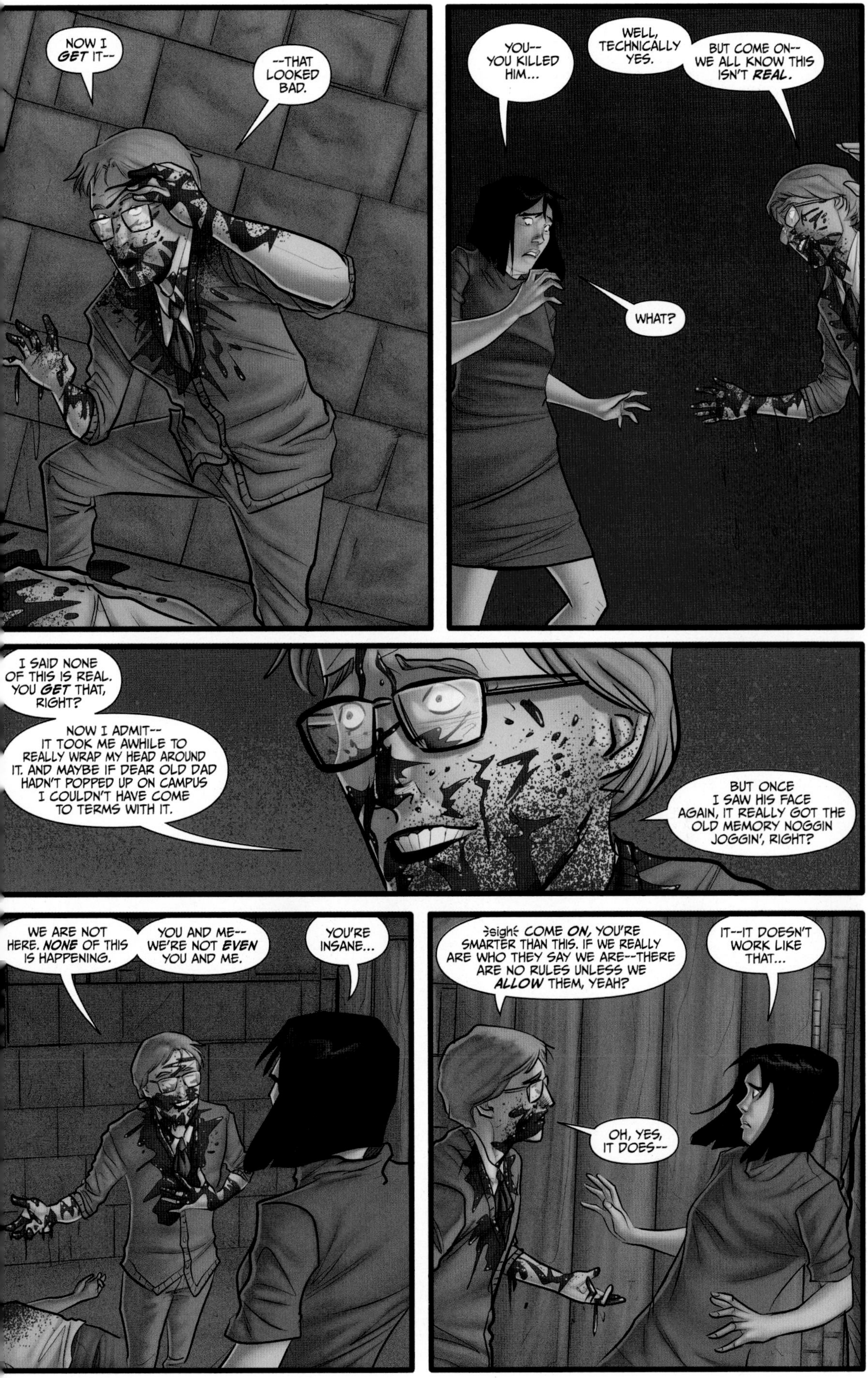
NOW I GET IT--
--THAT LOOKED BAD.
YOU-- YOU KILLED HIM...
WELL, TECHNICALLY YES.
BUT COME ON-- WE ALL KNOW THIS ISN'T REAL.
WHAT?
I SAID NONE OF THIS IS REAL. YOU GET THAT, RIGHT?
NOW I ADMIT-- IT TOOK ME AWHILE TO REALLY WRAP MY HEAD AROUND IT. AND MAYBE IF DEAR OLD DAD HADN'T POPPED UP ON CAMPUS I COULDN'T HAVE COME TO TERMS WITH IT.
BUT ONCE I SAW HIS FACE AGAIN, IT REALLY GOT THE OLD MEMORY NOGGIN JOGGIN', RIGHT?
WE ARE NOT HERE. NONE OF THIS IS HAPPENING.
YOU AND ME-- WE'RE NOT EVEN YOU AND ME.
YOU'RE INSANE...
sigh COME ON, YOU'RE SMARTER THAN THIS. IF WE REALLY ARE WHO THEY SAY WE ARE--THERE ARE NO RULES UNLESS WE ALLOW THEM, YEAH?
IT--IT DOESN'T WORK LIKE THAT...
OH, YES, IT DOES--

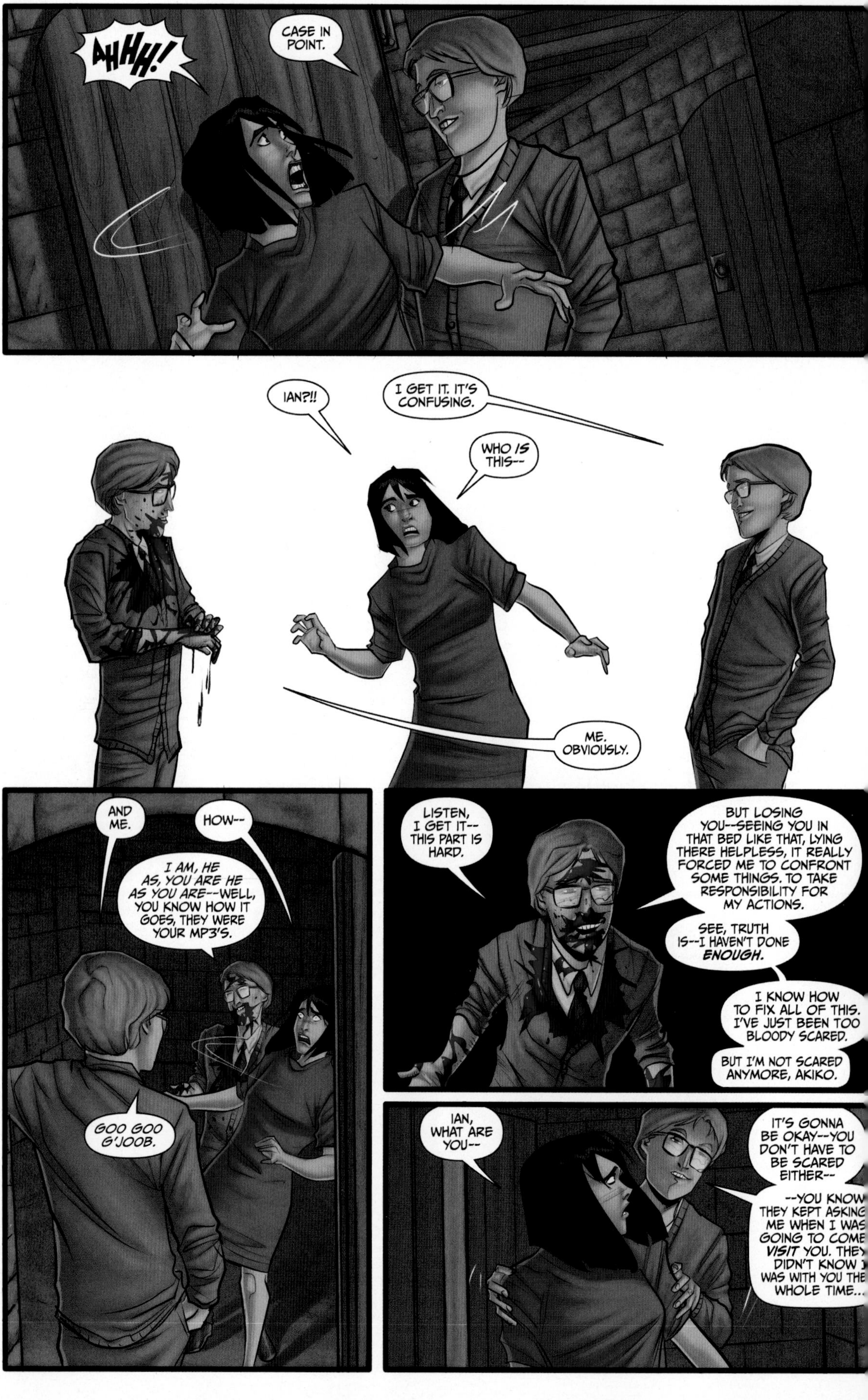
AHHH!
CASE IN POINT.
IAN?!!
I GET IT. IT'S CONFUSING.
WHO IS THIS--
ME. OBVIOUSLY.
AND ME.
HOW--
I AM, HE AS, YOU ARE HE AS YOU ARE--WELL, YOU KNOW HOW IT GOES, THEY WERE YOUR MP3'S.
GOO GOO G'JOOB.
LISTEN, I GET IT-- THIS PART IS HARD.
BUT LOSING YOU--SEEING YOU IN THAT BED LIKE THAT, LYING THERE HELPLESS, IT REALLY FORCED ME TO CONFRONT SOME THINGS. TO TAKE RESPONSIBILITY FOR MY ACTIONS.
SEE, TRUTH IS--I HAVEN'T DONE ENOUGH.
I KNOW HOW TO FIX ALL OF THIS. I'VE JUST BEEN TOO BLOODY SCARED.
BUT I'M NOT SCARED ANYMORE, AKIKO.
IAN, WHAT ARE YOU--
IT'S GONNA BE OKAY--YOU DON'T HAVE TO BE SCARED EITHER--
--YOU KNOW THEY KEPT ASKING ME WHEN I WAS GOING TO COME VISIT YOU. THEY DIDN'T KNOW I WAS WITH YOU THE WHOLE TIME...

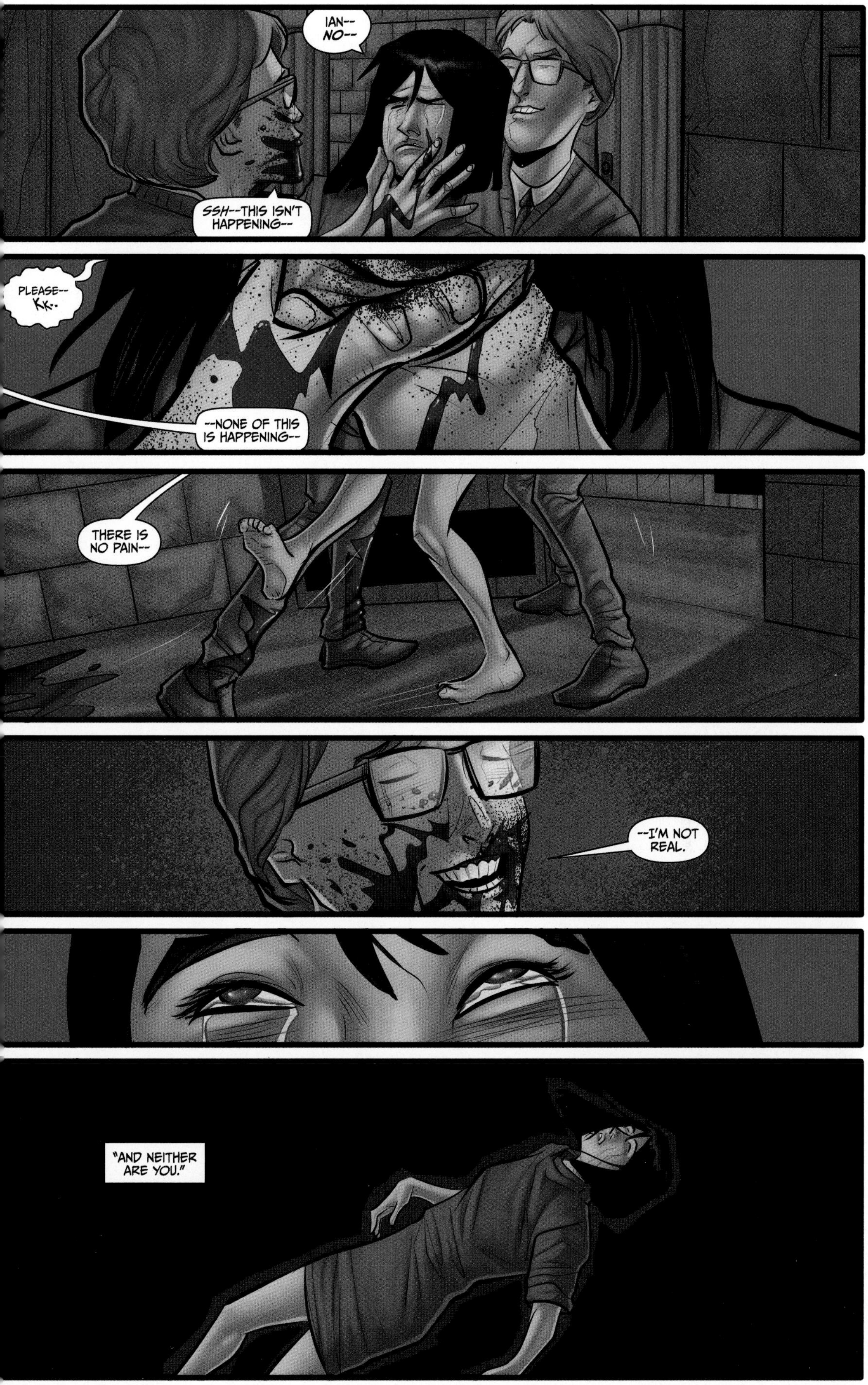

IAN--
NO--
SSH--THIS ISN'T HAPPENING--
PLEASE--
KK..
--NONE OF THIS IS HAPPENING--
THERE IS NO PAIN--
--I'M NOT REAL.
"AND NEITHER ARE YOU."

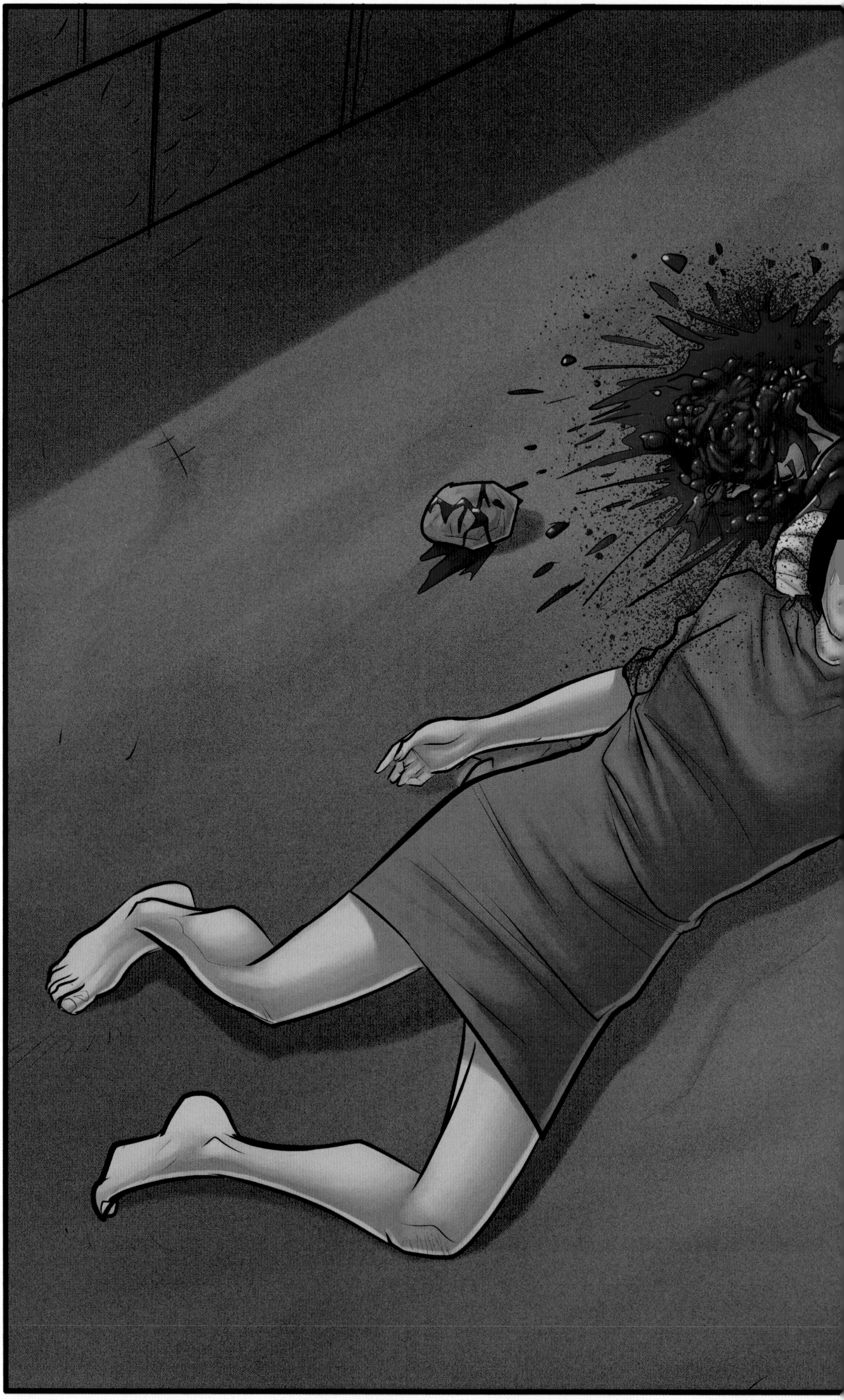

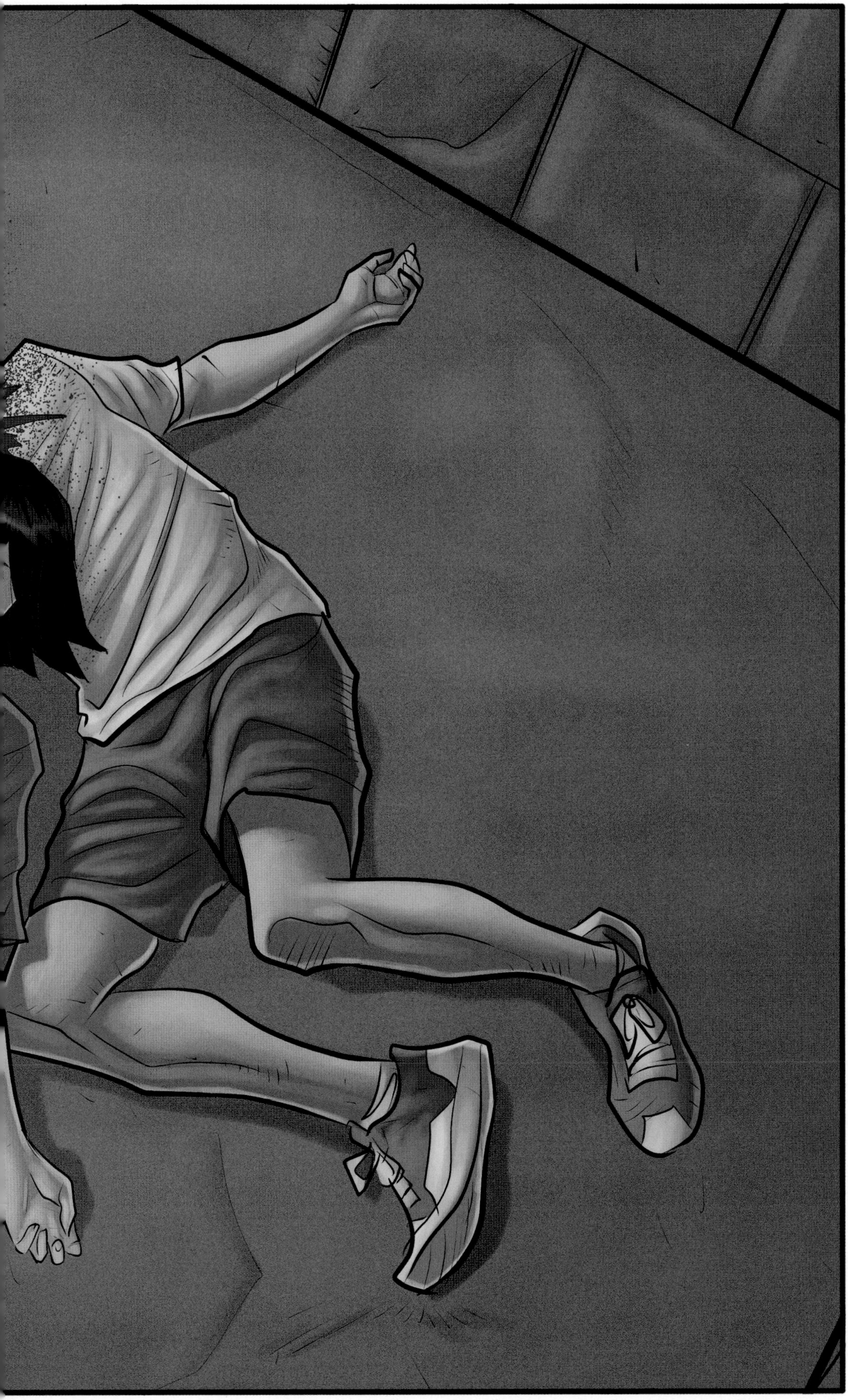

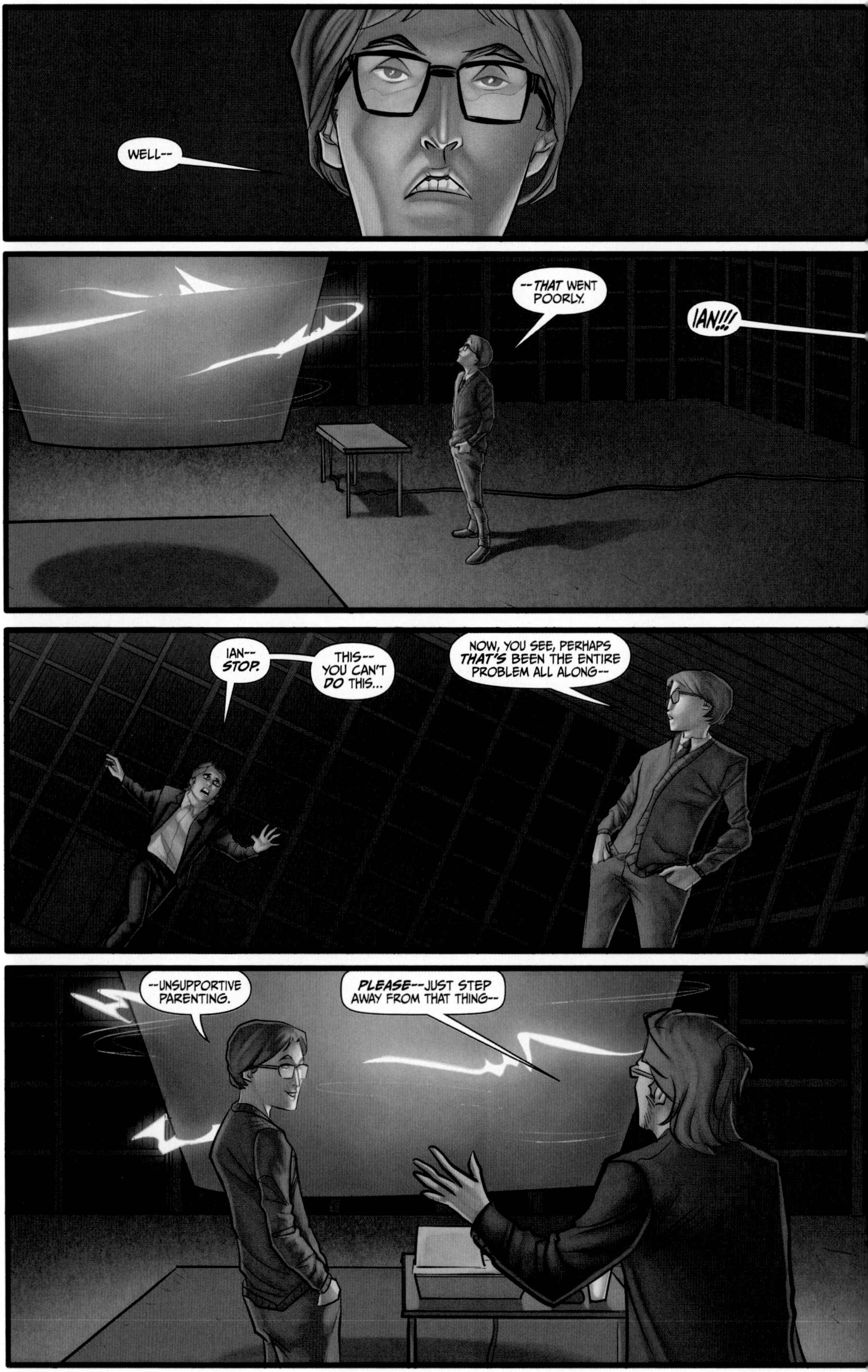
WELL--
--THAT WENT POORLY.
IAN!!!
IAN-- STOP.
THIS-- YOU CAN'T DO THIS...
NOW, YOU SEE, PERHAPS THAT'S BEEN THE ENTIRE PROBLEM ALL ALONG--
--UNSUPPORTIVE PARENTING.
PLEASE--JUST STEP AWAY FROM THAT THING--

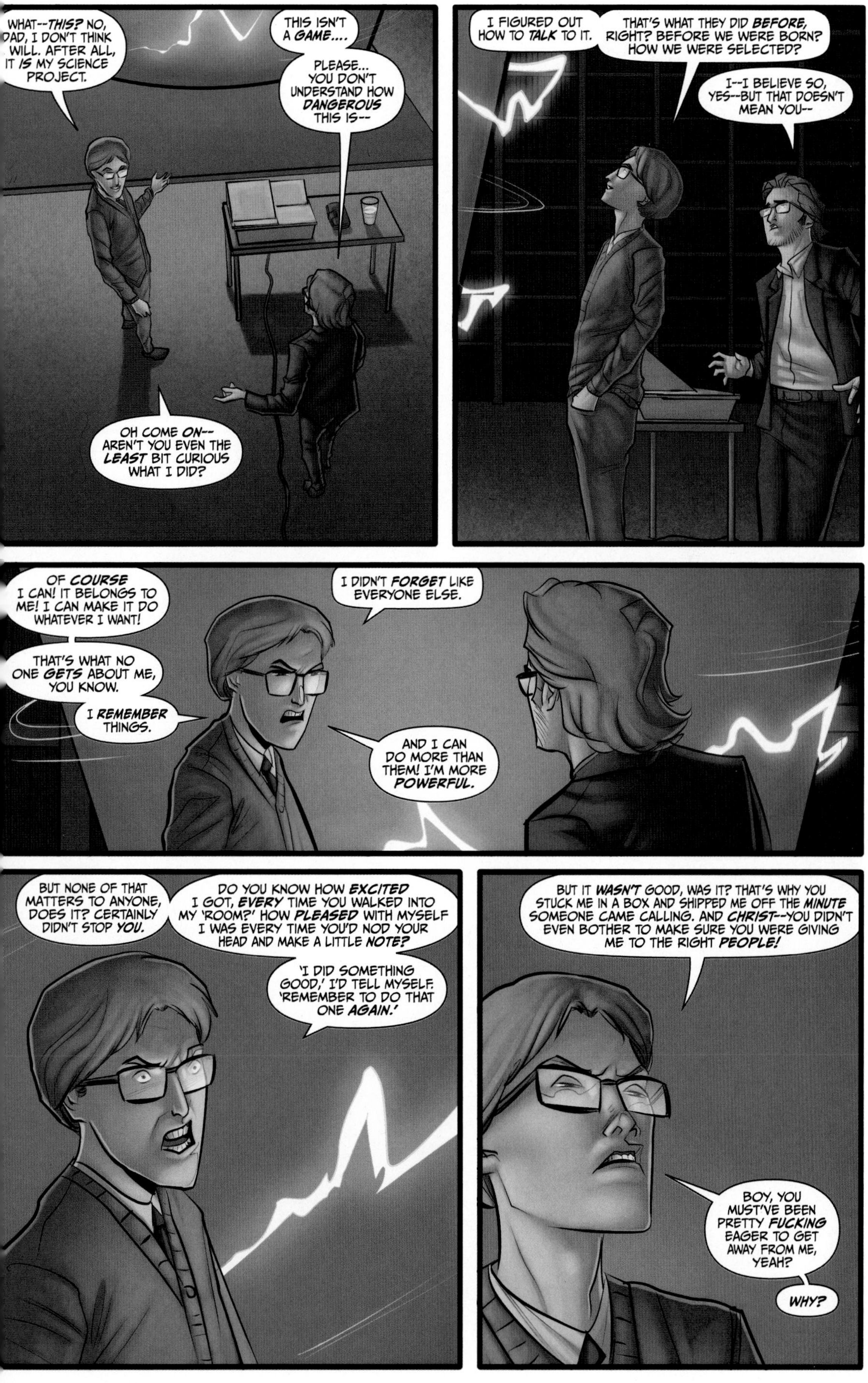
WHAT--THIS? NO, DAD, I DON'T THINK WILL. AFTER ALL, IT IS MY SCIENCE PROJECT.
THIS ISN'T A GAME....
PLEASE... YOU DON'T UNDERSTAND HOW DANGEROUS THIS IS--
OH COME ON-- AREN'T YOU EVEN THE LEAST BIT CURIOUS WHAT I DID?
I FIGURED OUT HOW TO TALK TO IT.
THAT'S WHAT THEY DID BEFORE, RIGHT? BEFORE WE WERE BORN? HOW WE WERE SELECTED?
I--I BELIEVE SO, YES--BUT THAT DOESN'T MEAN YOU--
OF COURSE I CAN! IT BELONGS TO ME! I CAN MAKE IT DO WHATEVER I WANT!
THAT'S WHAT NO ONE GETS ABOUT ME, YOU KNOW.
I REMEMBER THINGS.
I DIDN'T FORGET LIKE EVERYONE ELSE.
AND I CAN DO MORE THAN THEM! I'M MORE POWERFUL.
BUT NONE OF THAT MATTERS TO ANYONE, DOES IT? CERTAINLY DIDN'T STOP YOU.
DO YOU KNOW HOW EXCITED I GOT, EVERY TIME YOU WALKED INTO MY 'ROOM?' HOW PLEASED WITH MYSELF I WAS EVERY TIME YOU'D NOD YOUR HEAD AND MAKE A LITTLE NOTE?
'I DID SOMETHING GOOD,' I'D TELL MYSELF. 'REMEMBER TO DO THAT ONE AGAIN.'
BUT IT WASN'T GOOD, WAS IT? THAT'S WHY YOU STUCK ME IN A BOX AND SHIPPED ME OFF THE MINUTE SOMEONE CAME CALLING. AND CHRIST--YOU DIDN'T EVEN BOTHER TO MAKE SURE YOU WERE GIVING ME TO THE RIGHT PEOPLE!
BOY, YOU MUST'VE BEEN PRETTY FUCKING EAGER TO GET AWAY FROM ME, YEAH?
WHY?

DID I SCARE YOU, OLIVER?

WHAT? *NO,* IAN--I--

--I WISH THINGS HAD BEEN DIFFERENT, BUT THERE WAS AN AGREEMENT IN PLACE--AN *ARRANGEMENT*--

NOW *THAT* DOESN'T STRIKE M AS A VERY HONEST ANSWER

YOU KNOW, I'M PLANNING TO CHANGE SO *MANY* THING HERE IN A MOMENT--BU PERHAPS I COULD AD A FEW MORE THINGS WITH YOU IN MIND--

NO! WAIT--

--Y-*YES.* IS THAT WHAT YOU WANT TO HEAR?

YES, I *WAS* TERRIFIED OF YOU--TERRIFIED OF *ALL* OF IT... I'M A MISERABLE COWARD AND--AND--I NEVER SHOULD'VE LET THEM *TAKE* YOU--

SSH--THAT'S *ENOUGH*--

--YOU'RE FAR TOO *HARD* ON YOURSELF.

I MEAN, LOOK AT *ME*--

--*I* TURNED OUT ALL RIGHT IN THE END, DIDN'T I?

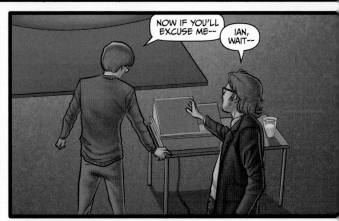

NOW IF YOU'LL EXCUSE ME--

IAN, WAIT--

I SAID GO!!!

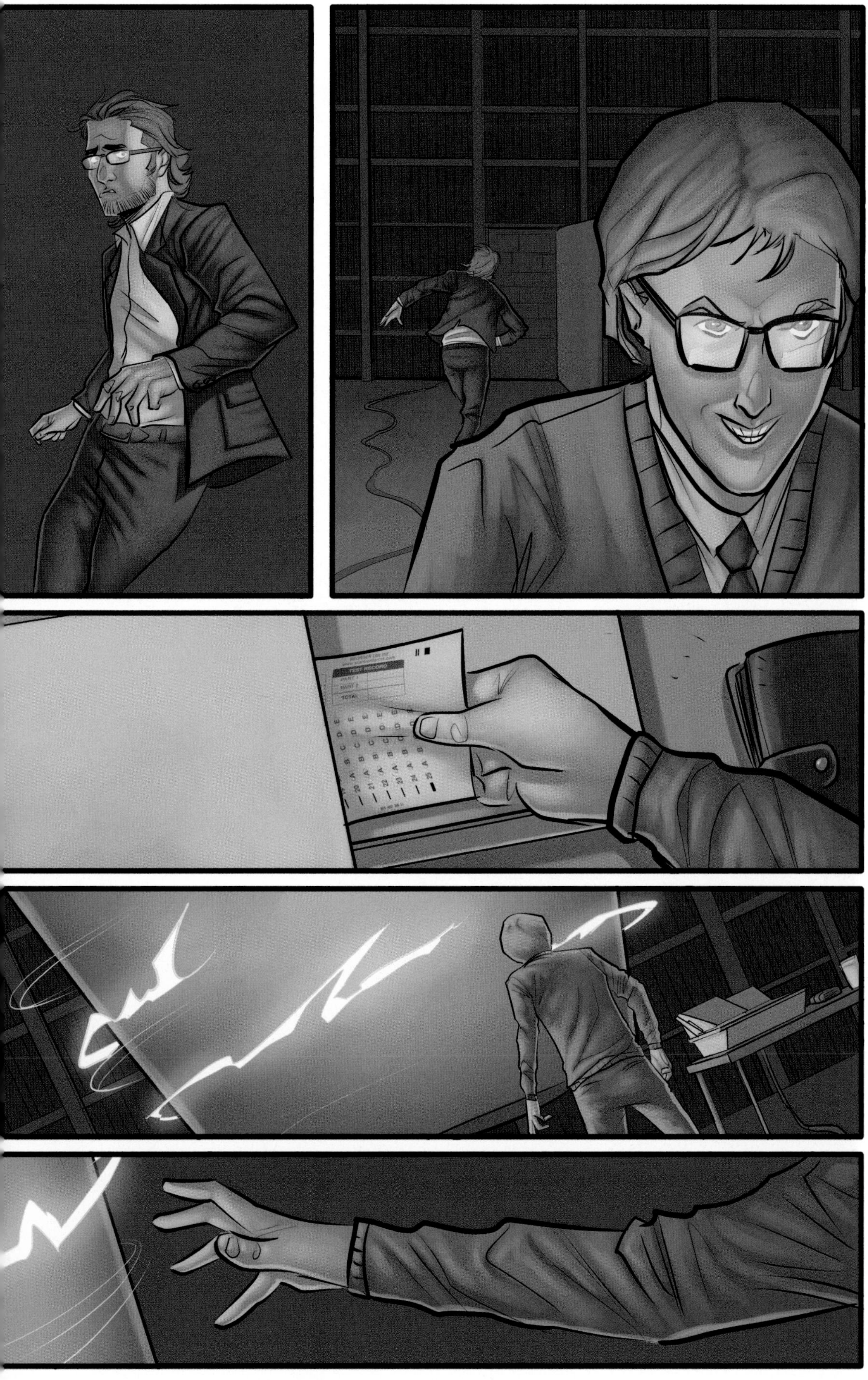
TEST RECORD
PART 1
PART 2
TOTAL

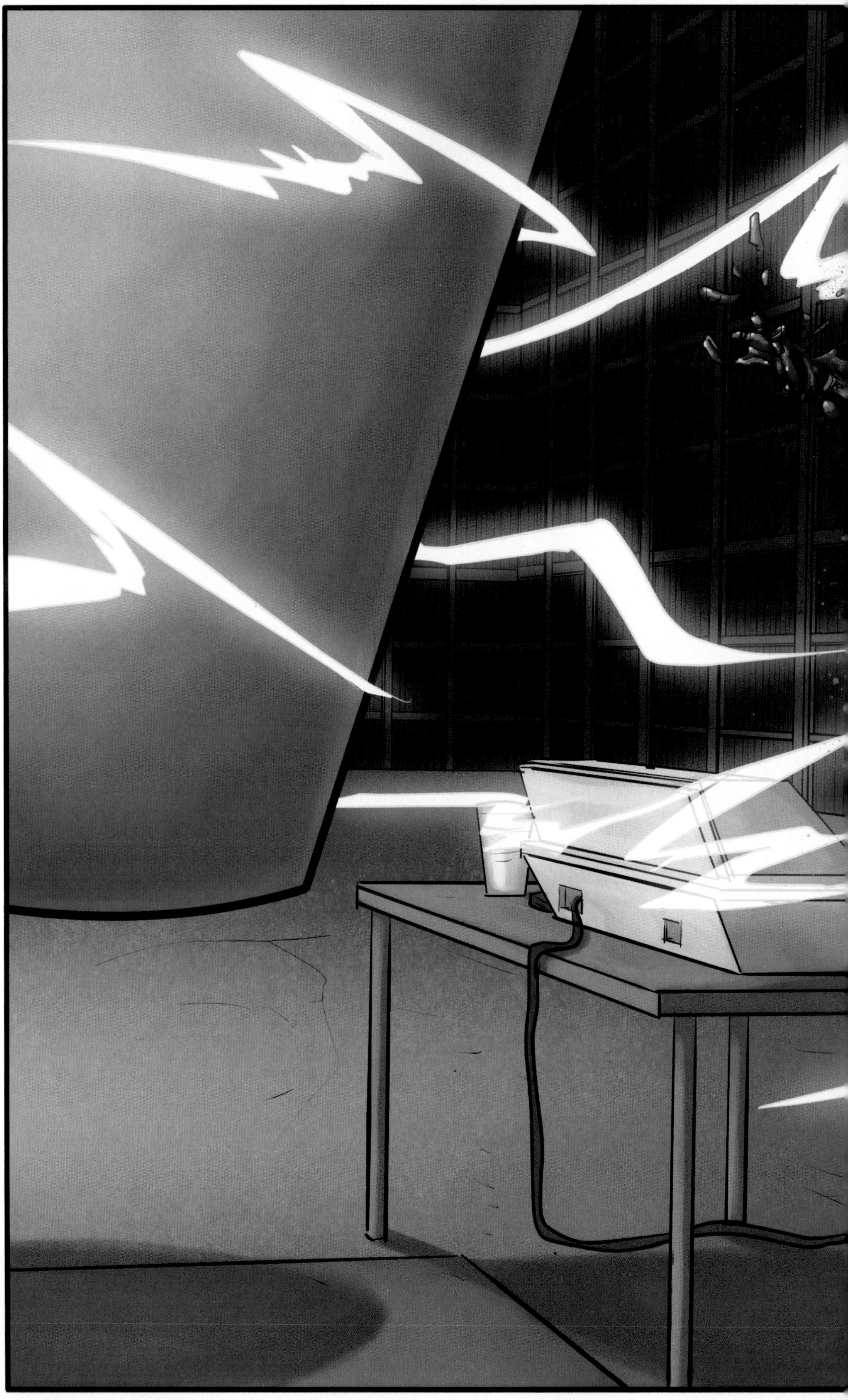

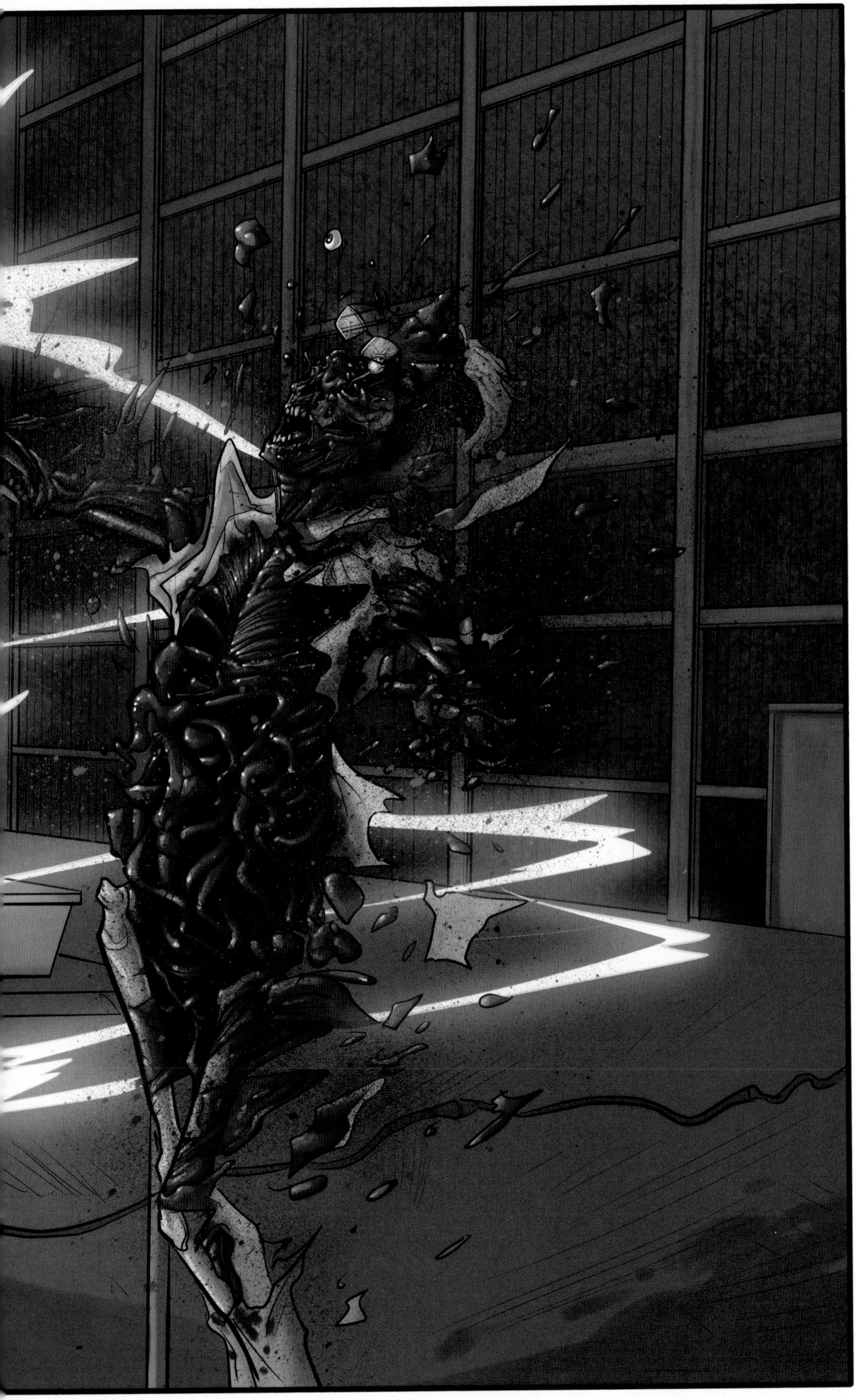

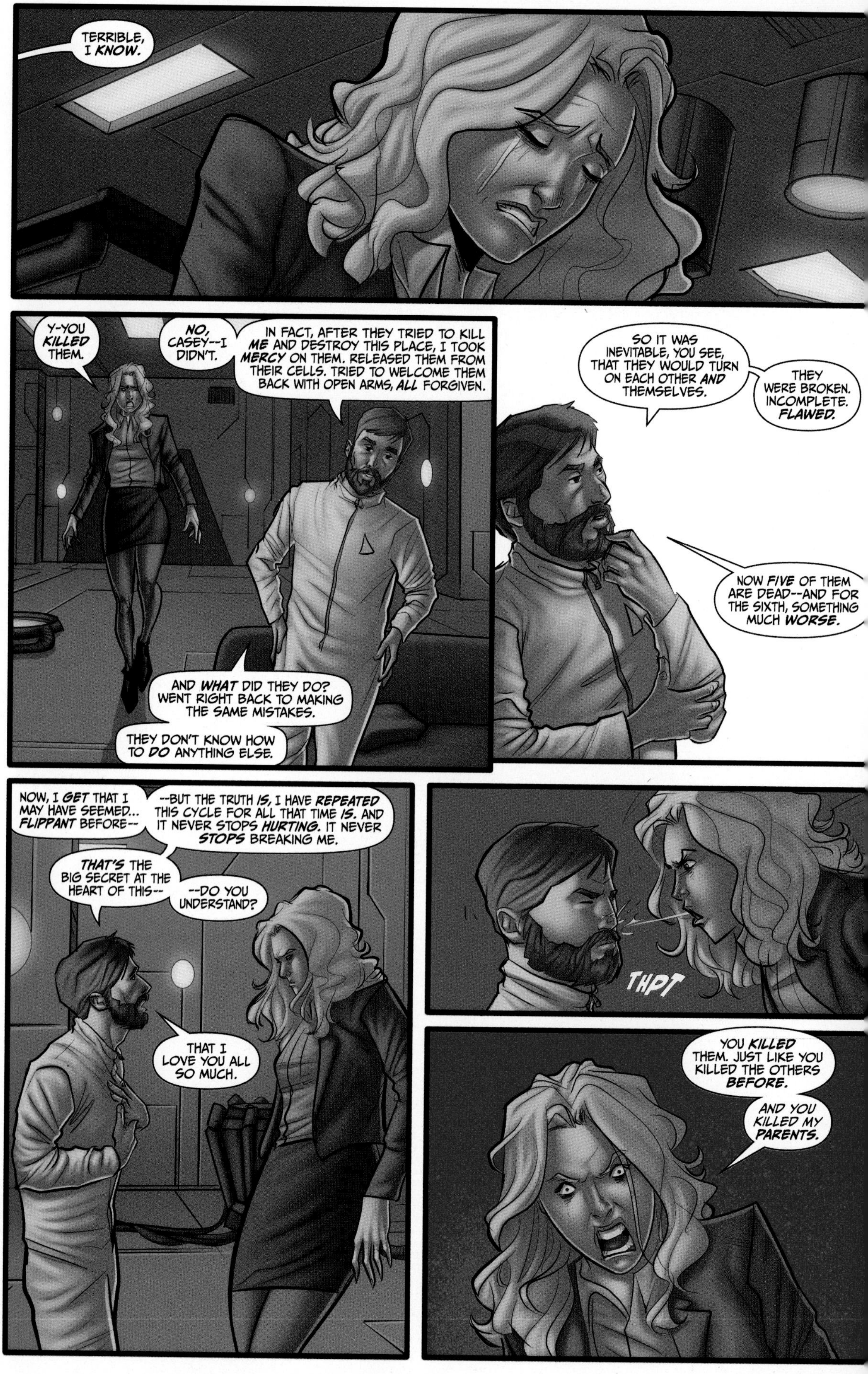
TERRIBLE, I KNOW.
Y-YOU KILLED THEM.
NO, CASEY--I DIDN'T.
IN FACT, AFTER THEY TRIED TO KILL ME AND DESTROY THIS PLACE, I TOOK MERCY ON THEM. RELEASED THEM FROM THEIR CELLS. TRIED TO WELCOME THEM BACK WITH OPEN ARMS, ALL FORGIVEN.
AND WHAT DID THEY DO? WENT RIGHT BACK TO MAKING THE SAME MISTAKES.
THEY DON'T KNOW HOW TO DO ANYTHING ELSE.
SO IT WAS INEVITABLE, YOU SEE, THAT THEY WOULD TURN ON EACH OTHER AND THEMSELVES.
THEY WERE BROKEN. INCOMPLETE. FLAWED.
NOW FIVE OF THEM ARE DEAD--AND FOR THE SIXTH, SOMETHING MUCH WORSE.
NOW, I GET THAT I MAY HAVE SEEMED... FLIPPANT BEFORE--
--BUT THE TRUTH IS, I HAVE REPEATED THIS CYCLE FOR ALL THAT TIME IS. AND IT NEVER STOPS HURTING. IT NEVER STOPS BREAKING ME.
THAT'S THE BIG SECRET AT THE HEART OF THIS--
--DO YOU UNDERSTAND?
THAT I LOVE YOU ALL SO MUCH.
THPT
YOU KILLED THEM. JUST LIKE YOU KILLED THE OTHERS BEFORE.
AND YOU KILLED MY PARENTS.

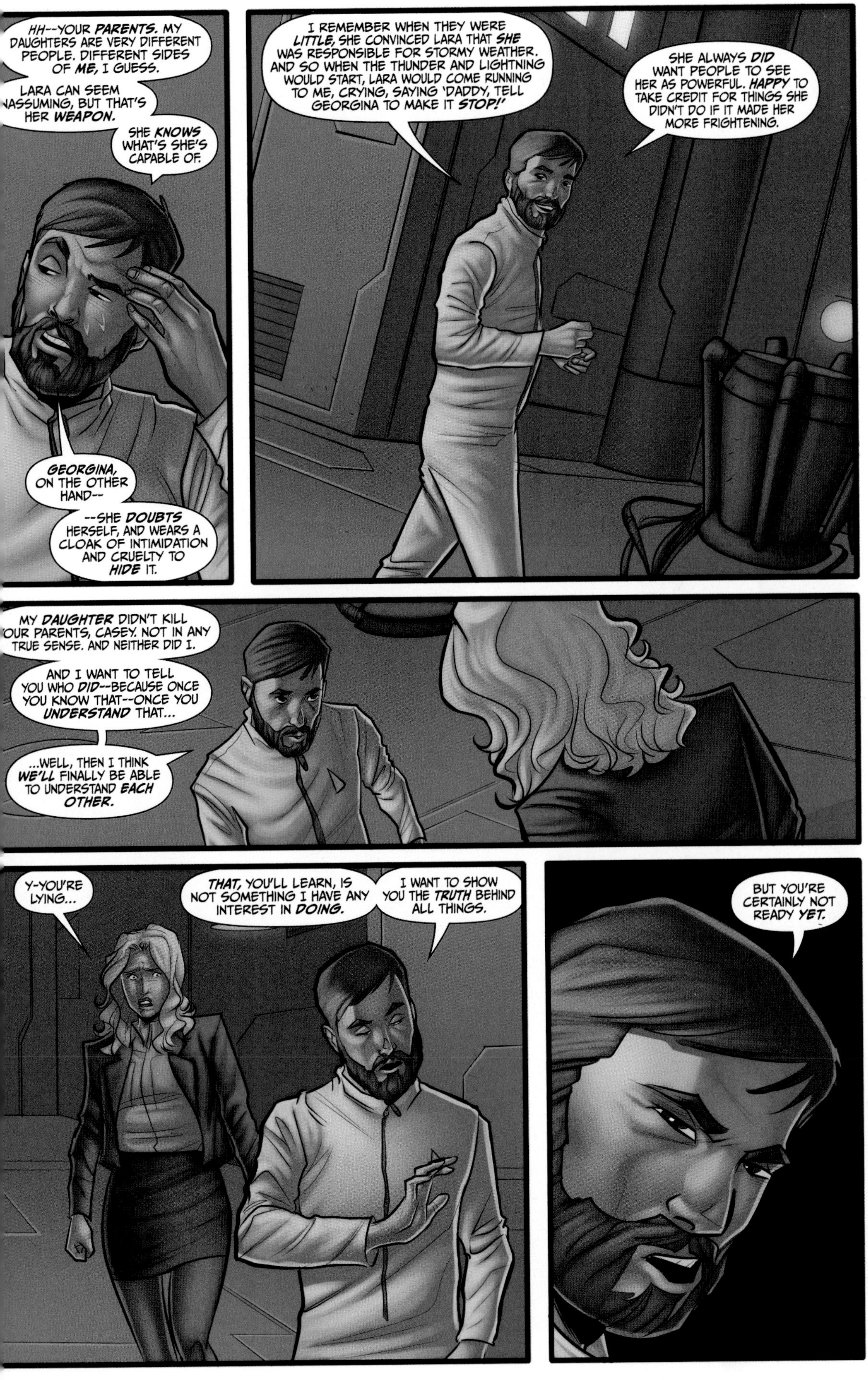
HH--YOUR PARENTS. MY DAUGHTERS ARE VERY DIFFERENT PEOPLE. DIFFERENT SIDES OF ME, I GUESS.
LARA CAN SEEM UNASSUMING, BUT THAT'S HER WEAPON.
SHE KNOWS WHAT'S SHE'S CAPABLE OF.
GEORGINA, ON THE OTHER HAND--
--SHE DOUBTS HERSELF, AND WEARS A CLOAK OF INTIMIDATION AND CRUELTY TO HIDE IT.
I REMEMBER WHEN THEY WERE LITTLE, SHE CONVINCED LARA THAT SHE WAS RESPONSIBLE FOR STORMY WEATHER. AND SO WHEN THE THUNDER AND LIGHTNING WOULD START, LARA WOULD COME RUNNING TO ME, CRYING, SAYING 'DADDY, TELL GEORGINA TO MAKE IT STOP!'
SHE ALWAYS DID WANT PEOPLE TO SEE HER AS POWERFUL. HAPPY TO TAKE CREDIT FOR THINGS SHE DIDN'T DO IF IT MADE HER MORE FRIGHTENING.
MY DAUGHTER DIDN'T KILL YOUR PARENTS, CASEY. NOT IN ANY TRUE SENSE. AND NEITHER DID I.
AND I WANT TO TELL YOU WHO DID--BECAUSE ONCE YOU KNOW THAT--ONCE YOU UNDERSTAND THAT...
...WELL, THEN I THINK WE'LL FINALLY BE ABLE TO UNDERSTAND EACH OTHER.
Y-YOU'RE LYING...
THAT, YOU'LL LEARN, IS NOT SOMETHING I HAVE ANY INTEREST IN DOING.
I WANT TO SHOW YOU THE TRUTH BEHIND ALL THINGS.
BUT YOU'RE CERTAINLY NOT READY YET.

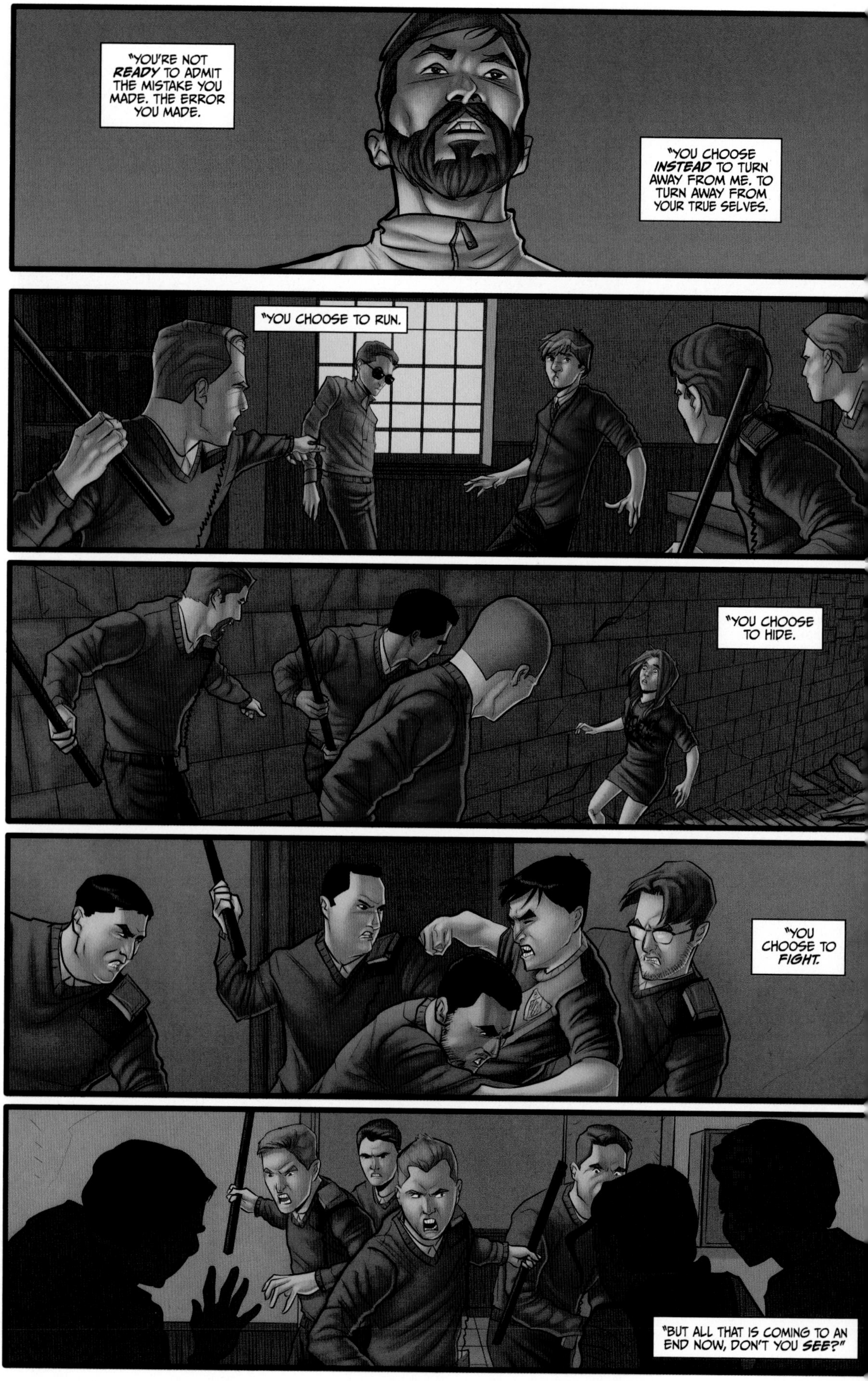
"YOU'RE NOT READY TO ADMIT THE MISTAKE YOU MADE. THE ERROR YOU MADE.
"YOU CHOOSE INSTEAD TO TURN AWAY FROM ME. TO TURN AWAY FROM YOUR TRUE SELVES.
"YOU CHOOSE TO RUN.
"YOU CHOOSE TO HIDE.
"YOU CHOOSE TO FIGHT.
"BUT ALL THAT IS COMING TO AN END NOW, DON'T YOU SEE?"

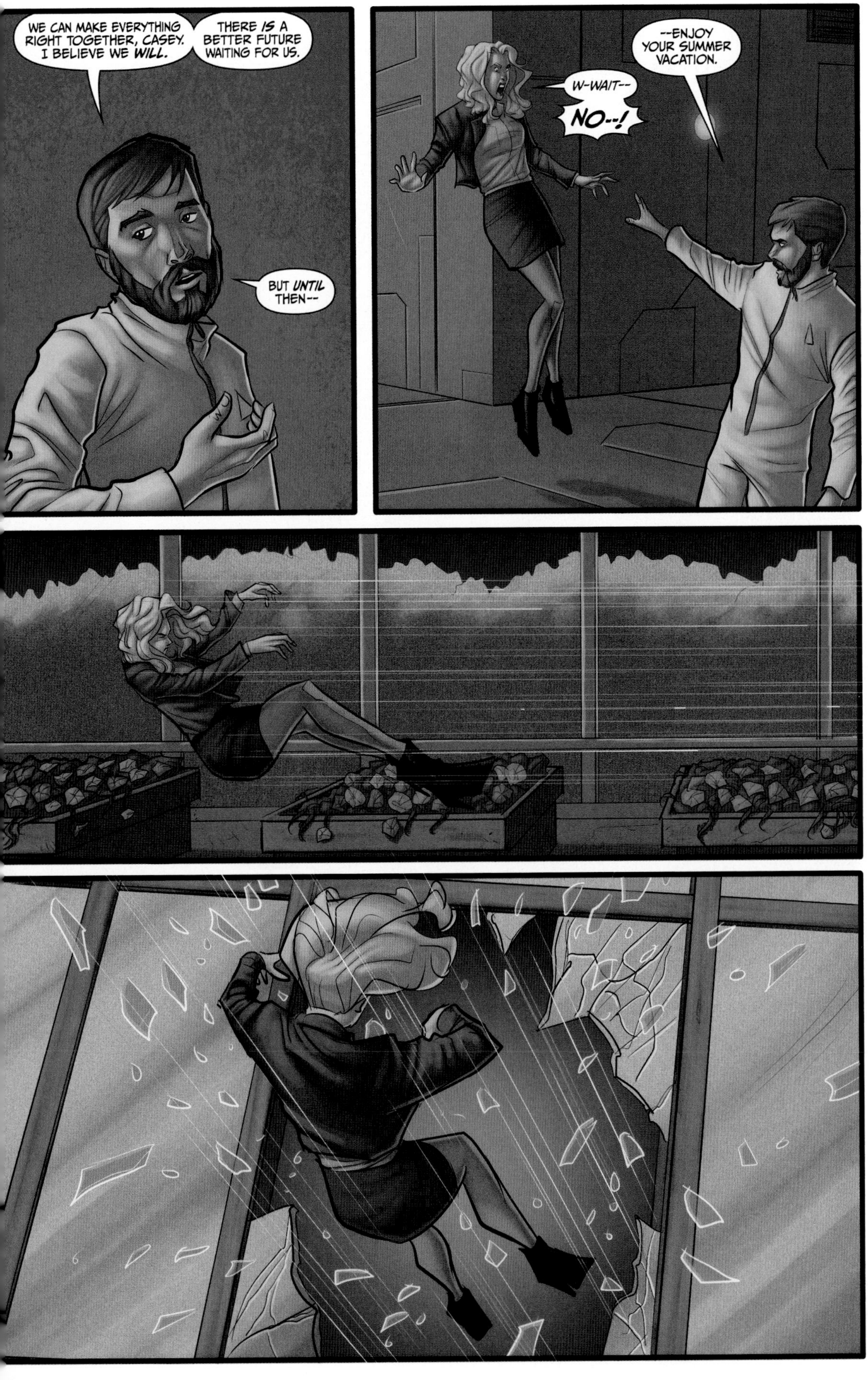
WE CAN MAKE EVERYTHING RIGHT TOGETHER, CASEY. I BELIEVE WE *WILL*.
THERE *IS* A BETTER FUTURE WAITING FOR US.
BUT *UNTIL* THEN--
--ENJOY YOUR SUMMER VACATION.
W-WAIT--
NO--!

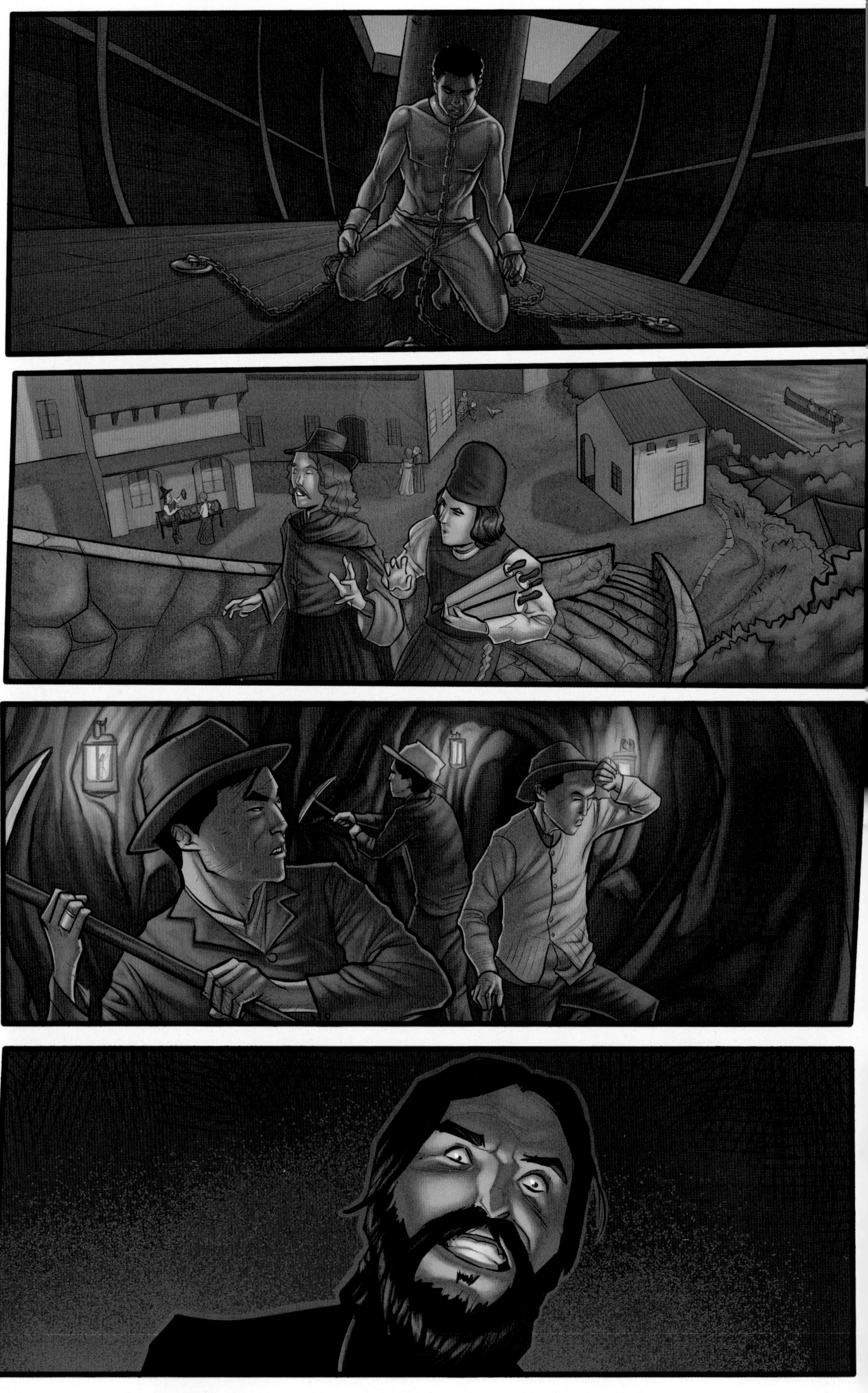

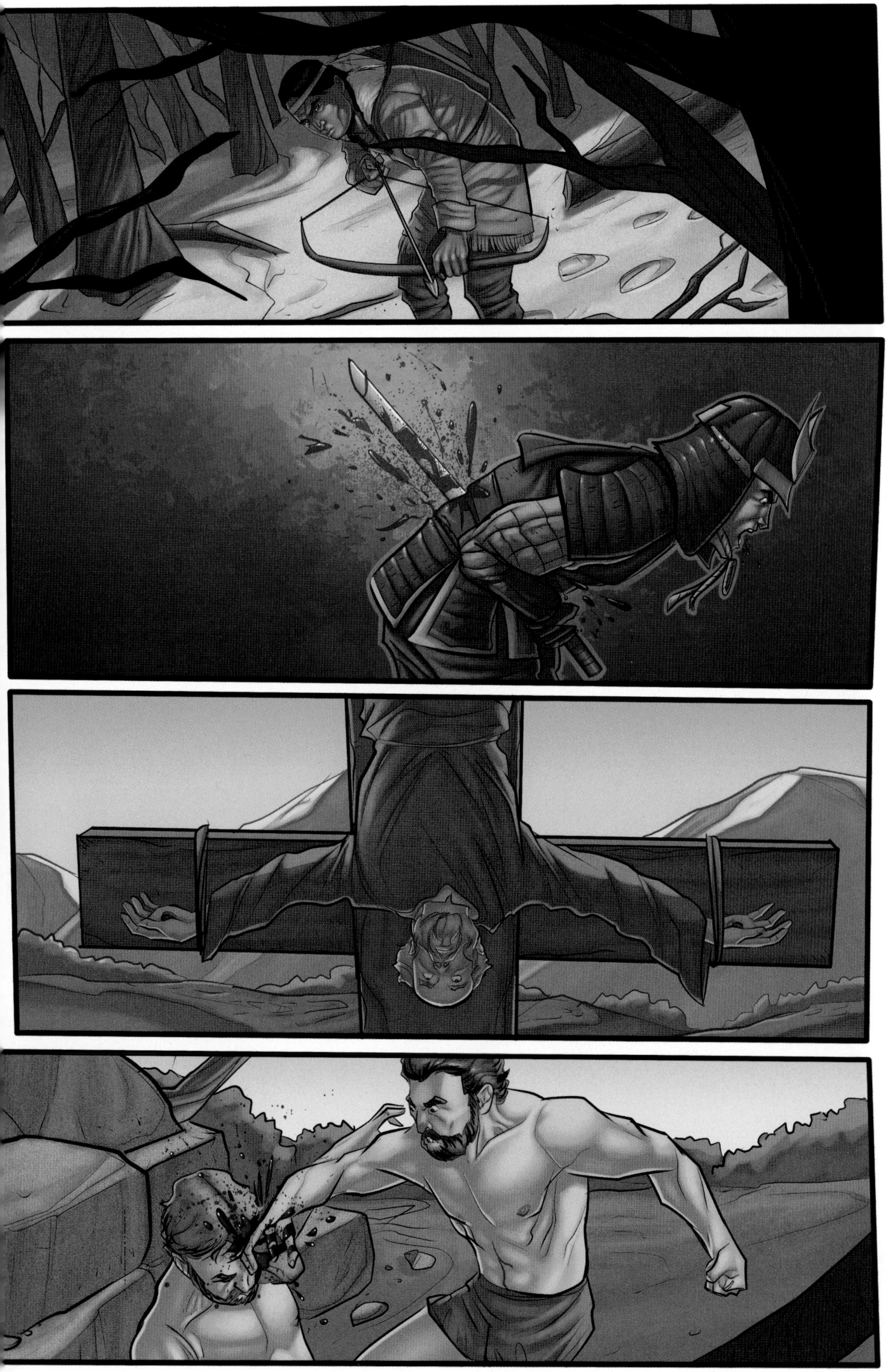

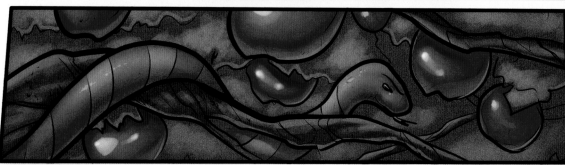

OH MY GOD. IS THAT--

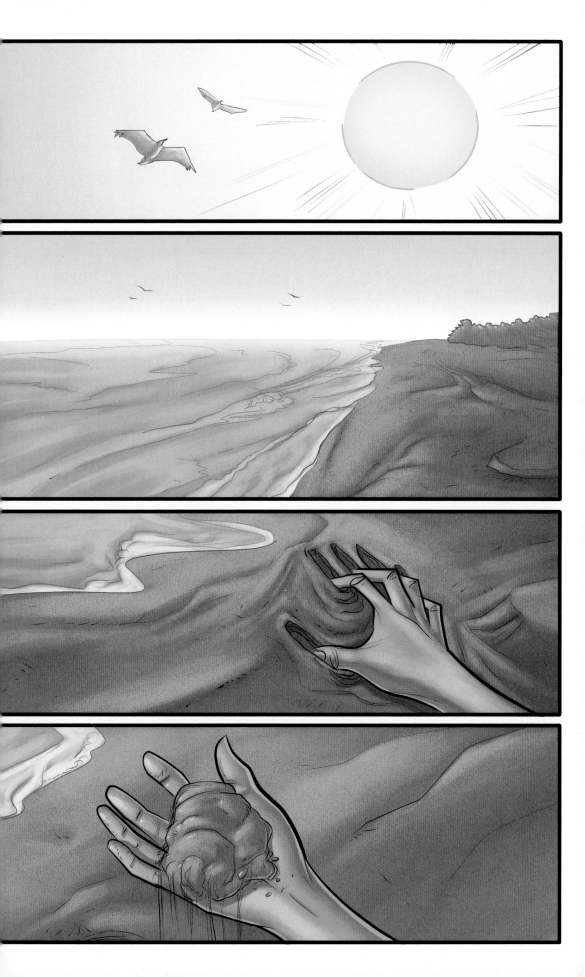

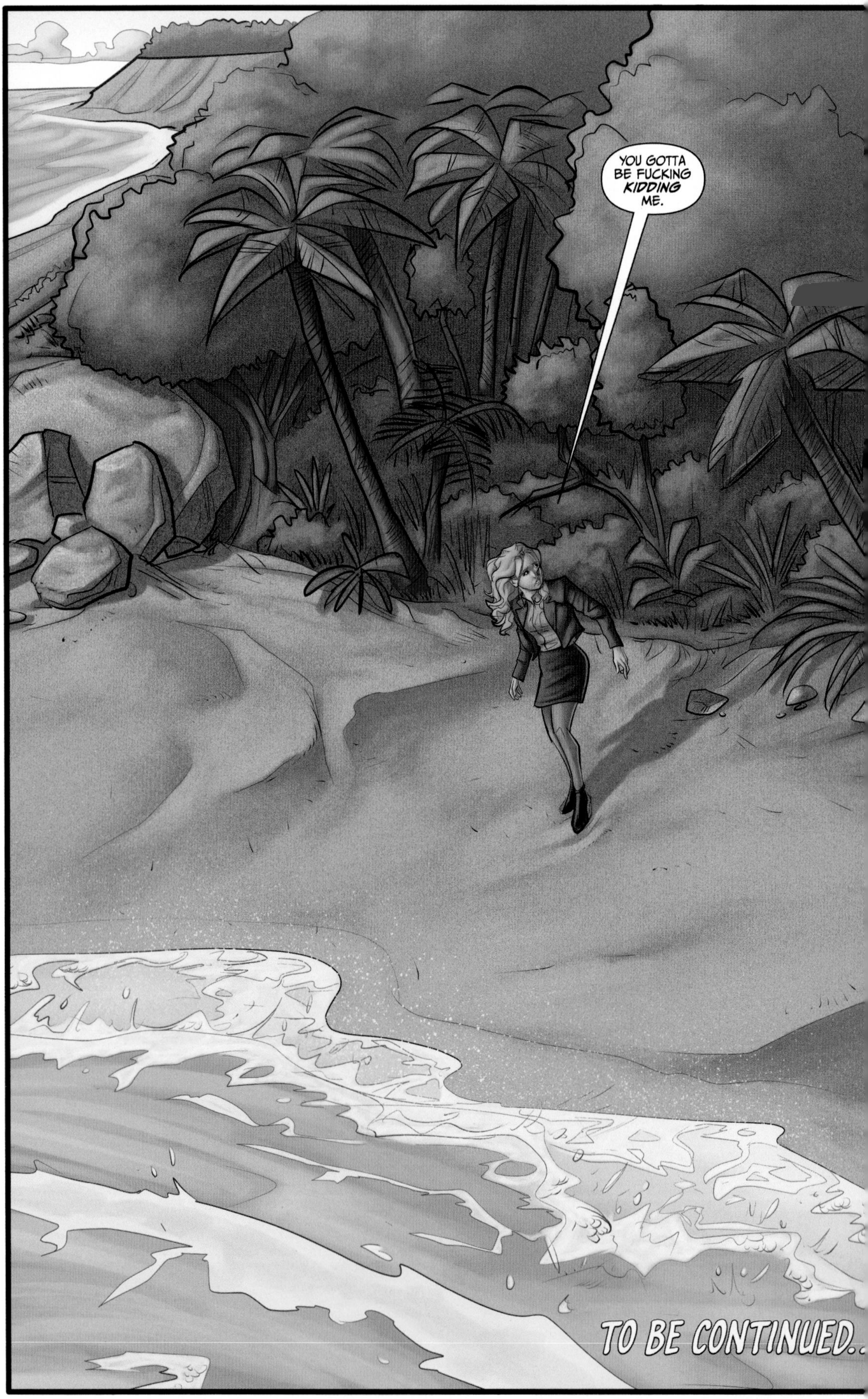
YOU GOTTA BE FUCKING KIDDING ME.
TO BE CONTINUED...

ART OF THE ACADEMY

FEATURING SELECT SKETCHES OF ARTIST

JOE EISMA

MGA

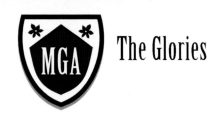

The Glories

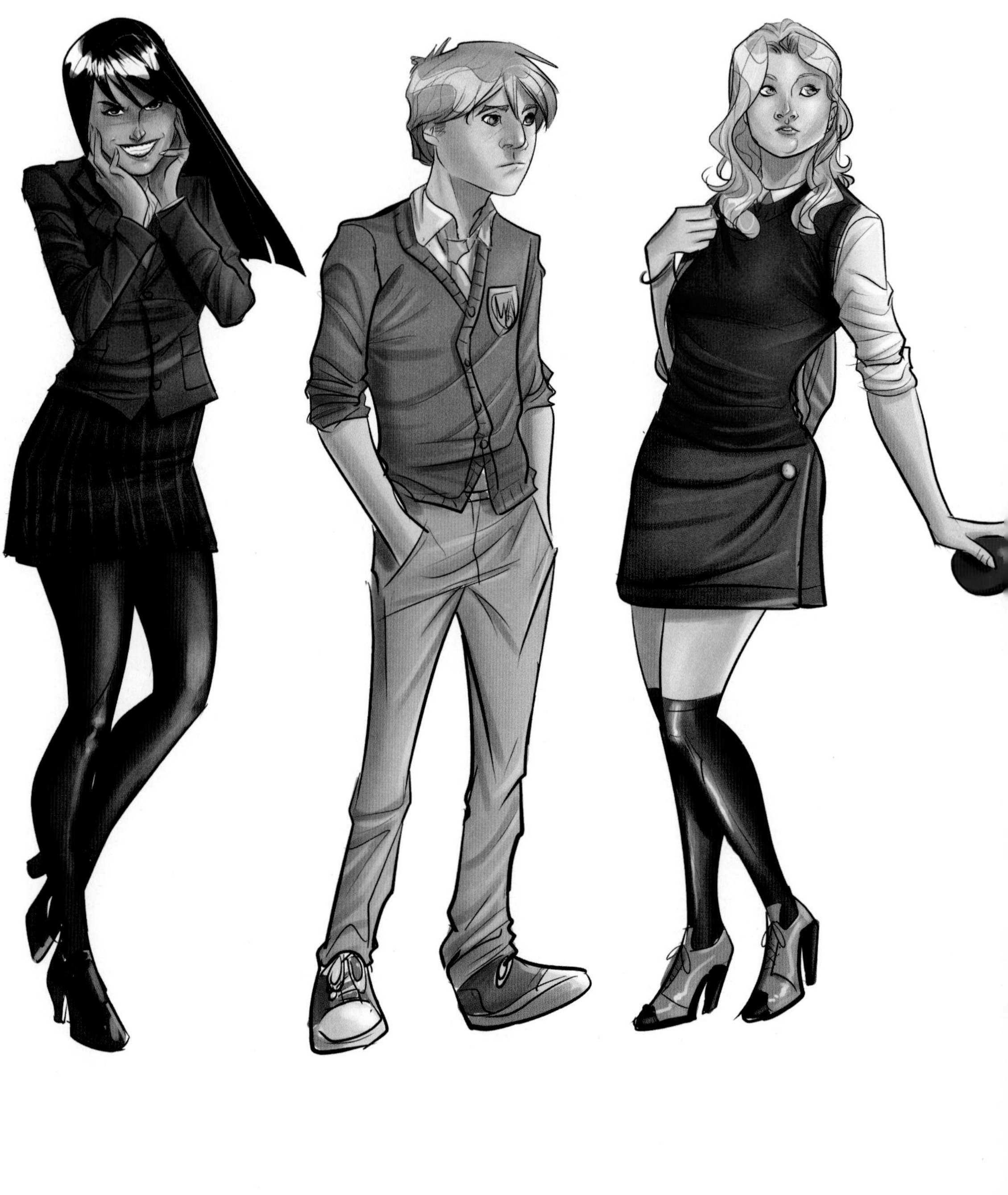

MGA

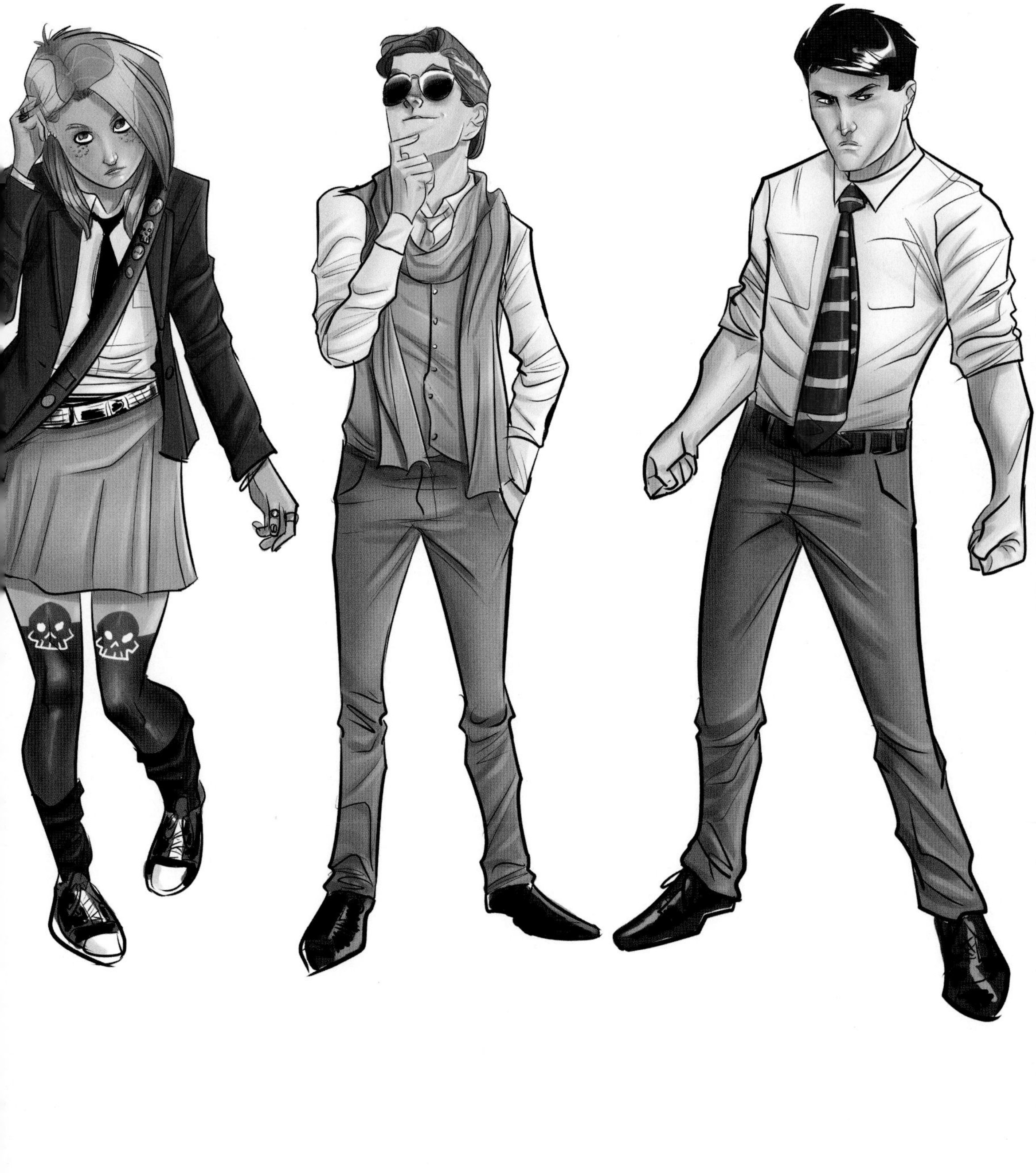

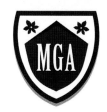

Guillaume

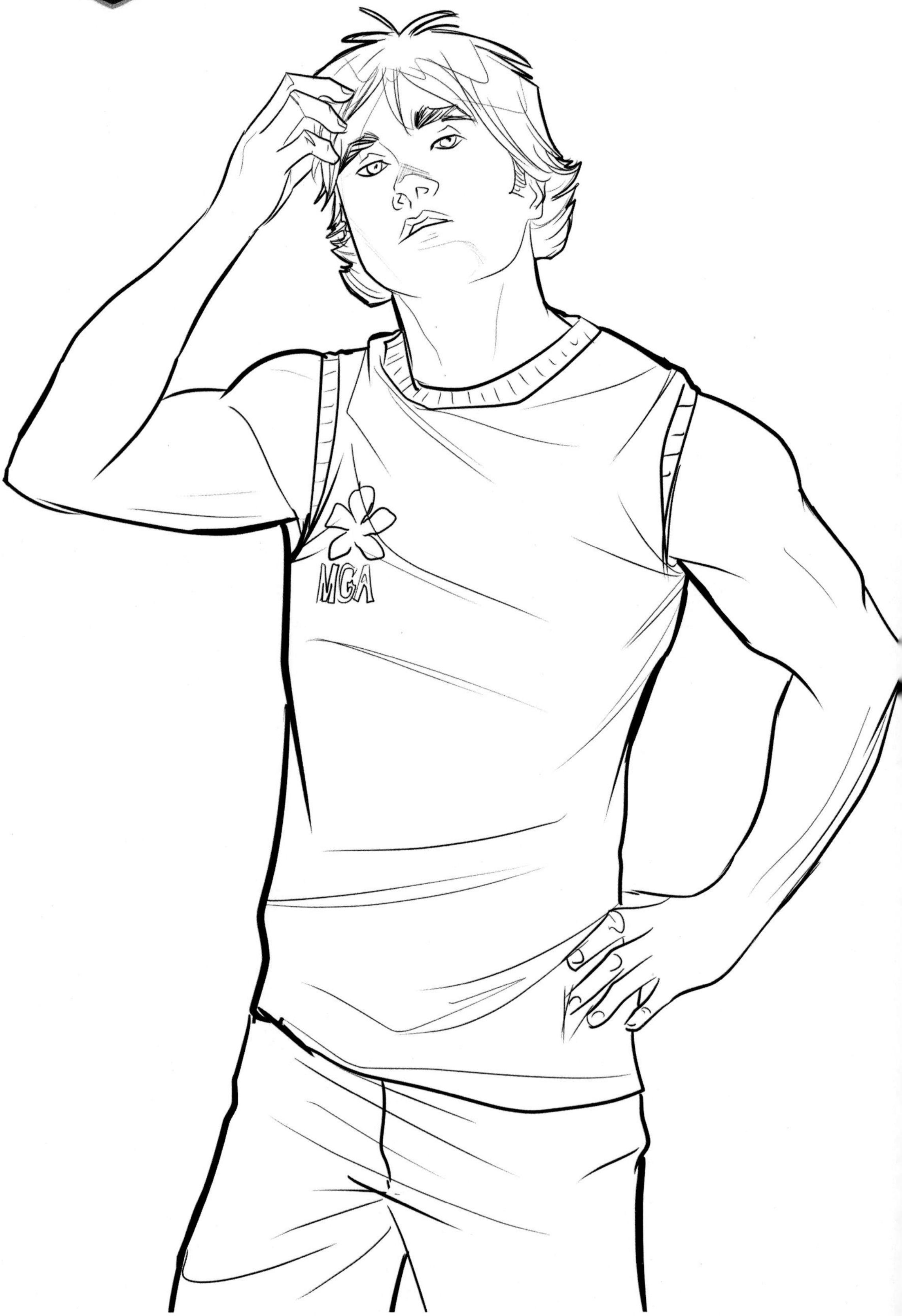
MGA

Jade

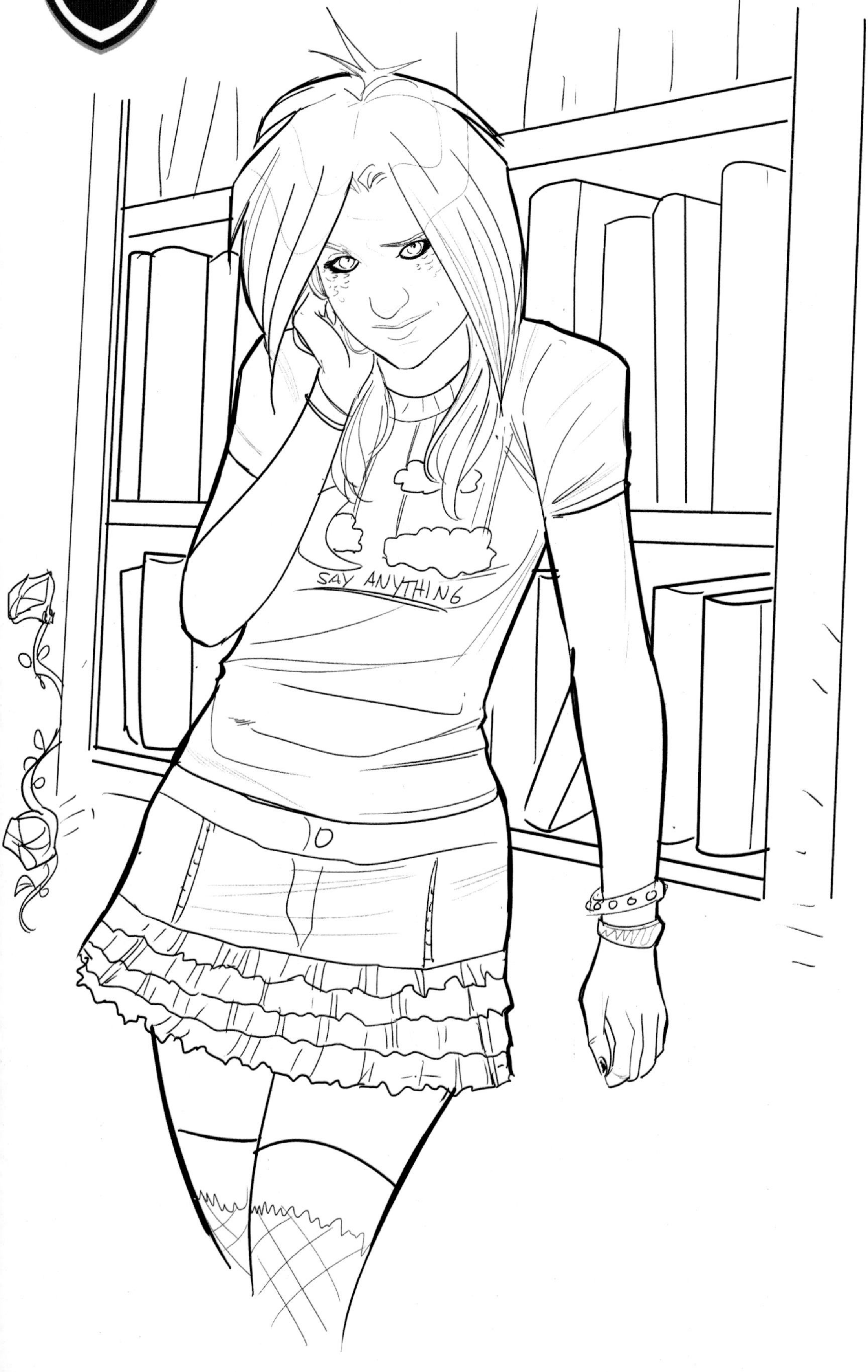
SAY ANYTHING

MGA

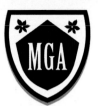

Casey, Jade & Hunter

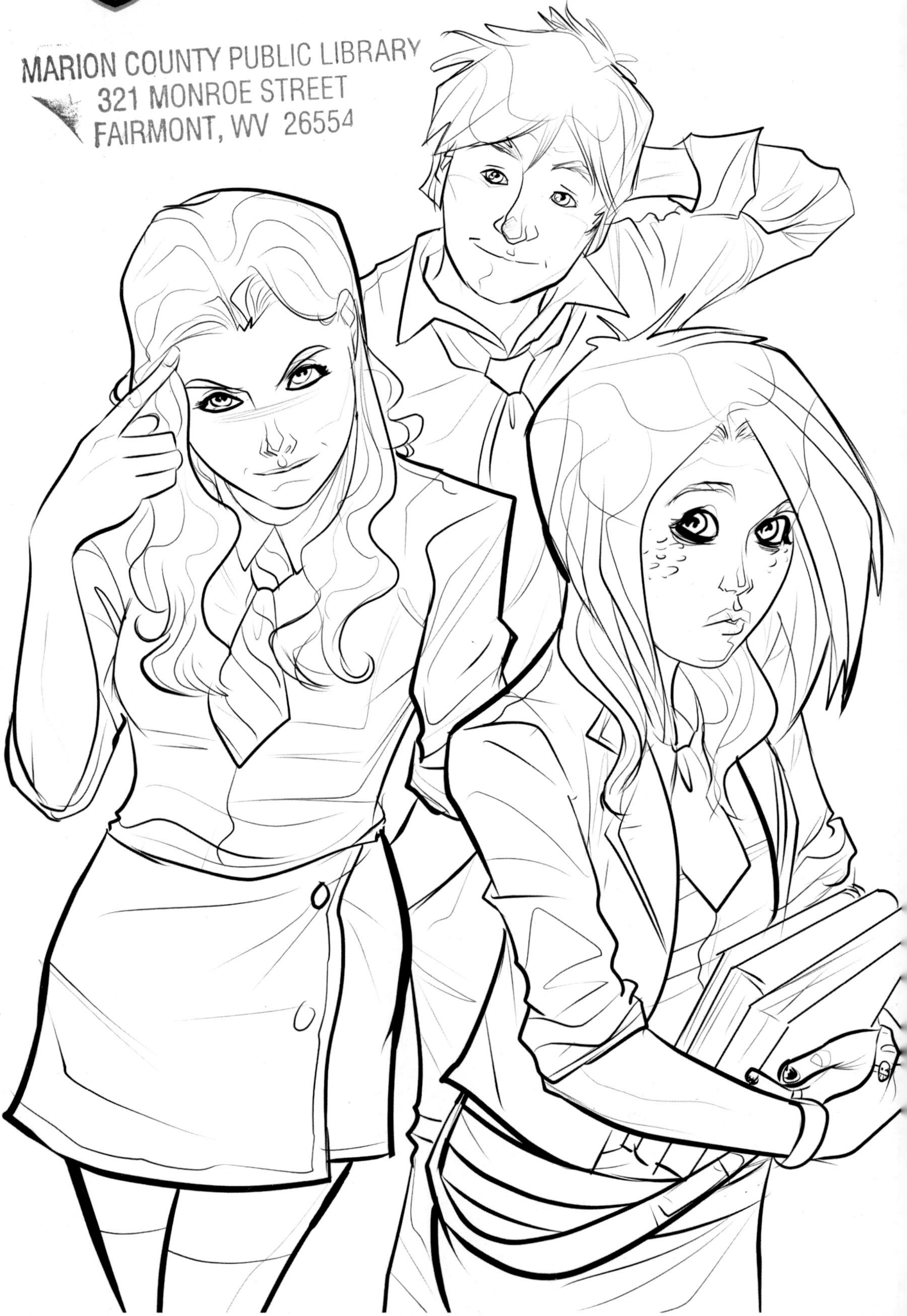